BUDWEISERS INTO CZECHS AND GERMANS

BUDWEISERS INTO CZECHS AND GERMANS

A LOCAL HISTORY OF BOHEMIAN POLITICS, 1848–1948

Jeremy King

PRINCETON UNIVERSITY PRESS   PRINCETON AND OXFORD

Published by Princeton University Press, 41 William Street, Princeton,
New Jersey 08540
In the United Kingdom: Princeton University Press, 3 Market Place,
Woodstock, Oxfordshire OX20 1SY

Second printing, and first paperback printing, 2005
Paperback ISBN 0-691-12234-2

The Library of Congress has cataloged the cloth edition of this book as follows

King, Jeremy, 1963–
Budweisers into Czechs and Germans : a local history of Bohemian politics,
1848–1948 / Jeremy King.
p. cm.
Includes bibliographical references and index.
ISBN 0-691-04892-4
1. Germans—Czech Republic—Ceské Budějovice. 2. Ceské Budějovice
(Czech Republic)—Ethnic relations—Political aspects. 3. Ceské
Budějovice (Czech Republic)—Ethnic relations—History—19th century.
4. Ceské Budějovice (Czech Republic)—Ethnic relations—History—20th
century. I. Title.

DB2650.C463 K56 2002
305.83'104371—dc21   2002025107

British Library Cataloging-in-Publication Data is available

This book has been composed in Galliard

Printed on acid-free paper. ∞

pup.princeton.edu

Printed in the United States of America

10 9 8 7 6 5 4 3 2

Contents

Illustrations

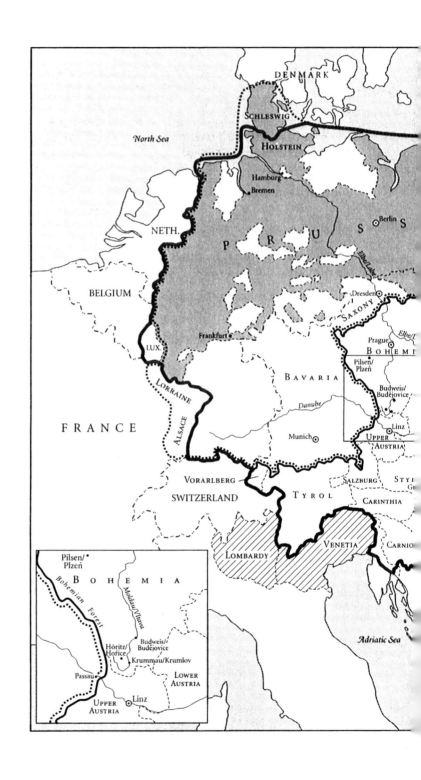

DENMARK

SCHLESWIG

North Sea

HOLSTEIN

Hamburg
Bremen

NETH.

P   R   U

S

⊙ Berlin

S

BELGIUM

Frankfurt •

LUX.

LORRAINE

ALSACE

FRANCE

BAVARIA

Danube

Munich ⊙

Dresden ⊙

SAXONY

Elbe/L

Prague ⊙

BOHEMI

Pilsen/
Plzeň

Budweis/
Budějovice

Linz •

UPPER
AUSTRIA

VORARLBERG

SWITZERLAND

TYROL

SALZBURG   STYI
G

CARINTHIA

VENETIA   CARNIO

LOMBARDY

Adriatic Sea

Pilsen/
Plzeň   •

B   O   H   E   M   I   A

Bohemian   Forest

Moldau/Vltava

Höritz/
Hořice   •

Budweis/
Budějovice

Krummau/Krumlov

Passau

UPPER
AUSTRIA

LOWER
AUSTRIA

Linz ⊙

Baltic Sea

RUSSIAN
EMPIRE

	Habsburg Monarchy 1867
	Boundary between Cisleithanian and Transleithanian parts of Habsburg Monarchy 1867–1918
	German Confederation 1815–1866
	Prussia 1867
	German Empire 1871–1918
	Territory lost by Habsburg Monarchy to Italy 1859–1866
	Territory acquired by Habsburg Monarchy 1878
	International boundaries
	Provincial, regional boundaries

SILESIA

öniggrätz/
radec Králové   SILESIA
AUSTRIAN

MORAVIA
◉ Brünn/Brno

GALICIA

BUKOVINA

OWER
nna ◉
STRIA

Buda ◉ Pest

Danube

HUNGARY

TRANSYLVANIA

CROATIA - SLAVONIA

BOSNIA AND
HERZEGOVINA
Sarajevo ◉

SANJAK OF
NOVI PAZAR

CENTRAL EUROPE
1848–1918

clb

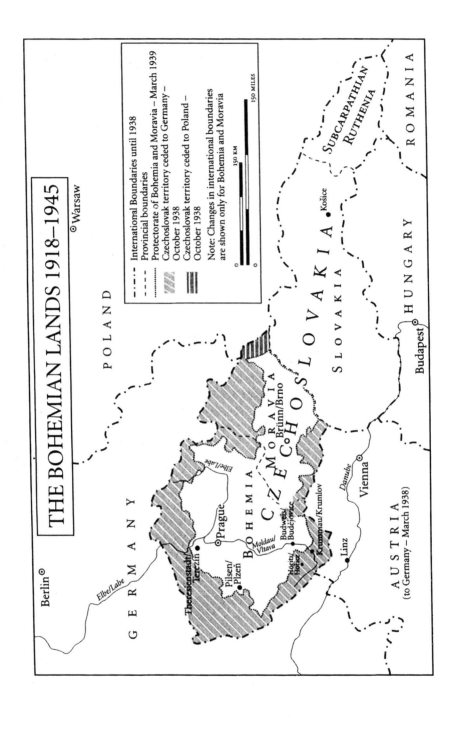

THE BOHEMIAN LANDS 1918–1945

⊙Warsaw

⊙Berlin

P O L A N D

G E R M A N Y

Elbe/Labe

Theresienstadt/
Terezín

Pilsen/
Plzeň

⊙Prague

B O H E M I A

*Moldau/
Vltava*

Elbe/Labe

M O R A V I A
Brünn/Brno ○

C Z E C H O S L O V A K I A

Budweis/
Budějovice

Hořice/
Horice

Krummau/Krumlov

Danube

Linz

Vienna ⊙

A U S T R I A
(to Germany – March 1938)

S L O V A K I A

Košice ●

SUBCARPATHIAN
RUTHENIA

R O M A N I A

H U N G A R Y

Budapest⊙

International Boundaries until 1938
‐ ‐ ‐ ‐ Provincial boundaries
Protectorate of Bohemia and Moravia – March 1939
Czechoslovak territory ceded to Germany –
October 1938
Czechoslovak territory ceded to Poland –
October 1938

Note: Changes in international boundaries
are shown only for Bohemia and Moravia

0   150 KM
0   150 MILES

BUDWEIS/BUDĚJOVICE, CIRCA 1890

1. Town Hall
2. Imperial-royal District Captainship and Post Office
3. The Sun Hotel
4. The Silver Bell Hotel
5. German gymnasium
6. Bishop's residence
7. Town Theatre
8. Deutsches Haus

9. Theological seminary
10. Cathedral
11. Imperial-royal district court
12. Beseda
13. Institute for deaf mutes
14. Barracks
15. St. Wenceslas Church
16. Czech gymnasium
17. Synagogue
18. Hardtmuth pencil factory

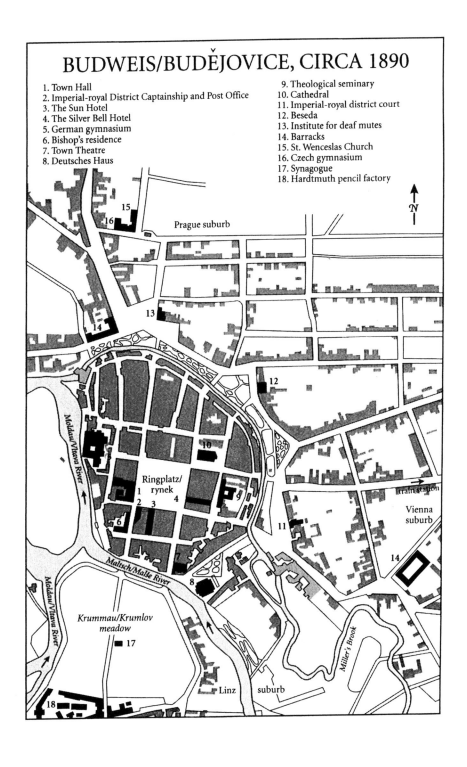

Preface

In 1986, I spent a day in Česke Budějovice, a charming Czech town due south of Prague, about three-fourths of the way to the Austrian border. An American, I had fallen in love with Czech literature several years earlier, in college. Then, in 1984, I had moved past fiction, during six weeks in Prague. Yet when I made my visit to Česke Budějovice, during a second stay in Czechoslovakia, I still had no idea that within the "Bohemian lands" of Bohemia, Moravia, and Austrian Silesia, the town had long counted as unusually mixed in national, Czech-German terms. I did know that during the Habsburg Monarchy, interwar Czechoslovakia, and the Third Reich, the rim of the Bohemian lands had been German, and the interior Czech. Thus the Czech-German conflict that was once so central to Bohemian politics had tended to unfold at arm's length. Budějovice had been one of the exceptions—but that fact I learned only several years later, as the Cold War ended and as I advanced through the doctoral program in History at Columbia University.

The face-to-face quality of national conflict in Budějovice, I came to think, made it a good site for a local study through which I might try to capture the history of Bohemian politics in a new way. Multiple historians of the Bohemian lands had already written valuable studies on "the nationality question." None of those studies, though, confined its geographical dimension in such a way as to permit considerable length in the chronological dimension and reasonable depth in the political one—which spanned the German and the Czech, the rich and the poor, the Christian and the Jewish, and much more. Scholars had provided considerable insight into the "Springtime of Nations" in 1848, when Czech and German leaders first took up important positions within formal political structures. Excellent work had been done on multiple aspects of the constitutional era between the 1860s and 1914; on the interwar Czechoslovak era of Czech democratic dominance; and on the Second World War, when Nazi Germany, in addition to annihilating Bohemian Jewry, drove almost all of Czech politics underground. At least the outlines were clear, finally, of the years between 1945 and 1948, when the restored Czechoslovakia eliminated German politics from the Bohemian lands by expelling its entire German population—and then became part of a quite different conflict, between East and West, as a Soviet satellite. The literature seemed to have covered all phases and sides in some fashion, but only piecemeal. In 1991, I returned to Budějovice and began my research.

Now, ten years later, I find myself humbled. The narrow story that I had set out to tell proved dauntingly deep and complex. Yet I also find myself surprised and heartened. My approach yielded sums different from my predecessors' parts in ways that I had not expected. Perhaps the best one-word introduction to those sums is "Budweisers." By it, I mean not bottles of the American beer but a certain kind of person from Budějovice—from whose German name, Budweis, the word derives. Budweisers awakened me to the roles played in national, Czech-German conflict by nonnational actors, and to flaws in narratives that revolved around "ethnicity." I came to see that conflict as only part of Bohemian politics between 1848 and 1948. I also came to think more historically about "Czechs" and "Germans," as well as about the "nation," a defining category of modern times.

I thank the many people and institutions that have helped me research and write this book. Colleagues and friends include Brad Abrams, Nadia Abu El-Haj, Catherine Albrecht, Celia Applegate, Karen Barkey, Steven Beller, Arthur Brenner, Rogers Brubaker, Audrey Budding, Peter Bugge, Gary Cohen, John Connelly, Bhavna Davé, István Deák, Hana Demetz-Rosskam, Lois Dubin, Elizabeth Dunn, Catherine Epstein, Tamás Fóti, Benjamin Frommer, David Good, Daniel Gordon, Frank Hadler, Eugenia and Robert Herbert, Eugene Hill, Peter Holquist, Charles Ingrao, Owen Johnson, Stephen Jones, Pieter Judson, Judit Kertész, Daniel Kovář, Hana Krejčová, Petr Křivinka, Rita Krueger, Jana Laczová, David Laitin, Hugh Lane, Andrew Lass, Alexander Loesch, Daniel MacMillan, Charles Maier, Edward Malefakis, Jan Mareš, András Márton, Jr. and Sr., Dávid Márton, Milan Mottl and family, Zuzana Nagy, Thomas Ort, Cynthia Paces, Jason Parker, Marko Prelec, Alon Rachamimov, Ágnes Réthy, Julie Rosenbaum and family, Robert Sak, Til Schuermann, Petr Šebesta, Holly Sharac, David Shengold, Alena Šimůnková, Wim Smit, Tim Snyder, Fritz Stern, Philipp Ther, Markéta Thonová, Stefan Troebst, Jon Van Den Heuvel, Brigitta van Rheinberg, Dan Unowsky, Katherine Verdery, Mark von Hagen, Veljko Vujačić, James Wald, Theodore Weeks, Jan Westfall, Nancy Wingfield, and Larry Wolff; an anonymous reviewer for Cornell University Press; and my fellow members in the Department of History at Mount Holyoke College. I have also learned much from my students, especially in my course "From Habsburg to Hitler: Bohemian Politics, 1848–1948."
    I am grateful to the following institutions for funding my research, travel, and writing: the Joint Committee on Eastern Europe of the American Council of Learned Societies, Columbia University, the Harvard Academy for International and Area Studies, the International Research and Exchanges Board, the Mellon Foundation, the National Endowment for the Humanities, the SSRC-MacArthur Foundation Program on Peace

and Security in a Changing World, the Woodrow Wilson International Center for Scholars, Mount Holyoke College, the American Academy in Berlin, the Austrian Cultural Institute, and the Center for Austrian Studies at the University of Minnesota. I also thank the following libraries and research institutions for allowing me access to their valuable resources: the State Archive, Museum, and Library, as well as the History Department of the University of Southern Bohemia, all in České Budějovice; Widener Library at Harvard University, Butler Library at Columbia University, Van Pelt Library at the University of Pennsylvania, and Williston Library at Mount Holyoke College. Jan Mareš, Director of the Regional Division of the State Library in České Budějovice, was particularly generous in sharing with me his time and knowledge. Criticism and support from him, as well as from all of the persons previously mentioned, contributed greatly to reducing the faults in my work.

Finally, I thank my mother, my father, my two brothers, and the rest of my family. Without them—and especially my wife, Katya King, and our two children (born two years apart on the name day of Wenceslas, the patron saint of Bohemia)—I could not have overcome the physical and metaphysical obstacles to completing this project. I only wish that our beloved Scout, also known as der Schkuh/Skautík, were still among us. May he live in memory as one of the finest American pooches ever to visit Budweis/Budějovice.

1 November 2001
South Hadley, Mass.

BUDWEISERS INTO CZECHS AND GERMANS

Budweisers into Czechs and Germans

"In Southern Bohemia, there are three nations, namely Germans, Czechs, and Budweisers." So, in and around Budweis/Budějovice, went an early twentieth-century saying in both the Czech and the German languages.[1] Embedded in it are an ahistorical assumption and a historical insight. Budweisers were no "nation." In the nineteenth century, though, what might be termed a nonnational or more-than-national category of Budweisers did exist. By excavating and understanding it, we can better understand Czechs, Germans, "nations," and modern politics more generally in the Bohemian lands.

In August 1861, months after the Habsburg Monarchy had begun moving in the direction of constitutional rule after a decade of repression, the mayor of Budweis/Budějovice made a public statement. A second middle school was being built, at which instruction would take place not only in German, as had long been the case at the original middle school, but also in the less prestigious Czech language. The mayor and the senior aldermen had decided on this new policy of "equality and progress." They had also decided to request that the governor of Bohemia assign a new school inspector to town, because the current inspector had an imperfect command of Czech. "Ultra-Germans," though, led by "Germanomaniac" [*deutschthümliche*] members of the town council, had objected. Claiming that the mayor had acted at the instigation of an "Ultra-Czech deputation," they had also questioned his honesty. He now responded by branding the talk of a deputation a lie and by stating the following, in the German language that both newspapers in town at the time employed:

> As regards myself, and claims that I circulate among Germans as a German, and among Czechs as a Czech, I am in truth proud to have learned how to do this. People will surely find my comportment quite natural, and all the more forgivable when they consider that it is desired by the government, in which both nationalities are to be represented. That I have been equally correct toward both is proved by my recent reelection as chief executive of the mature and worthy burghers of both tongues, who thereby expressed their considerable trust in me.[2]

The outcome was a compromise. The mayor—who called himself Franz Josef Klawik in German and František Josef Klavík in Czech—retained the support of the town council, yet the school inspector kept his post. Ultra-

Germans and Ultra-Czechs alike found reason for disappointment. That fall, dispute erupted again, this time over the classical high school, or gymnasium. The governor of Bohemia had recently ordered that here, too, instruction should be made officially bilingual, at least for those students who wished to learn both German and Czech. Eighteen of the thirty-six aldermen opposed this change, and in November, they succeeded in passing a municipal resolution that urged the governor to rescind his order. Only four aldermen, including Klawik/Klavík, voted against the resolution. Fourteen failed to attend the meeting.[3]

Ultra-Germans immediately attacked one of the four aldermen, Vicar Ottokar Haug, for forgetting his "completely German origins" and for going over "lock, stock, and barrel" to the other camp. He defended himself in a public letter, stating that he had not forgotten those origins and that he loved Germandom as he did his parents. He had dedicated his life, though, to the welfare of both his German and his Czech countrymen. To that end, he wished to help elevate the Czech language from a "mere peasant dialect." "Of a camp to which I have *gone over lock, stock, and barrel*," Haug continued, "I know nothing. As a priest, I strive only to promote culture, and know no other camp than that of Christian civilization." He concluded, "What the Germans already have, the Czechs should be able to strive for as well. This may produce passing tensions, but in the long run leads to peace."[4] The governor seems to have agreed with Haug, because the addition of bilingual classes to the gymnasium proceeded as planned.

What, then, were Budweisers? Klawik/Klavík defined himself as both a Czech and a German, and as a person committed to equality between the two "nationalities"—which he defined by "tongue." He claimed to have backing from both the municipal electorate and the state for his stance, but also labeled it "natural." Indeed, it was so natural, or at least seemed so natural, that he lacked a precise name for it. In German, the word *Budweiser* (the plural of which is also *Budweiser*) at first meant simply a person or people connected to Budweis/Budějovice. The equivalent in Czech was *Budějovičan* (plural *Budějovičané*). Gradually, through such conflicts as those just described, a second meaning developed, of a particular kind of person or people—or what Ultras came to call a "third nation." And in the 1870s, far away in the United States, there developed yet another meaning, a brand of beer marketed by two brewers in St. Louis named Anheuser and Busch. In Southern Bohemia, Czech-speakers succeeded in disambiguating the second meaning from the original, broader one by folding the word *Budweiser* into their language (sometimes spelling it *Budwajzr*, plural *Budwajzři*). In 1861, however, such changes were only beginning. Klawik/Klavík lacked a word in either language to distinguish clearly his category, which applied almost universally in town, from the competing and as yet marginal categories of Czech and German Ultras.

Haug, another Budweiser, considered himself a German, but not a Czech. Ultra-Germans agreed with Haug, at least about his German origins. Ultra-Czechs, for their part, did not try to claim him as one of their own men, even when they later threw their support behind him in an election. If he spoke Czech, he probably spoke it with a German accent, and made grammatical errors.[5] Certainly one did not have to be bilingual in order to count as a Budweiser. No hard data were ever collected concerning bilingualism in the Bohemian lands. But in 1865, *Budivoj*, a new Czech newspaper in Budweis/Budějovice, estimated that the rate there was about 60 percent. Other observers agreed that the figure in town, although unusually high, fell well short of 100 percent.[6] More important to being a Budweiser than bilingualism, according to the Budweiser view, was an insistence on defining Germanness and Czechness as a question primarily of language, and thus as a matter of no great importance in many aspects of life. Ultras, from this perspective, could try to make a political issue of nationhood, but would succeed in stirring up only "passing tensions." Or to quote a satire published early in 1861 by the *Budweiser Wochenblatt* [*Budweis Weekly*], a newspaper that took a Budweiser stance: all would end with "splendid reconciliation," "under the provision that for all eternity the Ultra-Germans are to speak nothing but Czech, the Ultra-Czechs nothing but German, and all others nothing but *reasonably*."[7]

Budweisers misunderstood and underestimated Ultras, however, and thereby committed a political error of the first order. Ultras, meanwhile, misinterpreted Budweisers, and thereby hit on a remarkably successful strategy. "Tell me," began a short "Conversation between Two Politicians," printed in 1863 by Budweis/Budějovice's Ultra-German newspaper, the *Anzeiger aus dem südlichen Böhmen* [*Gazette for Southern Bohemia*], "what does it mean when someone says that he's nationally uncommitted?" The answer: "You green fool, when nothing's at stake, then people say it, even when they aren't. But when something decisive comes up, then they simply go over to the Czech camp." Czech Ultras, like German ones, preferred to view "uncommitted" residents as closet Ultras or as Ultras in the making, rather than as Budweisers.[8] Or to stop using the vocabulary of the 1860s and to start using a more recent one: leaders of the German and Czech national movements understood potential recruits to be not so much nonnational or more-than-national individuals as Germans or Czechs of a latent, unconscious, ethnic sort. According to this view, the two "nations" were mutually exclusive and very important. National indifference was an inconvenient fact that national leaders denied and minimized. Indeed, they even nationalized it: hence, by about 1910, the amusing oddity of a "nation" of Budweisers.

In the spring of 1862, Czechs, Germans, and Budweisers clashed again—and the national contestants scored a victory. Three burghers, all Czechs, demanded that the *Liedertafel*, or Choral Society, in town change its informal policy of practicing and performing Czech songs "as conditions allow" to a formal policy of making every third piece a Czech one. Rebuffed by a German faction, the three men and others seceded to form a new choir, the *Beseda*—which means "chat" or "get-together" in Czech. In May, the *Budweiser Kreisblatt* [*Budweis District Newspaper*], a successor to the *Wochenblatt*, printed two letters to the editor (signed "*Ein . . . Budweiser*" and "*Der Budweiser*") that denounced German efforts at blaming the split on Czech intolerance. And in June, the newspaper skewered both national sides with hilariously hyperbolic prose, even while lamenting that the affair was dividing some families. Before long, the *Beseda* decided to sing only Czech songs at its first concert, by a vote of 30 to 33.[9]

Remaining members of the *Liedertafel*, meanwhile, gave a recital in November 1862 at which they performed Ernst Moritz Arndt's composition from 1813, "What Is the German's Fatherland?" Some burghers stood up as they sang the words in German, presumably to add emphasis to the claim that the German's fatherland reached "as far as the German tongue sounds." Other burghers, though, walked off the stage, removing their choir badges. Two weeks later, the now more German *Liedertafel* gave another recital, in a new German club, and sang the same song—not once but twice. It provoked a storm of cheers. But as the *Anzeiger aus dem südlichen Böhmen* reported with some annoyance, among the German-language cries of *hoch* could be heard Czech-language cries of *výborně*. Shouting "bravo" in Czech was how some members of the audience, and perhaps of the *Liedertafel* itself, saw fit to join in the German, anti-Czech enthusiasm. A Budweiser choir split into two choirs, one Czech and one German. Burghers now had difficulty expressing a Budweiser stance through song. When Wenzel/Václav Bernhart, an alderman, died in 1863, both choirs paid him their final respects, but separately—the *Liedertafel* at the church service and the *Beseda* at graveside.[10]

Today, when almost all politics is national politics, the Budweiser worldview may seem odd and confusing. It may seem trivial, too. Yet it can be understood, and should be—because Budweisers practiced a local variant on a form of politics that was once pivotally important in Habsburg Central Europe. How to name that form? Contemporaries often called it "Austrian," after one of the several names for the Habsburg Monarchy. Today's small nation-state of Austria, though, has complicated the meaning of the word. Joseph Roth, in his early twentieth-century fiction, came closer than almost anyone else to evoking and to naming the imperial

Austrian political ethos. He idealized and exaggerated, though, and used inconveniently long phrases: "a great mansion with many doors and many chambers, for every condition of man," for example, and "a powerful force with the ability . . . to unite what seems to be trying to fly apart." Historians have written of "local patriotisms," but in ways that miss the coming together of those disparate allegiances into a loose, overarching one.[11] Best, perhaps, are the old term "Habsburg-loyal" and a derivative: simply "Habsburg." They point to the Habsburg dynasty and to the nonnational and then more-than-national state that Klawik/Klavík invoked in defending his Budweiser stance. As Budweisers became Germans or Czechs, Habsburg loyalists more generally became national too. Peasants, burghers, nobles, and other Habsburg subjects gradually became Germans, Czechs, Poles, Ruthenes, Romanians, Slovaks, Hungarians, Serbs, Croats, Slovenes, Italians, or other nationals. The Habsburg Monarchy, which had long rested on the principle of rule by divine right, came to rest more and more on multiple national variants on the principle of popular sovereignty—not just on one, as in France, where all peasants and other subjects famously became Frenchmen.[12] The new, national forms of politics became an ever larger part of politics in the Habsburg Monarchy, which contained their mutual incompatibilities ever less successfully. Conflict among Budweisers, Czechs, and Germans in Budweis/Budějovice formed part of a contest for the Habsburg succession in Central Europe.

Budweisers, other Habsburg loyalists, and their state, however, did not disappear overnight, and in the meantime shaped the contest for their succession in vital ways. Between 1848 and 1918, by setting and enforcing many rules to the political game, the Habsburg state influenced powerfully the political content and demographic dimensions of individual national movements—which kinds of Budweisers tended to become Germans, for example, and which kinds Czechs. The Habsburg state was also more accepting of national movements than of other kinds of movements. That policy perhaps contributed to the failure by believers in class, religious, or racial conflict to make "the people" in popular sovereignty not "nations" but workers and peasants, Christians, or Aryans. After 1900, the Habsburg state even embraced a cluster of nationhoods, by moving to institutionalize them as subcitizenships among which citizens had to choose.

After the collapse of the monarchy in 1918, the contest for the Habsburg succession was reduced to a struggle of national movements or "camps" alone. The new states, including Czechoslovakia, turned out to be not so much contestants in their own right as resources controlled by this or that national movement. Nationhood triumphed, at least generically—in the Bohemian lands, in both German and Czech forms. Vicar Haug's "passing tensions" continued. Only a generation later did his prediction of a lasting national peace in the Bohemian lands come true after all. But that outcome was far from inevitable, and took a form that he had not wanted: a specifically national, Czech victory. That outcome also followed events that he could not have imagined: a world war, the disappearance of the Habsburg Monarchy, a Nazi occupation, a second world war, the Holocaust, and the expulsion of all Germans. The Bohemian lands became wholly Czech, and part not of Central Europe but of a Slavic East separated from the West by a nuclear Cold War.

Historians have long viewed the contest for the Habsburg succession, consciously or unconsciously, from national perspectives. A central consequence has been to misinterpret and to neglect the Habsburg state and Habsburg loyalties. In 1966, at a landmark conference concerning "The Nationality Problem in the Habsburg Monarchy in the Nineteenth Century," Arthur Haas made the telling criticism that there were "a dozen or so papers on the Slavic nationalities alone but none at all explaining the government's position."[13] Writ large, that criticism still applies today. Over the past two decades, a new consensus has emerged among scholars to the effect that nationhood is not ancient and natural, as nationals often think. Rather, it is modern and "constructed."[14] Yet almost all histories of Bohemian politics between the 1840s and the First World War still amount to mere variations on the long-standing national understanding of a German-Czech duel. German and Czech movements constructed themselves, runs the implicit argument, and did so in such a way as to reduce nonnational or more-than-national actors rapidly to political insignificance.[15]

Enabling historians' neglect of Habsburg politics has been an emphasis on ancient "races," "peoples," or "ethnic groups" instead. Czechness and Germanness supposedly did not emerge from Habsburg loyalties through a struggle over resources, but rather had always existed, in the form of ethnic Czechs and Germans. They "awoke" to national consciousness during the nineteenth century, above all through struggle against each other. The forebear to nationhood was not nonnational politics but nonpolitical ethnicity. As Jörg Hoensch wrote in his *History of Bohemia*, published in German in 1987, "the German national consciousness that burgeoned in the German states during the wars of liberation [against Napoleon] gripped only a few Germans in Bohemia." And as Zdeněk Kárník has explained more recently and more explicitly, "In varying intensity, the Bohemian lands were the settlement area for at least seven centuries of three ethnic groups: the dominant Czech one, a strong German minority, and a less numerous but nonetheless influential Jewish minority. . . . Only the nineteenth and twentieth centuries elevated these relations—with variations in timing and in intensity—to a relationship among modern nations." In various guises, this derivation of each new "nation" from an old ethnic community has long been dominant among Bohemian and other Habsburg historians.[16]

Historians, in using that derivation, have confused scholarly analysis with political practice. National leaders in the Bohemian lands during the nineteenth century often argued that Czech-speakers or German-speakers should add, and indeed were fated to add, a Czech or German consciousness to their Czech or German "origins," or ethnicity. That argument failed to convince Vicar Haug, yet proved remarkably successful in many other cases. In 1918, only irony made one person's comment about his youth in Prague during the 1860s unusual: "Like Molière's fellow who spoke prose without knowing it, we were Germans without knowing it."[17] The practical success of the ethnic argument, however, makes it no less misleading as an analysis of what happened. National approaches to nationhood generate what François Furet once called, in a different context, the "vicious circle" of "commemorative historiography," and what Daniel Gordon calls the "mimetic pitfall."[18] Historians can go beyond commemoration or mimesis. Although evidence abounds of solidarity among speakers of the same language long before the nineteenth century, other evidence testifies to bilingualism and to mutually unintelligible dialects of a Czech or German language that emerged only gradually, in contingent fashion.[19] If languages divided a population vertically, into protonational columns, then corporative and socioeconomic solidarities divided it horizontally, into Habsburg layers—and had far more institutional anchoring and sociological significance. Yet almost all historians have joined nationals in downplaying the gaps and flaws in the "nations emerged from ethnic groups" explanation as mere complications and exceptions.

The Jewish ethnic group that Kárník and other Bohemian historians add to the German and Czech ones is itself an exception—and not only because that group is defined primarily by religion rather than by language. Both in the 1840s and far back into the past, Bohemian Jews figured as a tightly bounded community, its members (some of whom had no language in common) defined consistently by multiple institutions and practices. One can state with considerable precision and confidence that in 1846, for example, Jews made up about 1.7 percent of the population in the Bohemian lands. (In Budweis/Budějovice, Jews were banned as residents between 1506 and 1849. Thereafter, in 1857 and in 1869, surveys tallied 166 and then 250 Israelites, or 1 percent and 1.4 percent of the population.)[20] This well-defined group, though, did not turn into a "nation." Between the 1840s and the 1930s, some Jews became Germans, and some Czechs; some of both also became Christians. A few became nationally Jewish, in the sense of Zionists. The Bohemian ethnic group for whose historical existence the best case can be made fits the ethnic explanatory model worst—unless one insists on viewing as predestined the unification of much of European Jewry into a modern "people" by the Nazi regime, through genocide. Better is a different explanation: ethnic groups are not national antecedents but national products, projected ahistorically yet with history-making effect into the past. Far from constituting distinct and robust categories of historical analysis, the ethnic group and the "nation" stand in a relationship of mutual and constitutive dependence.

For that matter, to think of "nations" as the successors to ethnic groups is to misunderstand nationhood. As Rogers Brubaker wrote in 1996,

> Countless discussions of nationhood and nationalism begin with the question: what is a nation? This question is not as theoretically innocent as it seems: the very terms in which it is framed presuppose the existence of the entity that is to be defined. The question itself reflects the realist, substantialist belief that "a nation" is a real entity of some kind, though perhaps one that is elusive and difficult to define.

Someone who is national understands a "nation" as a membership organization, as a large, real, and even countable community of people ("members") characterized by a specific "identity." Scholars, though, in order to explain such understandings, must exit them. And from the outside, "nations" are *imagined* communities, reifications of a modern form of legitimacy—nationhood—which might be defined as a set of mutually exclusive variants on the principle of popular sovereignty. To cite Brubaker again,

> Reification is central to the quasi-performative discourse of nationalist politicians which, at certain moments, can succeed in creating what it seems to presuppose—namely, the existence of nations as real, mobilized or mobilizable groups. . . . As analysts of nationalism, we should certainly try to *account* for this social process of reification—this process through which the political fiction of the nation becomes momentarily yet powerfully realized in practice. This may be one of the most important tasks of the theory of nationalism. But we should avoid unintentionally *reproducing* or *reinforcing* this reification of nations in practice with a reification of nations in theory.[21]

Historians of Habsburg Central Europe, then, have tended to write national histories, rather than histories of nationhood. Deep links between history-writing and national politics in the region during the nineteenth century, as well as the national nature of the societies within which historians have lived more recently, explain that pattern.[22] Yet history-writing concerning nationhood does not *have* to be national, and has not always been national in the same ways. The very term "ethnic" amounts to an innovation of the 1970s and 1980s—often misused, but also used to yield genuine insights.[23] Until its advent, after all, scholars of Habsburg Central

Europe had followed national leaders in regularly using the same vocabulary for nationally conscious and unconscious individuals, and thus in minimizing the distinction. Over the past several decades, social historians have pushed past vague understandings of national "awakening" to address why certain people did or did not become national at certain times and in certain ways.[24] Open displays of prejudice in favor of a particular "nation" have grown much less common among historians, and have yielded to national prejudice of a more subtle and generic nature—Czech *and* German, for example.[25]

Some scholars have even challenged ethnic master narratives. Already in 1981, Gary Cohen argued, in a study of the German movement in Prague, that socioeconomic standing accounted better than did ethnicity for how residents became national: as Czechs or as Germans. His book, the first chapter of which bears the title "From Bohemians to Czechs and Germans," shows that many poorer people became ethnically Czech only as they became nationally so. Cohen treats the pattern as far from exceptional or incidental. To be sure, the title of his book, *The Politics of Ethnic Survival*, almost invites readers to continue thinking of ethnicity as ancient and enduring. And his work remained within the spirit of its time by subscribing to what Brubaker terms a "groupist" understanding of nationhood, as well as by participating in the neglect of the state that characterized the pioneering generation of social historians. Yet after two decades, Cohen's analysis of nineteenth-century Bohemian politics remains unsurpassed. The few scholars who have joined him in undermining ethnic readings of the Bohemian past have tended not to be historians. Vladimír Macura, who helped to historicize the Czech language and who dissected the central ethnic metaphor of awakening, was a semiotician specializing in literature. Andrew Lass, who has emphasized the national, history-making role of historians and who has situated the making of a Czech ethnic group or folk in modern times, is an anthropologist. And Peter Bugge, who has provided an overview of Czech "nation-building" without embracing the Czech understanding of ethnicity or neglecting the state, is a historical sociologist.[26]

In 1899, Rudolf Hermann von Herrnritt, a professor of law at the University of Vienna, published a book that distinguished three interwoven strands to national politics in the Habsburg Monarchy: ethnic, historical, and centralistic.[27] He described the first strand as "very radical," and as resting initially on "purely theoretical ground." His second strand referred to understandings of certain "nations" as the successors to certain feudal orders or estates—the nobility of various duchies and kingdoms that became part of the Habsburg Monarchy between the sixteenth and eighteenth centuries. National leaders, by claiming their "nation" to be the heir to a small and real group in the past, bolstered their claims to political primacy within the Bohemian, Hungarian, or other Habsburg lands in the present.[28] Von Herrnritt's third strand, centralistic, contained understandings of the "nation" as the entire citizenry of a state. Today called *civic*, this strand posited a Habsburg or Austrian "nation" for the Habsburg Monarchy, akin to the French and American ones for France and for the United States.

During the 1990s, Jiří Kořalka and Pieter Judson published studies that confirm von Herrnritt's apparently forgotten argument that many of the nationhoods in the monarchy were once rich amalgams, rather than overwhelmingly ethnic. Complementing ethnicity in the Czech case, but rarely given full attention by historians before Kořalka, was a historical, "Bohemian state rights" strand. And complementing, even overshadowing, ethnicity in the German case for a time were historical and civic strands—the first of which von Herrnritt himself, a German, failed to see, and both of which Judson explained in masterful fashion, but not from beginning to end.[29] Already in the 1970s and 1980s, meanwhile, István Deák, Péter Hanák, Andrew Janos, and Katherine Verdery explored the complex interplay among ethnic, historical, and civic strands to Hungarian nationhood.[30] Those studies, like von Herrnritt's and others mentioned previously, all point in the same direction. Ethnicity was only one form of nationhood among several in Habsburg Central Europe, yet one that came to dominate the others by the early decades of the twentieth century. To this day, both in real time and retrospectively, ethnic understandings convert dynamic interaction among socioeconomic interests into conflict between statically defined groups and obscure the political roles of the state.

Budweis/Budějovice is an exceptionally good place through which to press the challenge to the historiographical consensus regarding politics in modern Habsburg Central Europe. Vicar Haug, an ethnic German, did not become a national one. Nor did quite a few other ethnic Germans in town. In part, that was because many of them, if not Haug, were also ethnic Czechs. The high local rate of biethnicity contributed to another pattern unusual in the Bohemian lands: both a German and a Czech movement were present, in roughly equal yet asymmetrical strengths. As was the case elsewhere, those movements used ethnic rhetoric. Individual choice and national competition, though, slowed ethnic nationalization in Budweis/Budějovice and stripped the process of much of its seeming naturalness and irreversibility. Nonethnic understandings of nationhood received unusual emphasis. Czech and German leaders, in their pursuit of power, also appealed openly to socioeconomic interests as well as resorted to raw coercion of Budweisers and of other residents—perhaps no more than elsewhere, but certainly more visibly for posterity, because of mutual national monitoring and denunciation. The Habsburg, Czechoslovak, and

Nazi states, meanwhile, confronted with the Czech-German conflict in miniature, recapitulated their policies for the Bohemian lands as a whole.

Local histories, despite having played significant roles in the scholarly literatures concerning such topics as working-class politics and Nazism, have played only a small role in the literature concerning nationhood. In the Bohemian historiography, Cohen's book is the only major contribution that focuses on a small territorial unit over a considerable span of time. Equivalent studies concerning other parts of Central Europe are few.[31] Farther afield, historians of late imperial Russia and of the Soviet Union have published superb studies in recent years of multinational politics in a nonnational or more-than-national state—but have heavily favored macropolitical approaches.[32] Historians of Western Europe have written a handful of pathbreaking local histories of nationhood. Only Peter Sahlins, however, focused on two nationhoods rather than on just one, and he did so not within one state but on the boundary between two: France and Spain.[33]

Local histories have their limits. A history centered on one town in Habsburg Central Europe cannot hope to explain the origins of national politics, which lie outside the region. Nor can such a study account for a pivotal national success in the region before 1848: the acceptance by Habsburg elites of the idea that Czech, German, and other "nations" existed, and rested at least in part on Czech, German, and other ethnic groups. A study centered on Budweis/Budějovice must also neglect a force that for some time played an important role in Bohemian politics as a whole, but played a minor one in town: the great landowning nobility. Its power, however, steadily declined, such that the triadic, Czech-Habsburg-German structure to politics in Budweis/Budějovice between 1848 and 1918 anticipated a Bohemian trend. Even national successes strictly within the town can be only partly explained through a local approach, because they form part of a global pattern in modern times. Yet such limits are actually quite broad. Within them, this book attempts to go beyond Czech, German, or Czech *and* German interpretations of Bohemian politics during the century after 1848—and in the process, to arrive at a better understanding of Czech and German nationhood.

Publications from Budweis/Budějovice provide the bulk of primary sources for this study. Before the collapse of Communism in 1989, one could have spoken of 1848 and 1948 as the beginning and end of a free press in the Bohemian lands. Censorship and other political constraints, tight during the 1850s and during the Nazi occupation, were relatively loose during the intervening eras of constitutional rule, as well as in the chaotic years of 1848–49 and 1945–47. The economic conditions for local publishing were also favorable. By 1864, a town with fewer than twenty thousand inhabitants, together with its surrounding countryside, was supporting a German newspaper, a Czech newspaper, and a Budweiser one (in German). Over the following several decades, periodicals printed in Budweis/Budějovice mushroomed in number and covered ever more of the shifting political spectrum. Institutions and individuals, meanwhile, added many nonperiodical publications: political pamphlets, associational reports, collections of documents, memoirs, histories, fiction, and more. Circulation figures and print runs, unfortunately, tended to remain a trade secret. But literacy rates, quite high in Bohemia already at the middle of the nineteenth century, officially exceeded 94 percent in 1900.[34]

Some comments about terminology are in order. In this book, the adjective "German" does not refer to the Germany that was founded in 1871. Nor do the nouns "Germans" and "Czechs," when used without "ethnic," refer to nonnational individuals who happened to speak a version of the German or Czech language. In direct quotations from German or from Czech, proper nouns are either translated into English or left in the original language. Otherwise, people, places, and things known in their time by both German and Czech names are called by both here, separated by a slash mark: hence "Budweis" in a quotation from a German-language source, "Budějovice" in a quotation from a Czech-language one, and "Budweis/Budějovice" in other contexts. Double naming was uncommon in the past, as was English-language writing about Habsburg Central Europe. To use only the Czech name or only the German name in English would be less cumbersome. Doing so, though, would favor one national side over the other, and neglect the third, Habsburg, dimension to Bohemian politics before 1918.[35] Historical practice, commemoration, or mimesis are one matter, and historical analysis another: scholars need not limit themselves to understanding the past only in its own terms. On the other hand, scholars should not tolerate anachronism. Thus this book does not follow the widespread practice—whose historical roots are explained in chapter 1—of translating *die böhmischen Länder/české země* as "the Czech lands." If they became Czech, rather than Bohemian, then that was only after 1945.

In English, "nation" is often used to mean "state," and "state" to mean a territory within a state. This book tries to avoid confusion by being consistent. "State" here means "country," in the sense of a membership organization that asserts, to quote Max Weber's classic definition, a "monopoly of the legitimate use of physical force within a given territory."[36] "Nation" means an imagined community at the heart of a certain kind of modern politics, and remains always in quotation marks—which signal critical distance from national uses of the term. "Nationhood," a word coined only recently, is used to replace "nationalism," which has a pejorative ring for many people. "Czechness" and "Germanness" are shorthand for Czech and German nationhood, i.e., loyalties and legitimacies expressed through reference to the Czech and German "nations."

"Ethnic," finally, means an understanding that a "nation" emerged from and rests on a homogeneous culture—defined in the Bohemian cases primarily by language, but also to some degree by religious heritage. In the United States, where nationhood has a strong civic component, "ethnic" often denotes a cultural quality that distinguishes some Americans from others: thus Italian-American, African-American, and so on, in the sense of Italian or African by ethnicity but American by nationhood and by citizenship. From an ethnic perspective in Habsburg Central Europe, though, someone Czech or German by nationhood must be Czech or German by ethnicity as well.

In the summer of 1918, Robert Scheu, a Social Democrat and journalist from Vienna who had little knowledge of Bohemia but excellent connections there, set out to "experience the national question" of the Bohemian lands, and to heighten that experience by visiting Czechs and Germans "where they mesh." He started in Budweis/Budějovice, where he quickly realized that "things of global significance are taking place. But these are silent events that stretch over decades and cause not the slightest stir—no more than does the transformation of a deciduous forest into a coniferous one, which often comes about as a consequence of a single frosty night, and subsequently brings about a climatic change." Originally, Scheu explained, the town had been German. Gradually, though, "through the work of generations of small people, massive dams have been undermined, to the point that the foundations can no longer bear the political superstructure. [Czech] [a]rtisans and small businessmen, united with intellectuals dedicated to the national cause, have conquered heavy industry and banking through tenacious work; they have founded schools, and gained space and ground. The Germans, as heirs [*als erbgesessen*], are on the defensive." Indeed, by the time Scheu finished writing an account of his expedition, in 1919, the Bohemian lands formed part of a Czech state—Czechoslovakia. Why, he asked, had Germans not been able to keep pace with their competitors? "Probably a dramatist could give us the answer, in a sweeping novel that laid bare the driving forces over several generations. I recommend Budweis to him as the setting for the plot."[37]

Scheu proves himself nationally quite tolerant in his account. Yet he was a German, and like most other nationals of his era and of subsequent ones in Habsburg Central Europe, he was blind to nonnational politics. Budweis/Budějovice had not been at first German, then more German than Czech, and then more Czech than German. Rather, it had long been Budweiser, or Habsburg-loyal—and German only in the purely linguistic sense that most residents seem to have preferred to speak German until some time after the middle of the nineteenth century. The transformation of which he wrote was both more complex and more vast than he succeeded in imagining. It involved not only a Czech triumph and a German defeat (whose dimensions in 1918–19 were dwarfed by those in 1945) but a national triumph and a Habsburg defeat—a transformation in the very nature of politics. Yet Scheu's recommendation of Budweis/Budějovice as a setting is a good one, as one novel and several histories that cover life in town over several generations show.[38] Like Scheu's own journalistic work, though, those others are quite national. And unlike it, they tend to neglect developments affecting the town from outside. No one has yet succeeded in laying bare driving forces by focusing on Budweis/Budějovice. This book takes up the challenge.

One

Politics in Flux, 1848–1871

In the year 1265, at the behest of Otto/Otakar II of Přemysl, the King of Bohemia, colonists speaking a Germanic language created a new settlement near the confluence of the Maltsch/Malše and Moldau/Vltava Rivers. A local knight known as Budiwoj provided inspiration for the new town's name: Buduoyz in Latin, and Budweis in the language that eventually crystallized into German. Budějovice, the Slavic or Czech equivalent, followed some time later. Little more than a sparsely settled swamp at first, the town lay approximately 100 miles due south of the royal capital, Prague, on the edge of the Central Bohemian plain. A small mountain range rose in the distance, marking where the neighboring duchies of Upper and Lower Austria began. More immediately, to the southwest, stretched the dense Bohemian Forest, through which intrepid travelers could reach Bavaria. Since well before the thirteenth century, the mountainous rim of Bohemia had been home to a population speaking Germanic dialects, and the low-lying core home to a population speaking Slavic ones. The linguistic border, "quite sharp, and almost without transitions" in most parts, nonetheless had its fuzzy areas and its discontinuities. Those areas now included Budweis/Budějovice.[1]

During the fifteenth century, the Bohemian lands were wracked by struggles between Catholics and "Hussites," as some of Europe's first Protestants were known. Throughout those struggles, as well as after them, Budweis/Budějovice remained Catholic, predominantly German-speaking, and loyal to the crown—which bore the name of Wenceslas [*Wenzel/ Václav*], Bohemia's first king and patron saint. In 1526, that crown fell to the Habsburg dynasty, which ruled the neighboring Austrian duchies. Bohemian nobles, however, chafed under its very Catholic rule, and started a revolt in 1618 by heaving two Habsburg officials from a window in the Prague Castle. Because of troubles in Hungary (whose Crown of St. Stephan the Habsburgs had also inherited in 1526), as well as in the Austrian duchies, the fate of the dynasty hung in the balance. So did that of Budweis/Budějovice, "the always loyal." One of only three Bohemian towns not to side with the nobles, it soon found itself under siege.

In November 1620, Ferdinand II of Habsburg emerged triumphant from the pivotal Battle of the White Mountain just outside Prague. He had several noble leaders beheaded, and integrated the Bohemian lands much more tightly with his other lands, thereby violating the historical rights of the Crown of St. Wenceslas. For a generation, armies continued to spread misery across Central Europe, in what has come to be called the Thirty Years' War. Already in December 1620, though, Budweis/Budějovice reaped rewards for its loyalty, including elevation to the status of free royal town. Over the following two centuries, as the Habsburg Monarchy became one of Europe's Great Powers, Budweis/Budějovice prospered. The linguistic border within the Bohemian lands did not change. But medieval Czech, which had figured next to Latin as a language of the court and of public life, yielded in many formal contexts to some form of German.[2]

During the Napoleonic wars, armies occupied Budweis/Budějovice more than once. Some Budweisers found themselves swept out into the wide world by the tumult. Those who returned brought new perspectives. Both the medieval fortifications ringing the town and legal distinctions between burghers and mere residents remained in place, as did many of the other barriers that had long prevented peasants from moving to town. Yet the insular, "home town" quality to life had been disrupted permanently. In 1812 or 1813, Matthäus/Matouš Zátka, a young merchant in a nearby village, succeeded in taking up residence in Budweis/Budějovice. Like others who had made that shift in the past, he had to switch languages, because the linguistic distinction between town and country remained, at least in attenuated form. As a prominent burgher wrote in 1821, "the inhabitants, largely Catholic and mixed only with a few Protestants, are exceedingly industrious, and given more to the German language than to the Czech one—which, however, most people speak, too." Yet Zátka's generation of transplants turned its back on the countryside less than had earlier generations. He and a few other newcomers sometimes got together to socialize in Czech, even as most residents continued to look down on the language and to use it much less with each other than with peasants buying or selling goods in town.[3]

Although the Bohemian lands counted among the more industrialized parts of the Habsburg Monarchy, Southern Bohemia lagged behind. Coal deposits were lacking, and the only natural resources available in abundance were graphite and lumber. A few noble families, including the Schwarzenbergs and the Buquoys, owned huge swaths of the countryside (much of it confiscated from rebel nobles after 1620), and did not promote vigorously the new kinds of economic activity on the rise elsewhere in the kingdom. Nor did the burghers of Southern Bohemia's towns. But in 1832, a small horse-drawn railroad connected Budweis/Budějovice to Linz and to the Danube River, in Upper Austria. In the opposite direction, toward Prague, state-sponsored regulation of the Moldau/Vltava River also improved the transportation network. Between 1832 and 1838, the weight of goods shipped through town tripled. A wool spinnery opened, and soon employed more than 140 people. In 1847, two major factories relocated to town from Vienna: L. & C. Hardtmuth's Earthenware and Pencil Factory, and a matchworks. The population of Budweis/Budějovice increased from about 6,800 in 1828 to 8,100 in 1832, and to 15,200 in 1851.[4]

Such dramatic demographic growth resulted in the growth of whole new residential districts just outside Budweis/Budějovice's walls—especially to the north and east, in what came to be called the Prague and Vienna suburbs. Inside the walls, the layout barely changed. At the center was the huge square, or *Ringplatz/rynek*, where various markets were held and around which stood a chain of buildings, linked one to the next by a covered promenade except at the four corners. One of those buildings, on one of the corners, was the town hall. Many others contained a workshop or store on the ground floor. Just off the *Ringplatz/rynek* was the cathedral, and next to it the Black Tower, from which a watchman continually surveyed the town for fires.

Only a few things are known about the thousands of men and women who joined Zátka in moving to Budweis/Budějovice during the first half of the nineteenth century. Protestant residents remained rare, and Jewish ones prohibited. As late as 1848, a policeman roused a man from his bed in a hotel on the *Ringplatz/rynek* and expelled him from town—for violating a long-standing ban not only on residence by Jews but on overnight stays. Most of the newcomers probably came from the surrounding countryside, were poor, and spoke more Czech than German.[5] Here a few comments about the Czech and German languages are in order.

Both Czech and German are Indo-European languages, and thus share many grammatical and lexical elements. Czech, however, belongs to the Slavic or Slavonian branch of the Indo-European family, and German to the Germanic branch. The distance between the two is enough to make Czech and German mutually incomprehensible. Then again, well into the nineteenth century, dialects and cultural registers in both languages varied so much that even two Bohemians who supposedly spoke the same language could fail to understand one another. Bilingualism, meanwhile, took more than one form. Those members of old Budweiser families who spoke Czech tended to do so in far less schooled fashion than they spoke German, having learned the Slavic language through interaction with countryfolk in the household or on the *Ringplatz/rynek*. Villagers in Czech-speaking areas often picked up some German in mirror fashion. But any such villagers who had a good education almost certainly had a firm command of German, because secondary schools were located in towns and used the German language. The Czech-speaking peasant lad who attended school for more than a few years often ended up able to read and write German better than he did his original tongue.

Bohemia's two languages were linked to each other asymmetrically, in ways that reflected historical complexities and relationships of power. But those links were changing. Already in the eighteenth century, the Habsburg state and the Catholic Church had begun to develop a dense network of elementary schools that reached into the Bohemian countryside, and promoted at least basic literacy in a standardized version of either German or Czech. Vicar Haug and people like him, guided by Enlightenment understandings of education, worked hard to make Czech less of a "peasant dialect," and more equal with German. Much the same was happening elsewhere in the world, too: mass literacy in newly codified vernaculars was emerging, in a complex give-and-take with the rise of centralized states and of social mobility. One scholar, Vladimír Macura, has written of a "shift in the center of gravity from an understanding of Czech culture as a partial cultural sphere within a culture tied to communication in German, toward an understanding of Czech culture as an independent and self-contained [celistvý] configuration."[6]

That process of standardizing, separating, and equalizing German and Czech, however, was slow and uneven. In the early 1840s, Johann Georg Kohl, a writer from Bremen (a German-speaking port some distance from the Habsburg Monarchy), journeyed by stagecoach from Prague to Budweis/Budějovice. Commenting on the "peculiarities of the Bohemian-German dialect" spoken by his fellow passengers, he wrote,

> I was not a little surprised at the systematic and consistent manner in which the good people modify our grammar and pronunciation to suit their own views. Sometimes Slavonian words are Germanized, and sometimes German words effectually disguised by Slavonian terminations, and at other times the strangest gibberish is produced by the least cultivated classes, who frequently mix up their German and Slavonian in so indiscriminate a manner, as to make their meaning unintelligible to any one not familiar with both languages. These remarks do not, of course, apply to the more educated classes.

Subsequent accounts by natives of Budweis/Budějovice confirm Kohl's impression, and show "systematic and consistent" mixing not only of Czech into German but vice versa.[7]

Kohl's observations about language in Budweis/Budějovice itself were less accurate. One could even call them distorted. He emphasized the German-speaking aspect of the town, to the point of omitting any mention of its Czech-speaking one. "The place is more completely German," he claimed, "than hardly any other town in Central Bohemia except Prague. For that reason, quite rightly, it is known to all the world only by the German version of its name: Budweis. All Germans, to be sure, will rejoice silently over this fact."[8] To Kohl, the town was German-speaking, and thus German. A German from outside the Habsburg Monarchy, he brought to it a national perspective of an ethnic type.

Yet Kohl viewed matters from a German perspective of a historical type as well. Until 1806, parts of the Habsburg Monarchy and of Prussia, together with the more than 300 sovereign territories that made up the political patchwork of West Central Europe, had belonged to the "Holy Roman Empire of the German Nation." Then the Habsburgs, its longtime heads, had dissolved the "empire" under pressure from Napoleon. That loose association of states, as many a student of history has heard, was actually not holy, not Roman, and not an empire. Nor was it German: the "nation" in its name denoted not a people in the modern sense but a feudal elite. Yet Kohl and other nationals ignored the vast differences between medieval and modern "nations," as well as between a medieval empire and a modern one, and saw in the Holy Roman Empire a first German state. Even before coming under Habsburg rule, the Bohemian lands had belonged to that "Germany." And since 1815, they had belonged to its successor, the German Confederation—a loose association of the same territories, organized now not into hundreds of states but into fewer than forty (above all, the Habsburg Monarchy and a greatly enlarged Prussia). Thus the Bohemian lands, and Budweis/Budějovice within them, were supposedly German.[9]

Kohl did not belong to the historical "nation" of royalty and nobility that continued to dominate politics in the "Germany" of his day. Indeed, his name, which lacked the noble predicate "von," means "cabbage." Yet by adding an ethnic strand to the historical one, he made himself an heir to that elite. So did many other speakers of German. The result was a "nation" open to linguistic assimilation, closed to the lower classes, and above other "nations" in Central Europe—although Kohl's brief remarks only hint at that configuration. He quite likely arrived at his assessment of Budweis/Budějovice as so "completely German," for example, by counting all wealthy residents as Germans (whether or not they spoke the language with a native accent) and by dismissing all poorer ones as members either of no "nation" or of one that was inferior. Czechs took it "very much amiss," Kohl wrote, when "we Germans" claimed that Prague and the rest of Bohemia were German. But "as ancient and modern lords we have the most perfect right on our side; so we shall continue to call Bohemia a German land, on right of our sword, our civilization, and our industry—a German land, in which the intruding Tshekhs are condemned to plough our fields."[10]

When Kohl visited Budweis/Budějovice, no official studies by the Habsburg state of language use in the Bohemian lands existed. From experience, the authorities knew where to post proclamations in Czech and where in German. The authorities also pursued a policy of bilingualism often enough to have developed for it a special term: "utraquism," which had originally denoted the heretical Hussite practice of taking the Sacrament *sub utraque specie*, or in both kinds—as bread and as wine. From Habsburg perspectives, however, questions of language mattered little. Only in 1841 was a small Statistical Office in Vienna enlarged into a Directorate of Administrative Statistics and granted enough resources to begin work on the first official study of language use throughout the monarchy. Perhaps because the head of the directorate, Karl Baron von Czoernig, relied in considerable measure on earlier, rudimentary studies that had recorded only one language for each person, his own study did the same. His reluctance to spread a person across more than one linguistic category (what Benedict Anderson calls the "impermissibility of fractions" for demographers) perhaps contributed as well to this reductionist decision.[11] Whatever the reasons, von Czoernig's *Ethnography of the Austrian Monarchy* placed the authority of the state behind an ethnic, mutually exclusive system of classification. Because his study barely mentioned Budweis/Budějovice and did not appear until the 1850s, and because his successors then avoided the subject of language or ethnicity for a generation, the effects of Habsburg support for ethnic understandings will not be discussed at length until chapters 2, 3, and 4 of this book. Here, however, one preliminary point must be made.

Von Czoernig's reams of data help make clear a question of majorities and minorities that lurks beneath the surface of Kohl's less systematic and less ethnic work. In one matter, von Czoernig's *Ethnography* proved Kohl correct. The Czech language indeed was dominant in the Central Bohemian plain, except in Prague, Budweis/Budějovice, and a few other towns. But von Czoernig's numbers also revealed something that Kohl had not mentioned: not only in the plain but in Bohemia as a whole (whose population was about 4.4 million), as well as in the Bohemian lands (6.4 million), Czech-speakers were in the majority, by a proportion of about 3:2. In the entire monarchy (approximately 36 million), on the other hand, Czech-speakers (3.9 million) numbered only half as many as German-speakers (7.9 million). And non-Habsburg parts of the German Confederation contained hardly a single speaker of Czech, but many additional millions of German-speakers. Depending on the historical territory that one chose, German-speakers could be seen as a minority or as a majority.[12] Kohl may or may not have known about that demographic pattern, and may or may not have cared. Whatever the case, his choice—the German Confederation—yielded a large ethnically German majority.

A Czech counterpart to Kohl's assessment of Budweis/Budějovice may be found in an *Ethnographic Survey of the Bohemian Kingdom*. Published in 1850, but based primarily on summaries of language use by parish priests in 1829, the survey was written (in Czech) by Josef Jireček, a man active in Czech circles in Prague. In his very first paragraph, he equated language with "nation" or "people" [*národ*], and argued that the state should collect data so that it might devise language policies that better served the population. He then explained that he had classified communities as "Czech," "German," or "mixed," according to "the language used by residents as their mother tongue in communal intercourse." Yet he barely used his third category, and thus followed Kohl in glossing over bilingualism. Jireček also admitted to contradicting his own classification system in the cases of Prague and of Budweis/Budějovice, both of which he labeled Czech. As justification, he offered only that residents of the capital were Slavic in their great majority, and that it would be "entirely frivolous" [*zcela daremné*] to classify a population on the basis of language alone. The implication, it seems, was that a person's language of daily use mattered less than did his or her "mother tongue"—and indeed, that "mother tongue" mattered less than did the mother's tongue, at least when the latter was Czech. If Kohl understood ethnicity in such a way as to welcome German gains through assimilation, then Jireček understood ethnicity in such a way as to resist Czech losses. His vocabulary of "population" and "majority" also signaled a more populist, less elitist stance.[13]

Like Kohl, but less so, Jireček complemented ethnic nationhood with a historical, territorial one. He concluded his study by highlighting Bohemia's ethnically Czech majority, and left all larger territories unmentioned. Serving him and many other Czechs as the ancient Czech "nation" was the Bohemian nobility. To be sure, Jireček was no more a nobleman than was Kohl.[14] And while nobles within the German Confederation tended to speak German well, many nobles in Bohemia spoke little Czech. Indeed, radical Czechs tended to agree with Kohl and with other Germans in understanding the Bohemian nobility not as Czech (or as Habsburg-loyal) but as German. Yet ties between nobles and Czechs were real, and mutually beneficial. Before 1848, the "imperial-royal" authorities—first under Emperor-King Francis (1792–1835) and then under his feeble-minded son Ferdinand (1835–48)—pursued a reactionary course, and placed tight restrictions on public life. One of the few initiatives of lasting political significance that the noble-dominated Bohemian Diet, or crownland parliament, succeeded in undertaking was to commission František Palacký, a Czech historian, to write a multivolume study of medieval Bohemia. Some Bohemian nobles also made a point of improving their command of Czech. By emphasizing the pre-Habsburg history of the Bohemian lands and their linguistic difference from the rest of the monarchy, as well as by building linguistic bridges to the Czech-speaking majority, Bohemia's historical elite bolstered its political position vis-à-vis the Habsburg state. Czechs, for their part, gained much needed support and legitimacy, as well as a

mythology that reinforced their self-image as a once great people debased
and unjustly dominated by an arrogant German "nation."[15]

Before 1848, Germans in the Bohemian lands actually numbered very
few. Kohl, an outsider, found no fellow Germans with whom to rejoice
during his brief stay. Nor have specialists in his era unearthed many Germans through research.[16] Czechs, although less rare, still made up only a
small minority. At the end of the 1860s, when Palacký, the Czech historian, said that the entire Czech "nation" might have perished had the roof
caved in on a single gathering forty years earlier, he was exaggerating. But
at any time before 1848, had he or Jireček visited Budweis/Budějovice,
they would have found only a few dozen Czechs with whom to lament a
German dominance that existed only in their national imaginations.[17] All
national assertions aside, the Czech-German linguistic divide ran through
many people, in undivisive fashion. And more significant for residents than
the German Confederation or the Bohemian lands was the much smaller
historical territory of the town. The central political struggles unfolded
not between Czechs and Germans but among burghers, unprivileged
town dwellers, peasants, and nobles, as well as among Catholics, Protestants, and Jews—in other words, among Budweisers and among other
varieties of Habsburg loyalists.

To sum up, individual languages and linguistic repertoires in the Bohemian lands during the first half of the nineteenth century were complex
and historically contingent. Broad structural transformations gradually
undermined the social asymmetry between the Czech and German languages. Even as that asymmetry faded, though, it found new expression
in national understandings of ethnicity—the Czech one centered on
"mother tongue" and on heredity, the German one open to linguistic
assimilation. Czech nationhood as a whole, for that matter, tended to be
more ethnic than historical, while German nationhood tended to be more
historical than ethnic. Czechness differed from Germanness, and even preceded it in the Bohemian lands, but also was linked to it through what
Vladimír Macura has called a "negative and analog tie."[18]

1848: Habsburg, Czech, German

In 1848, in the whole of Central Europe, an era of political flux began.
Until 1871, as things turned out, some of the most basic questions about
politics stood open. What should be the borders of individual states? What
should be the formal institutions through which politics was channeled?
Who should have access to them, and on what terms? To what extent
would traditional forms of legitimacy yield to popular sovereignty, and to
what extent would popular sovereignty take national forms? Answers and

a new stability came only slowly, with considerable upheaval. Several major wars took place; entire states vanished from the map; subjects moved far toward becoming citizens; and parliaments and constitutions gradually became fixtures of public life. Already in 1848, though, all the questions appeared in full force. And almost as quickly, at least part of one answer became clear. The "people" in popular sovereignty would be primarily national.

Early in March, news of "revolution" in Paris triggered off political upheaval in multiple capitals of Central Europe. By the end of the month, the Habsburg chancellor, Clemens Lothar von Metternich, had fled into exile; fighting had erupted in Vienna, Berlin, and Milan; the Habsburg Monarchy and Prussia seemed well on their way to constitutional rule; and Emperor-King Ferdinand had been forced to yield control over many state organs within the lands of the Crown of St. Stephan to the Hungarian movement. In Prague, Czech activists demanded linguistic equality, the unification of the lands of the Crown of St. Wenceslas, and the creation of a Bohemian administration responsible to a legislature elected on the basis of the broadest possible suffrage. And in Frankfurt, about 500 Germans—only two of them from the Habsburg Monarchy—designated themselves a "Pre-Parliament," and set to work organizing an election to a German Constituent National Assembly. Those self-appointed, mostly bourgeois men intended to unite the German Confederation into a single nation-state in liberal, constitutional fashion.

Political contradictions quickly became clear. Palacký and other Czechs opposed the holding of elections in the Bohemian lands for the German Constituent National Assembly. Some burghers in Prague, made into Germans almost overnight by what they considered the excessive nature of the Czech demands, resigned from a committee established to organize elections to a new Bohemian Diet. The emperor-king sanctioned that diet yet hemmed it in by issuing a constitution that superimposed a Habsburg or all-Austrian parliament on the Bohemian one. At the same time, the disoriented authorities allowed followers of the German Constituent National Assembly to do as they pleased.[19] By the end of April, three elections were in the offing in Bohemia, to three revolutionary legislatures. Each was designed to represent the inhabitants of a different historical territory, and each rested on a different kind of legitimacy: German, Czech, and Habsburg. Those legitimacies, furthermore, all contained a new, civic strand. Subjects were to become citizens—politically enfranchised members of a new or reformed state.[20]

In Budweis/Budějovice, the early news from the big cities prompted both celebration and concern. Leading burghers and officials quickly organized night patrols by a National Guard. A more accurate name, though, would have been "Bourgeois Guard," given its composition. And what little public disorder the Guard encountered during March and April involved not so much national conflict as conflict over class and religion. By the end of the month, however, German politics had crystallized locally in at least one form: *Der Löwe* [*The Lion*], a new newspaper edited by a longtime resident named Ernst Franz Richter. His first two issues barely mentioned "nations." But his third, dated May 6, discussed several political topics from a German perspective. One article attacked *Národní noviny* [*National News*], a new Czech newspaper in Prague, for claiming that Germans in Budweis/Budějovice were hostile to linguistic equality, and thus to Czechs. A second article reported on a meeting in Vienna of a newly founded "Association of Germans from Bohemia, Moravia, and Silesia for the Maintenance of Their Nationality," and stated that the Budweiser who had attended had been persuaded that the Czechs were attempting to oppress the Germans. And a third, on the front page, bore an untranslatable title—*Böhmen und Čechen*—which requires explanation.[21]

Until the 1830s or 1840s, both in German and in Czech, the words "Bohemian" and "Czech" were the same: as an adjective, *böhmisch/český*, and as a noun, *Böhme/Čech*. Some related terms coincided too. In German, for example, "Bohemia," "Bohemians," and "Czechs" were all expressed as *Böhmen*. The national implications of that overlap were enormous. When Bohemian nobles learned Czech, and when Czechs studied the Bohemian past, they could claim to be recovering their own language and history. When Jireček proclaimed Budweis/Budějovice to be Czech, he sounded credible, despite its patterns of language use. After all, the town was in Bohemia, and indeed, was sometimes called *Böhmisch* Budweis or *České* Budějovice in order to distinguish it from a town in Moravia with a similar name: Budwitz/Budějovice. In both Czech and German, "Bohemia for the Czechs!" sounded much like "Czechia for the Czechs!" in English.

The handful of Germans in the Bohemian lands, in combating such rhetoric, almost had to develop a new vocabulary. Over a decade or more, they did so by adopting the word *Čech* (sometimes respelled as *Tscheche*) from the Czech language to denote a Czech, and by creating *čechisch* (or *tschechisch*) as a companion adjective. Bohemia, or *Böhmen*, was thus a land whose inhabitants were not *Deutsche* and *Böhmen* (or as one variant had it, *Deutschböhmen* and *Stockböhmen*—with *Stock* meaning something like "true-born") but *Deutsche* and *Čechen*. Czechs objected vehemently to this change, and prevented it from occurring in Czech. Some Germans, though, pushed onward, and began to call themselves the real Bohemians. The article in *Der Löwe*, for example, bore the title *Böhmen und Čechen*—"Bohemians/Bohemia/Germans and Czechs."[22] Richter countered the widespread Czech rhetoric of "Czechia for the Czechs!" with "Bohemia for the (German) Bohemians!" Hardly do the enchanting rays

of freedom cast their smile on the glorious meadows of our fatherland,"
the article stated,

> and hardly do we call out our joyous and warm welcome to this long missed and
> anxiously awaited goddess, than discord rears its head. . . . As though at the strike
> of a wand, Ultra-Czechs [*Ultra-Čechen*] and German Bohemians [*Deutschböh-
> men*] have sprung up. They attack one another constantly, squandering precious
> time without achieving any more favorable result than rendering every attempt
> at unity impossible. . . . The German Bohemians form associations in order to
> protest against the excesses of the Ultra-Czechs in Bohemia. The Czechs wish
> to plant their banner everywhere again. They distinguish themselves sharply from
> the German Bohemians, and heated verbal battle has already been done on several
> occasions. May God grant that matters never come to blows.

The author—probably Richter—then explained what was at stake: *Anschluss*, or the inclusion of Bohemia in Germany. The Pre-Parliament in
Frankfurt had urged Budweis/Budějovice's town hall to organize the election of a delegate to the German Constituent National Assembly, which
was due to convene on May 18. But town hall was taking no action.

In mid-May, radicals in Vienna took to the streets and forced Emperor-
King Ferdinand to extend the franchise in the upcoming elections to the
all-Austrian Parliament, as well as to the Bohemian Diet. Indeed, he surrendered to the parliament the authority to write a constitution. In Bud-
weis/Budějovice, there formed a chapter of the Slavic Linden Tree, a new
Czech association with headquarters in Prague. Charter members numbered about 150, and included two sons of Matthäus/Matouš Zátka:
Ignaz/Hynek and Jakob/Jakub. As was the case in two-thirds of the electoral districts in Bohemia, elections in town to the German Parliament or
Constituent National Assembly failed to take place. Richter attributed that
outcome to the "machinations" of Ultra-Czechs at a crucial meeting of
voters.[23] More plausible, though, is that Czechs added their weight to a
Budweiser, Habsburg-loyal electoral majority, which prevailed against a
minority of Germans such as Richter.

At the beginning of June, the day after the opening of a congress of
Austrian Slavs—who thus signaled their opposition to the German Parliament—in Prague, Richter's *Löwe* printed an essay by someone who identi-
fied himself as a Slav by birth, but took the German side. Western Slavs
such as the Czechs, he argued, had far more in common with Germans
than with Eastern Slavs such as the Russians, and had to choose between
joining Germany or Russia. In the long run, independence from both was
not possible. Members of the Slavic Linden Tree, taking offense at that
article or at others in a similar vein, went looking for Richter, and found
him hiding in a pigsty. "Arrested," tried for his supposed crimes, and sentenced to death by hanging, Richter nonetheless made his way home un-

harmed. He then wrote an address to his readers in which he insisted that any apparent bias in his newspaper stemmed only from the fact that more Germans than Czechs were sending him articles for publication. Perhaps in an attempt at conciliation, he used the word *Böhmen* for "Czechs." Then again, he went on to say that he considered himself a *Böhme*, and always would. The Slavic Linden Tree, meanwhile, supposedly counted some Germans as members.[24]

In mid-June, as elections to the Bohemian Diet began, student and working-class radicals rioted in Prague. The Habsburg response marked an end to the revolutionary spring and a beginning to a revival of conservative fortunes. The imperial-royal army bombarded Prague, reestablished order, and disbanded some Czech organizations. The Slavic Congress collapsed, tainted by the riots through geographical association. In Budweis/ Budějovice, two radicals in the Slavic Linden Tree, both priests, were taken into custody. The Bohemian Diet never convened. But the Austrian Parliament did, at the end of July—days before a Habsburg military victory that sealed the fate of a bid for Italian independence in the south of the monarchy. Joining eighty-nine other Bohemian delegates in Vienna, as the representative of Budweis/Budějovice, was its aging deacon. He had run unopposed at the beginning of the month, in an election that had drawn only 200-odd men, one-fifth of the electorate.[25] Of the three legislatures proposed in the spring, only the Habsburg one had succeeded in getting off the ground in Bohemia.

One of the first resolutions passed by the delegates in Vienna concerned not national conflict but serfdom. At the beginning of September, they abolished the *corvée* and patrimonial courts. Yet when the parliament then turned to making lords and peasants into citizens with the same civil liberties, nationhood quickly took center stage. Considerable discussion centered on the internal boundaries and representative bodies of the monarchy, and how they should accommodate its "nations." In October, Budweis/Budějovice's representative resigned his seat, explaining that his priestly duties were considerable, and that he felt suspected of being a reactionary. His successor, Anton Robl, was a German Liberal. In the by-election, he prevailed against a nonnational, out-of-town candidate— Count Leo/Lev Thun, until recently the governor of Bohemia—by a thin margin.[26]

Palacký, who sat in the Austrian Parliament, had outlined the leading Czechs' program already in April, in a widely circulated letter to the Pre-Parliament in Frankfurt. Bohemia's tie to the Holy Roman Empire and then to the German Confederation, he argued in the letter, had never been of much importance to "the Czech/Bohemian people, the Bohemian estates" [*das böhmische Volk, die böhmischen Stände*]. *Anschluss* to the new Germany had no historical justification, and was out of the question.

Palacký rejected the opposite extreme, too: becoming part of a pan-Slavic, Russian empire. He also intimated strongly that the Czech "nation" was too small and weak to survive between the German and Russian colossuses as a sovereign state. Much more in the interest of Czechs, and indeed of all Europe, was the preservation of the Habsburg Monarchy. Preservation, though, required transformation. The Habsburg state, he wrote,

> has long mistaken and denied the actual juridical and moral basis to its existence: the principle of complete equality of rights and respect for all the nationalities and confessions united under its scepter. . . . If the bond that binds a number of nations into a political whole is to be firm and enduring, . . . each nation must harbor the certain hope of finding defense and protection in the central authority against any possible excesses by neighbors. Then one will even make haste to endow that central authority with sufficient powers to make the furnishing of such protection possible.[27]

Palacký placed his hopes in a Habsburg Monarchy divided up into federal units, each one the domain of a different "nation." Made multinational in supposedly egalitarian fashion, that state would in fact prevent Germans from dominating Czechs—and indeed, perhaps allow Czechs to dominate Germans within the Bohemian lands.

In June, however, the Habsburg suppression of the Bohemian Diet ruled out Palacký's maximal goal of "restoring" control over the whole of the Bohemian lands to a supposedly ancient Czech "nation." Over the following months, he proposed less ambitious variants on that solution. On the parliamentary committee responsible for drafting a constitution, he even floated the idea of creating an autonomous territory that included only ethnically Czech areas. That tack would have required that he jettison the historical strand to Czech nationhood—although through his writings, he had probably done more to develop that strand than any other person. Palacký seems also to have stood open to a civic understanding of nationhood, such that ethnic Germans might have become part of his Czech or Bohemian "nation." Over the course of the summer and fall, however, he and other Czech leaders sided increasingly with Habsburg leaders—who were less than enthusiastic about civic institutions, and now were rapidly reasserting political control. The Czech change in course, besides reflecting political realities, coincided with a programmatic Czech emphasis on opposing the German movement, which dominated the "Left" in the parliament.[28]

That "Left," it should be noted, was not Marxist but liberal. In Budweis/Budějovice, *Der Löwe* emphasized that *Anschluss* would be to a constitutional Germany in which Germans and non-Germans would enjoy the same rights. But how equality among individuals would translate into equality between the German and Czech "nations" remained unex-

plained. And German reactions to Czech understandings of equality, furthermore, tended to betray arrogance and intolerance, as well as impatience with supposed reactionaries and social inferiors. In July, Richter
printed a letter from Frankfurt by Franz Schuselka, a native son who had
left town quite young and then, outside the Habsburg Monarchy during
the 1840s, had become a leading German Liberal. "It filled me with deep
pain to hear that Czech terrorism rules in Budweis, too," he wrote, without giving any specifics.

> To tell the truth, the dear *German* residents of Budweis are to blame. My lovely
> home town must have undergone quite a change; in my time it was decidedly
> German! Hopefully the German Bohemians will now come to full conscious-
> ness. Eventually the raw brutality of the Czechs must outrage even the most
> tolerant of souls. Everyone who means well for Austria and for Bohemia is
> obliged to work against the drive of the Czech legions [*der Čechomannen*] to
> become the rulers. German or Russian? That is the fateful question. Whoever
> wishes to be a Slav(e) in Bohemia should do so. But the German, too, must have
> a right to free development.[29]

In December, Richter printed an article entitled "Reflections on German and Austrian Unification." The author argued,

> Once the equality of all nationalities is constitutionally guaranteed, one can lay
> to rest any fears that the German character might exercise any other influence
> over nationalities connected to it than that until now—the influence of a greater
> civilization. And should some or all of these nationalities thereby disappear into
> the German one, in the course of completely free national life, then this would
> be a peaceful conquest of a sort probably unprecedented in the history of man-
> kind, a conquest of freedom. It would also be proof that the given race [*Volks-
> stamm*] was no longer viable.[30]

The author considered liberal principles universal, supranational. But he
also expected that a triumph of liberalism would be a triumph of Germanness. Ethnic Czechs, once made citizens of a German state, would
exercise their freedom in order to become part of the superior German
"nation."

Not all Germans in Bohemia were so confident. Already at the end of
August, Bohemian German members of the Austrian Parliament had gathered for a congress. There they, like Palacký, had nearly abandoned historical nationhood, and had called for the redivision of the monarchy into
ethnic units. Central to understanding that retreat is the Habsburg recov-
ery of control. In September, the imperial-royal army began the conquest
of Hungary. In October, troops smashed an uprising in Vienna. Prince
Felix von Schwarzenberg, newly installed as chancellor and as foreign minister, charted a resolutely conservative course. On December 2, Emperor-

King Ferdinand abdicated in favor of his eighteen-year-old nephew, who became Emperor-King Francis Joseph. And throughout the fall and winter, the German Parliament in Frankfurt shrank. Its remaining members pinned their fading hopes on creating a Germany that included no part of the Habsburg Monarchy—a smaller Germany, rather than a greater one.[31]

Prussia, however, which would necessarily have dominated a smaller Germany, was experiencing a revival of conservative, dynastic fortunes, too. At the end of 1848, the king of Prussia, Frederick William IV of Hohenzollern, disbanded a constituent Prussian Parliament that he had allowed earlier in the year, and imposed a conservative constitution. The German Parliament, desperate, still offered him the imperial crown in the spring. Frederick William rejected the offer, perceiving correctly a fundamental clash with his own understanding of nationhood—which over the preceding months had grown reactionary and almost exclusively historical. As he explained to a friend, "Should the thousand-year-old crown of the German Nation, which has rested for forty-two years, be given away again, then it is I and my EQUALS WHO WILL GIVE IT AWAY. Woe to him who usurps that to which he has no right."[32] All claims by commoners such as Kohl to the contrary, only princes could belong to the German "nation." Soon thereafter, the German Parliament collapsed.

The Austrian Parliament, meanwhile, had continued its deliberations. In January 1849, von Schwarzenberg succeeded in piecing together a majority, including Czech delegates, that voted to shelve discussion of Article I of a draft constitution, according to which "all powers of the state originate from the people [*Volk*]." But he and Francis Joseph had already decided to follow the Prussian example. They disbanded the parliament and imposed, or "octroyed," a constitution early in March. Centralist, as opposed to the federalist draft elaborated by the parliament, the octroy paid only lip service to national equality. And a supplement restricted the right to vote in town council elections to the minority of men prosperous enough to pay a direct state tax. Those voters, furthermore, were now divided into three electorates, or "curias," such that the elite that paid two-thirds of the taxes also controlled two-thirds of the seats. A similarly plutocratic suffrage came into force for the Bohemian Diet. In Prussia, King Frederick William IV imposed a three-class suffrage, too, for the all-Prussian Diet. There, though, adult males paying no tax kept the right to vote that they had gained in 1848. Unlike in the Habsburg Monarchy, the third curia could be understood to represent the entire population—the third estate.[33]

Over the following several years, while the Prussian regime cultivated its three-class sham of universal male suffrage, the Habsburg regime rejected the principle of popular sovereignty outright, and turned instead to a naked neo-absolutism. During 1849 and 1850, the authorities reimposed censorship and disbanded associations. Public life in the monarchy all but ended, smothered under a blanket of political repression. Francis Joseph then suspended his own constitution, and put a stop to any further elections. Yet he did not wind the clock back to the reactionary days of Francis and of Ferdinand. Rather, the new emperor-king wound it back further, to the enlightened absolutism of their predecessors, Maria Theresa and Joseph II. During the 1850s, the Habsburg state abolished internal tariffs, enacted a pathbreaking law on corporations, promoted railroad construction, and created an influential network of Chambers of Commerce and Trade. In 1859, new trade regulations swept away guild restrictions and established occupational freedom. Such reforms, together with the abolition of serfdom, sped economic development and cleared the way for a huge wave of migration from the countryside to the towns.[34]

In 1848, residents of Budweis/Budějovice had faced a fundamental question for the first time: did they want to belong to a German state, to a Habsburg one, or to a Czech or Bohemian one within the monarchy? The distinctions and implications, however, had been unclear, and answers had been both confused and unenthusiastic. In March 1849, when notables organized a public celebration on the anniversary of the 1848 "revolution," attendance was poor.[35] One year had only been enough time for Budweisers to begin thinking as citizens. Yet helping to structure that preliminary thought about citizenship had been the national categories of "Czech" and "German"—even when the citizenship in question was Habsburg.

After 1848: Habsburg, Federalist, Centralist

At the end of the 1850s, neo-absolutist rule collapsed. Causes included the ruinous state of imperial finances and the unification of Italy (which involved a military defeat for the Habsburg Monarchy, as well as the loss of Lombardy). Francis Joseph, desperate for funds, agreed to establish a quasi-parliament. He quickly found himself pushed—but also pulled—to concede more. On the one hand, the Hungarian movement sought a restoration of the autonomy won in 1848. On the other hand, banking circles made loans contingent on the creation of an all-Austrian legislature with significant powers of budgetary oversight and taxation. Other players quickly took sides in what became a defining political question over the following decades: federalism or centralism? Political conservatives and Czechs, along with Hungarians, took the federalist side.[36] German liberals, for reasons that will be explored shortly, took the centralist one.

During the winter of 1860–61, the emperor-king first decided on a
federalist course, and then reversed himself, having found the resistance
of centralists too strong. With the "February Patent," he brought into
being an Austrian Imperial Council, or Parliament, with broad jurisdiction. In a concession to the Hungarian movement, the Austrian Parliament could meet either as a full body or as a narrower one concerned only
with "Cisleithania," or the non-Hungarian lands of the monarchy. Many
members of the Upper House were to be appointed by Francis Joseph,
while members of the Lower House were to be elected by the crownland
diets—whose powers were otherwise not great. Those diets were to rest
on suffrage systems much like those created in 1849 and then suspended
shortly thereafter. The electorate for the Bohemian Diet, for example, included about 6 percent of the population, and was partitioned into four
curias: great landowners (aristocrats, numbering only in the dozens), with
seventy seats; urban males paying at least ten florins in a direct state tax,
with seventy-two seats; rural males paying the same amount (but voting
indirectly, through electors), with seventy-nine; and Chambers of Commerce and Trade, with fifteen.[37]

The February Patent also permitted a revival of electoral politics at the
municipal level—where town councils were now meant to serve as a weak
federalist counterweight to the Imperial Council. Like diet electorates, the
town council ones were small, and strongly tilted toward elites through
the use of curias. Here the curias usually numbered three, and were defined by tax payments as well as by social status. (Burghers, for example,
could vote in the third curia even if they had paid less than the minimum
of one florin in a direct state tax.) In Budweis/Budějovice, each of the
three curias created in 1861 elected twelve aldermen. And in the municipal
election held at the end of the winter, about 8 or 9 percent of residents
could vote—not secretly but "publicly, without shyness."[38]

That election, the first in a decade, was not contested by parties. Indeed,
an ordinance prohibited public discussion of political issues. At a meeting
held for the purpose of assembling a single list of twelve candidates for
the third, largest, and least wealthy curia, 306 voters (of 838 who could
have attended) divided over the candidacies of two men who had distinguished themselves as national leaders in 1848: Ignaz/Hynek Zátka and
Anton Robl. Zátka won nomination with 56 percent of the votes, and
Robl with 44 percent. No other pair, though, had a nationally polarizing
effect. And chosen by two-thirds of the voters was Franz Josef Klawik/
František Josef Klavík, the Budweiser whose actions later in 1861 were
discussed in the introduction. In the actual election that followed, Zátka,
Robl, and Klawik/Klavík, together with Vicar Haug, all won a seat on the
town council. Klawik/Klavík, who had been serving as mayor since the

late 1850s, was now confirmed in the post by the aldermen.[39] Fault lines within the electorate were not primarily national.

In mid-March, the Budweis/Budějovice Chamber of Commerce and Trade, which was dominated by wealthy businessmen, elected two German Liberal factory-owners to the diet: Peter Steffens and Karl Hardtmuth. Rural voters surrounding the town elected Zátka and a lawyer, Wendelin/Vendelín Grünwald—who, like Zátka, was a federalist and had been active in Czech circles during 1848. The municipal electorate, though, chose Klawik/Klavík. He, unlike Steffens and Hardtmuth, avoided siding with centralists in the diet when it met during April in Prague. And unlike Zátka and Grünwald (as well as the bishop in town, Johann Valerian Jirsik/ Jan Valerian Jirsík, whose office entitled him to a diet seat), Klawik/Klavík refused to join Palacký and nearly eighty other federalist delegates in signing a protest. In it, they claimed to represent a Czech-speaking majority that was intent on recovering Bohemia's historical rights, but had been reduced to an artificial minority in the diet by the electoral system.[40]

Klawik/Klavík's neutrality on pivotal issues, however, rendered him almost irrelevant. Between about 1861 and 1863, loose factions emerged in the Bohemian Diet and Austrian Parliament. One, led by Palacký and his son-in-law, František Ladislav Rieger, called itself the Bohemian/ Czech National Party [*Česká národní strana*]. It had a small liberal wing and a larger Catholic one—politically conservative, but in many respects attuned to the plights of Bohemia's many poorer people. Another faction was made up of federalists among Bohemia's great landowners. Already at the beginning of 1861, their leader, Count Heinrich/Jindřich Clam-Martinic, had met with Palacký and Rieger to discuss the possibility of an alliance. Opposition by the landowners to a revision of the diet suffrage (in other words, to an undermining of the power provided them by the curial system) proved a stumbling block. But the two groupings gradually developed a common federalist, or "Bohemian state rights," stance. Even when they voted together in the diet, though, they remained a minority. And making up the majority were not neutrals, who numbered little more than a dozen, but centralists. Indeed, adherents of the February Patent commanded a majority even among the great landowners, thanks to considerable pressure exerted by the Habsburg government during the elections.[41]

The centralists in the Bohemian Diet clustered in several factions, all having in common a liberal belief in the importance of creating unified markets and a strong secular state. All factions were also predominantly German. The meaning of "German," though, was changing. Throughout Central Europe, German Liberals had all but abandoned hope of transforming the German Confederation (revived in 1851) into a Greater German nation-state. Hungarians, in contrast, were now regaining hope of

Figure 1. Franz Josef Klawik/František Josef Klavík (1798–1878). Mayor of Budweis/Budějovice, 1858–1865. Courtesy of the State Regional Archive in České Budějovice.

transforming the Hungarian lands into something at least approaching a nation-state, as a federal unit within the Habsburg Monarchy. For German Liberals in the monarchy, that left the non-Hungarian, or Cisleithanian, territories lumped together in the narrower Austrian Parliament. Despite having little historical resonance and only a German ethnic plurality, Cisleithania did have a bourgeois stratum that was disproportionately German and centralist. And thanks to the curial system, as well as to the Habsburg decision to favor centralists, that bourgeois stratum now commanded a majority in many electoral bodies. Such contexts encouraged German Liberals to develop a new strand of German nationhood, centered on the enfranchised citizenry of Cisleithania, and to do so in ways that complemented the ethnic strand less than the historical—or at least historical-cultural, if not historical-territorial, strand. As Pieter Judson has argued, German Liberals reinterpreted their "nation" by the mid-1860s as an elite more capable of representing and serving the interests of lesser social and national elements in Cisleithania than could those elements themselves. To a historically rooted understanding of German superiority, Liberals added a bourgeois and meritocratic, civic one. The proper political stance of lower-class citizens was passivity and deference. Through self-improvement, though, they could earn enfranchisement and membership in the Cisleithanian "nation," which happened to speak German.[42]

In Budweis/Budějovice, during the second half of 1861, perhaps the most bitter public disagreement concerned language use in schools. As was explained in the introduction, the town council became divided after the Bohemian governor approved the conversion of some secondary schools in town from German-speaking to bilingual, or utraquist. The following year, the male choir split into a German-singing *Liedertafel* and a Czech-singing *Beseda*. As in the diet, those disputes took on a bipolar rather than tripolar structure. Because Czechs did not propose to make the schools entirely Czech-speaking, for example, Klawik/Klavík and Haug placed themselves quite close to the Czech position when they advocated "equality and progress." Some other Budweisers, when they recoiled from the idea of putting a "peasant dialect" on par with German, placed themselves quite close to the German position—which Ernst Franz Richter, as the new editor of the *Anzeiger aus dem südlichen Böhmen*, stated succinctly at the beginning of 1862: "True equality . . . demands precisely that the gymnasium in Budweis be preserved for the Germans of Southern Bohemia."[43] Prominent Budweisers, pushed into taking linguistic sides, seemed thereby to have taken national ones. Local politics mapped onto the federalist-centralist struggle in ways that brought the Czech-German dimension to the fore.

The Austrian Parliament, meanwhile, succeeded in passing laws that gave more room to the press and to associations. In 1864, Czechs founded a newspaper in Budweis/Budějovice, *Budivoj*. They also expanded the activities of the *Beseda*. By then, Budweis/Budějovice also had a gymnastics club, or *Turnverein*, with 150 members and with ambitions of serving the town as a volunteer fire squad. Mayor Klawik/Klavík, though, insisted on hiring full-time professionals instead.[44] He may have done so in part because elsewhere in Central Europe, decades previously, gymnastic drill had become a potent expression of German nationhood, as a substitute and even preparation for military resistance to Napoleon's occupying armies. And helping to revive that past, early in 1864, had been a much discussed war. The Habsburg Monarchy and Prussia, intervening in a long-standing and complex dispute, had invaded Denmark and seized two duchies that many Germans considered German: Schleswig and Holstein. The duchies straddled the border of the German Confederation, and could be argued to have German ethnic majorities.

When elections to Budweis/Budějovice's town council took place in June 1865, they featured competing slates for the first time. "The Party of Progress" promised to promote trade and industry and to reduce taxes. It also argued, in *Budivoj*, that the composition of the town council should reflect the fact that both Czechs and Germans lived in Budweis/Budějovice. Yet the party's candidates were actually not so much Czechs and Germans as Czechs and Budweisers. Its ticket for the third electoral curia, for example, included Zátka, Grünwald, Klawik/Klavík, and the municipal deacon, Johann Schawel/Jan Šavel—who had been leading separate pilgrimages for German-speaking and Czech-speaking Catholics to a holy site in the Bohemian Forest each summer for the past several years. Leaders of the ongoing campaign against utraquism in the schools, meanwhile, ran as candidates of a different party, provocatively called "The True Party of Progress." Led by Alderman Eduard Claudi (who spoke German with a Czech accent), it had the backing of Richter's *Anzeiger*, opposed the reelection of Klawik/Klavík, and ran neither Schawel/Šavel nor any other priest. The True Party also included three token Czechs among its thirty-six candidates, and issued a poor Czech translation of its program, which focused on economic issues. A "Middle Party," finally, ran too, centered on Klawik/Klavík and led by a factory-owner. It failed, however, to distinguish itself from the Party of Progress, many of whose candidates were the same.[45]

In the third curia, which voted first, the Party of Progress candidates won all twelve seats, with a slim majority of the 950-odd votes cast. Candidates of the True Party, though, received two-thirds of the vote in the smaller second and first curias, and captured the remaining twenty-four seats. At least officially, ballots were now secret, and the voter stood free to choose any twelve candidates. Yet in most cases, he chose a straight party ticket. And the biggest exception, a bloc of about sixty men in the

third curia, bucked the ticket of the True Party of Progress not in order
to reach across political lines but in order to draw them more deeply—by
refusing to vote for the three token Czechs. Since 1861, enfranchised
residents of Budweis/Budějovice had drifted into two broad camps, both
containing Budweisers. One camp was more populist, Catholic, federalist,
and Czech. The other was more elitist, liberal, centralist, and German. Its
leader, Claudi, now replaced Klawik/Klavík as mayor.[46]

Weeks later, Emperor-King Francis Joseph and his advisers reversed
themselves and turned toward federalists. Motivating the change of course
were two forces: the Hungarian movement, which continued to deny and
to undermine the legitimacy of the political restructuring undertaken in
1861, and Prussia, whose hugely ambitious chancellor, Otto von Bismarck, was behaving less and less like an ally and more and more like a
foe. The Habsburg leadership sought to come to terms with its strongest
domestic opponent in order to face a foreign opponent from a position of
greater strength. In September, the emperor-king suspended the February
Patent. That fall, thanks to government pressure on great landowners,
federalists won a majority in elections to the Bohemian Diet. Yet the Bohe-
mian/Czech National Party and other federalist factions quickly proved
themselves a greater obstacle than centralists had been to a settlement of
matters with the Hungarian movement. By 1865, many centralist leaders
were willing to make an exception of Hungary (or to be more precise, of
the lands of the Crown of St. Stephan), such as to allow the creation of a
"dual" monarchy, divided into a centralized Cisleithania and an autonomous "Transleithania," or Hungary. Federalist leaders, in contrast, sought
to make Hungary the rule. Besides promising to sap more of Francis Joseph's power, that approach was far more complex. Multilateral negotiations dragged on.[47]

The following summer, Bismarck provoked the Austro-Prussian War.
The decisive battle, fought near Königgrätz/Hradec Králové in Northern
Bohemia, ended with a Prussian victory. Bismarck persuaded his king,
William I of Hohenzollern, to exclude the Habsburg Monarchy from the
German Confederation, and to transform that loose collection of states
into a tighter, smaller one: the North German Confederation, whose new,
democratically elected parliament obscured a reality of dominance by William I and by the three-class Prussian Diet. Francis Joseph, for his part,
turned to intense negotiations with the Hungarian leadership. The federalist majority in the Bohemian Diet, excluded from those negotiations,
responded by refusing to send delegates to an Austrian Parliament convened that winter for the purpose of approving a dualist, Habsburg-Hungarian "compromise" [*Ausgleich/vyrovnání*]. Habsburg leaders responded
by reversing course again, at least in Cisleithania. Francis Joseph dissolved
recalcitrant diets, and his ministers ensured that the new elections ended

in a triumph for centralists. In the Bohemian Diet, members of the new centralist majority (including Claudi, who had run unopposed in Budweis/Budějovice) reached an understanding with Francis Joseph. They would send delegates to the Parliament, and assure that it approved the compromise. In exchange, the emperor-king would reinstate the February Patent in Cisleithania and permit liberal centralists to make significant additions to it.[48]

Weeks after the Austro-Prussian War, *Budivoj* had risked police action by calling Austria's defeat a "divine judgment" and by blaming it on misguided policies of centralization and Germanization.[49] As matters turned out, though, Königgrätz/Hradec Králové was followed by a tighter Habsburg embrace of liberal centralism, rather than by its rejection in favor of federalism. The lands of the Crown of St. Stephan, to be sure, gained their own parliament, and became a Hungarian state within the Habsburg one. But in Cisleithania, the Austrian Parliament now possessed far more power than did the crownland diets. And although the emperor-king retained almost complete control over foreign policy and over the military, he gave his sanction at the end of 1867 to a set of "Fundamental Laws" passed by the Austrian Parliament. Amounting to a liberal constitution, they established a Cisleithanian citizenship, equality before the law, parliamentary immunity, something approaching freedom of speech and freedom of association, and much more—and were joined within months by further legislation that separated the Catholic Church from the state in matters of education and of marriage.

Budivoj exaggerated in equating centralization with Germanization. But to some degree, the centralist, Liberal victory of 1867 indeed was a German victory, too. On the surface, article 19 of the Fundamental Law concerning civil liberties seemed nationally egalitarian, and thus more Czech than German: "All races in the state have equal rights, and every race has the inviolable right to preserve and cultivate its nationality and language. The equality of all languages native to the crownlands [*landesüblichen Sprachen*] is recognized by the state in schools, government agencies, and public life." Yet "race" and "nationality" remained undefined, and Liberal deputies from Bohemia succeeded in adding an important qualification: "In lands inhabited by more than one race, public schools shall be organized in such a way that every race has adequate opportunity for education in its own language, without being forced to learn a second language of the land." The Austrian Parliament, furthermore, failed to specify how or by which state agency article 19 was to be implemented and enforced.[50] The effect was to favor the linguistic status quo, and thus German over Czech. Through dominance of the new Cisleithanian government and of the Austrian Parliament, Liberal centralists also possessed considerable power to assist the German side in myriad disputes.

From Dualism to Trialism?

In Budweis/Budějovice, for example, Liberal members of the government helped representatives of the first and second municipal curias deal a blow to Czech-language education. In 1866, when federalist fortunes had still been good, Habsburg officials had begun to consider establishing a separate, Czech-language gymnasium in town, as an expansion of the utraquist classes established a few years previously in the primarily German-language gymnasium. But in June 1867, a majority of the aldermen decided to answer a formal communication from the Ministry of Education by recommending against such action, and by refusing any municipal funds for it. Dissenters could do no more than submit a minority opinion, in which they underscored that their curia, the third, was the largest and therefore the most representative of the population as a whole, and that most students in the German-language gymnasium were from outside town and were native speakers of Czech. (Richter's *Anzeiger*, in contrast, emphasized that "the elite of the population in Budweis is German.") The ministry decided not to expand the utraquist classes. Indeed, in December, a decree ordered them terminated in town.[51]

Here Bishop Jirsik/Jirsík intervened, by offering to pay from his own pocket for the construction of a primarily Czech-language gymnasium. His motives were both Czech and Catholic. As the head of Budweis/Budějovice's seminary, whose graduates provided the bishopric with most of its new priests, he had long relied on the gymnasium as a source for novices. Jirsik/Jirsík wished, furthermore, that new priests be capable of serving in any parish, whether the congregation spoke German, Czech, or both. In 1865, *Budivoj* had criticized him for ruling out the possibility that a growing shortage of novices who spoke German as a native language might lead someday to a shift from bilingual instruction to instruction exclusively in Czech.[52] Now, though, the new hostility of the gymnasium to Czech seemed likely to drive away Czech-speaking peasant sons—the kind of students that experience showed most likely to choose a career in the Church. Only four months after the decree ordering an end to the utraquist classes in town, Jirsik/Jirsík presided over groundbreaking ceremonies for two buildings, side by side: his primarily Czech-language gymnasium and a church dedicated to St. Wenceslas.

Attendance at those ceremonies was staggeringly high. From far afield, thousands of villagers converged on Budweis/Budějovice, wearing their Sunday best and riding brightly decorated carts. Over the spring and summer of 1868, similar open-air gatherings took place across the Bohemian lands, and increasingly took on the character of political demonstrations. Bohemian federalists organized the *tábory*, or rallies, as part of an attempt

Figure 2. Johann Valerian Jirsik/Jan Valerian Jirsík (1798–1883). Bishop in Budweis/Budějovice, 1851–1883. Courtesy of the State Regional Archive in České Budějovice.

to force a conversion of the dualism of the 1867 Compromise into a "trialism" that would accommodate Bohemian state rights.[53]

This embrace of more populist tactics signaled that the weight of the great landowners within the federalist camp was decreasing. In May, a delegation traveled from Budweis/Budějovice to Prague in order to attend groundbreaking ceremonies for a Czech/Bohemian National Theater. Federalist great landowners participated, but were vastly outnumbered by the crowd. In June, another delegation from Budweis/Budějovice attended celebrations of Palacký's seventieth birthday. (Days later, Catholics, Czechs, and others from in and around the town celebrated the seventieth birthday of Jirsik/Jirsík in similar fashion.) And in August, Zátka and Grünwald joined seventy-nine other nonaristocratic delegates to the Bohemian Diet in signing a Czech "Declaration" written by Rieger and other leaders of the Bohemian/Czech National Party. (Jirsik/Jirsík no longer had a diet seat, having resigned it in 1863.) The "Declarants" proclaimed a boycott of the diet, restated the state-rights program, and claimed backing for their stance from "the entire Bohemoslavonic nation, which numbers five million souls in all the lands of the Bohemian Crown." ("Bohemoslavonic" [českoslovanský/böhmisch-slawisch], a relatively new term, meant "Czech" in a broader ethnic sense, and allowed Czechs to refer unambiguously to all Czech-speakers, including those living outside Bohemia, without taking the politically disadvantageous step of distinguishing, as Germans had done, between "Bohemian" [böhmisch/český] and "Czech" [tschechisch/český].) At the expense of consistency, the declaration also invoked a "historical-political Bohemian nation," and implied that the supposedly unanimous Czech-speakers (for which five million was an inflated figure) made up the majority of that bilingual people.[54]

On October 3, Jirsik/Jirsík's private gymnasium opened its doors, with nearly 300 students. Some Catholics disapproved, and expressed their displeasure on October 4 by stalking out of the cathedral before Jirsik/Jirsík could conclude a Mass on the name day of the emperor-king. Contributing to the tensions were new diet elections (in which most Declarants won reelection, and then refused to fill their seats), more demonstrations, and the declaration of a state of siege in Prague. Jirsik/Jirsík, in what may have been a sardonic protest against national interpretations of his politics, turned to a new educational project: creating an institute in town for deaf mutes.[55]

Inconclusive federalist-Habsburg-centralist struggle followed for nearly two years. Francis Joseph pursued secret negotiations with federalists, not only from the Bohemian lands but from elsewhere, including Galicia. Yet he left Liberals—or "Constitutionalists," as they often called themselves—in control of the ministries and of the Parliament. In 1869, Liberal legislation established a network of state-funded primary schools, in a stab at the Church, and required all children to receive formal education for at least eight years. When elections to the town council took place that summer in Budweis/Budějovice, federalists decided on a course of boycott, although doing so meant losing control of the third curia. "It is better to step completely to one side," argued *Budivoj*, "and to wait until matters change in Austria. As long as the current cabinet rules in Vienna, we can work here to good benefit only by taking care to harden and to strengthen ourselves privately." One sign of such private strengthening was the founding in town of a chapter of the Czech *Sokol* [Falcon], or gymnastics club, modeled closely on the German *Turnverein*.[56]

The next summer, Bismarck provoked a war with France. Francis Joseph exploited the moment in order to reverse his domestic position yet again, this time only in the Bohemian lands. Once more, he called new diet elections and ordered imperial-royal officials to influence the outcome, now to the advantage of federalists. Centralists could do little, in part because in the spring, the emperor-king had replaced the Constitutionalist prime minister with a Galician aristocrat. In the rural district surrounding Budweis/Budějovice, Zátka easily won reelection on August 23. And in the town itself, Zátka's young son August, a reserve officer in the imperial-royal army who had just received his law degree, distinguished himself as a campaign leader for the Party of Progress. It chose not to identify itself closely with the Bohemian/Czech National Party, and ran not a Declarant but someone capable of attracting swing votes: Vicar Haug. He barely lost, by a count of 420 to 427. In a letter of thanks to his voters on August 28, the vicar emphasized that it was possible, as a good German, to side with Czechs in seeking autonomy for Bohemia.[57]

On August 30, days before Prussia scored a crucial victory over France at Sedan, the Bohemian Diet convened in Prague. The following month was consumed by intense negotiations: the federalist majority refused to elect delegates to the Austrian Parliament before winning concrete concessions, and Francis Joseph refused to make those concessions before the federalists had conceded the legitimacy of the central legislature. In an imperial rescript issued on September 26, however, he did announce his willingness to respect the rights of Bohemia, and to submit, as king of that crownland, to a formal coronation. Two days later, on St. Wenceslas day, Bishop Jirsik/Jirsík consecrated the newly completed St. Wenceslas Church in Budweis/Budějovice. Thanks in part to railroad lines that had just established a new link with villages to the east and west, as many as 30,000 people attended. *Budivoj* interpreted the festivities as an emphatically national, Czech demonstration. Federalist members of the diet, meanwhile, continued to refuse to send delegates to the Parliament.[58]

Francis Joseph's response was to change the electoral system. Henceforth, he decreed, Bohemia's delegates to the Lower House were to be elected directly by four curias modeled closely on the ones established in 1861 for the diet. *Budivoj* expressed the hope that in the Budweis/Budějovice electoral district, every loyal Bohemian [*Čech*], whether German or Slav, would vote for Grünwald. And August Zátka gave a speech radical enough to trigger an investigation by the authorities. Through the fall, as Prussia's armies besieged Paris, the tug-of-war in Cisleithania continued. Early in November, Grünwald fell short of a majority in town (437 to 549), but prevailed in the electoral district as a whole, which included several smaller towns of Southern Bohemia. Overall, federalists (including Clam-Martinic and seven other great landowners) captured thirty of Bohemia's fifty-four seats, and continued their boycott of Vienna.[59]

In January 1871, at Versailles, the King of Prussia was proclaimed the ruler of a new, second "German Empire"—the Prussian-dominated North German Confederation, expanded to include the southern states of Bavaria, Baden, Württemberg, and Hesse-Darmstadt, as well as France's territories of Alsace and Lorraine. A united but smaller Germany had been created, with blood and iron and without the Habsburg lands of the former Holy Roman Empire. Weeks later, Francis Joseph encharged an aristocrat with assembling a Cisleithanian cabinet inclined toward federalists. Chosen as the minister of education was the author of the ethnographic survey discussed earlier in this chapter, Josef Jireček. He and another minister became the first Czech members of an Austrian cabinet. In Budweis/Budějovice, Bishop Jirsik/Jirsík insisted to the 100-odd members of a new Catholic Association that religion should bring people together without regard for nationality. Yet the association held its meetings on less than neutral ground: a newly erected clubhouse for the *Beseda*.[60]

Over the spring and summer, the new cabinet hammered out a detailed agreement with the Bohemian federalists. Eighteen "Fundamental Articles," designed for enactment as a Bohemian constitution, assigned powers of autonomy to the kingdom—powers that closely resembled those assigned to Hungary in 1867. (Moravia and Silesia, less important to great landowners than to Czechs among the federalists, were not included.) Modifications to the Bohemian Diet suffrage promised to give federalists a secure majority, without going so far as to provoke an aristocratic veto. And a draft Nationalities Law promised to restructure much of Bohemian politics—by establishing separate Czech and German school systems, by guaranteeing national equality in public offices, by providing for a redrawing of administrative, juridical, and electoral districts in accord with nationality, and by creating Czech and German diet curias (to which great landowners and some other delegates needed not belong) with special powers in specific national questions. Implicitly and imprecisely, the draft law, written in large part by Rieger, the Czech leader, defined nationality in ethnic terms.[61]

Shortly before the Bohemian Diet convened to approve this remarkable settlement, or "compromise," yet another election took place in Budweis/Budějovice. Mayor Claudi had resigned his diet seat, without any explanation. Again, the Party of Progress downplayed its Czechness, running an attorney and knight active in Catholic circles, Adolf von Jungmann/z Jungmannů. His opponent, predictably enough, was a Constitutionalist. Nominating him, though, in a telling shift toward national terminology, was not the True Party of Progress but an "Election Committee of the Germans in Budweis." Days after the defeat of von Jungmann/z Jungmannů on September 9 by a vote of 520 to 488, the *Budweiser Kreisblatt* (which continued to cover matters from a nationally neutral perspective) printed a letter. The author, a federalist named Johann Faber, accused a centralist in town of having said "better to become Prussian than Czech."[62]

When the diet convened, the liberal minority proclaimed a boycott— in the name of the German people. Budweis/Budějovice's town council passed a resolution expressing support. The Ministry of Education, for its part, made public a decision to take over the financing of the Czech-language gymnasium from Bishop Jirsik/Jirsík. In Prague, early in October, the rump diet ratified the Fundamental Articles and the Nationalities Law. "A new epoch has begun in the history of Central Europe," a Czech newspaper rejoiced. "An independent Slavic state has been created in the heart of the continent, as an answer to the restoration of the German Empire." Jirsik/Jirsík's Catholic Association, after a discussion both in Czech and in German, unanimously passed a resolution calling the liberal boycott unjustified and unpatriotic.[63] Only Francis Joseph's sanction of the legislation was needed in order to seal the federalist victory.

That sanction never came. At the last minute, opposition not only by Constitutionalists in Cisleithania but also by the Hungarian elite and the German Empire persuaded Francis Joseph to reverse direction yet again. He appointed a new Bohemian governor and Cisleithanian prime minister, and henceforth sided resolutely with the Constitutionalists. They did not object to a severe crackdown on federalists, although it included an illiberal suspension in Bohemia of the civil liberties guaranteed in the Fundamental Laws. The Constitutionalists regained a majority in the diet (with Claudi defeating von Jungmann/z Jungmannů by a vote of 606 to 462), and ended their boycott, while Bohemian federalists, or at least Czechs among them, resumed theirs.[64] In Galicia, the nobles who dominated electoral politics arrived at an informal but effective federalist arrangement with the emperor-king, and kept up their part of the pact by voting consistently in the Austrian Parliament with the government. The larger, Cisleithanian coalition of federalists collapsed.

Czech leaders in Budweis/Budějovice reacted to the defeat of trialism with a surge of anger—directed at, among other people, Jews. Indeed, even before the defeat, *Budivoj* had begun to focus in disproportionate fashion on the Jewish voters in town, who made up only 5 percent of the diet and Austrian Parliament electorates. "In elections in Budějovice," the newspaper had claimed just before the Diet election on September 9, "the Constitutionalists owe thanks for their electoral victories above all to the Jews, whom they have tried to keep on their side at all costs. If the Jews were to vote with us, or at least abstain, the Czech side would emerge the victor from every contest." The editorial had concluded with the threat that Czechs would remember who voted how. Two months later, immediately after the definitive derailment of the Bohemian compromise, Czechs were urged to make no purchases from German or Jewish merchants at an upcoming fair: "Each to His Own [*Svoji k svému*]!" The following week, *Budivoj* published an anti-Semitic article.[65]

Budweis/Budějovice's Jewish population did tend to have liberal and German sympathies, for good reasons. All of the 250 Jews registered in the 1869 census were relative newcomers to town, usually from rural areas of the Central Bohemian plain. Encounters there with the traditional anti-Semitism of Catholic, Czech-speaking peasants had been common. So had less intimate and less dismaying encounters with German-language culture, in part because of laws dating from the late eighteenth century that had required Jewish children to attend German-language elementary schools. More recently, the *Beseda* in town had decided to accept "honorable and intelligent Jews" as members—but only a year and a half after splitting off from the *Liedertafel*. Liberal leaders had been more welcoming. Liberal deputies had also consistently emphasized achievement over birth, and had crafted the Fundamental Laws, which separated church from state and established legal equality for all citizens.[66]

Budivoj did not acknowledge the realities that made Czech, conservative, Catholic, and federalist stances less appealing than German, liberal, anticlerical, and centralist ones to most Jews. Nor did it allow that Jews might be Germans or Czechs, rather than a "nation" apart. Instead, *Budivoj* pandered to Czech anti-Semitism and made Jews into scapegoats for the actions of Francis Joseph—on whom direct attacks were taboo. In December 1871, just before still another election to the Parliament, the newspaper singled out Jewish voters for unfriendly attention. The front page carried three separate appeals. The first, signed by the "Election Committee of the Friends of the Compromise," was written in German and called on burghers to vote for Grünwald rather than for his opponent (whose principal backers supposedly included a baptized Jew). The second appeal, signed by the "Czech Election Committee," was written in Czech and delivered a straight national pitch. And the third, signed by "The

Czechs of Budějovice, your peace-loving fellow citizens who do you no wrong," was written in Czech, and called on all fifty-four of the Jewish voters by name to abstain. Jews intending to appear at the polls were warned that they would be assumed to have come in order to vote against Grünwald.[67]

Two days later, armed gendarmes stood in the snow on the *Ringplatz/ rynek* and made certain that Czech threats and dreams of disenfranchising Jews did not come true. Grünwald lost in Budweis/Budějovice by a tally of 489 to 584, but prevailed in the electoral district as a whole. *Budivoj* soon printed a letter from him, in which he expressed his thanks to supporters in both Czech and German. In the same issue, the Czech Electoral Committee also thanked Czech voters, together with "a small cluster of German voters who voted with us." "Finally," the statement continued, "we thank the Jews of Budějovice, who have pronounced themselves our clear political opponents, casting off the mask of hermaphroditism [*obojetnost*]. Decided adversaries we find preferable to fawning hypocrites. We will forgive those who have no homeland and have lost their language that they do not understand the struggle for these two estates [*statky*]. We regret, however, that these people ask not on which side lies right but instead which party rules."[68] Yet if Jews really were "decided adversaries" of Czechs, then Czechs bore at least half the responsibility. And whatever the politics of Budweis/Budějovice's Jewish residents, they were finding, as had Klawik/Klavík and Jirsik/Jirsík, that taking sides in the German-Czech struggle was increasingly difficult to avoid.

Conclusion

The political flux that had begun in 1848 came to an end in 1871. A Greater Germany did not come into being. Instead, Prussia completed its expansion, through victorious wars against Denmark, the Habsburg Monarchy, and France, into a smaller German Empire. The Habsburg Monarchy, which had divided into a dual monarchy after losing the Austro-Prussian War, stopped short of further division into a trialist one. To the south, Piedmont-Sardinia capped its transformation into Italy by seizing Rome. In the Prussian and Piedmontese cases, the dynasties that controlled the upper reaches of the state met with considerable success in claiming national legitimacy. They supposedly restored, or at least partly restored, a lost German and Italian unity. In the Habsburg case, on the other hand, it was the Hungarian movement that met with greatest success in claiming national legitimacy, *against* the dynasty. Hungarian leaders supposedly restored, or at least partly restored, a lost Hungarian sovereignty.

Nearly surrounded by the German Empire, Italy, and Hungary was Cisleithania, or what came to be known as the Austrian half of "Austria-Hungary." Here, as in the three emergent nation-states, much of politics now unfolded within a constitutional order of civil liberties and of elected legislatures with carefully delimited powers. That continued to be the pattern, in fact, until the First World War. Yet Cisleithania was fundamentally different. In the German Empire, Italy, and Hungary, the major factions all claimed to speak for the same "nation," and collaborated in suppressing non-Germans, non-Italians, or non-Hungarians who challenged the rules of the game. In Cisleithania, when centralists and federalists spoke of domestic conflict in national terms, that conflict was often between two "nations," rather than within one. Politics had moved in the direction of becoming not so much national as binational or multinational. The state apparatus, however, remained for the most part Habsburg. Some ministers and officials were national—usually German. Yet they served at the pleasure of Francis Joseph and over the objections of federalists, and could do little to nationalize the imperial-royal civil service, the army, or the law.

Germanness and Czechness in Cisleithania, meanwhile, in the process of moving toward the political fore, had changed considerably, even while remaining linked by a "negative and analog tie." German leaders had abandoned their historical focus on the territory of the Holy Roman Empire and had shifted to a more realistic, civic focus on the territory of Cisleithania. At the same time, they had pushed the historical-cultural, or elitist, strand to Germanness in civic directions, and had reduced their emphasis on ethnicity. Czech leaders, in contrast, had retained their emphasis on ethnicity and had become more populist—through *tábory*, through invocations of "five million souls," and, for that matter, through attempts at harnessing base popular sentiments such as anti-Semitism. One result was that the weak historical-cultural strand to Czechness had grown weaker still. Federalist great landowners had become less important to the Czech movement. They, as well as ethnic Germans in the Bohemian lands, had become less Czech in Czech eyes. Yet the historical-territorial strand to Czechness remained. German-speaking Bohemians might not count as Czech, but the land on which they lived did.

The strength of the Czech and German national movements, however, should not be exaggerated. Nor should the extent of their conflict with traditional, Habsburg forces. In Budweis/Budějovice, national leaders had succeeded in forcing a choice on some Budweisers between Czech and German. That choice, though, concerned only thin slices of life: elections, in which the great majority of Budweisers could not vote; associations, which the great majority could not or did not join; the press, which many people did not read; and schools, which were only beginning to offer a choice between Bohemia's two languages. Typical was not the treasonous statement of "better to become Prussian than Czech," but rather an attempt by the *Beseda* and *Liedertafel* to outsing one another in the presence of the Bohemian governor.[69] The national movements competed with each other over which was more Habsburg-loyal.

Two

A More Broad and National Politics, 1871–1890

The common people of our town are Czech, and
thus far, this precious material has not enjoyed
our attention.
  —*August Zátka, 1882*

We wish to draw all strata of the German citizenry to the great national project.
  —*Josef Taschek, 1884*

In Budweis, the two competing parties must demonstrate their congenital strength. Whichever side
proves itself, over time, to be stronger must necessarily be accommodated by each government, in
accordance with the law.
  —*Count Eduard Taaffe, 1888*

In Budweis/Budějovice during the 1870s and 1880s, public life expanded. Elections, associations, schools, and the press ceased to exhaust
the list of principal political spaces, and a bourgeois elite, together with
imperial-royal officials, ceased to exhaust the list of principal political
actors in town. Municipal enterprises, the census, new and less local associations, the labor market, and both shops and shopping became important
arenas for contestation. So, for that matter, did many nonbourgeois—at
the same time that they became political actors in their own right.

Politics also became more national, even as nationhood itself changed.
Constitutionalists grew more German, and less liberal. Their opponents
grew more Czech, and less Catholic. German leaders became somewhat
less elitist, while Czech leaders reduced their emphasis on Bohemian state
rights. Both came to think of nationhood in more ethnic terms. Both
national movements also expanded demographically and spread out from
their original, fairly specific tethering points along the political spectrum.
The expansion and change both of nationhood and of politics more generally, however, were incremental, not revolutionary. August Zátka and Josef
Taschek, new leaders of the opposing movements in Budweis/Budějovice
from the early 1880s, followed up only in part with action on their claims
to the "common people of our town" and to "all strata of the German

citizenry." Organizations came to include many lower-middle-class individuals, but continued to exclude working-class ones. In some senses, Count Eduard Taaffe, the Cisleithanian prime minister between 1879 and 1893, did "accommodate" the stronger, German side in town, led by Taschek. But before, during, and after Taaffe's term in office, the state was dominated by nonnational elites, and actively shaped the political field. State policy, for example, largely defined the lower-middle class that Taschek and Zátka set to embracing. The strength of the two increasingly national parties in town, for that matter, became more equal over time—less because of their "congenital" natures than because of ongoing dynamics in which the Habsburg authorities, both intentionally and unintentionally, played major roles.

Public and Private

Months before the enactment of the Fundamental Laws in 1867, workers in Budweis/Budějovice had begun tearing down the medieval ramparts that by that point served only to choke the town. *Budivoj* found strong symbolism of a national sort in the event. "With the demolition of this bulwark," the newspaper commented, "legal continuity is sundered. Demolished is the historic right of our Teutons not to know Czech."[1] Mayor Claudi saw things differently, perhaps in part because he and other Constitutionalists dominated the town council. In the mid-1860s, through legislation understood by Habsburg policymakers as a counterbalance to the centralist February Patent of 1861, town councils throughout Cisleithania had gained a measure of autonomy almost without parallel in Europe. "Communes" [*Gemeinden/obce*] had won extensive latitude in important fields, including education, taxation, language policy, and public utilities. Urban communes, or municipalities, had retained control over the granting of burgher status and, thus to some degree, over the contours of the third municipal curia.[2] At about the same time, as part of a Europe-wide trend, the size of municipal government had begun to mushroom. During the late 1860s and early 1870s, the town council in Budweis/Budějovice oversaw not only the razing of the old town walls but also the illumination of streets by a new gasworks, the drastic reduction of cholera outbreaks by a new sewage system and waterworks, and more.

Such projects gave Liberal and German aldermen tangible ways to promote Germanness and to discourage Czechness. Czech leaders, in an open letter to the mayor in February 1869, complained that whenever the *Liedertafel* sponsored a dance, lamps belonging to the new gasworks lit up the streets until dawn. The lamps outside the German *Casino* burned brightly all the time. But around the site for a *Beseda* gathering, the lighting often left much to be desired.[3] The municipal gasworks, waterworks, police force, and slaughterhouse, through their creation or expansion, also presented new opportunities for patronage. Some German factory-owners had already begun to demand that employees vote for certain candidates, join certain associations, and enroll children in certain schools. By the beginning of the 1870s, Mayor Claudi was beginning to demand much the same from people on the municipal payroll. In some other towns, Czechs and their allies dominated municipal government, and used it against Liberals and Germans. Throughout the Bohemian lands, municipalities became a central site of national politics.[4]

As an institutional check on municipalities, the Habsburg authorities had instituted a network of district captainships in 1868. They fit into a larger pattern, whereby autonomous organs in Cisleithania tended to be paired with an organ of "political administration," controlled from Vienna. Diets, for example, were paralleled by governors. Diets and town councils were elected "from below," albeit by a small minority of residents. Governors and district captains (whose individual districts usually included a number of communes) were appointed from above. A district captain could overrule municipal actions if they clearly violated the law and could even call in army units to maintain order. Overall, the role of the captains "cannot be sufficiently emphasized," to cite an expert on the topic.[5] In Budweis/Budějovice, Constitutionalists thus faced weaker Czechs and Catholics, but also the Habsburg authorities.

The state also made its presence felt in the local economy. In 1872, the Imperial Austrian Tobacco Monopoly opened a cigar and cigarette factory in town. Employees, who numbered about 500, seem to have done as they pleased in linguistic and national matters without fear of being fired. That freedom, though, may have derived from a perceived insignificance. Imperial-royal officials during the 1870s, even more than national leaders, understood public life to concern only males of substance. Women, though, made up the bulk of tobacco workers, and almost none of the men among them earned enough money to qualify for the vote in municipal, diet, or Austrian Parliament elections.[6]

In September 1871, the town council ignored petitions submitted by the Catholic Political Association, together with a recently founded Czech Political Association, and voted to cancel the annual municipal subsidy to an elementary school administered by the Piarist religious order. The school, which stood almost alone in town in allowing pupils not yet fluent in German to speak in Czech, had to close. Four months later, at a meeting of the Czech Political Association, August Zátka motioned that Czechs should build their own, private schools. His proposal passed, although some members argued that the Czech movement lacked resources, and that such matters were the responsibility of the state in any case. Zátka immediately set to work organizing a School Foundation [*Matice školská*], taking as his model several Czech foundations elsewhere with similar goals. He issued an appeal addressed to the whole of the Czech "nation," and within a year raised enough money to launch a boys' elementary school. Less combative residents, meanwhile, delivered another petition to the town council, requesting funding for Czech-language schools. A reply came in the form of a fine for violation of the submission protocol.[7]

Zátka's initiatives signaled Czech disillusionment with the Habsburg authorities in the wake of the trialist debacle, as well as a sharpening of Czech-German conflict. But his initiative also signaled greater Czech confidence. Ten years previously, the *Beseda* had been the sole Czech association in town. But by now, it had expanded from a mere choir into an umbrella social club at the center of a small network of Czech associations. Indeed, in 1870, a *Beseda* building had gone up in town, complete with a restaurant, a ballroom, and smaller spaces in which those associations could meet. Members had pledged their property as collateral for the mortgage. Jan Neruda, a Czech writer in Prague, visited town shortly after the clubhouse opened. He arrived in the evening, via one of the new railroad lines, knowing no one in town: "Porters and callers for hotels, here as everywhere else, greet [one] at the train station," he wrote.

> But among the cries is suddenly heard: "*Beseda—Beseda!*" and, magnetically drawn, we are soon seated in the omnibus and riding to the Czech *Beseda* of Budějovice. . . . The *Beseda* building is completely new, with a beautifully decorated restaurant and a hall so elegant that none of the Prague halls can match it, a spacious garden, billiards, skittles. . . . Here the traveler can find lodgings and all else very cheaply, yet of high quality. And besides, here he feels immediately at home, among his own people. "Whoever listens up right away to a Czech call at the station is in any event our man," the Czechs of Budějovice think quite correctly, and they treat each person as a beloved guest.[8]

The *Beseda* might not have welcomed Neruda, however, had he not been bourgeois. Membership in the club remained restricted to businessmen, teachers, civil servants, and the like, and totaled, after the expulsion of about forty men who had fallen behind in paying their dues, only 284 in 1872. The social profile of Constitutionalists or Germans—who built a German House [*Deutsches Haus*] in 1872—was similar, but slightly more exclusive. The *Liedertafel* and other associations that filled the German House roughly paralleled the Czech associations in size, but had higher dues and more spacious quarters, in a reflection of greater wealth.[9]

In the spring of 1873, when elections to town hall came due, Mayor Claudi campaigned at the head of a "German and Constitutionalist Party." Many of its leading members (but not Claudi) signed a public denunciation of their opponent as the "Czech Party," and claimed that the goal of

Czechs in town now was to "put the Fundamental Articles into effect piecemeal [*im Kleinen*], because the attempt failed wholesale [*im Großen*]." Yet that opponent, rather than identifying itself as a local branch of the Bohemian/Czech National Party, campaigned as the "Burgher Party." The name was misleading. So too, though, was a solely national name. One of the leaders, Adolf von Jungmann/z Jungmannů, was more a Catholic and a nobleman than a Czech. And the attempt by Germans and Constitutionalists, in their public denunciation, to dismiss such men as Vinzenz Paschek/Čeněk Pašek, Josef Täubl, and Johann Faber as candidates "whom the Czechs have patented as Germans" signals the presence of a Budweiser contingent.[10]

When the third curia voted in mid-May, Grünwald, the older Zátka, von Jungmann/z Jungmannů, and another Burgher Party candidate—all of whom the German and Constitutionalist Party had placed on its own ticket as well—won election with between 739 and 755 votes (about 58 percent) each. Eight years previously, Grünwald and Zátka had polled more than 880 votes from a smaller electorate, and had led a sweep of the curia by the Party of Progress. Claudi, as head of the True Party of Progress, had received only about 400 votes, and had needed to run again, in the first curia. Now he and five other Constitutionalists won seats in the third curia easily, with vote tallies just under 700 (about 54 percent). Two men running only as candidates of the Burgher Party rounded out the winners, with 570 votes each.[11] The new electoral results indicated that Claudi had used his time as mayor well, and had enlarged the third curia (above all through the granting of burgher status) to German and Constitutionalist advantage. They also indicated that many voters had voted nationally. But that was not all. Claudi had taken some care to maintain his support from Budweisers by not pushing Czech-German conflict too far.

During the brief campaign for the second curia, the Burgher Party listed Jews as two of its twelve candidates. That play for Jewish votes was unconvincing, though, because in the third curia, the only one in which the party had any hope of capturing seats, it had run an all-Catholic slate. The *Kreisblatt* (which had recently abandoned its Budweiser stance) wrote of a "newly concocted stunt born of Czech cunning." The German and Constitutionalist candidates received slightly more than two-thirds of the 338 ballots cast. Four days later, on May 30, the first curia voted. Here, in what could be called a stunt born of German cunning, the German and Constitutionalist Party listed the town rabbi on its ticket. Most enfranchised Jews had already voted in the third curia. Running a Jew there, though, might have given the Burgher Party an opportunity to capture more seats, by trumping nationhood with religion. In the first curia, in contrast, the German and Constitutionalist Party was confident of victory. Sixteen of the ninety-three voters abstained, including Bishop Jirsik/Jirsík and Deacon Schawel/Šavel. Nine voted a straight Burgher ticket; six split their ballots between the two parties; and the remaining two-thirds elected the German and Constitutionalist Party's apostles, including the rabbi, to three-year terms. The *Kreisblatt* trumpeted that *"Budweis rests more firmly than ever on the foundations of Germandom and of loyalty to the law and the Constitution."* Claudi, reelected as mayor, excluded Grünwald, Zátka, and other opponents from the important committees.[12]

Czech and Catholic leaders, it was becoming clear, had no hope of capturing a share of power in town hall any time soon. They thus turned their attention elsewhere. In 1876, as had been the case in 1869, they boycotted elections to the town council in all three curias. Meanwhile, in the fall of 1873, Claudi added a position in the Austrian Parliament to his position as mayor. As had been the case in previous elections, the centralist candidate prevailed over the federalist one within town. This time, though, the state-rights candidate, Hynek Zátka, could not accumulate a majority in the rest of the electoral district—because the rest was no more. Liberals in the Austrian Parliament, together with Francis Joseph, had consolidated their majority through an electoral reform, part of which was the gerrymandering of Budweis/Budějovice into the smallest electoral district for the Austrian Parliament in Bohemia.[13]

During the 1870s, as Czechs and Catholics in Budweis/Budějovice turned their backs on the municipal government, Germans and Constitutionalists became ever more entwined with it. The *Anzeiger aus dem südlichen Böhmen*, signaling perhaps a retreat from the countryside, changed its name to the *Budweiser Zeitung* in 1873. The following year, the gymnastics instructor of the *Turnverein* went on the municipal payroll, and participation in German-style gymnastics became required in all municipal elementary schools. The town council made the necessary room in some pupils' schedules by demoting the Czech language to an elective subject. Yet Constitutionalists did not have so much power through town hall as to be able simply to ride roughshod over their opponents. In May 1878, the royal Bohemian School Council (recently divided into German-language and Czech-language sections) initiated proceedings to take over the school that the Czech School Foundation had opened in 1873, and to finance it from public funds. Thanks both to Czech self-help and to modest support from the state, educational opportunities in the Czech language in town ceased to shrink and before long began to expand.[14]

Utraquist activities in town continued, but changed in meaning. The year 1874 saw the consecration in the cathedral of the parade flags of the Association of War Veterans, with a phalanx of Czech and Catholic clubs facing a phalanx of Constitutionalist ones. Founded two years previously, the club had already published its statutes in a carefully utraquist pamphlet. "Headquartered in Budweis, the Association has German and

Czech [*böhmisch*] as its languages," read the text in German, while the version in Czech read that "Headquartered in Budějovice, the Association has Czech and German as its languages." In both cases, however, there immediately followed a statement that commands given within the association would always be in German. The policy mirrored that of the army. Although officers on active duty were required to study any tongue spoken by more than 20 percent of the enlisted men in the regiment, those men had to know the "language of command"—which consisted of eighty-odd cries in German, such as "March!" and "Open fire!"[15] The attempt to guarantee at least a minimum of mutual comprehensibility between any two soldiers, at the price of making one language more equal than the rest, promised to save Austrian lives on the battlefield. In Budweis/Budějovice, though, no lives were at risk when veterans marched in parades. And the scrupulous implementation of utraquism called attention to the slight inequality.

Budweis/Budějovice also gained a volunteer fire department. Claudi revived the idea that his predecessor as mayor, Klawik/Klavík, had vetoed in the mid-1860s: to enlist gymnasts in order to fight fires—if not wars—for free. Claudi refrained, though, from turning the new, vitally important organ of public safety into a German outpost. He did so perhaps because the consequences for his political cause would have been serious had a Czech's house burned to the ground. Eighty-eight firemen, drawn both from the *Turnverein* and from its Czech equivalent, the *Sokol*, protected the town henceforth from conflagration.[16] Utraquism was changing into "either-or," rather than "both," and into a question of Czech and German nationhood, rather than just of the Czech and German languages.

In May 1879, the *Beseda* and the *Liedertafel* broke with years of an almost total mutual boycott, and attended unveiling ceremonies for the statue of a local hero: Adalbert/Vojtěch Lanna, a boatbuilder and industrialist who had died in 1866 and who, as a Budweiser, had contributed to Czech and to German causes. The *Kreisblatt* called on its readers to treat members of a Czech singing club from Prague warmly when they visited town.[17] Political developments on high help to explain this suspension of the usual emphasis on differences. In 1878, the Habsburg Monarchy had gained control of the Ottoman territories of Bosnia and Herzegovina in the Balkans. Some Liberal Germans had been so bold as to question the wisdom of acquiring backward and Slavic areas. Relations between the Liberal-dominated government and Francis Joseph, who considered foreign policy his own domain, had deteriorated rapidly, and the cabinet had resigned in July 1878. Since then, caretaker prime ministers had been trying to piece together a new coalition even a fraction as stable as the old. Czech delegates to the Austrian Parliament continued to boycott it, but strong voices among them called for a more constructive approach. On one and the same page, the *Kreisblatt* completed its coverage of the unveiling and reported that the emperor-king had dissolved the Lower House of the Austrian Parliament. New elections were in the offing, and Bohemian politics stood more open than at any time since 1871. "The mood of the times," the newspaper commented, "speaks powerfully for a compromise with our Czech fellow inhabitants. The quarrel, which has lasted for years, now seems likely to end to the benefit of the [Austrian] Empire."[18]

A German Turn toward Ethnicity

The Austrian Parliament elections, held in June 1879, concluded in Budweis/Budějovice with a victory by Claudi. Yet in many districts, thanks in part to Habsburg pressure, non-Constitutionalist candidates prevailed. Francis Joseph then turned with the assignment of forming a cabinet not to a Constitutionalist but to a Bohemian aristocrat and childhood playmate, Count Eduard Taaffe. A Czech journalist in Vienna, writing some years later as a longtime acquaintance of Taaffe, summed up the man as follows:

> Count Taaffe was born so to speak without any clear nationality. . . . What is certain is that he was neither a Czech nor a German, although he was reared in German fashion. . . . Nor was the father of Count Eduard a German in the modern sense. And this lack of nationality explains many an advantage, but also many a fault to his politics. . . . Whoever is born blind has no hope of distinguishing colors; whoever belongs to no nation cannot be open to national feelings and passions. For this reason, Count Taaffe was to a certain degree objective and unbiased with regard to national strivings.[19]

Certainly Taaffe possessed sufficient objectivity to recognize that, without at least some national members of the Bohemian contingent in the Lower House, he could not assemble a majority. To conservatives, to federalist great landowners, and to the noble-Polish bloc from Galicia, he succeeded in adding fifty-odd deputies from the Bohemian/Czech National Party. Almost overnight, Czech leaders shifted from organizing boycotts of the Austrian Parliament to organizing ministries.

That fall, Francis Joseph complemented Taaffe's antiliberal "Iron Ring" of conservative, federalist, Catholic, and Slavic national representatives in the Lower House by concluding a secret defensive alliance with the German Empire, directed against Russia. Both the Dual Alliance and the monarchy's occupation of Bosnia and Herzegovina carried the imprimatur of the German chancellor, Bismarck, and both signaled that Francis Joseph had come to terms with the outcome of the Austro-Prussian War of 1866. The Habsburg Monarchy, surrendering its ambitions in the West,

turned toward the South and East.[20] From national perspectives, the twin
Habsburg initiatives of 1879 seem contradictory: Cisleithania's prime
minister concluded an agreement with Slavs against Germans at home,
while the monarchy as a whole did the reverse abroad. Yet the course
taken also had important nonnational dimensions. It served the dynastic
interest, and for that reason proved durable.

Taaffe could not reward the Bohemian/Czech National Party for its
participation in his coalition by implementing trialism. But in a memorandum submitted to Francis Joseph late in 1879, leaders of the "Czech
Club" in the Parliament set a lower price. They pointed to article 19 of the
Fundamental Laws, and called on the state to institute linguistic equality.
Taaffe responded quickly. In the spring of 1880, a decree ordered courts,
district captainships, and additional imperial-royal offices (but not the
army) to cease favoring German in the Bohemian lands, at least in public
dealings. This new policy boosted the career prospects of officials raised in
Czech-speaking environments, because secondary-school education and
employment had already rendered them overwhelmingly bilingual. Imperial-royal civil servants who spoke only German, on the other hand, faced
a dilemma. They could limit themselves henceforth to serving in districts
and on cases in which only German was used, thereby crippling their
chances for advancement, or they could tackle the humiliating chore of
mastering a language widely regarded as culturally inferior, yet dauntingly
difficult for non-Slavs.[21]

Budweis/Budějovice's town council joined many municipalities and associations across Cisleithania in condemning the so-called Stremayr decree
(named after Taaffe's Minister of Justice). The aldermen passed a resolution in June that branded the decree an "attempted rape of the German
race in Bohemia." The very next month, Constitutionalists and federalists
managed to settle on a common ticket for elections to town hall. But the
agreement rested on a misunderstanding at best, and on deceit by Claudi
at worst. No sooner did the elections end than Constitutionalists, who
continued to hold a large majority of the Council seats, repeated their
1873 performance and blocked the appointment of even a single Czech
or Catholic to the important committees.[22]

In September 1880, in another protest against the Stremayr decree, the
town council signed on as a charter member of a new organization with
headquarters in Vienna: the German School Association [*Deutscher Schul-
verein*]. Its purpose was to establish German-language schools in areas of
the monarchy where German-speakers were so few that state-funded education took place in another language. A Constitutionalist alderman motioned that the municipality should join by donating 100 florins. His motion, the *Kreisblatt* reported, "passes with all votes—against the six Czech
ones. After the balloting, loud calls of 'Bravo!' resound in the auditorium.

Alderman Dr. Wokáč attempts to register the protest of the Czech aldermen in the minutes." Vokáč also attempted to introduce a motion that
the council should make a comparable contribution to a Czech cause.
Claudi and his allies simply ignored the proposal.[23] Gone was the conciliatory national mood that had characterized public life in town only a year
ago.

Vokáč may have recognized in the German School Association not only
a rival to Zátka's Czech School Foundation but also that highest compli-
ment, imitation. The new organization, like Zátka's, relied heavily on ethnic rhetoric and called for donations so that it could win children—few of
them burgher offspring, and none of them enfranchised—for the national
cause. Both organizations attempted to tie together citizens of Cisleithania who lived dozens and even hundreds of miles apart.[24] Ousted from
Habsburg ministries and stripped of a long-standing linguistic privilege,
Constitutionalist leaders had responded almost immediately by emphasizing their Germanness more. They had done so, furthermore, by taking a
step away from their elitist, historical-cultural rhetoric and toward a more
populist, ethnic one.

December 1880 saw another national conflict over language, although
in this instance the Habsburg role was more inadvertent. In a census
scheduled for repetition every ten years, the Habsburg Monarchy for the
first time sought to learn about language use, person by person. In answer-
ing one of the questions on the census form, heads of household had to
declare, for themselves and for members of their family, a "language of
daily use" [Umgangssprache/obcovací řeč]. In professional publications,
Cisleithanian demographers distinguished language explicitly from "nation" or "nationality"—which no question in the census so much as mentioned. As Adolf Ficker, president of the Austrian Directorate for Administrative Statistics, had explained in public lectures already in 1869 and
1870, when the decision to poll language a decade hence was being made,
"in many towns of Bohemia and Moravia, Southern Styria, and Carniola,
many families undeniably exist which still prefer to make use of German
in their own midst, without thereby wishing to renounce their Slavic nationality [Nationalität]."[25] His "nationality" related to language in complex ways.

Ficker, in his lectures, had pointed to two guiding principles for demographers: "the person polled must be able to give a positive answer to the
questions asked, and the census taker must be able to ascertain the correct-
ness or incorrectness of the answer without extensive investigation." He
had then stated that the Directorate of Administrative Statistics concluded, on the basis of experience accumulated in population surveys during the 1840s and 1850s, that "nationality is *not* a phenomenon allowing
of individual communication, that it may not be derived from the individ-

ual or sought of him, and as a consequence may not be determined by the mechanical means of the census." The official understanding of "nationality" emphasized social relationships more than did German and Czech leaders, who tended to emphasize individuals, "members" of a "nation" or "race." The official stance that "nationality" or nationhood of any sort could not be polled in the census found consistent confirmation by Cisleithanian courts over the following two decades.[26]

Even had Cisleithanian demographers concluded that they could poll "nationality" or nationhood, they had little reason to do so. More relevant to the state was a purely linguistic issue. Administrators and policymakers, in order to serve, govern, and communicate with a given population, needed to know which language or languages it spoke and read—at least in the course of public activities. From this focus derived the term "language of daily use." Other countries, and even the Hungarian half of the monarchy, tended to collect data on the "mother tongue" of citizens. Hundreds of thousands and even millions of Habsburg subjects, however, used the language (or languages—Ficker had explicitly acknowledged the existence of many utraquists) of their early childhood only within the confines of the home, if at all.[27]

"Mother tongue," in fact, had no place in a survey carried out according to truly scientific principles. The term, like "nationality," proves highly elastic upon closer examination. In the Hungarian half of the monarchy, official guidelines to the census eventually made the disarming confession that "the possibility cannot be excluded that the mother tongue of the student is other than that of his mother, particularly if he has acquired a language different than that of his mother in school or through other intercourse." Ficker, until his death in March 1880, consistently advocated polling "family language" instead. The Ministry of the Interior, however, apparently wishing to emphasize still more the social, the public, and even the territorial aspects to language, decided that month to poll "language of daily use."[28]

Both Ficker and his successors among census officials were well aware that language was no simple matter. They badly distorted the results of the census, however, by making it deaf to bilingualism. Those polled could claim only one language, from a specific list. Why? Since the early 1870s, states in Europe had been attempting to coordinate their censuses in multiple ways. The tendency in linguistic matters, anchored in a resolution passed at the International Statistical Congress in St. Petersburg in 1872, was to allow each person to claim only one language. Delegates from the Habsburg Monarchy rejected the interpretation, put forward by some other delegates, that languages were a proxy for nationalities, and for that reason had to be polled in mutually exclusive fashion. Yet Cisleithania, in an effort to make its statistics comparable with those of other countries, abided by the one-language principle.[29] The domestic, homogenizing zeal of Europe's nation-states, by force of interstate example and under cover of scientific objectivity, contributed to eliminating from the census the option of claiming to speak both German and Czech, and to leaving unknown how many of Budweis/Budějovice's residents were bilingual.

By allowing only one language per person, state demographers provided to ethnic nationhood a boost that was as great as it was unintentional. The Habsburg authorities required that everyone make a formal declaration in favor of a single language, at least once every ten years. In some cases, the name of a language and of a "nation" coincided—although the official designation in the census for Czech was "Bohemian-Moravian-Slovakian." No language bore the same name as the monarchy; inhabitants did not have the option of responding to the language question with "I speak Habsburg." Because the census contained no question about "nationality," national leaders could claim all the more plausibly that the question about language was really about national affiliation.

In Budweis/Budějovice, the novelty of the language question made for much confusion in December 1880. Political leaders, however, leapt to assist residents with the choice forced on them, offering multiple interpretations—sometimes convoluted, consistently self-serving—of what "language of daily use" meant. The *Kreisblatt* wrote on December 18 that "if . . . a German in a district with a mixed population *knows both languages of the province* (be it German and Czech, German and Slovene, or German and Polish) and uses the non-German one in his business dealings frequently, but converses in his family and with relatives and friends in the German language, then the language 'that the person uses in regular intercourse' is *German*."[30] Four days later, the newspaper published a "Call to Germans in Bohemia" from Dr. Franz Schmeykal, a leader of the Constitutionalist community in Prague and in Bohemia more generally. By the rules of logic, his appeal contradicted the previous one. Still, Schmeykal's possessed a more honest ring, arguing as it did that people who felt themselves to be Germans, whatever language they might employ in their day-to-day activities, should answer the language question with "German."[31]

The next issue of the *Kreisblatt* offered still another reason why readers should claim German as their language of daily use. Citizens who failed to fill out their forms correctly, an official notice warned, risked penalties of up to twenty florins or four days in jail. The catch? The imperial-royal Statistical Central Commission had assigned the task of checking the forms to town hall. Georg Groh signed the notice, as deputy mayor. Some Czechs must have remembered him as the man who, among other things, had resigned his post as a substitute alderman in 1862 in order to protest an attempt by Mayor Klawik/Klavík at keeping municipal schools utraquist. Groh could be trusted to police the census as much as a cat, in its master's absence, could be trusted to watch over a caged canary. Indeed, the *Kreisblatt* hinted in the New Year that feathers had been flying, reporting without details that the municipal Census Commission was issuing numerous summonses to residents in connection with questionnaire errors. On January 12, the newspaper also reprinted an article from the *Reichenberger Zeitung*, in the north of Bohemia, on high passions there in the wake of the census. According to the article, "language of daily use" should have been abandoned in favor of "nationality." "That way many a Czech resident, whose language of daily use here after all is only German, could at least justify how he filled out his form; he could have answered truthfully, and scenes of which no one can approve could have been avoided."[32]

During the countdown to the census, Constitutionalists attempted to intimidate municipal employees into declaring German as their language of daily use, whatever they spoke outside the workplace. Threats did not stop a Czech, who taught (in German) in one of the town schools, from writing the following on his census form: "language of administration and of education, German; language of daily use, Czech."[33] (Writing in German, he used the word *böhmisch*—not *tschechisch*.) The man kept his job but may have had his answer corrected for him by town hall.

The census results, when published in 1881, surprised leaders on both national sides in town. Czech-speakers numbered far more than Germans had feared or than Czechs had hoped, and had finished in a dead heat with German-speakers, 11,812 to 11,829. (In confessional terms, the population broke down into 22,782 Catholics, 969 Jews, and 72 Protestants.) Only eleven residents had listed a language other than Czech or German.[34] They presumably devoted their days to delivering soliloquies—or more likely, had joined many other people in stating not language of daily use but national affiliation. In 1880, poorly paid workers in the tobacco factory—or, for that matter, all women and children and most adult males—remained barred from participation in elections to the town council, the Chamber of Commerce and Trade, the Bohemian Diet, and the Austrian Parliament. But democracy ruled in the census, where *everyone* had a vote (albeit one cast indirectly by most women and by minors). Indeed, to use words written in 1910 by one of Ficker's successors as official head of Cisleithanian demographers, "Even where the obligation to vote exists, the voter who does not want to take sides has the option of submitting an empty ballot or one filled out with a name carrying no political significance. But in the census, one is demanded to answer [questions] in a certain sense, under penalty of legal action!"[35]

Both national movements in Budweis/Budějovice "won" the census carried out by the Habsburg state. One of the winners, though, won more. No less than Czech leaders, German and Constitutionalist ones had campaigned hard, and thus implicitly had accepted the census results in advance as a measure of relative national strengths. Those results had made Germans balloon in number to more than ten thousand, at least on paper and to some people. Yet on the new, quantitative and ethnic turf of the census, the German and Liberal movement lost the enormous advantage that it enjoyed over the Czech movement on the old, qualitative turf of town hall, curial elections, and formal politics more generally. Czech leaders, by achieving a form of numerical equality with their opponents, on terms that those opponents accepted, had achieved a milestone victory.

Mayor Claudi and his allies did not respond to the twin shocks of the Stremayr decree and of the census results by becoming more egalitarian in their handling of language issues. To the contrary, the Constitutionalist majority in the town council passed a resolution in 1881 banning the use of Czech during council meetings. The district captain overruled the resolution, as did the Bohemian governor on appeal. Claudi rephrased the ban on Czech—and was overruled again. Over several years, Czechs repeatedly appealed both to the authorities and to the conscience of Germans in town hall. Constitutionalists, for their part, kept municipal lawyers on the case. When the council mandate expired in 1884, Constitutionalists placed only two Czechs on its slate, which swept to victory. (Von Jungmann/z Jungmannů also won election, but now as a member of the opposing ticket.) The two Czechs may have wished to decline the dubious honor of being elected, but could not: Hynek Zátka and several other men had attempted to withdraw their own involuntary candidacies in 1869, only to learn that the law forced them to serve out the council term foisted on them, on penalty of the loss of voting rights for six years.[36]

Between 1879 and 1881, three German and Liberal representatives in Budweis/Budějovice's Chamber of Commerce and Trade died in office. In accordance with the bylaws of the chamber, the runners-up in the elections—federalists—replaced the deceased representatives until, like them, their terms expired. Members of the shrunken Constitutionalist majority, frightened by this development and by ominous trends in the electorate, postponed the next round of voting. Then they attempted to stuff the electoral commission with allies when the Ministry of Finance would tolerate no more delay. Such trickery only angered many voters in the countryside, who in May 1883 helped to elect eight Constitutionalists and twelve Czechs and Catholics to the Chamber Council.[37] Constitutionalists lost control over the chamber's seat in the Lower House of the Austrian Parliament, over two seats in the Bohemian Diet, over a valuable channel of communication to the Ministry of Finance, and over eight full-time jobs in the chamber's offices in Budweis/Budějovice.

At the constituent meeting of the new Chamber Council, representatives of the victorious coalition elected as their president the scion of one

of Bohemia's richest and oldest noble families, Prince Franz von Lobko-
witz/František z Lobkovic. After this bow to federalist great landowners,
additional bows followed in the direction of other key constituencies. In
the Tabor/Tábor district of the chamber, a bloc of Jewish voters had abandoned the Constitutionalist ticket and had decided the outcome in one
curia. In 1885, the Chamber Council filled its seat in the Lower House
with a Jew. Czechs, for their part, gained linguistic equality in the chamber's publications, as well as the replacement of German with Czech as
the language of administration.[38]

A New Generation

In 1883, Grünwald moved to Prague. His departure, combined with the
aging of Hynek Zátka and others, cleared the way for August Zátka to
assume the mantle of Czech leadership in town. By now thirty-six years
old, with his own law offices, Zátka had settled down, marrying Klawik/
Klavík's granddaughter, Johanna Klawik/Jana Klavíková, in 1878. Since
Zátka's first, somewhat wild public appearances in the early 1870s, he had
matured into a principled and charismatic leader, equally gifted at war-
room strategizing and at rallying crowds with impassioned speeches.[39]
Recognizing the central Czech advantage—mounting strength with every
year—he worked consistently to choke off impulsive calls from the ranks
for frontal charges, without depressing morale. *Zátka*, by coincidence,
means "stopper" or "cork" in the Czech language.

By the following year, 1884, a changing of the guard had begun in the
Constitutionalist camp, too. Deputy Mayor Groh retired, and Mayor Claudi
died that fall. For the next several years, a cluster of men ran the party
and town hall: Wendelin Rziha, an attorney who apparently had begun his
political career elsewhere as a Czech (Vendelín Říha); Anton Franz
Taschek, a merchant; and several others. Yet none of those burghers succeeded in bending the others to his will. Rather, with time, Taschek's
son Josef did. This graduate of the engineering faculty in Vienna, only
twenty-seven years old in 1884, had set to work immediately upon his
return to Budweis/Budějovice in the late 1870s at constructing a personal political machine within the world of liberal associations. In electoral politics, the first results of his efforts showed in the summer of 1884,
with his election to the town council as an alternate. This was followed
by his designation as deputy mayor in 1890, as member of the diet in
1893, and then as mayor in 1903—the nearly mechanical outcome of
harnessing the local wheels of power and patronage, and then of due
diligence in lubricating them.[40]

Like Claudi, Taschek found his very Germanness called into question by Czechs—on ethnic grounds. Sometimes, as Zátka delighted in pointing out, Taschek made Czech-inspired grammatical errors in the German language. *Budivoj* reminded its readers that Taschek's father had come to Budweis/Budějovice in the 1840s from the Czech-speaking village of Bernardice and had signed on as a charter member of the *Beseda* in 1862 before rethinking his loyalties. For that matter, *Budivoj* noted that the family name was a Czech one, and lay at the root of the word "*taškář*"—meaning "rascal."[41] Taschek was "really" a Czech, and thus the worst kind of German. As a Czech saying goes, *Poturčenec horší Turka*—"worse than the Turk is the Turkish convert."

Constitutionalists, in a sign that their understanding of ethnicity continued to differ from the Czech understanding, did not question Taschek's Germanness. Nor did they claim that Grünwald was a German because of his name, or that Zátka was a German because he spoke German as a native. Czech understandings of ethnicity, as has already been noted, tended to stress native command of a language, and to classify as "Czech" anyone who spoke both languages of Bohemia equally well. (Czechs did make exceptions when doing so helped the cause. Zátka's mother, for example, had learned Czech only as an adult; here is part of why German counted as one of the "mother tongues" of her oldest son. But she counted as a Czech to Czechs—who did not poke fun at the very national names of her last two sons: Vlastimil and Dobroslav. Here supranational understandings of women as minors—such that their nationhood, like their citizenship, hinged on that of a father, husband, or son—played a role.) Constitutionalist and German understandings of ethnicity, in contrast, tended in cases of bilingualism to emphasize what Constitutionalists had always seen as important: individual action and conviction. Taschek was German because he spoke German, acted like a German, and claimed to be a German—any accent or errors notwithstanding.[42]

In those parts of the Bohemian lands where almost everyone spoke only one language, the new, jointly national emphasis on ethnicity promised to render the nationalization of two "peoples" easier. Czech and German leaders, by agreeing on who belonged to which national movement, could hinder each others' recruitment efforts less, and could make nationalization seem more natural and inevitable. But in places such as Budweis/Budějovice, where the proportion of utraquists was unusually high, the difference between Czech and German ethnicity allowed both national movements to claim many of the same individuals. As Zátka and Taschek began to look past burghers and bourgeois to an entire people, each leader pursued an internally consistent view of who his people were. Yet the result was not a productive division of nationalizing labor. Rather, thousands of utraquists became sites of Czech-German contestation. A person's nation-

Figure 3. Josef Taschek (1857–1939). German Liberal leader and mayor of Bud-
weis/Budějovice, 1903–1918. Courtesy of the State Regional Archive in České
Budějovice.

ality depended on who was doing the ascribing. Even for people speaking only one language, nationalization became less a question of nature and of inevitability than of choice—not only between Czech and German but between national and nonnational. Because the rhetoric of ethnicity had Czech and German variants, Budweis/Budějovice's many utraquists did not "break" or completely disable the rhetoric. Yet by clashing, the two variants stripped the Czech and German ethnic convergence of at least part of its accelerating effect on nationalization.

Both Taschek and Zátka worked harder than their predecessors at splitting utraquist associations and at heightening the national qualities of middle-class clubs already dominated by one national movement or the other. The First South Bohemian Association of Soldiers and Public Officials, founded on a utraquist basis in 1880, did not remain that way for long. When the president led the board in rejecting applications for membership from Zátka and from two other men late in 1882, Czech members staged a revolt. In January 1883, on a floor vote, they revoked the board's action and impeached the president, replacing him with Zátka. There followed an exodus by Germans from the club, which transferred its headquarters to the *Beseda*. (In 1884, members nonetheless attended Claudi's funeral.) Both the *Turnverein* and the *Liedertafel* added the word "German" to their name—although a majority of the gymnasts rejected the change in 1882 and agreed to it, at Taschek's urging, only on a second vote in the following year. The *Liedertafel* also adopted a new emblem: a swan with spread wings over oak leaves and a lyre on a band in the black, red, and gold German colors.[43]

In the fall of 1883, a bust of Joseph II of Habsburg went up in town, in a sign that Constitutionalist leaders continued to strengthen their emphasis on Germanness, and to do so in ethnic ways. A century previously, Joseph II had sought to improve and to centralize the governance of his far-flung lands. To that end, he had attempted—and failed—to make German a sort of Habsburg *lingua franca*. Taschek, together with German leaders throughout Cisleithania during the early 1880s, seized on the monarch's promotion of the German language and made him a new national hero. Taschek also exploited the unveiling of the bust to lend his still heavily middle-class movement a more populist appearance—by recruiting villagers to attend. For them, Joseph II's improvement of peasants' legal position vis-à-vis nobles probably meant more than did his language policy (whose national motives existed only in the imagination of Germans and of Czechs). The bronze took up a position directly opposite the *Beseda*, where it provoked Czechs daily over the following decades.[44]

Immediately after the unveiling, Taschek held a meeting at which he proposed forging closer links between Germans in Budweis/Budějovice and German-speakers living in the nearby countryside. The German

Union of the Bohemian Forest [*Deutscher Böhmerwaldbund*] came into
being as a result, with Taschek serving as president. In 1884, the *Kreisblatt*
explained that the mission of the association was to "bring laborers and
domestic help as fresh elements to the Germans of this town so as to put
an end to the inundation with Czech factory workers and maids. The
apprentice and maid from [the Bohemian Forest], and if necessary from
[Upper] Austria, must be mobilized. It should no longer be so that prominent German businesses in Budweis have Czech managers who bow and
scrape on the job in front of their employers, then take part assiduously in
the sappers' work of the Czechs in the *Beseda.*" In another report on the
Böhmerwaldbund, the newspaper insulted Czechs again, even while borrowing the central Czech ethnic metaphor of national consciousness as a
natural state to which individuals awaken from a deep sleep: "In wide
circles, there still rules an alarming indifference in national matters. In the
long term, this can only bring about the worst, given that our Czechs,
allied with the feudals and with the clericals, use every possible means to
pull the nightcap farther over the eyes and ears of the plain and honest
German [*dem deutschen Michel*]."[45] Constitutionalist leaders were taking
poorer people more seriously as potential national recruits. Those leaders
also agreed now with Czech leaders that people who arrived in town speaking only Czech translated much more easily into Czechs than into Germans. In less than liberal fashion, Taschek attempted to influence who
joined the labor market in town, thus conceding that sheer numbers mattered more than he liked in the Czech-German struggle.

The *Böhmerwaldbund*, although geographically more focused than the
German School Association, differed less from it than from the men's
choirs and social clubs that had characterized both national movements
during the 1860s and 1870s. Membership in the new type of associations
was more broad, not only in the class, numerical, and territorial senses but
in a gender sense as well. Emphasis lay less on face-to-face encounters of
middle-class males who already knew one another than on pulling together small financial contributions from a large number of men and
women. Those contributions or dues, furthermore, went not so much to
self-celebration as to projects that benefited others—strangers made ab-
stractly familiar through their nationalization. Less than a year after the
founding of the *Böhmerwaldbund*, more than 7,000 members belonged
to it through forty-eight chapters, one in Budweis/Budějovice and the
rest scattered over the Bohemian Forest and beyond. At about the same
time, the local chapter of the German School Association (also headed by
Taschek) claimed that the number of its female members alone had now
passed 500.[46]

Older national clubs in town tried to adjust to this new model, Czech
ones often with greater success. Months after the founding of the German

School Association in 1880, Zátka's Czech School Foundation had become part of a pan-Bohemian association, the Czech Central School Foundation. Both of the gymnastics clubs in town had done much the same even earlier. The size and the social composition of the *Turnverein*, though, stagnated. Only 194 men belonged in 1890, despite an effort during the late 1880s at recruiting lower-middle-class members with free lessons. The *Sokol* pulled ahead, counting 320 members by 1894. (Anyone inclined to take literally the *Sokol* slogan, "Every Czech a *Sokol!*" though, has to draw sobering conclusions even from that higher figure.) Both gymnastics clubs, like the *Beseda*, the *Geselligkeitsverein*, the *Liedertafel* (which added a small women's choir), and additional associations, failed to take off into geometric growth. Instead, they continued to be predominantly middle-class, local, and male.[47] In electoral contests, trends were similar. Local Constitutionalists and federalists had already tied themselves into larger political networks some time ago. But under Zátka's leadership, Czechs and Catholics gradually became more open about their affiliation with the Bohemian/Czech National Party, and discontinued names such as the Burgher Party. Both of the major "parties" in town also became more worthy of that name, by growing beyond small clusters of notable men.

The Czech "Each to His Own" campaign, as well as a German equivalent, began to influence the purchasing decisions of a broader cross-section of town residents. District captains and judges frowned on calls to boycott, and the Cisleithanian Supreme Court eventually ruled that they violated the constitutional rights of shopkeepers and that instigators could be punished with jail terms of up to six months. Yet prosecutors put next to no one on trial—because people were not so dim-witted as to require incitement explicit enough to meet legal standards of proof. Owners of businesses came under pressure to make a declaration of national colors and to surrender one part of their clientele in order to keep another. In 1885, the *Böhmerwaldbund* issued an address book or directory for Budweis/Budějovice that ascribed a nationality to business owners through different typefaces. The National Bohemian Forest Union (NJP), founded by Czechs in response to the *Böhmerwaldbund*, condemned the publication. But once the Czech business community in town stood on firmer legs, the NJP published a directory of its own, in 1894.[48] The very existence of such directories, of course, indicates that even shoppers who assumed that every business owner had a national affiliation sometimes could only guess at what it was.

In June 1884, in a sort of inaugural speech as Grünwald's successor, Zátka proposed ways to weave more densely the Czech institutional web that, radiating outward from the *Beseda*, was beginning to cover the town. He urged the creation of a new *Beseda* of the People, on the model of the original *Beseda* and of the derivative *Beseda* of Artisans and Tradesmen, founded in 1882. "The common people of our town are Czech," he claimed, "and thus far, this precious material has not enjoyed our attention." The attention that he now proposed included founding more schools. Zátka also made a case for establishing a German-language newspaper and a club which, conservative and nonconfrontational, might draw national neutrals in the direction of the Czech movement. In keeping with the long-standing Czech practice of combining ethnicity with a more historical, state rights nationhood, he pointed out that some German-speakers, especially imperial-royal officials, army officers, priests, and Jews, might become Czechs. "Perhaps the slogan of reconciliation might find an echo among burghers as well. There is plenty of material for a conciliatory German association. In elections to the diet, Austrian Parliament, and town council, Czechs would not hesitate to vote for honorable men, even if they were Germans by birth, and such candidates could win if they had, in addition to Czech votes, a relatively small number of German ones. For Jews, such a German conservative association could serve as a bridge over which to escape from German-national captivity."[49] Such people felt more comfortable in German-speaking settings, Zátka apparently believed, but they disagreed with some or all of liberal and German politics. By demanding less than the German movement did and by offering more, the Czech movement might win adherents.

Czechs followed through quickly on Zátka's proposals. The *Beseda* of the People, founded in December 1884, lured lower-middle-class people by charging no dues and by sponsoring cheery gatherings—where the club motto, "Czech children belong in Czech schools," probably figured prominently. A new Czech high school, funded entirely through private donations, opened its doors in September. By 1885, there were 2,396 children in Budweis/Budějovice acquiring an education primarily in the Czech language, nearly seven times as many as in 1870. Zátka's wife became the president of a new Czech women's association dedicated to raising money for girls' schools; the NJP opened a lending library in town; and the *Beseda* undertook construction of a new wing.[50]

Attempts at making Czechs out of German-speakers yielded less inspiring results. When elections to the Parliament took place in November 1884, neither Zátka nor other local leaders of the Bohemian/Czech National Party ran. Instead, they persuaded a retired army officer with an impeccable record and with no clear nationality, Franz/František von Kopřiva, to do so. As a Czech historian phrases the matter, the hope was that he would prove appealing to voters for whom "the state idea meant more than the national cause." The town council, which had the right to appoint half of the members for an electoral commission encharged with policing the polls, appointed Constitutionalists. The district captain, who appointed the other half, appointed federalists—in an effort to help a candidate who was certain to join Prime Minister Taaffe's coalition. By a count of 429 votes (39 percent) to 671 (61 percent), von Kopřiva lost to Josef Schier, a merchant. The tally marked only a 2 percent improvement on the showing by a more Czech candidate, Vokáč, against Claudi in 1879.[51]

Early in 1886, a Czech-funded semiweekly, the *Budweiser Bote*, commenced publication—in German, and employing what it claimed, without a trace of irony, was a "truly *progressive, conservative perspective.*" Perching precariously at the point where German, Czech, and nonnational views diverged, the newspaper promised that it would "advocate steadfastly the true rights and needs of the *German people*, but devote full consideration and generous recognition at the same time to the efforts and interests of the other peoples of our fatherland." At best, the *Bote* may have succeeded during its decade-long existence in luring a handful of nationally neutral burghers, officials, and Jews closer to the Czech cause. The "Union" club, founded for the same purpose at the end of 1884, proved a similar letdown, developing into little more than a license for a small cluster of Budweisers to socialize with one another in the *Beseda* in German. Zátka had the Union dissolved in 1889.[52]

The Five-florin Men

Neither Zátka nor Taschek succeeded in altering the national balance within the middle-class electorates that they, as new leaders, had inherited. Instead, they confirmed and deepened that balance together. A decision at the highest Habsburg level, however, ensured that formal politics now preoccupied an additional social stratum as well. Taaffe, seeking to consolidate his Iron Ring coalition, pushed a bill through the Austrian Parliament in 1882 that reduced from ten florins to five the tax threshold at which men became qualified to vote for candidates to the central legislature, as well as revised the structure of the great landowners' curia in Bohemia. Somewhat later, he also helped bring about an expansion of the electorate of the Bohemian Diet, whose Constitutionalist majority had yielded to a fragile federalist one in 1883. When the first Austrian Parliament elections to be held according to the new franchise occurred in the summer of 1885, the number of ballots cast in Budweis/Budějovice increased by nearly 40 percent. One of the Constitutionalist responses was to begin a boycott of the Diet in 1886. Federalists, meanwhile, rushed to embrace the shopkeepers, low-ranking officials, and less wealthy artisans who made up the "five-florin men." They, in fact, were the audience at which Zátka aimed the new *Beseda* of the People.[53] Although Czechness

remained emphatically ethnic, as opposed to civic, Czech leaders were
becoming reconciled to the centralist state, at a price to the civic component to Germanness.

Even as the "emperor's minister," as Taaffe called himself, opened up
electoral politics to lower-middle-class males, he clamped down on the
working class. In 1874, Marxists had founded an Austrian Social Democratic Party, taking advantage of the political rights guaranteed citizens
in the Fundamental Laws. In 1881, though, and especially after several
attempted assassinations of police officials by anarchists in Vienna during
1883 and 1884, Taaffe curtailed those rights, first through decrees and
then through temporary legislation that once again made political organization among workers extremely difficult. The measures closely resembled
the repression ordered several years previously in the German Empire by
Bismarck. In a further reflection of upper-class and bourgeois fears of the
lower social orders, both states also enacted paternalistic labor legislation—establishing limits on the length of the working day, for example,
as well as creating accident and sickness insurance programs.[54] The nonnational leadership of the monarchy sought to increase the size of the electorate without opening up the political spectrum to include Marxism.

As Taaffe had hoped, many five-florin men cast their first votes for non-
Constitutionalist candidates. In Budweis/Budějovice, Schier had defeated
von Kopřiva in 1884 with 61 percent of the vote. But in 1885, Schier
squeaked by with less than 52 percent, and the Constitutionalist parliamentary contingent shrank from 106 seats to 87. Five-florin men narrowed the local German and liberal margin of victory in elections to the
diet as well—where a federalist majority had replaced a liberal and German
one in 1883. That year, Claudi had defeated Grünwald, 955 votes to 529,
while in 1885, Schier won election unopposed. But in 1887, after the diet
suffrage reform, Zátka polled 1,047 votes to Schier's 1,363. Schier, who
had joined other Constitutionalists in walking out of the diet in 1886,
was reelected again in 1888. That time, though, he triumphed by a score
of only 1,337 to 1,207, and then had to resign amid charges of fraud.
Across Cisleithania, the Constitutionalist Party, with its patrician style and
with its platform (emphasizing liberty, the individual, the need for the
separation of church from state, and the benefits of allowing markets—
not traditions and bureaucracies—to allocate resources), alienated many
of the new voters. They often felt wronged by the capitalist system that
the liberal creed celebrated, and they embraced not so much reason and
progressive practices as collectivities, inherited bonds, faith, and market-
inhibiting institutions such as guilds.[55]

Yet the suffrage reform did not have the simple effect of undercutting
Constitutionalists to the benefit of parties in Taaffe's Iron Ring. Many
five-florin men in the Bohemian lands found the state-rights option no

more attractive than the German and liberal one. Neither set of leaders, after all, paid much attention to problems that plagued the *petit bourgeois*. Without the external impulse of Habsburg-driven enfranchisement, impulses internal to the national movements might not have sufficed to trigger the decisive opening up of associational life, especially on the Constitutionalist side. That interpretation, at least, helps to explain why new, poorer participants in clubs often clashed with a bourgeois leadership anxious to instruct and to control them. For political entrepreneurs who touted themselves as neither Constitutionalist nor federalist, prospects suddenly brightened.

Less to the right or to the left of the Constitutionalist Party than belonging to a new political dimension altogether, an unstable array of "German National" or *völkisch* (meaning "populist" or "folk") factions emerged during the 1880s. Radical, contradictory, simultaneously innovative and backward-looking, leaders of these new parties tended to have more diverse social origins than the Constitutionalist notables they battled, and to court support less through appeals to reason and to the public good than to emotion and to self-interest. *Völkisch* leaders were more emphatically national than Constitutionalist ones, and also much more emphatically ethnic. Language defined the "nation" for them much more than did citizenship, enfranchisement, and achievement more generally. So did religious origin; the German National parties soon began excluding Jews, even baptized ones.

In Budweis/Budějovice, Prague, and several other cities, the rise of German Nationals, with their political anti-Semitism, gave German Liberals cause for concern. On the one hand, the Constitutionalist Party needed to court the five-florin men for their votes in diet and Austrian Parliament contests. On the other hand, should the German-Jewish, Liberal coalition that had formed in the 1860s dissolve in the acid bath of *völkisch* agitation, federalists would probably make political gains. In Budweis/Budějovice, for example, Czechs and Catholics might increase their share of power in town hall. Then again, repeated lapses by Czech leaders into anti-Semitic outbursts signaled that Jewish voters had no real alternative to the Constitutionalist ticket, and could be appeased with little more than token gestures. Those gestures, such as placing several Jewish candidates on the Constitutionalist ticket in each municipal election, offended anti-Semitic Germans. But such Germans numbered few among that electorate, while in diet and Austrian Parliament elections, higher federalist pressure compensated for higher German tensions. No formal *völkisch* opposition to the Constitutionalist Party emerged in town during the 1880s.

In German associations, on the other hand, from which Czechs were absent, ranks began to split as early as 1884. Taschek signaled the openness of the *Böhmerwaldbund* to Jews by writing the statutes so as to exclude all questions of religion from discussion, and by placing a Jewish attorney, Israel Kohn, in charge of administration. The constituent meeting of the Budweis chapter, held shortly after Zátka's course-setting speech to Czechs in June, attracted what the *Kreisblatt* called people from "all circles of our comrades in origin [*Stammesgenossen*]"—workers, teachers, factory owners, lawyers, and so on. Taschek, in a speech, proclaimed that "We wish to draw all strata of the German citizenry to the great national project." Yet Johann Hrusa, the director of the local branch of the Discount Bank and an alderman, objected at the meeting that the Germanness of some members "could easily be doubted." Perhaps he was not referring to Kohn. And even if Hrusa was, he perhaps had a point, all anti-Semitism aside: several years later, Kohn had to deny a claim by *Budivoj* that he had once been a member of the *Beseda* and had professed Czech national feelings while serving as a clerk in August Zátka's law office. Whatever the case, the *Budweiser Kreisblatt* began to criticize the *Budweiser Zeitung* in 1884 for betraying the Liberal cause. By the end of the decade, tensions between Liberals and *völkische* had surfaced in the *Turnverein*, and the anti-Semitic stance of a social club called *Germania* had prompted the leaders of multiple Constitutionalist associations to join in denouncing it as un-German and as harmful to the German cause.[56]

Ethnic Germans, 50 percent of Budweis/Budějovice's population according to the 1880 census, were widely believed to be losing ground. At less local levels, the figures were considerably lower (although also more stable, as it would turn out, from census to census): about 37 percent in Bohemia, about 35 percent in Cisleithania, and about 25 percent in the monarchy as a whole. Having no real power to lose, *völkisch* leaders railed with growing irresponsibility at real and imagined enemies, and devised radical solutions to the minority status of their race or people. Some of those solutions, perhaps involving the abandonment to Slavdom of Budweis/Budějovice and of additional German "islands," were federalist— not in historical but in ethnic ways. German-speaking areas of Cisleithania should be welded together, without regard for the historical boundaries of the crownlands. A few extremists, willing to risk arrest, even swept both citizenship and the centralist-federalist distinction aside and pushed ethnic rhetoric to the logical but treasonous conclusion that German-speakers in the Habsburg Monarchy and in the German Empire (and indeed, in territories that had never belonged to the Holy Roman Empire) belonged together. Another, often complementary set of *völkisch* musings addressed the problem of Slavic majorities through a superimposition of German-Liberal elitism, with its historical-cultural and civic roots, onto German ethnicity. Like Liberal leaders, *völkisch* ones rejected the principle of one man, one vote. But if Liberals had instead backed curias defined by wealth and merit, *völkische* proposed a far more vague and broad elite. They focused not on superior individuals but on a superior, Aryan "race" or "nation" entitled to a privileged relationship with the state, whether that state was Cisleithania, the Habsburg Monarchy as a whole, or some sort of Greater Germany. Czechs, Jews, and other non-Germans, whatever their numbers, were entitled to no such thing, or even to autonomy.[57]

While *völkisch* Germans built fantasy castles in the air, liberal Germans defended real castles on the ground. In Budweis/Budějovice, Taschek worked to maintain the advantages that his party had—above all, control of town hall. Here the restrictive municipal franchise was pivotally important. Yet it also undermined, no less than did Czech "sappers," Taschek's new bridges to the Bohemian Forest. *Budivoj* wrote in 1888 that "since the founding of the well known '*Böhmerwaldbund*,' one can observe a German increase in the lower strata of the local population. . . . 'Taschek,' the wonderful lad of that Bernardice native and Greater German who made good, is recruiting not only maids and apprentices to come here from German areas but other kinds of laborers too." But the newspaper leapt to ethnic conclusions about how German and how liberal those German-speaking newcomers felt. Liberal condemnations of anti-Semitism as un-German perhaps did not contribute much to winning them over. Nor did Constitutionalist opposition to an expansion of voting rights. As Zátka noted years later, "It was a misfortune for the [Liberal] Germans that they were wealthy." Or to cite Gary Cohen's study of the German community in Prague, "By cultivating the self-image and collective life of a cultured and propertied elite, the German middle classes . . . could make it nearly impossible to build a broader popular base."[58]

For federalist leaders, the Habsburg expansion of the Austrian Parliament and diet electorates pushed politics in a different direction. As on the other side of the Bohemian political divide, five-florin politics tended to be more stridently national, populist, and anti-Semitic. But the Bohemian/Czech National Party already made heavy use of an ethnic rhetoric and had no significant Jewish constituency to hold leaders back from matching step for step the anti-Semitic demagoguery of new rivals. Ethnic rhetoric, furthermore, yielded a demographic majority for Czechs within the historical boundaries of the Bohemian lands and thus gave Czech leaders a powerful incentive to pursue a democratization of civic institutions in the Bohemian lands, rather than a racialization or a territorial redefinition. Indeed, the new and more radical style of politics among Czechs developed somewhat earlier and in considerable measure within the already existing Bohemian/Czech National Party. Even when some leaders seceded from the party in 1874 in order to found the Czech National Liberal Party [*Národní strana svobodomyslná*], they did so more as reformers than as rebels. Quickly labeled "Young Czechs," they took issue with the social conservatism and with the Catholicism of "Old Czechs" (as members of the original party came to be known, to their disadvantage), and questioned the close alliance with federalist great landowners. Yet Young Czechs, like Old Czechs, maintained a historical, state-rights rhetoric next to an ethnic one. And unlike *völkische*, Young Czechs maintained organizational unity. They also made their first major mark not with utopian and rash proposals but with the pragmatic objection during the 1870s that the Czech boycott of the diet and of the Austrian Parliament was yielding no results. That challenge to civic negativism helped to bring about the Iron Ring.

During the 1880s, five-florin men helped to make the National Liberals or Young Czechs a major force in Bohemian politics. Yet the Czech movement as a whole remained far more united than the German one. Young Czech leaders worked closely with Old Czech ones until the late 1880s and argued that two parties could serve the Czech "nation" better than could one.[59] The flip side to that argument was that, in pockets of Czech weakness, a one-party structure remained justified. And indeed, in Budweis/Budějovice, Zátka's Old Czechs did not face a branch of the Young Czech Party until the end of the decade. Even then, Czech clubs experienced nothing like the tensions in German ones between Liberals and *völkische*. In Budweis/Budějovice, the unusually even balance of Czech and German strength delayed and softened a central outcome for the Bohemian lands as a whole of Taaffe's enfranchisement push: greatly increased Czech-Czech and German-German competition.

Why, contrary to Taaffe's expectations, did lower-middle-class politics take on primarily national forms, and spur a greater nationalization of middle-class politics—in the sense that Constitutionalists became more German and federalists more Czech? Across Europe, as well as beyond it, politics was becoming more national. In Cisleithania, the parties that dominated politics at the beginning of the 1880s were already partly national. Even before Taaffe's enfranchisements took effect, those parties (and especially the Bohemian/Czech National Party) had begun to recruit and to nationalize lower-middle-class males. Because runners-up in winner-take-all elections get no prizes, political entrepreneurs who sought power by courting the new voters had to court at least some of the old voters as well. Useful in that context were national rhetorics. They proved flexible enough to accommodate considerable change in the social composition both of the national movements and of Bohemian politics more generally. As will be shown in the next chapter, furthermore, the Czech and the German movements in Budweis/Budějovice thrived not only on conflict with one another but also on internal conflict as well. Both movements, once internally articulated, succeeded in reaching more residents than ever before and also in reaching deeper into individual lives.

Taaffe only made incremental additions to electorates. He did not transform them and the party system by enfranchising vast numbers of people all at once. From Habsburg perspectives, the politics that mattered was not local. As Taaffe stated in 1888, "In Budweis, the two competing parties must demonstrate their congenital strength. Whichever side proves itself, over time, to be stronger must necessarily be accommodated by each government, in accordance with the law."[60] He left municipal electoral orders unchanged, and provided few incentives for politicians to found parties that professed loyalty to the Habsburg Monarchy in nonnational ways. Instead, he focused on boosting already existing parties that made up part of his Iron Ring. Habsburg policy was at most boldly conservative, not revolutionary. And as is the case with most policies, it had some unintended consequences.

As the Czech and German movements grew socially more inclusive, a subtle yet momentous transformation took place. "Liberal" and "Constitutionalist" had used to overlap considerably with "German." Now the Czech and the German movements both claimed a Liberal party. The reverse, though, did not hold true: no liberal movement existed with subordinate Czech and German parties. The Right-Left political spectrum and the Czech-German conflict, for some time roughly parallel, were becoming hierarchically ordered. Both Czech and German Liberals were now less liberal than they were national. Non-Liberal voters, too, tended now to decide first on their national loyalties, and only then on how they viewed the Church, "equality," and individual candidates and issues. The Habsburg injection of the lower-middle class into electoral politics challenged the Czech and German establishments, but the more complex politics that resulted was all the more emphatically national.

In 1866, the Habsburg Monarchy had lost a major war with Prussia. As Pieter Judson has pointed out, however, Constitutionalists in Cisleithania had experienced the military defeat less as a nationalizing event than as confirmation that their own, only partly national course was correct. Indeed, they had exploited Francis Joseph's weakness after 1866 to win significant political victories—above all, the enshrinement of their principles in the Fundamental Laws, and the almost uninterrupted control for more than a decade of key Cisleithanian ministries. During those years, Liberals had claimed, as exceptional individuals, to represent the best interests of all—without regard to class, for example, or to language.[61] The Germanness of Cisleithanian liberalism had remained weakly defined and often secondary, and the Germanness of Prussia and of the Germany created in 1871 had remained distant.

In 1879, shortly after the Habsburg Monarchy's "victory" in claiming Bosnia and Herzegovina, Liberals had lost their positions within the state apparatus. The new holders of at least some of those positions had been federalists. That development, far more than the war of 1866, had led to a redefinition and strengthening of Germanness in Budweis/Budějovice and in the Bohemian lands. Indeed, that reversal had led to a redefinition and strengthening of nationhood more generally within Bohemian politics. Constitutionalists had become less liberal and more German, and Germanness had become less civic and more ethnic. Constitutionalists had not become German or ethnic enough, though, to prevent the emergence of a new, *völkisch* wing to the German movement. Although inconsistent, that new wing might be characterized as indifferent to the question of centralism or federalism, and hostile to civic understandings of Germanness. *Völkisch* leaders also pushed historical-cultural, elitist Germanness in populist directions, such as to place even the most lowly speaker of German over any speaker of Czech. Federalists, meanwhile, had become more Czech, while Czechness had continued to become more populist. Czechness had also grown less anticivic—in the sense of remaining primarily ethnic, with a secondary emphasis on the historical unity of the Bohemian lands, but becoming reconciled to the centralist structure of Cisleithania. The two blocs that, together with Habsburg leaders, made up the principal players in Bohemian politics were becoming more national, and the two nationhoods more similar, even as basic asymmetries persisted.

Old Politics and New

In 1888, *Budivoj* estimated that three or four thousand "Czechs" in Budweis/Budějovice either remained indifferent in national matters or "pass themselves off as Germans so as not to spoil things for themselves with 'the lords.'"[62] That claim amounted to a wildly optimistic exaggeration of the breadth of national sentiment in town. Only recently had the institutional structures of either national movement begun to include the lower-middle class. Both movements continued almost to ignore families below the five-florin tax threshold—who made up an absolute majority of the population. Both movements devoted more attention than previously to females, but still far less than to males. Even among middle-class males, Budweiser components persisted into the late 1880s and beyond. Higher-ranking civil servants, for example, fit poorly into the national scheme of things and had reasons not to accommodate to it. The same holds true of genuinely liberal (as opposed to nationally liberal) individuals who spoke only Czech and of devoutly Catholic burghers who spoke only German.

Army officers remained largely nonnational too. In 1860, an author had written that "the Austrian armed forces form a society in and of themselves, one could almost say a nationality." A generation later, men on active military duty, like almost all women, continued to be denied the vote in any election. Officers also continued to associate above all with each other. From the mid-1880s, the *Beseda* and the *Geselligkeitsverein* each counted an officer among the members of its board. But those two men, together with their comrades in arms, belonged to both clubs simultaneously. This double, group form of membership, ordered by the army command, weakened the national content to dances and to other forms of socializing with civilians.[63]

Some priests had strong national sentiments and clashed with a part of their congregation as a result. But at higher levels of the Church administration in town, where policy was made and where funds were allocated, individuals did not divide clearly into Czechs and Germans. In February 1883, Bishop Jirsik/Jirsík died. Over the following decade or more, Czechs annointed him a national hero, commemorating the day of his death every year and collecting funds to erect a statue in his honor. The next bishop, an imperial count, acted with scrupulous national impartiality during his tenure—which was cut short in 1885 by his elevation to archbishop in Prague, and then to cardinal. His successor in Budweis/Budějovice, Martin Josef Říha, a professor at the seminary, was of far more humble origins, yet displayed the same "strict impartiality." Germans did not celebrate his birthday as Czechs did, but German newspapers found little cause for national complaint right up to Bishop Říha's death in 1907. And the Liberals who dominated town hall made him an honorary burgher in 1899.[64]

Many middle-class Jews remained weakly national as well. They did so, though, not so much by their own decisions as because of anti-Semitism in both national movements. The very shape of the synagogue, built in 1888, expressed strong assimilationist desires. It was, in the words of an architectural historian, "the most obviously church-like structure created for Jewish worship" in all Europe during the nineteenth and twentieth centuries, and a signal that members "were almost hoping to be mistaken for local Catholics." This assessment finds confirmation in a fictionalized family history written by Norbert Frýd, a Jew born on Budweis/Budějovice's *Ringplatz/rynek* in 1913. Jews in town, he claims, regularly referred to the synagogue as "the church"—a designation that Frýd judges justified, given that the building "was in the fashionable neo-Gothic style, with two pointed towers, stained windows, and an organ that made it resemble a Catholic sanctuary far more than a synagogue."[65] Budweis/Budějovice's Catholic population was becoming more national. But the Jewish population, by embracing Catholic appearances, failed to enter completely into the trend. Czech and German acceptance of Jews was less than complete—whatever liberal Germans said to the contrary.

Above the middle classes and mostly beyond Budweis/Budějovice's boundaries were aristocrats. They continued, although less than in times past, to play major roles in politics, through institutions such as the great landowners' curias in the diet and in the Lower House of the Austrian Parliament, through the Upper House as a whole, and through posts such as Taaffe's. A handful of high nobles also wielded considerable clout more locally. The Schwarzenberg family, for example, owned dozens of breweries, mills, and additional enterprises in Southern Bohemia, staffed by more than 2,000 officials and employees. The head of the lesser, Orlik/Orlík branch of the family, Charles (1824–1904), was a leading federalist and a close political associate of Old Czechs. And the head of the main, Krummau/Krumlov branch, Prince John Adolf (1799–1888), "behaved in friendly fashion toward the Czech nation" during the final years of his life, according to *Budivoj*. Yet neither man counted as national. John Adolf did contribute thirty florins to the *Böhmerwaldbund* upon its founding in 1884. Considering that his family owned approximately one-third of the entire Bohemian Forest, though, the contribution counts as a minor one—and in any case, found a Czech counterbalance in John Adolf's status as a founding member of the *Beseda*. "The late Prince's ideal," wrote *Budivoj* in its obituary in 1888, probably glad that he had not become a German, "was a position above the national parties."[66]

The German and the Czech movements made little attempt to "swallow" aristocrats, Jews, or Budweiser holdouts among the bourgeois. Instead, national attention shifted during the 1880s to the many Budweisers of the lower-middle class. Socially speaking, Zátka, Taschek, and other national leaders probably had little in common with individual shopkeepers, clerks, and the like. As a group, such people in Budweis/Budějovice arguably had less power than a single Schwarzenberg. Yet in the new politics, emerging beside the old across the monarchy (and for that matter across Europe), victory went not to the gourmet but to the gourmand. The old was a politics of quality. The new was a politics of quantity. And in the context of that new politics, the lower-middle class more than made up for a lack of refinement, as compared to "higher" nonnational elements, with greater numbers and with a greater ease of ingestion.

The last Budweiser to have played a significant role as a political leader had been Klawik/Klavík, during the 1860s. Since then, Budweisers had been Habsburg-loyal in mostly reactive ways, as followers. In Budweis/Budějovice, that left as Habsburg leaders only the district captain and a few other imperial-royal officials (as opposed to municipal ones, for example, who almost had to be German). And those imperial-royal officials were much less leaders than administrators or soldiers. Outside town, there was the rest of the imperial-royal civil service and military, as well as the immensely powerful figure of the emperor-king. But they, together with great landowners and with other practitioners of the old politics, saw no great need to weld Budweisers, Praguers, and so on into some sort of "people." National leaders—less powerful and less shielded from the daily, local rough-and-tumble than were men such as Francis Joseph, Taaffe, and Prince John Adolf—almost had to understand better the implications of popular participation in politics. With hard work, those national leaders met the Habsburg challenge of suffrage reform. They began to digest a whole new following. One consequence was an increase in tensions within both national movements. But another, as will be seen, was a new robustness—manifested in organizational structures, in membership figures, and in a growing confidence that national fortunes might rise and fall, but "nations" would remain. All this occurred gradually and within limits. National and nonnational modes of action remained complementary in many ways, not contradictory. The old, grand politics and the new, more gritty one collided only in some arenas. And even then, Czechness or Germanness by no means implied disloyalty to the state.

The opening and closing dates of this chapter, 1871 and 1890, also frame Bismarck's years as chancellor of the German Empire. That is a coincidence, as well as an indication that the whole of Central Europe was caught up in some of the same developmental trends. Links between Germanness in Budweis/Budějovice and abroad remained weak. Dominating the political horizon in town in 1871 was not the unification of Germany but the collapse of the Bohemian state-rights effort at converting the monarchy from a dualist state into a trialist one. More important in the history of Czech and German nationhood in the Bohemian lands than the military alliance with the German Empire in 1879 was Taaffe's formation that same year of his Iron Ring. Thereafter, conflict between federalists and centralists arguably became a dimension of conflict between Czechs and Germans, rather than vice versa. In 1890, not so much Bismarck's dismissal by the young and rash Emperor William II marked the beginning of a new era as did another attempt, discussed in the next chapter, at a restructuring of politics through a Bohemian compromise.

In 1890, for the first time, workers across the Habsburg Monarchy celebrated the first of May with public processions. In Budweis/Budějovice, fewer than 200 men and women dared to participate, and thus to defy both their employers and the intimidating presence of intensified police patrols.[67] The year before, a united Austrian Social Democratic Party had been founded again, while in 1891, antisocialist legislation in Cisleithania expired. Politics began to open wider still and to include not only an additional social stratum but also a movement that claimed to represent a nonnational or at least multinational "people"—the proletariat. Here was a new challenge for Budweis/Budějovice's Czech and German movements.

Three

Free-for-All, 1890–1902

I accept with pleasure the assurances of the loyalty and dynastic fealty of the town of Budweis, and I express to you my warm thanks. I am convinced that the inhabitants of this town of both nationalities will always maintain their loyal Austrian ways [spoken in German]. I sincerely wish that all of you will compete, with all your strength, for the public good in peace, and that you will thus contribute to the prosperity and progress of the town [spoken in Czech].
  —*Emperor-King Francis Joseph, 1895*

In a time when the fratricidal struggle against class-conscious workers is conducted with unprecedented loutishness on the hot soil of nationality struggles, and when often a solitary critical word suffices to ensure that he who pronounced it is branded a traitor to his fatherland and driven to the political slaughterhouse by his enemies as an enemy of the nation, we feel doubly the weight of our task.
  —Jihočeský dělník, *a Social Democratic newspaper in Budweis/Budějovice, 1897*

[W]e will smash your brewery to smithereens. We know your weak spots, and it is not an audit but something else that will break your neck. . . .
Here you have our ultimatum. An eye for an eye, a tooth for a tooth! We do not want to conquer Town Hall but we have a right to the third curia, and we will not allow anyone to strip us of it!
  —Budivoj, 1902

During the final decade of the nineteenth century, public life in Budweis/Budějovice continued to expand. The Czech and German movements participated in that deepening and broadening of political participation but did not create it. Or if they did create it, then it created and re-created them as well, in a complex process with causes and consequences that in no way remained limited to national matters. Habsburg leaders, for example, played a major role in pulling lower-class men into politics. So did Social Democrats, or Marxists. The unity of both national movements came under new strain. Indeed, the Marxist insistence on the primacy of class signaled at least the possibility of supplementing or replacing the national and Habsburg categories that had structured politics thus far.

Between the national movements, within them, and across the whole of the growing political field, conflict found expression in ever sharper language and even in physical clashes. The trend toward greater ideological complexity, in contrast, proved short lived. The German and Czech movements, rather than breaking into pieces along class or other lines, became more differentiated and articulated. Politics as a whole, rather than swinging in a less national direction, swung in a more national one. Not only Social Democrats but also Habsburg leaders, including Francis Joseph himself, thought more and more nationally, even as they sought solutions to mounting national problems. The new class complexity remained. But national leaders, and especially Czech ones, succeeded at accommodating their organizations to it, and at making national questions trump class questions much more often than vice versa.

Intranational Conflict, Nationalizing and International Dynamics

In the early 1890s, national politics in Budweis/Budějovice "caught up" somewhat with national politics elsewhere in the Bohemian lands, by becoming internally more divided. Yet the Old Czech-Young Czech division and the Liberal-*völkisch* one did not set back the national movements as a whole. Even as hostility between individuals on the same national side increased, nationhood in a generic sense became more central to politics. Intranational conflict also pushed the German and Czech camps farther apart; national sentiments became deeper and more intense.[1] The following discussion presents this complex dynamic through the example of the aftermath in Budweis/Budějovice of the Bohemian Compromise, a pact signed in 1890 but never implemented.

Early in January 1890, Prime Minister Taaffe called together Old Czechs, Liberal Germans (known at this point as the "United German Left"), and both centralist and federalist great landowners for negotiations in Vienna. By the end of the month, all parties to the talks had settled on legislation, to be passed by the Bohemian Diet, that reworked administrative boundaries, diet curias, language policy, and more. At the heart of

the Bohemian Compromise lay a partial nationalization of Bohemian politics. In the diet, the curia of the great landowners (with seventy seats, of
which about one-fourth were Constitutionalists, and the rest state-rights
advocates) and the curia of the Chambers of Commerce and Trade (with
fifteen seats) were to remain unchanged. But the urban and the rural curias
(with seventy-two and seventy-nine seats) were to yield to a Czech and to
a German one (whose sizes the agreement did not specify). The Stremayr
language decree of 1880 was to lose effect in solidly German-speaking
areas. District boundaries, when redrawn, were to correspond as closely as
possible to "national" ones. By that term, the negotiating parties apparently meant ethnic boundaries, as recorded in the language question of
the census.[2]

Through the Bohemian Compromise, Old Czechs and their aristocratic
allies hoped to strengthen the Iron Ring, and thus to shore up their erod-
ing power. The quid pro quo was an administrative partition, or federalization, of Bohemia along ethnic lines, and thus a retreat from the historical,
state-rights doctrine that underpinned Czech-aristocratic cooperation.
Liberal Germans and their own aristocratic allies stood to gain both concrete concessions and political ammunition against intranational *völkisch*
opponents—in large part by embracing the *völkisch* program of ethnic federalization. Here the major sacrifice lay in conceding the legitimacy of the
Bohemian Diet by ending the Liberal boycott. Taaffe, finally, expected to
gain not only an end to the German boycott and a strengthening both of
the Old Czechs and of the Iron Ring but also an overall reduction in
national tensions. In exchange, he and the state that he represented agreed
to write nationhood into the constitutional structure of Bohemia. The
implications of this step were remarkable—as will be seen in the next chapter. For now, it will be noted only that the Bohemian Compromise of
1890, like the Habsburg-Hungarian Compromise of 1867 and the failed
Bohemian Compromise of 1871, stood to make politics in one area of the
monarchy more national. Yet unlike the agreement of 1867, and much
more evenhandedly than the nonagreement of 1871, the Compromise
of 1890 stood to reorganize politics in *bi*national, Czech *and* German
fashion.

By excluding both the Young Czechs and the *völkisch* parties from the
negotiations, however, the makers of the Bohemian Compromise miscal-
culated colossally. Only the year before, Young Czechs had fared very well
in elections to the diet, nearly quadrupling their number of mandates in
the three nonaristocratic curias, from ten to thirty-nine, and thereby reducing the Old Czech contingent from eighty-nine to fifty-eight. Now,
by branding the Bohemian Compromise a defeat for Czechs and by attacking Old Czechs as sellouts to Germans, Young Czechs could turn
their exclusion to political advantage. And that they did. Over the follow-

ing two years, Young Czechs torpedoed the Bohemian Compromise in the diet. They also pushed Old Czechs almost entirely out of the Lower House of the Austrian Parliament in elections held in 1891. And in diet elections held four years later, the Young Czech Party captured ninety mandates and left only three to Old Czechs (as well as four to other Czech parties). Slightly later, Liberal Germans experienced a defeat too, although a less devastating one. The Old Czech and Liberal German attempts at regaining a monopoly on national political representation backfired, to the advantage of Young Czechs and of *völkische*. Taaffe, with his drive to restore his Iron Ring, ended up weakening it.

In Budweis/Budějovice, the Old Czechs did not fare as badly as they did elsewhere in Bohemia—again, in large part because the Czech movement in town faced a strong German opponent. Zátka and several other Old Czech leaders in Southern Bohemia counted among the few men who retained their seats in the diet and in the Austrian Parliament. Yet now a local chapter of the Young Czech Party, recently founded, shattered the informal ban on Czechs attacking Czechs in public. In the fall of 1890, when town council elections came due, Young Czechs insisted on running a ticket separate from the Old Czech one. They thereby destroyed all hope, however slight, of capturing the third curia. "Better a German than an Old Czech," radicals among the Young Czechs supposedly argued.[3]

Old Czechs in town attempted to counter this rude challenge by redoubling their efforts. Only weeks after the municipal elections, Zátka threw his party into an all-out campaign to "win" the census, scheduled for the end of the year. *Budivoj*, which remained affiliated with the Old Czechs, urged readers to bring their census forms in to the *Beseda* for help in filling them out. The newspaper also underscored that the Bohemian Compromise pending in the diet would give new importance to the language question. Speakers of Czech or of German, if they exceeded a certain number or proportion, were to gain linguistic rights in municipal schools and administration. "Let us prove with deeds that we are Czechs!" *Budivoj* urged. "Let our motto be that he who is Czech by descent and origins reports as his language of daily use *his mother tongue, Czech!*"[4]

Old Czechs did not stop there. Acting on a proposal by Zátka, they organized a private census parallel to the Habsburg one. Not language of daily use but nationality, understood in a Czech ethnic sense, was the focus. Zátka added a third category, though, to "Czech" and to "German": not "mixed," as in Josef Jireček's survey forty years previously, but *odrodilec*. Perhaps best translated as "person who has renounced his or her birth and origins," the term seems to have applied to native speakers of Czech who claimed to be Germans—including, presumably, Josef Taschek. How residents who spoke *both* languages as mother tongues ended up within the three-part scheme remains unclear. Without doubt, however, the amateur demographers ignored the long-standing objection of their Habsburg counterparts to counting nationhood. No matter how German some people felt, they were really Czech, or fell at best into the category of *odrodilec*. The private census did violence to the scientific methods of demography, to the national sentiments of some Germans, to the nonnational sentiments of Budweisers, and to Habsburg legitimacy. Yet Zátka and his associates saw their census as more accurate than the official one. It, a local Czech publication later claimed, "limps far behind truth and reality."[5]

Germans responded with anger to the Czech census. Town hall—hard at work trying to turn the official tally into an ethnic headcount of the German variety—sent its police force to stop the Czech volunteers from going door to door through the entire town. The law, however, provided no grounds for confiscating data or for prohibiting Zátka's squads from finishing out their rounds. Indeed, the district captainship may have given Old Czechs more room for maneuver than the law required. Taaffe was still hoping to see the Bohemian Compromise pass in the diet, and had every reason to support a member of his coalition against Liberal Germans. Days before the Habsburg census, an official proclamation in Budweis/ Budějovice emphasized the right to decide for oneself on a language of daily use.[6] The government was already committed, in the Bohemian Compromise, to interpreting nationality in ethnic terms. Now, by letting Old Czechs poll mother tongue, the government indicated a willingness to interpret ethnicity in Czech terms.

In April 1891, the imperial-royal Statistical Central Commission made public the results of its census. Budweis/Budějovice now officially had 11,642 residents speaking more German than Czech (a loss since 1880 of 1.5 percent) and 16,585 residents speaking more Czech than German (a gain of 40 percent). The Czech movement could claim to have seized a commanding demographic lead, and to speak for almost 59 percent of the population. Old Czechs, though, pushed their quantitative advantage, and published their own, rival data: 17,223 Czechs and 9,639 Germans. According to these numbers (which excluded military personnel, probably because the soldiers stationed in town at the time spoke more German than Czech), Czechs made up 64 percent of the population, slightly higher than the official figure for Bohemia as a whole. The *odrodilec* group disappeared—folded, it seems, together even with such people as Taschek, into the Czech total.[7]

During 1891 and 1892, the hostility of Young Czechs toward Old Czechs in Budweis/Budějovice escalated dramatically. Young Czechs founded a separate, "Civic-Political" *Beseda*. In June 1891, at a meeting of the Czech Political Association (which coordinated Czech electoral campaigns), Young Czechs blamed Zátka for the Czech defeat in the recent municipal elections, and lambasted him for backing the Bohemian Compromise. Zátka replied in a tone that was no less new: he announced that he was resigning from the association. Those present, including the Young Czechs, reacted to this piece of melodrama with another, and unanimously elected him president. The following year, Zátka made a broader threat to withdraw from all politics, after Young Czechs, playing to the lower-middle class, had accused him and the several businesses that he owned of pushing Czech tradesmen into bankruptcy. Also during 1892, a Young Czech leader in town announced that his party would boycott the next elections unless a new cohort led the effort. *Budivoj* gained a Czech competitor—which settled before long on calling itself the "Southern Bohemian Correspondent" [*Jihočeské listy.*][8]

Zátka in fact did lay down many of his leadership positions during 1892. But first, in a speech on June 28, he countered Young Czech criticism by calling for the creation of a Czech Statistical Office [*popisný úřad*]. "I would suggest," Zátka explained,

> that Czech families be subjected to an interrogation on the basis of a questionnaire aimed at learning who goes shopping where. Questions would be both general in scope, for the head of the family, for the wife, and for the children— and particular, by individual occupations. Should the population prove willing to submit to such an interrogation and to tell the truth, we would gain a vivid understanding of the degree to which Germans depend on a Czech clientele. We would also learn which trades and businesses in town were not being plied by Czechs, and set about recruiting Czech entrepreneurs to fill them.

Additional goals, Zátka continued, were to find who was dependent on whom, where children attended school, and who had German relatives. "It is necessary to have all the threads connecting our people with our opponents in order that we might sever them."[9]

In 1884, Zátka had first taken bold action to make Czechs out of lower-middle-class residents. Now he sought not only to do more of the same but also to raise for everyone the stakes of what being Czech meant. In 1884, he had just cut (or had seen cut) a thread of his own, perhaps at some personal financial cost, by ceasing to serve as legal counsel to Taschek's father. Now Zátka tried to intensify the "Each to His Own" campaign. On this goal, Young Czechs were in full agreement. They responded, though, not with support but with the claim that Zátka purchased items regularly from Germans and from "renegades." Zátka lashed back in kind. In 1893, he revealed that Vojtěch Holanský, a Young Czech leader in town, had voted until recently for German candidates in elections. Holanský tried to explain away his past by pointing to pressure exerted by his former employer, a Liberal German. Holanský also responded to the embarrassment (which Old Czechs did not let anyone forget for years) with action. He and other Young Czechs seized control of the *Sokol* in 1894, and left Old Czechs little choice but to resign and to found their own club.[10]

Young and Old Czechs, by questioning each others' Czechness, pushed it in a more intensely anti-German direction. Czech organizations, furthermore, rather than losing members as a result of the constant feuding, apparently gained them. As a local chronicler of the *Sokol* wrote in the 1920s, "Through this dispute among the brothers, the number of members in Č. Budějovice increased considerably."[11] Yet both Czech parties remained solidly middle and lower-middle class. Despite disagreeing heftily over the Bohemian Compromise, over the Church, and over additional issues, Old Czechs and Young Czechs agreed on where to draw the line between practice and rhetoric, between active and passive Czech "citizenship." Even as the factions, in sparring, changed Czechness, they continued to agree on its definition. That agreement helps to explain patterns not only in Budweis/Budějovice but outside it. Many Czech voters switched from one party to the other during the early 1890s, simply substituting Young for Old.

With some delay, the Liberal-*völkisch* division shaped German nationhood in partly similar ways. It became more anti-Czech, for example. Yet here agreement on fundamental points was lacking. Liberals did not emphasize the ethnic strand to Germanness nearly as much as did *völkische*. Much more so than the clash between Old Czechs and Young Czechs, the one between Liberals and *völkische* amounted to a clash between classes: middle and lower-middle. Like the *Sokol*, the *Turnverein* contended with growing internal tensions. But the official, Liberal history of the *Turnverein*, published in 1912, blamed the troubles on "common people," using the term in a negative sense. Liberal leaders, faced with calls to make membership hinge not on merit or on competence but on descent, refused. *Völkische*, blocked in their drive to exclude Jews and to capture the club for less wealthy men such as themselves, ended up resigning in 1898. Absent was a dynamic like the Czech one, in which factions competed at laying down an ever more dense organizational grid within the lower-middle class. Division within German ranks during the 1890s was less complementary and had fewer nationalizing effects.[12]

Czechs fought Czechs, Germans fought Germans, and as a part of the process, both Germans and Czechs severed many a thread connecting them. Many threads, though, remained. The distance between Czechness and Germanness in Budweis/Budějovice widened, but neither national movement turned against the state. When Francis Joseph visited the town in September 1895, in connection with military maneuvers nearby, the two national movements outdid one another in attempts at linking themselves to him. Both the *Deutsches Haus* and the *Beseda* sported lavish decorations. Young Czech, Old Czech, *völkisch*, and Liberal clubs gathered along the emperor-king's route from the railroad station, in a well-organized yet unmistakably genuine display of devotion. Taschek, as Deputy Mayor, made a short speech of welcome "in the name of the inhabitants of the always loyal town"—in both Czech and German. Francis Joseph, in his reply, acknowledged the division of the population into "nationalities," and, also speaking in both languages, made clear how he expected them to act, both toward each other and toward the state: "I accept with pleasure the assurances of the loyalty and dynastic fealty of the town of Budweis, and I express to you my warm thanks. I am convinced that the inhabitants of this town of both nationalities will always maintain their loyal Austrian ways [in German]. I sincerely wish that all of you will compete, with all your strength, for the public good in peace, and that you will thus contribute to the prosperity and progress of the town [in Czech]."[13] Here, as in the Bohemian Compromise, was an understanding of Germanness and of Czechness as mutually exclusive yet also as compatible, equal, and important forms of loyalty to the state.

Socializing Nationhood, Nationalizing Socialism

During the 1890s, the predominantly middle- and lower-middle-class national movements faced a new challenge, brought on in part by their own successes. Habsburg leaders came to believe that the injection of social concerns into politics would help alleviate national tensions—and abandoned the stance that poor men had no right to vote. Social Democrats suddenly found that they had more freedom of political movement. A continued failure by national parties to embrace "the masses" now threatened to expose nationhood for what, thus far, it had been for the working class: an inclusive rhetoric that masked exclusionary deeds.

Völkisch leaders, in their early years, had planted one foot on either side of the moving line between men with the vote and men without it. Social Democratic leaders, in contrast, made no serious effort to court any enfranchised part of the population during the early 1890s. Instead, they targeted poor people, especially urban ones: factory workers, maids, and the like—many of them female, and thus with even less chance of winning enfranchisement any time soon. The core Marxist doctrine of class conflict helps to explain this strategy. For Social Democrats, the middle classes constituted not potential allies but necessary and central enemies. The Social Democratic Party offered not incremental modifications to an already dominant political model but a fresh and even revolutionary approach. That freshness found reflection in nonnational aspects to the structure of the party. The Austrian Trade Union Commission, closely

linked to the Social Democatic Party, organized itself according to industry branches, not "nations." Many Social Democratic associations in the
Bohemian lands were utraquist.[14]

Taaffe's Iron Ring coalition, in the meantime, was rusting. In a maneuver of a type that the prime minister had famously labeled "muddling
through" [fortwursteln], he turned again, as in the early 1880s, to the idea
of firming up his parliamentary position by enfranchising a new swath of
the population. In persuading Francis Joseph to permit this risky tactic,
Taaffe and other top government officials—treading a path similar to one
blazed some years previously by Benjamin Disraeli in Great Britain—argued that poor men (who, besides women and children, were the only
substantial group left to enfranchise) often lacked national consciousness.
Such people, contrary to received wisdom, could be won for progovern-
ment parties in their struggle against the radical national ones.[15] The nonnational dimensions to Social Democracy partly confirmed that peasants
and workers would not vote automatically for Young Czechs or for völkische. And Socialist rhetoric, although in some sense even more radical
than theirs, paired up with a strong practical focus on winning an expansion of electorates—on working within the system. Because expanding
the franchise was precisely what Taaffe proposed to do, he could hope to
tame even those new voters who, instead of becoming conservatives, became Social Democrats.

In the fall of 1893, Taaffe presented a surprise in the form of an electoral
reform bill proposing universal male suffrage in elections to the Austrian
Parliament. The curia system hollowed out the proposal, by giving the
many new voters disproportionately few seats. Some substance, though,
remained. Viktor Adler, the head of the Social Democratic Party, considered the bill serious enough to embrace it. He showed his support by
ordering an immediate reduction in Socialist agitation—just then taking
on impressive proportions—for electoral reform. Galician members of the
Iron Ring, on the other hand, as well as many great landowners, considered the bill serious enough to oppose it. They and the German parties in
the opposition, in fact, brought Taaffe and his government down. The
Iron Ring was no more.

That Christmas, seventy-odd Social Democrats from the Bohemian
lands and beyond held a "congress" at a pub in Budweis/Budějovice. Far
from tapping into deep local roots, the meeting counted among the first
showings in town of the united Austrian Social Democratic Party's flag.
Only that year had the first Socialist periodical begun publication locally—
and it had folded after only three issues. A Workers' Beseda existed, with
a partly conspiratorial past reaching back several years before the relaxation
of police pressure in 1891. But the club strayed beyond the limits of its
nonpolitical statutes only at considerable risk. As late as 1894, the public

prosecutor sought (unsuccessfully) to put twenty-nine members behind bars. Labor union activity dated only from 1892, and Budweis/Budějovice had as yet known no strikes.[16]

All the men in attendance at the so-called congress spoke Czech, and, indeed, made up an unofficial "Bohemoslavonic Social Democratic Party" within the larger Cisleithanian or Austrian one. The delegates passed two resolutions. One reaffirmed the commitment to fighting hard for universal suffrage. The Young Czech Party had come out only recently and reluctantly in favor of electoral reform, and a continued prominence of the issue promised to cause embarrassment and internal strains for that opponent. The second resolution consisted of an organizational plan for making Bohemoslavonic Social Democrats a clearly defined group within the larger party. Henceforth, as the Austrian party agreed early in 1894, a Czech-speaking and a German-speaking Social Democratic association were to exist side by side in many places, and to subscribe to the same party platform.[17] Social Democracy, as it reached Budweis/Budějovice, became more national, in ethnic ways.

Both the Social Democratic understanding of nationhood and the competition with national parties (especially Czech ones) help to explain this shift. Leaders of the party by no means simply rejected national worldviews in favor of a class-based one. Instead, they combined the two. Adler had even started his political career, early in the 1880s in Vienna, as a member of a *völkisch* party—despite his Jewish ancestry. After his conversion to Marxism, he had continued to understand Germanness in primarily ethnic terms, and to see himself as a German. Indeed, he saw himself as *more* German than Liberals or than *völkische*. As he wrote in 1887, the "Lords Bourgeois" concealed the fundamental political conflict, which was between bourgeoisie and proletariat, behind a national facade. The effect was to keep the working class divided and weak, and thereby to protect "dirty moneybag interests." Social Democrats, in contrast, represented the cause of the "whole people, all the way down to the poorest, starving miner."[18]

Adler and other Social Democratic leaders joined national leaders in accepting the reality of ethnic "nations." But Social Democratic leaders defined "nations" from the lower classes up, rather than from the middle classes down, and denied the centrality or even the necessity of national conflict. "Nations," rather, had common interests—and those could best be realized under socialism. Yet leaders of the Austrian Social Democratic Party, for all their multinational (as opposed to nonnational) cosmopolitanism, often imagined the better future toward which they worked in German ways. In the 1850s, both Karl Marx and Friedrich Engels had seen no good prospects for Czechs, with their supposedly "backward" culture, and had expected them to become Germans. Such thinking had meshed closely with liberal and German currents of the era. Adler's Germanness featured a thinner historical-cultural strand, but he still assumed that German-language culture was the standard toward which workers in Cisleithania should strive. "In Austria, German is the language of Social Democracy," he explained. "It is a matter of complete indifference to us, as Germans, whether the Czechs learn German. But as Social Democrats, we must strongly wish it."[19] Adler, like Marx and Engels, was no worker. Rather, he had a medical degree and a considerable inheritance—as well as a considerable dose of middle-class national thinking. Such people, in their role as Social Democratic leaders, contributed to the nationalization of working-class politics.

Czech-speaking workers, in the minds of Social Democratic leaders, were Czech workers. As such, those workers had reason to wish for a reorganization of the party along national lines. "Nonnational" organization seemed, in practice, to mean favoring German and Germans over Czech and Czechs. Czech-speaking Social Democratic leaders had further reason for desiring a nationalization of the party: competition from Czech parties. Up to 1893, those parties had done little to anchor themselves within the working class. The Workers' *Beseda*, for example, sounded like a logical addition to the palette of *Besedas* that Czechs had already founded in Budweis/Budějovice. But Zátka, Holanský, and other Czech leaders had shunned it from the beginning. Elsewhere in the Bohemian lands as well, only the efforts by Taaffe and by Social Democrats to expand the electorate for the Austrian Parliament jolted national leaders into action. Thus may be explained the Young Czech *volte face* regarding electoral reform in 1893, as well as ever louder Czech claims that Czech-speaking Social Democrats were the unwitting stooges of their German superiors in the party.

The state, meanwhile, was becoming more difficult to govern. Taaffe's successors found themselves turning, like him, to the idea of recasting the electorate of the Austrian Parliament in an attempt to gain a stable majority acceptable to Francis Joseph. In 1896, the prime minister, Count Casimir Badeni, won passage of a major reform bill. A new fifth, or "universal," curia came into being, with seventy-two delegates as the representatives of all literate males at least twenty-four years old. Men paying less than four florins (or eight crowns, since a currency reform between 1892 and 1894) annually in direct state taxes could vote only in the new curia. Men paying more could vote a second time, in one of the already existing mass curias (urban, with 118 seats, and rural, with 129). The electorate for the Lower House swelled to include more than three million new voters, and more than 20 percent of the population—as opposed to less than 8 percent in 1882. Cisleithania joined the German Empire in being able to boast, unlike Great Britain, of some sort of universal male suffrage. Yet the legis-

lature remained limited in its powers and was far from genuinely democratic. In Bohemia and several other crownlands, voters in the new curia
(like voters in the rural curia everywhere) were to elect candidates only
indirectly, by casting ballots for electors. The Chambers of Commerce and
Trade continued to control twenty-one seats in the second curia, and
fewer than 6,000 great landowners continued to control eighty-five seats
in the first.[20]

In February and March 1897, the first elections to the Austrian Parliament occurred since Badeni's reform. Social Democrats captured almost
38 percent of the direct vote in the fifth curia across Cisleithania. Electors,
though, handed the party only fourteen of the seventy-two seats. Young
Czechs, in contrast, profited from the electoral system, and emerged with
nine seats in the fifth curia and with sixty of the 425 seats overall. Indeed,
Young Czechs now had the largest contingent in the Lower House, while
the Old Czech contingent (from which the more conservative and Catholic leaders had recently split) nearly disappeared. Liberal Germans, whose
"United German Left" had won 108 seats in 1891 and had then divided
over the following years into mutually hostile factions, lost multiple seats
to *völkisch* or to Catholic German parties with populist and anti-Semitic
platforms. The new parliament featured only a small nonnational or less
national contingent, in considerable measure because of the timidity of
the electoral reform. Both international and intranational polarization,
meanwhile, continued, and made the task of putting together a governing
coalition all the more difficult.[21]

In Budweis/Budějovice, the election in the new, fifth curia had a nationalizing effect on working-class politics—and to a lesser degree, a socializing effect on national politics. Old Czechs and Young Czechs joined
in backing Zátka; Liberal Germans and *völkische* closed ranks behind a man
named Herbst; and Social Democrats fielded a candidate whose Czech-
language name, Němec, means "German." The election of electors, in late
February 1897, resulted in a rough three-way tie: 1,526 votes for Zátka in
town, 1,503 for Herbst, and 1,212 for Němec. Those first results probably
overstated the appeal to lower-class males of national programs, because
factory owners and town hall had pressured their employees to vote nationally, and had thereby boosted parties already possessing more money
and experience than did Budweis/Budějovice's Social Democratic neo-
phytes.

In each ward where no candidate had won a simple majority, the law
dictated a runoff election between the top two vote-getters. Here Czechs
hammered out a deal with Social Democrats, or at least claimed later to
have done so. In the Prague Suburb ward, where Zátka and Němec were
the runoff candidates, Czechs conceded the election in advance. In exchange, supposedly, Social Democrats were to vote for Zátka both in the

Vienna Suburb and downtown, where runoffs pitted him against Herbst. A more credible explanation for Zátka's surrender without a fight is that he had nothing to gain by going head-to-head with Němec in a heavily working-class part of town. To the contrary, the Czech movement stood to lose not only an election but the ability to speak with any credibility in the name of the many Czech-speakers who lived there. Whatever the case, Zátka carried both of the other wards in town against Herbst. In wards outside town, though, Herbst fared better. Němec did not, and thus failed to qualify for the final electoral round. On March 12, all electors gathered to decide between the two national candidates. Czechs, pointing to Zátka's concession of victory to Němec in the Prague Suburb, now called on the Social Democratic electors to reciprocate by voting Czech. They either abstained, though, or cast their ballots for Herbst—perhaps because his backers had succeeded in outbidding Zátka's, perhaps because Herbst's approach to the issues sounded more convincing or less Catholic, and perhaps because some of the Social Democratic electors harbored German national sentiments. Zátka lost, although he could have prevailed with all the Social Democratic electors' votes.[22]

Social Democrats, according to Czechs, had shown their true colors—and those were German. At the end of March, when the new parliament convened, the five Czech-speakers among the Social Democratic delegates seemed to confirm that assessment by issuing a statement that enraged many Czechs. The delegates, "as Czechs and as Social Democrats," rejected the Bohemian state rights program, calling it a "digging up of dog-eared privileges and documents." Only days before, Young Czech delegates, together with federalist great landowners, had publicly affirmed their commitment to that program as a common foundation for their parliamentary activity. (The sole Old Czech delegate, elected by members of Budweis/Budějovice's third curia, had endorsed state rights, too. He was Prince Friedrich von Schwarzenberg/Bedřich ze Schwarzenberga, brother of the Charles mentioned in the previous chapter.)[23] Young Czechs, having all but eliminated Old Czechs, had followed them in recognizing the usefulness at least to paying lip service to the nonethnic rhetoric, and thus to maintaining the Czech-aristocratic alliance. And Czech Social Democrats had called attention to the implications of that tactic for the lower classes.

Days later, on April 5, Prime Minister Badeni contributed to a worsening of relations between Czechs and Social Democrats, and indeed to a dramatic heightening of Czech-German tensions. In an attempt to woo the Young Czechs, without whom he had little hope of assembling a majority, Badeni issued a decree requiring many imperial-royal civil servants in Bohemia to pass language exams both in German and in Czech by 1901. An almost identical decree, concerning Moravia, followed on April

22. Liberal Germans and *völkische* immediately objected. The Social Democratic Party, including its Bohemoslavonic branch, sided with the German parties on the issue, mostly because Badeni had addressed through administrative fiat a matter that by right required legislation. Even after Czechs dug in their heels on the matter, Social Democrats continued to side with Germans. As a result, the Social Democratic Party found itself swept up in a mounting wave of German-Czech agitation. It took the form of ever larger demonstrations during the summer, as well as a looming government crisis.[24]

Young Czechs in Prague, furious at the Social Democratic Party, orchestrated the formation of an association of "national workers"—or what, within a year, came to be known as the Czech National Social Party [*Strana národně sociální*]. In June, meanwhile, at the sixth all-Austrian Congress of the Social Democratic Party, delegates voted unanimously for a sweeping restructuring, or nonterritorial federalization. It turned the party into a loosely coordinated set of German, Czech, Polish, Slovene, and additional national sections. Czech Social Democrats stood behind the proposal, which transformed their Bohemoslavonic branch to the party from the exception into the rule.[25] Social Democracy functioned as a channel for the exporting of nationhood, in generic form, from Bohemian politics to working-class politics elsewhere in Cisleithania.

Budweis/Budějovice, despite its tardiness during the 1880s in gaining a local chapter of the Young Czech Party, gained a local chapter of the new Czech national workers' association immediately. It employed a rabidly anti-Social Democratic rhetoric and gained a growing working-class following. Besides almost forcing Social Democrats into German arms, the association cultivated remarkably friendly relations with the Old Czech and Young Czech Parties. In October 1897, as the crisis over Badeni's language policy escalated further, elections took place in town to the board of a workers' health insurance fund. Czech National Socials, backed by the Czech establishment, ran against a joint German-Social Democratic slate, and won. Months later, when workers in a local, Czech-owned business decided to fight for Sundays off, National Socials sabotaged the effort. In 1885, a German-language handbook on Cisleithanian politics had commented of the Young Czechs, or National Liberals, that "in those cases where national interests come into conflict with liberal ones, liberal principles are sacrificed in favor of the national interests."[26] Now one could substitute "social" or "working-class" for "liberal" in the sentence, and apply it to the emergent party.

In one sense, though, the new addition to the Czech political palette was different. The Young Czech Party, in many ways, had resembled the Old Czech one. Both had attempted to appeal to all enfranchised Czech-speakers—with the outcome that one had ended up almost replacing the other, at least in the Austrian Parliament and in the Bohemian Diet. Neither party had taken much initiative before the mid-1890s at building support among the working class. Now, after the Austrian Parliament elections of 1897, the National Social Party signaled a new model: an articulation of Czech politics along class lines, in response to changes in state policy and to a threat from Social Democracy. At the same time, a consensus on Czechness continued. The creation of a new party did not reflect, like the Liberal-*völkisch* split, fundamental disagreement over national goals. Rather, the Czech movement gained an organizational flexibility that permitted a more effective pursuit of power under changed circumstances. "To keep workers part of the *national* body," wrote *Budivoj* at the beginning of 1898, "must be the unceasing effort of all decent people on our side."[27] The ethnic use of the verb "to keep" rather than "to win" was nothing new. But with such rhetoric, Zátka's newspaper now supported the nationalizing practice of National Socials. He and they worked together at turning workers into Czechs of a more anti-German and middle-class sort than what Social Democratic leaders, for their own part, envisioned.

In December 1897, Social Democrats in town founded a Czech-language newspaper. "In a time," wrote *Jihočeský dělník* [*South Bohemian Worker*] in its inaugural issue, "when the fratricidal struggle against class-conscious workers is conducted with unprecedented loutishness, on the hot soil of nationality struggles, and when often a solitary critical word suffices to ensure that he who pronounced it is branded a traitor to his fatherland and driven to the political slaughterhouse by his enemies as an enemy of the nation, we feel doubly the weight of our task."[28] Yet even as Social Democrats felt doubly burdened, the new, more national structure to their party doubly divided them in Budweis/Budějovice—into Czechs and Germans, and into nationalists and socialists. Here a new organizational model meant not so much articulation as confusion, and signalled not so much strength as weakness.

No German National Social Party paralleled the Czech one. A new German Peasants' Union, defying the limits of its name, did develop a presence in Budweis/Budějovice. Otherwise, German-speaking workers had few political alternatives to the Social Democratic Party. It shared with the *völkisch* parties a primarily ethnic understanding of Germanness. But differences with them, as well as with the German Liberal parties, dwarfed the differences of Czech National Socials with Old and Young Czechs. German Social Democracy, after all, figured less as the working-class wing to the German movement than as the German wing to the working-class movement. Consensus on the very nature of Germanness, already weak, grew weaker.

Meanwhile, much more in competition with *völkische* than with Social Democrats, a Christian Social Party gained some ground. Anti-Semitic, like *völkische*, Christian Socials differed by not being anticlerical. Indeed, they moved progressively closer to the Church, as well as to the Habsburg dynasty and state. The party even attempted for a time to subordinate its national perspective to a religious one, and to win a following among Czech Catholics. As a Christian Social in Budweis/Budějovice wrote in 1896, "The Jews have united, and stand as Hebrews under one command, attacking us politically from two sides [Liberal and Social Democratic]. . . . Only the cooperation of *both nations* can save Budweis from Judaicization [*Verjudung*], and lift trade and commerce." The parallels of this effort to the class-based, Social Democratic one deserve emphasis. Yet the religion-based effort quickly failed, in considerable measure because of Czech Catholic parties that succeeded the Old Czech Party, especially in the Bohemian and Moravian countryside. The Christian Social Party failed, in fact, to expand beyond strongholds in Vienna and elsewhere in the Austrian duchies.[29] There, if not in Budweis/Budějovice, it complicated German politics still more. Together, Liberals, *völkische*, Social Democrats, and Christian Socials contributed to an internal articulation of Germanness, and to its expansion. But Liberals tugged in the direction of merit, *völkische* in the direction of race, Social Democrats in the direction of class, and Christian Socials in the direction of religion. The Czech movement was more unified. The competition it posed, as well as Czech successes both at making Social Democrats more national and at preventing Christian Socials from becoming less so, helped the German movement escape still greater division.

With electoral reform, the Habsburg leadership had sought to use working-class males to its own ends, while keeping those men politically contained. But as with the five-florin men in the 1880s, the results had been different than what prime ministers and their advisers had expected. Pseudo-parliamentary governance in accordance with Francis Joseph's wishes had not grown easier. Rather, it had grown more difficult. The new voters had not tamed and hemmed in the national parties. Rather, the national parties had expanded their social profile. Habsburg policymakers, rather than choking the national movements, had succeeded only in force-feeding them another segment of the population. The Czech movement in particular had not only survived the experience but had emerged larger and stronger than ever. The Marxist movement had gained new room for maneuver, but on a field structured far more along national coordinates than along class ones. Even as Habsburg policymakers struggled to contain and to steer national politics, finally, they continued to view national movements as less dangerous than a Marxist one. After the expiration of anti-Socialist legislation in 1891, the Habsburg authorities continued to

hinder Social Democratic activity more than they hindered national equiv-
alents. (The district captainship in Budweis/Budějovice, for example, confiscated the inaugural issue of *Jihočeský dělník* cited earlier.)[30] Zátka,
Taschek, and other national leaders enjoyed not only the advantage of
having inherited political vantage points from the previous generation but
the advantage of seeming more respectable and more loyal to the Habsburgs.

A Leap into Violence

As a whole new realm of working-class politics opened up, middle and
lower-middle-class politics continued to become more radical and more
national. It also became less local—but not in the sense that local events
lost significance. Rather, events reverberated over larger territories. Happenings in separate places grew more related and similar, in a reflection of
national successes at imagining into existence broad communities of
Czechs and of Germans. Middle-class politics also led the way in a cross-
class turn toward violence.

During the fall of 1897, the Czech-German struggle over Badeni's language decrees escalated out of control. Before calm returned to Cisleithania, a series of political explosions shook up community after community, and signaled a new phase not only in the Czech-Habsburg-German
dynamic but in the history of the monarchy as a whole. Although the
decrees directly affected only a small number of people, Germans demonstrated by the thousands—not only in the Bohemian lands but in Vienna
and even in Graz, where almost no Czechs lived. In a vicious cycle, Czechs
turned out in huge numbers too. One side or the other set to smashing
windows, and the practice spread like wildfire. From the German Empire,
the public followed the events with intense interest. Theodor Mommsen,
the famous historian, even intervened from Berlin by publishing an open
letter in Vienna's premier Liberal newspaper. His exhortation to Germans
in Austria reflected the extraordinary passions of the moment, and fanned
them higher: "*Be tough*! The Czech skull is impervious to reason, but it is
susceptible to blows."[31]

In the Lower House of the Austrian Parliament, the German parties,
still backed by the Social Democratic one, filibustered, screamed, banged,
and threw ink pots—thereby blocking not only regular business but the
all-important decennial renewal of economic terms to the Compromise of
1867. The government, desperate, contributed to undermining the legitimacy of the legislature at the end of November by having the obstruction-
ists removed with force, thereby infringing on their parliamentary immunity. More German riots followed, and they succeeded at last in bringing

down Badeni. His successor, who lacked a parliamentary majority and had to rely on the extraordinary powers granted him under dire circumstances by one of the Fundamental Laws, prepared to rescind the language decrees. Mark Twain, the American author, happened to be living in Vienna at the time. He summed up the furor as follows: "The Badeni government came down with a crash; there was a popular outbreak or two in Vienna; there were three or four days of furious rioting in Prague, followed by the establishing there of martial law; the Jews and Germans were harried and plundered, and their houses destroyed: in other Bohemian towns there was rioting—in some cases the Germans being the rioters, in others the Czechs—and in all cases the Jew had to roast, no matter which side he was on."[32]

Budweis/Budějovice did not count as one of the towns where riots broke out in the final months of 1897. Residents there perhaps acted more cautiously than did residents of more one-sidedly national Vienna and Graz or Prague. The *Budweiser Zeitung* published apocryphal tales of a Czech who had run amok and tried to kill Germans, and of a Czech maid who had committed suicide out of fear that Germans were going to murder her. But the Liberal German newspaper compensated for its almost *völkisch* tone by setting such happenings at some distance, in the Cisleithanian capital, and by printing sober political commentary at the same time. *Budivoj*, for its part, provided partial confirmation of Twain's argument that Jews served both national movements in the political storm as a lightning rod. The Old Czech newspaper descended into crude anti-Semitism similar to that of the *völkische*—if not into incitement of the sort that would have brought out crowds and brought in Habsburg censors.[33]

Chance had it that winter that Budweis/Budějovice faced municipal elections, for the first time since 1890. The town council had seen its mandate expire already in 1893. But Taschek, afraid of losing the third curia to Czechs, had made sure that officials in town hall took their time in preparing the electoral rolls. Once laid out at last for inspection in 1895, those rolls had proven deeply flawed, to the advantage of Germans. Czech appeals and German counterappeals had dragged on for more than two years.[34] After New Year's in 1898, the news suddenly broke that the time for balloting at last had come. A campaign as hard hitting as it was brief—the elections were scheduled to begin on January 18—combined with the Badeni fiasco, and with Czech hopes of a breakthrough in the third curia, to generate an ominous mood.

On January 6, the same day that *Budivoj* announced that town council elections were imminent, Czech leaders held a rally at the *Beseda* in a show of solidarity with Czech-speaking minorities in mostly German-speaking towns. Zátka, Holanský, and Prince von Schwarzenberg/ze Schwarzenberga addressed the crowd, which by one count numbered 3,000. Czech

Social Democrats, who arrived as a group, found the entrance barred: only "firm and loyal Czechs" could attend. Czech national consciousness of a Social Democratic sort, in other words, was false—although people with that consciousness remained ethnically Czech. *Budivoj* claimed that the Prince had said in his speech that under the present circumstances, "*everyone must be either Czech or German, and that there is no place here for amphibians.*" In a commentary, the new Social Democratic newspaper, *Jihočeský dělník*, focused on the exclusion of the working class from the upcoming municipal election. "The lords of the Czech electoral committee, just like the bourgeois Germans, care only about the autocratic rule of one nationality, about power, rather than about the serious social tasks facing the town." A window repairer, meanwhile, took out an advertisement in *Budivoj* that displayed both a sense of humor and an assessment of the situation as less tense than elsewhere in Cisleithania. "No demonstration, not even a hailstorm," the advertisement read, "and yet here and there plenty of broken windows, guaranteed repaired cheaply and well."[35]

The elections, which commenced less than two weeks later, were simultaneously solemn and epic, outrageous and absurd. Both Czech and German leaders had had special ballots printed up for use by individuals in the third curia who stood under pressure from their employers. Containing a printed list of the "right" candidates on the inside, the ballots sported either a neutral brown or the colors and symbols of the "wrong" party on the outside. Taschek, for the first time, included no token Czechs on the united German candidate list. Zátka included no Jews on the united Czech one, offering instead feeble excuses and a less than ringing condemnation of anti-Semitism. Social Democrats fielded no list at all, in an admission of their weakness in the municipal electorate. Amid great suspense, and to cries on both national sides of bribery and of fraud, 713 men in the third curia voted openly for the Czech list, and 350 covertly. They lost to nearly 1,200 Germans and German sympathizers, 100 of whom wrapped their vote in a neutral or Czech disguise. On average, each German candidate defeated his Czech counterpart by fewer than 120 votes. Voter B., *Budivoj* claimed, had offered his ballot to the highest bidder. After gulping down payments from both Czechs and Germans in the form of five goulashes, two sausages, two portions of Emmenthal cheese, and nine sardines, he had contracted such a bad case of indigestion as to miss the election. *Jihočeský dělník* reported in less detail, but wrote of the "terrific willingness to be bought" of the Czech bourgeoisie and of a "regular auctioning off of votes."[36]

On January 21, municipal officials announced the third curia results to a crowd—far larger than the electorate—on the *Ringplatz/rynek*. Only these results mattered, because in the second and first curias, yet to vote, Taschek's Liberals possessed such an advantage that the Czech leadership had decided on a course of boycott. The people on the square, prepared by their leaders for a Czech victory, reacted to defeat with rage, and then with violence. If Germans could dominate the town council for yet another term, they could not keep control of the streets. Part of the crowd turned into a mob, which tore through town that evening. In a rampage made all the more frightful by its targeted nature, the rioters smashed more than 2,500 windows, all in buildings widely understood as German. The *Deutsches Haus*, the *Kreisblatt* editorial offices, Taschek's house, German-language schools, and Jewish shops counted among the hardest hit. Units of the army joined with the municipal police to reestablish order. The authorities made more than sixty arrests immediately, and dozens more over the following days.[37]

Even Zátka had contributed to directing the anger of the mob at Jewish targets. Days before the election, in a speech, he had claimed of the approximately 120 Jewish voters in the third curia that "the results of the election are in their hands." Yet in the very same speech, he had admitted that "Czech" voters in the curia who might end up voting for the German ticket numbered nearly twice as many. *Budivoj*, for its part, seemed to attempt to justify the anti-Semitic aspect to the destruction, arguing that "in spite of the fact that this time the Czech side accommodated [Jews] perhaps even with excessive willingness and kindness, they went *almost without exception* with the Germans." Indirectly, the *Budweiser Zeitung* agreed with this assessment of how most Jews had voted, writing that "the just cause has triumphed; the strong, tried and tested bulwark of Germandom in Southern Bohemia today stands, in defiance of every onslaught, more proud and fortified than ever. . . . But let thanks be said especially to the German Jewish voters of Budweis who, unswayed by all threats to harm them in their livelihood, placed the great cause of our people higher than their purely personal interest . . . the Jews are an auxiliary squadron from which the German electorate in Budweis receives a powerful influx."[38]

Frustrated at the polls, part of the middle-class municipal electorate had decided to switch from casting ballots to casting stones. Disenfranchised individuals had joined in, "voting" by helping to cover sidewalks with shattered glass. Whether Zátka and other Czech leaders had attempted to prevent the violence or had calculated that it would benefit their movement remains unclear. After getting through 1897 without erupting in riot, Budweis/Budějovice had exploded over a long stewing issue, the control of town hall. Hardly any of the few people in town who would have been forced by Badeni's decree to demonstrate proficiency in both German and Czech would have had difficulty doing so. More immediate and gripping, more nationalizing and radicalizing than the decree was the German victory in the municipal third curia—an outcome that, given the extensive powers of the municipality in Cisleithania, affected all residents, enfranchised or no, in multiple and significant ways. Yet Badeni's policy and its failure had provided a context, while riots elsewhere had provided a model. Budweis/Budějovice's riot, despite its specific and local roots, signaled a huge jerk toward both a radicalization and a spatial homogenization of national politics.

The day after the riot, as preparations for balloting in the second and first curias began and as troops patrolled the *Ringplatz/rynek*, Budweis/Budějovice experienced a total eclipse of the sun. Over the next several weeks, newspapers published apocalyptic accounts of vote buying and of businessmen having fired employees at the polls. Economic pressure found application not only by richer against poorer but vice versa, through boycotts. A butcher named Borovský took out an advertisement in *Budivoj* in order to deny rumors that he had voted for the German list. Indeed, he claimed that he had cast a ballot marked on the outside with the Czech insignia—an insignia that, as both he and his readers knew, bore no necessary relationship to the names inside. Perhaps the rumors concerned another butcher, Peřina. He outraged the new Czech National Social newspaper in town, *Stráž lidu* [*The People's Sentinel*], by abandoning Czech in favor of German as his language of daily use in the census at the end of 1900. That outcome might confirm the rumors, or might indicate only their value as self-fulfilling prophecy. Suspected rightly or wrongly of national disloyalty and boycotted by Czechs as a result, Peřina may have had little choice but to join the enemy after the 1898 municipal elections in order to stave off financial ruin. A financial motive certainly figured prominently in another case. "Jewish capital," sneered *Jihočeský dělník* in February 1898, "has found a dedicated supporter in a national worker, *Sokol* member, etc., by the name of Fr. *Hovádka*, who has accepted the position of shop foreman in Kohn's [German] Jewish factory. . . . [A]fter the patriotic brawls, he disappeared with no warning, and is now sorely missed by many a pub owner—who find sorrow not in his loss [to the national cause] but in his unpaid debts."[39]

No sooner did elections to the second and first curias end than Zátka and a team of lawyers set to work filing complaints and appeals with the authorities. Town hall, meanwhile, reimbursed shopkeepers and homeowners for the full cost of having broken windows repaired.[40] The Czech repairman whose advertisement was cited earlier probably failed to get any of that work, despite the spike in demand. By taking on the role of ex post facto insurer, the municipality forced Czechs to foot part of the bill, through their taxes. German taxpayers with unbroken panes had to accept their share of the expense as part of the mounting price of keeping the town in German hands. Social Democrats and Budweisers had to pay, too. Not only Czechs could complain of taxation without representation.

Long after all traces of broken glass in Budweis/Budějovice had disappeared, the threat of renewed Czech violence hung in the air. For that matter, after the Badeni debacle, the Habsburg Monarchy as a whole suddenly seemed less permanent, less legitimate. Observers joked about the "Monarchy until further notice." In 1899, the major German parties in Cisleithania succeeded for once in agreeing on a joint statement. The "Whitsun Program," like *völkisch* programs from the 1880s, envisioned a solution to national tensions through an ethnic federalization of Cisleithania, as well as through a privileging of Germans. That same year, the Social Democratic Party also called for a national redrawing of internal borders. That program, though, attempted to be nationally fair, and signaled a move not away from the state but toward it. For the first time, the party stated clearly a commitment to preserving the monarchy. Social Democratic leaders seem to have realized after 1897 that national politics might lead to the replacement of the monarchy with something less to their liking. Yet the party almost had to grow more national in order to remain in the political running.[41] And the state that Social Democrats backed now regularly lacked a government with a parliamentary majority, let alone the way and the will to implement sweeping plans, national or otherwise, for reform.

Budweis/Budějovice, ca. 1900

How did matters stand in town as a new century dawned? Elections, associations, education, the economy, religious affairs, and other issues featured strong national divisions. Habsburg institutions such as the district captainship, when they figured prominently in politics, tended to do so as targets of national anger. Both German and Czech newspapers accused government officials loudly and often of discrimination—a strong sign of national impartiality. Francis Joseph himself, also a Habsburg institution, stood legally and even socially beyond reproach. People of all stripes seem to have revered him, in no small part because he had refrained since 1868 from making anything but the most well-meaning and formulaic public pronouncements. (That year, he had let slip a negative remark about the new Opera House in Vienna, only to learn that this expression of majestic displeasure had driven one of the architects to commit suicide.) But now Francis Joseph was seventy years old. And his nephew and heir, Francis Ferdinand, had vehement likes and dislikes. More important, he also had plans for his reign that, if ever implemented, seemed certain to incense both German and Czech leaders.[42]

On demographic and ethnic turf, the Czech movement continued to fare better than the German one in Budweis/Budějovice. In the 1900 census, speakers of Czech and speakers of German increased in number as compared to 1890—but at rates of 41 percent for the former and of only 32 percent for the latter. According to the official tally, approximately 23,400 residents spoke more Czech, and 15,400 spoke more German. For the first time, the Habsburg authorities unambiguously conceded to household employees the right to answer the question about language independently of the family for which they worked. Some maids who spoke only German on the job used the opportunity to claim "Czech"—not their language of daily intercourse but their national affiliation. Czech leaders, who repeated their private survey, came up with different numbers: 27,000 and 11,700. The *Böhmerwaldbund*, meanwhile, accepted the official tally, but attempted to deny its implications. "The absolute numbers of the census results," argued the journal of the liberal association in 1901, "are not the correct standard for measuring the relative significance of a national group in a particular district or region. Of far greater meaning is the tax contribution, the degree of education, and other cultural markers."[43] And yet, people who interpreted the data as a key measure of the Czech and German national movements did so with greater justification than in 1880 or in 1890.

Two Czech publications, in 1900 and in 1904, claimed that of the 140-odd clubs in town, 73 or 74 were Czech, 60 or 61 were German, and only 8 or 9 utraquist. (A German publication, in 1904, noted simply that there were more than fifty German clubs, and ignored the rest.) Three of the utraquist ones, including the Association for the Construction of a New Cathedral, centered on religious matters. The remaining six tended to concern themselves with the social welfare of small and marginal groups: deaf mutes, for example, and released felons. Then again, the publications either made no mention of Social Democratic associations, which included competition for the two Czech *Sokols* and for the two German *Turnvereine*, or categorized the Czech-speaking ones as Czech and the German-speaking ones as German. That approach probably simplifies a complicated political stance too much.[44]

Zátka and Taschek continued to dominate national politics in town, even as elsewhere their parties became mere components to Czech and German multiparty systems. More sympathizers with the Czech cause than with the German one qualified for the vote every year, but the curia system delayed and attenuated the political implications to the trend. So did fraud, to which German leaders resorted ever more regularly. Taschek's abuses of public authority mounted especially in the manipulation of tax registers, proxy votes, and ballots—which appeared miraculously in the urns well after the death of the owners.[45]

A sea change was under way in Budweis/Budějovice's schools. In the late 1880s, Czech-language classrooms had grown so crowded that many children had been able to attend only in half-day shifts. According to Czechs, town hall had intentionally withheld funds so as to pressure parents to transfer their children to better funded, German-speaking schools. Instead, many families had made great sacrifices in order to scrape together tuition for one or the other of the educational institutions administered privately by Czechs. Other families had received Czech scholarships. The law ordered the creation of new public schools using a particular language if private schools in that language achieved a certain level of enrollment for a set number of years. Time after time, Czech leaders provided the required proof from one of their schools, and turned the financial burden over to the Habsburg authorities. The Czech movement then used the resources thus freed up to launch a new school. "We must look upon school enrollment as elections," Zátka declared in September 1898. Three years later, enrollment in Czech-language primary and secondary schools surpassed German-language enrollment for the first time.[46]

At risk of being stranded in a no man's land as politics became ever more national was the Jewish community. Among Germans, *völkisch* views continued to gain at the expense of Liberal ones. At the turn of the century, though, only two Jewish families in Budweis/Budějovice enrolled their children in schools having Czech as the language of instruction. Additional signs of tension between Jews and Czechs abound. Budweis/Budějovice differed from Prague, where a crossover by many Jews to the Czech side in the census occurred between 1890 and 1900.[47] But the disparity, rather than reflecting greater Czech friendliness in the royal capital, probably reflected the greater power of Liberal Germans in Southern Bohemia vis-à-vis local Czech opponents. Or to view the issue from another perspective: Jewish voters, through their importance to maintaining the German grip on town hall, helped ensure that national radicals played a smaller role in Budweis/Budějovice than they did elsewhere in Bohemia. A decisive turn toward radicalism would have spelled political disaster on the German side, while on the Czech side, German control of the municipality discouraged Czech division.

Zionism, a Europe-wide Jewish national movement that began during the 1890s, had Austrian roots, most notably in Theodor Herzl. Another form of Jewish national movement, which centered not on exit from Europe but on organization within Europe as a national minority, also had Habsburg roots—especially among the more numerous and less assimilated Jews of Galicia and of the Bukovina, far to the east from Budweis/Budějovice.[48] By the turn of the century, neither Zionism nor "Jewish diaspora nationalism" had gained any sizable following in town, or in Bohemia. In those new currents, though, exist parallels to the nationalization of Marxism and of political Catholicism. Jewish nationalists, Social Demo-

crats, and Christian Socials each continued a nonnational political tradition, in considerable part by reframing it in national terms.

Another amphibian group, the officer corps, continued to serve as a
vivid visual reminder—during the daily promenade on the *Ringplatz/
rynek*, for example—of Habsburg authority. Officers also continued to dis-
rupt national categories, and thus to call them into question, however
inadvertently. From the mid-1890s, the Young Czech newspaper, *Jihočeské
listy*, had criticized the behavior of army officers at the *Beseda* repeatedly.
In 1898, as the town council elections unfolded, the Young Czechs had
attacked again, this time taking umbrage at the failure of the corps to
attend a Czech Shrovetide ball on January 19, the second of three days
designated for voting by members of the third curia. At the end of the
month, as many a window in town still awaited repair, the officers resigned
as a group from the *Beseda*. The club retaliated by vowing not to allow
the playing of military music on the premises.[49]

German newspapers also found fault with army officers. Within days of
the resignation by the officer corps from the *Beseda*, the *Budweiser Zeitung*
published an article called "Czech Army Language in Budweis." At the
funeral on January 28 of a major, wrote the newspaper, "regimental drum-
mer Zajic, rather than using the command *Ruht* [German for 'At ease!'],
said *pohodlně* [the Czech equivalent] to the military band at graveside. For
now we will satisfy ourselves with recording this fact and reserving the
option of returning later to this most recent attempt at Czechization."[50]
The incident calls to mind the linguistic tensions among veterans in town
during the 1870s. Now, though, a sign of national sentiment came not
from veterans but from a man on active duty within a central Habsburg
institution. The *Budweiser Zeitung* tried to equate Czech demands for
linguistic equality with disloyalty to the state. Yet a cry of "*ruht*" could
cover treasonous thoughts just as easily as could "*pohodlně*." After all, the
German word served as a command not only to Habsburg soldiers but to
soldiers of the German Empire as well—a power made no less foreign by
its status as an ally.

A national spirit also permeated the economy. Czechs in Budweis/Bu-
dějovice had first attempted to create an industrial enterprise in 1872.
Their sugar refinery, however, had failed quickly, victim of a poor harvest
and of the fiscal crisis that gripped much of Europe in 1873. A second
attempt had not come until 1886, when the Czech movement in town
had possessed August Zátka at its head, solid backing from a burgeoning
middle class, and the political and legal talent to set up not one manufacturing facility but several. The Commercial and Industrial Association, as
the new arm to the movement had called itself, had adopted a model relatively new to Cisleithania, and hardly known in Budweis/Budějovice at
the time: that of the shareholder-owned corporation. Through it, Boards

of Directors could put to work not only their own capital but the savings of more humble folk. The results were remarkable from the start, thanks to an economic upswing, to competent managers, and to a policy of plowing a large part of profits back into each business. By the mid-1890s, the town had a Czech enamelware factory, fertilizer plant, barrel works, screw factory, and pencil factory, each with several dozen employees.[51]

German factories in town, Czech leaders claimed, belonged in most cases to outsiders, to Jews or to Czech "renegades," not to the local burgher families that held sway in Liberal German politics. Zátka mocked those families in speeches. Mass production, he claimed, had knocked the bottom out of their artisanal enterprises. Burghers, rather than preparing their sons for changing times, had neglected education and had encouraged an unhealthy adherence to long-standing family business practices. As for daughters, the typical burgher aspired at best to marry them off to army officers. Some truth resided in these charges, as at least one German author admitted. The Hardtmuths had moved their pencil manufacturing operations to Budweis/Budějovice from Vienna in the 1840s, and Franz Westen, owner of a new enamelware factory, had come to town in the early 1890s from Styria. Indeed, he had worked at first as a salaried expert for none other than the Czech Commercial and Industrial Association.[52]

Yet if few German burghers excelled in private business, their leaders worked to make up for this deficiency by excelling in public enterprise. During the 1880s and 1890s, several barracks went up around town at great expense—not to the Ministry of War but to the municipality. Members of the town council argued that they would recoup the investment from rent paid by the Habsburg regiments, as well as from increased tax revenues generated by the stationing of more soldiers in town. Whether or not such expectations of long-term public payoff were realistic, the private construction firms—invariably German-owned—that town hall commissioned to erect each project profited immediately.[53]

Jobs and profits, Liberal German leaders hoped, would translate into votes. During the electoral campaign in January 1898, the *Budweiser Zeitung* had emphasized the role of town hall's Liberal German leadership in making Budweis/Budějovice "a town of schools, officials, pensioners, and garrisons." Taschek himself had pointed with pride to new barracks and schools, as well as to a municipal slaughterhouse: "From the erection of such public state buildings the municipality naturally derives great benefit, inasmuch as its result is an influx of elements capable of gainful employment. One can only wish that such people would come in ever greater numbers. The Czech influx, on the other hand, consists for the most part of people who are nothing and have nothing."[54] Taschek and his political associates also exploited their control of town hall to finance new businesses and tourist attractions. Yet the annual Passion Plays that the *Böh-*

merwaldbund organized in the Bohemian Forest, in the village of Höritz/ Hořice, proved a continual financial drain on the municipality. So did an omnibus venture within the town limits. Partly as a result, Budweis/Budějovice ran large budget deficits and imposed on residents the highest tax rates in all Bohemia.[55]

In 1885, Czech companies and institutions had employed fewer than 120 workers and managers. By 1900, that figure had increased to almost 700. To be sure, the Hardtmuth pencil factory alone employed more than 1,000 men and women by the turn of the century, and was by many accounts a German bastion. Yet the Czech movement had made considerable progress toward what Czech publications consistently phrased as a liberation of Czech workers from the bondage of German employment. Czech leaders, as usual providing impossibly precise figures, claimed that Czechs had paid only 30.5 percent of municipal taxes in 1890 but 38.1 percent in 1900. In 1902, Czechs captured control over the last of the small businessmen's associations in town.[56]

The Social Democratic movement also made progress, but of another sort. In April 1899, workers stopped building a new barracks on the outskirts of town and persuaded several thousand other men and women to put down their tools, too. Leaders demanded a reduction in the length of shifts, an increase in wages (bricklayers earned slightly more than two crowns a day at the time), and recognition of the first of May as a holiday. More than two weeks of daily demonstrations followed, including some violent confrontations that provoked the intervention of the municipal police and the army. The strikers won at least some concessions. After the German firm that was overseeing the construction of the barracks had joined other firms in granting a small wage increase, work resumed on the second of May.[57]

Nationalizing Beer

An example of how national loyalties had come to shape economic activity lies in the production, marketing, and consumption of beer. The Burghers' Brewery in Budweis/Budějovice, established in 1795, was the property of those individuals who owned the nearly 400 buildings downtown. To sell a building was to lose one's share in the brewery. Until the 1860s, no other business in town had possessed brewing rights, and laws had regulated tightly which beer could be sold where within Cisleithania. The brewery had thus paid reliably plump dividends—which had found reflection in real estate prices and in the social profile of the owners. That profile, in turn, had found reflection in politics. In 1871, *Budivoj* had objected to the participation of the Burghers' Brewery in elections to the Austrian

Parliament. A majority of the owners of the brewery, in other words, had decided to use its vote in the Chamber of Commerce and Trade to back a Constitutionalist candidate.[58]

The deregulation of the beer market, together with the development of an ever more dense railroad network over which beer could be transported quickly, cheaply, and packed in ice, had signaled new dangers, but also new opportunities for the Burghers' Brewery. On the one hand, the *Beseda* and other Czech establishments had begun switching to other, less German suppliers, such as the Schwarzenberg brewery in Krummau/Krumlov. Attempts by German Liberals at blocking this aspect of the "Each to His Own" campaign—by exploiting control over town hall in order to link the issuance of liquor licenses to long-term contracts with the Burghers' Brewery, for example—had failed. On the other hand, vast new markets had opened up. In the early 1870s, an old-fashioned faction had lost control of the Board of Directors of the brewery, and an opposing faction (including members of the Taschek family, but also of the Zátka one) had set a bold new course: modernizing and ramping up production, as well as pushing the sales force farther afield. Small quantities of Budweiser beer had soon traveled even to the United States. Little profit had resulted from that particular export drive, but something else had. Two men in St. Louis, Eberhard Anheuser and Adolphus Busch, had appropriated the Budweiser name for an unrelated brew, and then had gone on to make it one of the first coast-to-coast American brand names.[59]

Closer to home, the Burghers' Brewery had fared better. By the mid-1890s, it owned multiple installations besides the beer-producing plant itself: several restaurants near town, including one at the site of the Passion Plays in Höritz/Hořice; refrigerated warehouses in Brünn/Brno, Graz, Innsbruck, Trieste, and additional cities of Cisleithania; and also warehouses in such places as Zagreb, Berlin, Hamburg, and Munich. Production had nearly tripled since 1871, to 114,000 hectoliters; the number of employees in Budweis/Budějovice had sextupled, to more than 200; and the dividend had jumped from 100 to 400 crowns—more than half of what a bricklayer could hope to earn in a year. The Burghers' Brewery, despite its antiquated ownership structure, had become a modern manufacturing facility. To the extent that the brewery was German, it seemed to disprove Zátka's claim that German burghers in town made poor businessmen.

The Germanness of the brewery, however, had reached a high point during the late 1880s or early 1890s, and thereafter had yielded to a more generic nationalization. At the beginning of the 1890s, the Czech Savings Bank had managed, through subterfuge, to purchase a brewery-linked building on the *Ringplatz/rynek* from a burgher allied with Taschek. Liberal German leaders, made suddenly aware of a new threat, had mobilized to defend the brewery, and for that matter the center of town—only to realize gradually just how powerful the Czech push was. By 1900, Czech families and businesses made up almost one third of the owners. Zátka himself continued to own at least one brewery-linked house.[60]

Well before 1900, Zátka had decided to complement the Czech attempt at gaining control of the Burghers' Brewery with a more radical strategy: founding a new, Czech brewery that would capture market share from the German-dominated one. In 1895, a Czech Shareholders' Brewery had come into existence in town. Rejecting the model of the Burghers' Brewery, which just then was celebrating its centenary, the new company had organized itself as a corporation instead. Like other Czech companies, it had raised capital by issuing stock in denominations small enough that even individuals of modest means could afford a share or two. By 1902, the Czech Shareholders' Brewery had more than 6,500 shares outstanding.[61]

The new business had proved an immediate success. The *Beseda* had signed up as one of the first regular customers, and from that point on could claim the distinction of being a Czech establishment that served Czech beer. So, before long, could more and more restaurants and pubs, including one called "The Czech/Bohemian German" [*U českého Němce*]. Open and explicit in financial dealings in a way that the Burghers' Brewery had never been, the Czech Shareholders' Brewery timed annual reports and dividends to coincide with those of the rival company. Regular drinkers of the new brand probably included all shareholders. In hoisting a glass, they could quench their thirst, increase the value of their assets, and serve the national cause all at once. The annual summer festival of the Shareholders' Brewery soon became a major Czech fund-raising event. Germans, meanwhile, also stood free to drink the beer—which, like its competitor, carried the name "Budweiser" in German. At the request of some buyers in Styria, the Czech Shareholders' Brewery even shipped bottles with labels that contained no mention of anything Czech or Bohemian. By 1900, the new Brewery had 130 employees in Budweis/Budějovice. It had also already given shareholders some tidy profits, and perhaps some beer bellies. The following year, when Czech-language schools in town first surpassed German-language ones in enrollment, the Shareholders' Brewery outstripped the Burghers' Brewery in barrels produced.[62] Such remarkable achievement set new standards in town for enterprise.

The spectacular feat of outproducing a major firm after only six years also indicated that something was rotten in the Burghers' Brewery. Indeed, its beer seemed to have declined in quality—in a development related to a dramatic widening in the Liberal-*völkisch* divide. In the late 1890s, Leopold Schweighofer, a German *völkisch* leader and the owner of a brewery-linked house, had launched a campaign against the Liberal German faction (headed, as in town hall, by Taschek and by Kohn) that dominated the brewery's Board of Directors. The young and brash Schweighofer, in his quest for victory against Liberals and for growth more in line with that of the Czech Shareholders' Brewery, proved willing to pact even with house-owners downtown who were Czechs.[63] "Better a Czech than a Liberal German," he and his followers seem to have reasoned in their angrier moments, and "Better a Czech than a Jew." To Czechs who owned a stake in the Burghers' Brewery, Schweighofer held out not only hope of better management but a chance to bloody Taschek and to neutralize the company as a political factor. After all, the brewery could influence how its employees behaved—not only at the ballot box but in school enrollment decisions for their children, in associational life, and so on. By definition, a *völkisch*-Czech coalition would not exercise its power to the advantage of either national movement.

The combination of Czech pressure and of *völkisch* rebellion weakened the Liberal grip on the Burghers' Brewery. Once the Liberal faction lost its ability to shroud financial data in secrecy, Schweighofer discovered that Taschek, his father, Kohn, and their associates had been selling the Burghers' Brewery ice, wood, coal, and hops at grossly inflated prices. The motive for this swindle remains unclear. Liberal leaders may have sought to profit personally, or they may have acted on behalf of their party—which needed ever more cash to keep members and voters in line. Quite likely brewery funds ended up diverted both to private and to German public ends. Wherever the money went, *völkisch* and Czech brewery owners found that expressing shock over its absence served their aims. Some of Taschek and Kohn's previously passive allies, appalled and angered by the new revelations, began to side with the rebels. Liberal members of the board denied everything and refused to step down.[64]

In October 1900, just as town residents were gearing up for the census and for elections to the Austrian Parliament, Schweighofer went public with his allegations. The speech he made provides a perspective committed all too rarely to paper on an important issue: how Taschek's party commanded loyalty or obedience from followers. "It would be interesting to know," Schweighofer said,

> how many votes for [the Liberals] would remain if everyone could vote as he thought. But one person owes money to the Savings Bank and another has a promise of a loan. The first is a municipal employee, the second an official of an institution—the Brewery, the Savings Bank, the "Bee" Loan Cooperative— dependent on them in another way. A third person is subject to the Town School Board, a fourth rents his lodgings from one of their people and is threatened

with eviction. A fifth, meanwhile, who owns a house, finds himself threatened
with termination of his lease by a renter belonging to their party. Craftsmen
they threaten with no more work, businessmen with boycott![65]

In the Liberal German political economy, all was linked in a seamless web
having town hall at its center. Indeed, town hall itself owned nearly a
dozen brewery-linked buildings, while the brewery held at least one vote
in the very small and very powerful municipal first curia.[66] This structure
made for political strength, but also for economic inefficiency. The brewery, under Taschek and Kohn, had no real bottom line, and insufficient
incentive to streamline operations as the market demanded. If the thousands of shareholders and employees of the Czech brewery found that
what was good for the Czech movement also benefited them individually,
then only the elite among German owners of the Burghers' Brewery could
claim the same. For other Germans, national and personal interests coincided in much sloppier fashion.

Schweighofer and other *völkische* fought Taschek and his Liberals with
more abandon than Holanský and other Young Czechs fought Zátka and
his Old Czechs. Unlike Holanský, Schweighofer succeeded in wresting
control from his intranational nemesis over a major institution; in January
1902, he won election as Chairman of the Board of the Burghers' Brewery,
backed by *völkische* and by Czechs. Immediately, that coalition faced a test.
Liberal leaders had been exerting their influence within companies in an
attempt to assure a Czech defeat in elections, now overdue, to the town
council. Early in February, Czech leaders learned the extent of that attempt (whose details are explained in the next chapter), and reacted with
a vehemence—and confidence—that would have been inconceivable a decade previously. *Budivoj*, less concerned with the fortunes of Schweighofer's Czech allies among the owners of the Burghers' Brewery than with
Czech political fortunes more broadly, warned Schweighofer to rescind
the previous chairman's pro-Liberal measures. Otherwise, "we will smash
your brewery to smithereens. We know your weak spots, and it is not an
audit but something else that will break your neck. . . . Here you have our
ultimatum. An eye for an eye, a tooth for a tooth! We do not want to
conquer Town Hall but we have a right to the third curia, and we will not
allow anyone to strip us of it!"[67]

In 1900, Schweighofer had countered Liberal charges that he was betraying the national cause by arguing that the Burghers' Brewery "*is not
a political enterprise. Rather, it is a purely commercial one,* purely economic.
Neither Germans nor Czechs nor Jews count in it, but simply numbers
and success." He had drawn the line at cooperating with Czechs in elections. Now, though, in order to deal another blow to his intranational

Liberal opponents, he risked lifting his national, Czech opponents to a big electoral victory—and losing money. If Schweighofer hesitated, then he did not hesitate very long. He gave in to the Czech pressure, and rescinded his Liberal predecessor's measures. In April, the new management that Schweighofer headed filed suit against former members of the board, and erected a Czech-language sign to complement the German-language one at the entrance to the factory compound.[68]

Originally a brewery of Budweiser burghers, then an increasingly Liberal and German one, and then a mostly German one with a seditious Czech minority, the Burghers' Brewery (and for that matter, Budweis/Budějovice as a whole) had become a factionalized *völkisch*-German-Liberal-Jewish-Christian-Czech hodgepodge. Between 1901 and 1905, the company paid out no dividend. Eventually, Taschek and his allies had to repay tens of thousands of crowns, if not the nearly two million crowns sought in lawsuits. The Czech Shareholders' Brewery, meanwhile, continued to thrive. Then again, how Czech it was stands open to question. Schweighofer claimed in 1902 that Germans owned almost half of all shares.[69]

As the case of the breweries illustrates, the structure of individual companies reflected their owners' national loyalties. The structure of those loyalties, in turn, continued to reflect early Czech-German socioeconomic disparities—and contributed, paradoxically, to reducing or even to reversing them. To some consumers, the two brands of beer may have seemed quite similar. But their political aftertastes differed radically. The Czech one was strong, open, and promising, while its rival smacked of corruption, decline, and discord. The former brew figured both as product and as producer of a Czech capitalist society characterized by strong cross-class bonds and by growing confidence. The latter, to the extent that it could be called German, served as symbol of a divided community whose increasingly illiberal leaders feared the future. As a Czech-German hybrid, finally, beer made by the Burghers' Brewery embodied the growing problems of containing a mutually exclusive, mutually reinforcing national dynamic within a Habsburg framework.

The Czech movement could have sought out unexploited economic niches for its ventures. Instead, it founded company after company directly opposite established German firms: the Shareholders' Brewery opposite the Burghers' Brewery, the National Pencil Company opposite Hardtmuth's, the First Budějovice Enamelware Factory, Inc. opposite three small, family-run enamelers, and so on. A few of the Czech startups drove their German enemies out of business. Several failed themselves. Most did neither, instead hauling the sleepy local economy into modern times and tightening the national grip on business and on public life as a whole.

Conclusion

During the 1890s, the Czech movement in Budweis/Budějovice had proved successful at maintaining a fundamental unity even while undergoing rapid change and growth. Key elements had been the development of internal articulations, which found expression in an emergent multiparty system, in an ever larger set of associations, and in the ownership structure of businesses. Whether rich or poor, whether anticlerical or devoutly Catholic, individual Czechs could take pride in "their" brewery in town. Differentiated organizational structures provided attachment points for every Czech—which the entire movement defined consistently, in primarily ethnic fashion.

The German movement, in contrast, featured mutually hostile factions. Until the 1880s, Pieter Judson has argued, German-speaking bourgeois males in Cisleithania had used the universalist language of liberalism to conceal even from themselves their particularist interests.[70] Then, after the political shocks of 1879–80, an ethnic strand to Germanness had emerged—less elitist, unambiguously national, and more like the dominant strand within Czechness. During the 1890s, the Liberal and *völkisch* strands had failed to converge on a consistent, overarching understanding of Germanness. Meanwhile, in an echo of the Liberal-German pattern of the 1860s and 1870s, working-class Germans had found perhaps their strongest advocate (and maker) in the Social Democratic movement, despite its location partly outside the German camp. In similar fashion, at least in some parts of Austria, the Christian Social Party had become a foremost representative of German political Catholicism—yet had developed in less national and in more Catholic directions than Czech counterparts. In the German Empire, Bismarck had waged domestic battles during the 1870s and 1880s against both Social Democracy and political Catholicism. In the more complex setting of Cisleithania, too, the Germanization of many workers and Catholics involved considerable intranational dissonance. Czechization unfolded with greater consistency and success.

Despite these Czech-German differences, politics as a whole in Budweis/Budějovice had grown more national. Why? First, the national movements had been able to meet the challenge of a more pervasive politics from a position of strength. Neither movement controlled the state, but for some time now, both had played central roles in electoral politics and in associational life. Second, the national movements had each other. Social Democratic leaders did not have the good fortune of finding major opponents who understood themselves primarily in class terms. Nor did would-be leaders of Catholic or Aryan movements succeed in pairing off with a credible movement in a struggle on whose religious or racial axis the contestants agreed. German and Czech leaders, in contrast, did agree. In their struggle against each other, they generated a powerful framework for interpreting, however inaccurately, nearly any event on the political field. Politics might pit burghers against officials, Bohemians against Budweisers, rich men against poor, Catholics against Jews, and any of those against themselves, or against Czechs or Germans. But from national perspectives, all those conflicts reduced to a competition for resources between Czechs and Germans. Nonnational loyalties figured merely as less-than-national ones. Even when Habsburg loyalties figured as more-than-national ones, they did so as a mere adding together of national parts, as a common political language for the national communities within the country. Budweiser, burgher, Bohemian, and other nonnational categories were becoming secondary—and not only for adherents of national movements.

Four

Toward a Multinational State, 1902–1918

> It is to the advantage of both [the German and
> the Czech] races to exchange for the ups and
> downs of debatable, contested, and cross-cutting
> demands a firm and secured basis in law. . . .
> [O]nly the constant power of the law . . . can
> guarantee the peaceful and uncontested posses-
> sion of national rights to the parties, and peace to
> the state.
> —*Government position paper, 1900*

> [On an electoral committee,] strictly speaking,
> there were actually three Czechs! There was
> Taschek, the son of a native of Bernardice—
> Czech blood. There was Bitzan, the offspring of
> Czech millers, and there was Watzek, whose
> name is also suspicious.
> —*August Zátka, 1906*

> [W]hoever possesses the vote or is required to at-
> tend school must declare to which nation he be-
> longs. That, incidentally, was always a difficult
> question. . . . It is a matter for the individual to
> declare to which nation he belongs.
> —*August Zátka, 1918*

During the 1870s, 1880s, and 1890s, Habsburg leaders had partly con-
strained, partly accommodated, and partly ignored national movements,
within the limits of a nonnational constitutional order. In the new century,
as cracks in that order widened, efforts at reforming it began to yield results.
In Budweis/Budějovice and elsewhere, in piecemeal but fairly consistent
fashion, the three major political players hammered out agreements that
pushed nationhood, a vague political principle, in the direction of a formal
status—akin in some ways to citizenship. "Nations" started becoming constituent members of Cisleithania, recognized by the law and proportionally
equal before it in the exercise of significant political rights. In a trend with
few European parallels, the state began to become multinational.

For national leaders, the reforms marked a tremendous gain. They also seemed to mark a consolidation of the Habsburg status quo, because of their multinational, more-than-national, and thus, in some sense, once again nonnational nature. A national state nationalizes politics specifically. Modern France, for example, has long been nationalizing its politics to French advantage. Cisleithania, however, nationalized politics generically, not necessarily to German, Czech, or any other advantage.

In becoming a legal category, nationhood had to lose some of its ethnic essence. Habsburg leaders refused to permit legal definitions of nationhood that centered on language or on any other ascribable and putatively objective factors. Zátka and other national leaders, in order to improve their chances of anchoring nationhood in the constitutional order—through a legislative package dubbed the Budweis/Budějovice Compromise, for example—had to concede that it was "a matter for the individual to declare to which nation he belongs." At the same time, though, those leaders continued in their words and deeds to define nationhood ascriptively, primarily in terms of "blood"—or to be more accurate, of ethnicity. To Zátka, Taschek counted deep down ("strictly speaking") not as a German but as a Czech. And to *völkische*, some Liberals counted deep down not as Germans but as Jews. A consensual resolution of this tension between legal and practical definitions of nationhood probably could not have been found. The same holds true of the tensions between German privilege and German weakness, between Czech underdog past and Czech majoritarian future, and between the territorial nature of state power and the nonterritorial ways in which political players increasingly sought to nationalize it. Sooner or later, the multinationalization of the state that got under way in the new century probably would have destroyed the German-Habsburg-Czech triad that had come to frame politics in the Bohemian lands. The outbreak of war in 1914, however, interrupted the experiment. And in 1918, with the destruction of the Habsburg Monarchy, a resumption of that experiment became impossible.

National Enfranchisement

During the winter of 1901–2, elections to Budweis/Budějovice's town hall did not take place, although they should have. The three-year term of the incumbent council had expired, but Taschek, as Deputy Mayor, had failed to set the electoral machinery in motion. That was because the Czech movement now probably had a majority in the third curia—which Taschek and other German leaders did not think they could afford to surrender. Both Czechs and the Habsburg authorities, however, forced Taschek to proceed. He turned to massive fraud. Czechs responded with fraud of their own, and the authorities spent the next four years sorting out the mess. The German and Czech movements succeeded in circumventing the nonnational law, and in adding many followers to the municipal electorate. At the same time, Czech-German differences threatened to paralyze town hall or to take on violent form again, as in 1898. Incentives mounted for the Czech movement, the German movement, and Habsburg leaders to collaborate in working out a new framework for politics in Budweis/Budějovice.

In January 1901, as the result of new Cisleithanian legislation, town hall had lost its long-standing power to deny nonnatives of town "domiciled" status. Almost anyone continuously resident for ten years could now claim it as a right. Originally developed in connection with poor relief, that status now held little significance. But in Bohemia, being domiciled in a town lowered a barrier to membership in the third municipal curia. The nondomiciled male had to pay a direct state tax in town—by owning real estate or a business, or by earning approximately 1,300 crowns a year— for the three years that preceded the drawing up of electoral rolls. The domiciled male, in contrast, had to pay such a tax for only one year. During 1901, more than 2,200 residents had taken advantage of the amendment to win domiciled status in Budweis/Budějovice. For some of the men in this group, the change in official domicile made the difference between qualifying or not qualifying for the vote.[1]

Those men, like nondomiciled ones who were just meeting the stiffer, three-year requirement for the first time, were far more likely to vote Czech than German. Almost half of Budweis/Budějovice's population had been born elsewhere. And elsewhere, according to census results, was a mostly or overwhelmingly Czech-speaking district of Bohemia in 75 to 80 percent of all cases. Yet even German Liberals now understood Germanness to a considerable extent in ethnic terms, and thus excluded people who did not speak German at least as a second language. The German organizational infrastructure at the economic bottom of the municipal electorate, furthermore, was not nearly as robust as the Czech equivalent. And among the men now qualifying for the vote through tax payments, those with strong German feelings often had the vote already. Germans on the town council, in their successful drives to keep the third curia German in the elections of 1890 and of 1898, had awarded burgher status (and together with it, domiciled status, as well as enfranchisement, regardless of tax payments) to nonvoters for whom reliable Germans had vouched.[2] Now Taschek needed to take new and more drastic action if he was to prevent the Czech movement from capturing the third curia.

Act Taschek did, in three progressively more desperate waves. First, in November 1901, he had the Revenue Office in town hall send bills to many of the Czechs who paid a direct state tax, and thus were members of the third curia. The bills were for municipal taxes that many of the men had already paid. (Payment only of a direct *state* tax entitled a resident to vote. But the law disqualified any such taxpayer whose *municipal* tax obligations stood more than one year in arrears.) Many Czechs paid again, so as not to see themselves struck from the electoral rolls. Some German members of the curia, meanwhile, mustered the cynical courage to refuse paying tax bills that were *bona fide*. Taschek, desperate for every German voter he could find, did not disqualify the delinquents. Rather, he papered over the shortfall—using, perhaps, the double payments by Czechs. The freeloaders profited from their Germanness, in a way that fostered no great love between leaders and led in the movement. This covert infighting, in fact, formed a sideshow to the Liberal-*völkisch* struggle, just then reaching an open climax in the Burghers' Brewery.[3]

Second, in December, Taschek began surreptitiously enlisting unenfranchised, domiciled men who were beholden to Liberals to declare, falsely, an income in excess of 1,300 crowns during the previous year, and to pay the state tax on that income. By so doing, the recruits qualified for the vote in the third curia. By January, they numbered 564. Nearly 140 of them worked at the Hardtmuth pencil factory, and more than 110, including 48 policemen, worked in town hall. At first, Czechs did not know about the maneuver. *Budivoj* noted with suspicion on December 10, though, that the Burghers' Brewery (still under Liberal control) had just paid state taxes for sixty-odd employees who did not earn enough to owe anything. Creative accounting by Taschek in town hall seems to have complemented such private sector donations. Money flowed from corporate and municipal slush funds to the state, resting only briefly in individual hands as taxes due. Men who were less German might have liked to keep some of the cash, as payment in advance for service to be rendered at the ballot box. But the threat of dismissal seems to have limited that practice, and to have allowed the German movement to create more German voters with the finite funds at its disposal.[4]

The Czech movement responded by creating its own "counterfeit" voters, who quickly came to be known as "one-year volunteers" (a cynical reference to officer candidates destined for the reserves of the army). Again, men lined up to pay real taxes on unreal income, often with other people's money. The Czech movement, though, could not tap public funds, and controlled fewer jobs. Its "volunteers" more often really *were* volunteers, moved by appeals to decency, to democracy, and to sacrifice for the common (or at least national) good.[5] Together, the Czech and German actions gave new meaning to the definition of taxation as a redistribution of income. National leaders paid the state for the opportunity to enfranchise poorer men, to nationalize them somewhat, and to sway the results of an election.

Taschek's third move, late in January 1902, signaled that the Czech counterfeits probably numbered enough to neutralize his own. As Czech leaders and the district captainship pushed town hall hard to stop shilly-shallying with the elections, the Liberal majority of the town council secretly awarded burgher status—and thus a vote in the third curia—to ninety-six men. On the same day, the Liberal majority publicly awarded honorary burgher status to twenty-six more men. During the previous century, only thirty-two men had been awarded that status, which carried with it enfranchisement not in the third curia but in the first. On February 2, Zátka suggested in a speech that this padding of a curia in which Czechs had few votes signaled Liberal fears that retired army officers and dignitaries in the curia would abandon or split the German ticket. Indeed, such people probably were repelled by the Liberal mismanagement of the Burghers' Brewery, by the Liberal-*völkisch* scandal there, and by Taschek's less than honorable attempts at influencing the outcome of the municipal elections. A newspaper founded recently in town by the German Peasants' Union judged on the same day that Taschek, in creating the honorary burghers, had seized on "the most unnatural of imaginable means." And *Deutsche Volkswehr* [*German National Guard*] had summed up the *völkisch* reaction the day before by calling Taschek "the misfortune of the Germans of Budweis." Only hours after Zátka's speech, town hall at last put the electoral rolls on display. On them, as Czech watchdogs quickly discovered, were not only the 26 new honorary burghers but the 564 third curia "counterfeits," the 96 new regular burghers, and an additional 226 regular burghers created just the day before.[6] The whole town now learned of what had been going on behind closed doors.

Who were the 322 (96 plus 226) new regular burghers? Liberals seem to have slapped together a list of non-taxpaying men who were likely, if enfranchised, to vote German and thus to lift the German ticket to a narrow victory. "Likely," rather than "certain," had had to suffice, it seems, because a deadline imposed by the district captain had ruled out the usual time-consuming vetting and calculation. This scenario accounts for otherwise inexplicable mistakes. Several of the new burghers denied having signed the applications submitted in their names. None of the new burghers was Jewish—a fact that had the potential to exacerbate tensions between Jewish and non-Jewish Liberals. The municipal statutes required that aldermen vote on the awarding of regular burgher status through formal balloting, but they had voted through a mere show of hands. Barely half the draftees in the third curia, finally, even lived in Budweis/Budějovice.[7] Taschek perhaps had already awarded burgher status to all the non-taxpaying men in town whom he trusted. Then again, he may have hoped, by enfranchising residents of Oberplan/Horní Planá, Kaplitz/Kaplice,

Pilsen/Plzeň, Prague, Linz, and Vienna, to increase their interest in the outcome of an election in a middling South Bohemian town.

With due deliberation, the Habsburg authorities reacted to the German challenge that the electoral rolls represented. In the second week of February, the district captain, Francis Joseph Křikawa (whose Habsburg-loyal given names complemented a surname with a German "w" and with a Czech *háček*, or diacritic, over the "r"), canceled the additions to the third curia, citing the failure to observe proper voting procedures. Yet no technical glitches marred the "German swindle" (to use *Budivoj*'s term) in the first curia, and Křikawa let stand the additions to it. Prosecutors weighed opening a criminal investigation in connection with the forging of applications for burgher status, but did not, probably because a Liberal closing of the ranks stifled all evidence. Liberal lawyers, proving themselves unintimidated, desperate, or both, appealed Křikawa's cancellation. Rumors circulated that Taschek's nominal superior, an elderly and ailing Liberal, was appalled, and was considering resigning as Mayor.[8]

Among Czechs, meanwhile, bile flowed copiously as they digested what their national opponent had done. Protest rallies gave Zátka and other participants an opportunity to vent their anger—or, from German perspectives, to engage in incitement. *Budivoj* published, with appropriately caustic commentary, the names of all the new voters manufactured by Liberals, and of all the aldermen who had participated. The newspaper also made its threat, cited in the previous chapter, to smash the Burghers' Brewery to smithereens. Schweighofer, who had just become chairman of the board, responded by rescinding the tax payments made on behalf of sixty-odd employees. Budweis/Budějovice came up for discussion in the Austrian Parliament, national boycotts tightened; and Czech tussles with the town police contributed to dangerously high tempers.[9]

Czech leaders turned not only to the Czech public and to the streets but also to the law. A volunteer staff worked feverishly and submitted a mountain of paperwork to the appropriate municipal commission at the end of the eight-day period allotted for objections to the electoral rolls. Those rolls contained 216 names in the first curia, 808 in the second, and 5,442 in the third. But in a stunning achievement, the Czech objections (some against the inclusion of people seen as Germans and others against the exclusion of people seen as Czechs) numbered more: 7,714. The municipal commission, dominated by Liberals, quickly rejected the great majority. Czech lawyers then appealed to the district captainship—which determined that it lacked jurisdiction. Further appeals regarding this and related matters joined briefs from the Liberal side in wending their way through the Bohemian bureaucracy and through the imperial-royal administrative courts.[10]

Figure 4. Franz Josef Křikawa/František Josef Křikawa (1851–1932). Imperial-
royal district captain in Budweis/Budějovice, 1896–1913. Courtesy of the State
Regional Archive in České Budějovice.

Figure 5. Postcards of Budweis/Budějovice, ca. 1900. "Greetings from Budweis"—a view of Town Hall (*top*). "Greetings from Budějovice"—a view of the
town center (*bottom*).

Czech leaders also turned to the government. So did Liberal ones. Taschek and Kohn, during a two-hour audience in Vienna with the Cisleithanian prime minister, Ernest von Koerber, asked him to overrule the district captain's overruling of the 322 additions to the third curia. Koerber, however, urged instead a German-Czech compromise. Czech leaders, when they showed up to plead the other national side to the case, met with substantially the same response.[11] Liberal leaders had committed no crime, if only because legislators in the Austrian Parliament and in the Bohemian Diet, failing to foresee that one day political leaders would stoop so low, had left loopholes.

From the Social Democratic perspective, this German or Czech maneuvering amounted only to specific swindles within a generically national swindle of the proletariat. As *Jihočeský dělník* wrote in March, "We are truly indifferent as to whether the Czech or the German bourgeoisie rules in town hall; neither the one nor the other suits us." Neither German nor Czech leaders backed a version of the electoral rolls that even vaguely approximated the confidential rolls of the recent census. Rather, both sides sought to expand the municipal electorates selectively, through means that ensured that new voters would not be able to express Social Democratic, Christian Social, Budweiser, or other loyalties at the urns. Back in 1895, on the day of Francis Joseph's arrival in town, *Budivoj* had complained about the laws governing elections to the Bohemian Diet. "*[E]very government*," the newspaper had told its readers, "whether having a majority of the nation behind it or no, *has succeeded . . . in securing a majority, through elections, to the Bohemian Diet.* For the [electoral] orders were not and are not composed according to purely constitutional principles with the goal that, through free elections, expression should be given in the Diet to the opinions and principles of the majority. Rather, all is for the benefit of the government, whatever its principles and ambitions, so that decisions might be made in parliamentary fashion even against the conviction of the majority."[12] Now Social Democrats made a similar complaint against the national movements in Budweis/Budějovice.

Jews in town by now were spread unevenly across overlapping Habsburg, Social Democratic, liberal, conservative, Czech, German, and even Zionist camps, and had no single stance. Nor did either national movement pursue a single policy toward Jews. On the German side, Liberal-*völkisch* friction revolved in large part around "the Jewish question." Tensions among the Czech parties sometimes found expression through arguments over the same issue. In June 1902, *Budivoj* urged Zátka's less anti-Semitic stance on readers, writing that "*no one* has the right to excommunicate anyone from the nation." Every Czech voter, the newspaper continued, possessed equal value, whatever his religion, provided that he did his duty at the polls and sent his children to Czech-language schools. "*More than this we do not wish of anyone*; whatever anyone should do in addition is a voluntary sacrifice."[13] The pleading tone and counterfactual ring to the article, however, hinted that the author had one eye on powerful anti-Semitic currents among his readership and the other on electoral math—and little concern for Jews themselves. He titled his article "The Jewish Question in České Budějovice," but made no mention of what ranked arguably as the most important event affecting that question in the last decade: the Czech attack on Jewish shops and houses in 1898.

The German movement had delayed the municipal elections and had attempted to win them unfairly. The Czech movement had frustrated German intentions, at the price of delaying the elections still further. Between 1902 and 1906, imperial-royal officials and judges disentangled thousands of individual cases and several legal knots. Both national parties celebrated greater and smaller victories along the way, and both appealed defeats. Meanwhile, the incumbent town council remained in power. Taschek, apparently unable to imagine anything good at the end of this pause, worked to prolong it. Indeed, after drawing up the list of voters practically with his own hands, he had had German lawyers file more than 1,500 objections to it—perhaps in order to insulate his movement from fallout over any of his nationally motivated additions or omissions, and to gain a legal lever with which to stretch out adjudication.

While waiting for Czech, German, and Habsburg legal experts to settle on a single version of the electoral rolls, residents could rest assured that they had witnessed the making of history. The electoral rolls prepared by Taschek's administration, besides excluding many Czech "one-year volunteers," excluded more than 80 percent of the population. Yet those rolls still contained more than twice as many names as had the rolls used in 1898. Habsburg leaders had long set the pace at which the lower classes gained representation in representative bodies and had tried to ensure that the franchise reforms of the 1880s and 1890s for diets and for the Austrian Parliament gave new voters a choice among national and nonnational (or at least less national) parties. But now the national movements had seized the initiative in determining when and how a more mass politics reached Budweis/Budějovice's town hall. National leaders and imperial-royal officials had averted a repetition of the 1898 outbreak of physical violence. Yet their deeds and misdeeds, actions and inaction had wreaked damage to the myth of the monarchy as something all-powerful, unquestionable, natural, and perpetual—in a word, legitimate.

None of these developments had necessarily altered the outcome of the elections, still pending. But the national movements, rather than simply canceling out one another, had accomplished a great deal together. They had made the news in Prague, Vienna, and elsewhere, thereby linking a local contest to the larger German-Czech struggle. Czech leaders had gained political capital from having forced their German opponents into a morally indefensible position. German leaders had gained proof that, in the absence of their unusual methods, the Czech party would steamroller to power—or at least to a sharing of it. Strategy sessions, demonstrations, and a flat-out mobilization of manpower and of money had created a chain of memorable events. Not only the opposing teams of lawyers, ward bosses, accountants, and hangers-on who had worked themselves ragged preparing tax and electoral rolls, objections, and appeals but also large numbers of residents had experienced the tug of war as a defining moment of national self-defense and cohesion. District Captain Křikawa, in contrast, had found himself trapped between mutually exclusive imperatives, certain no matter what he did to give offense in such a way as to create or to reinforce national feelings. His hands tied by the law and by a refusal on the part of higher-ups to intervene, he had lost the power to ensure timely elections or to address effectively the larger Czech-German conflict. It was by now the central, although far from sole, fact of politics in Budweis/Budějovice.

German Fear, Czech Ambition, Habsburg Restraint

Czech and German leaders, in their struggle over the municipal electorate in 1901–2, had hit upon new and potent methods of nationalization. Parallel to these methods, older ones continued to be used, becoming not less important but simply more routine. Choir rehearsals, outings, dances, and ceremonies figured less prominently in the national press than had been the case in the 1880s. But this change by no means signaled a weakening of the national movements. Rather, the shift reflected their success at making nationhood the major backdrop before which many minor conflicts took place. *Budivoj*, the *Budweiser Zeitung*, *Jihočeské listy*, *Deutsche Volkswehr*, and additional newspapers printed ever larger issues. These publications had ever less room to report in detail on any given national activity, though, because such activities numbered so many.

Now the propagation of nationhood in new generations and the deepening of what nationhood meant to national residents took up more time for Czech and German leaders than did the nationalization of Budweisers. Through associational life, elections, schools, boycotts, and businesses, through international (in the sense of Czech-German), intranational, and national-Habsburg conflict, the national division of souls continued. That this differentiation occurred asymmetrically in town, more to the advantage of Czechs than Germans, no longer surprised anyone. That pattern, however, generated German fear and Czech ambition. Government policies, meanwhile, signaled Habsburg restraint or even resignation.

In August 1903, German and Czech gymnasts faced off in Budweis/ Budějovice. The Liberal *Turnverein*, well in advance of the summer, had begun organizing a three-day fest for clubs belonging to the Maltsch-Moldau District of a new German gymnastics association—distinguished from others by the refusal to exclude Jews. The *Sokol*, dominated by Young Czechs, had then decided to hold its own, rival fest in town at exactly the same time. Liberal leaders had repeatedly requested the district captain to ban the Czech gathering. August came, and with it, almost 4,000 Czech gymnasts (fewer than 400 of them from town). Not nearly as many German gymnasts exercised and feasted in the safety of the *Deutsches Haus*, which was festooned with flags—including not only the Austrian red-and-white and the Habsburg black-and-yellow but also the German black-red-and-gold, supposedly in honor of visitors from the German Empire. The official history of the *Turnverein*, published in 1912, makes clear how embattled Liberals felt: "We did not allow the circumstance that all *völkisch* associations had left us in the lurch and ignored our celebrations to stop us from making a show, unfrightened, of the German colors in town during the hurly-burly of the Czech celebrations. . . . The welcoming dinner had the character of a fierce defense against the invasion of the Czech *Sokol*."[14]

The real military, as opposed to Budweis/Budějovice's national paramilitaries mounted on vaulting horses, continued under Habsburg control—barred from participation in elections, segregated in barracks, hemmed in by glorious traditions, and bound by an oath of loyalty directly to the emperor-king. The so-called Sausage Affair of 1905, however, signaled the success of the Czech and German movements in town at reaching the rank and file in that central Habsburg institution. During September and October, the Social Democratic Party staged impressive demonstrations, taking serious talk of electoral reform for both the Hungarian Parliament and the Bohemian Diet as an invitation to revive the struggle for universal suffrage. (The Austrian Parliament, it will be remembered, had seemed to feature universal male suffrage since 1897. But the curia system continued to give far more weight to the rich man's ballot than to the poor one's.) At the end of October, days before a renewed round of marches, sensational news arrived from Russia: the Tsar, rocked by Japan's defeat of his navy in 1904 and by revolutionary upheaval at home since January 1905, had proclaimed that he would create an all-Russian legislature, to be elected democratically. Within forty-eight hours, in Vienna, Prague, and Graz, huge numbers of workers turned out for half-celebratory, half-ominous parades. Clashes with the authorities occurred, and the conflict threatened to veer out of control.

On November 3, Francis Joseph intervened. He ordered his Cisleithanian prime minister, Paul Baron von Gautsch, to reverse course and to prepare legislation that would bring about a more genuine form of universal male suffrage for the Lower House. The shift in policy became public on the evening of November 4. The next two evenings, several thousand working-class men and women filled the *Ringplatz/rynek* in Budweis/ Budějovice. In many other cities as well, Social Democratic leaders brought workers together in order to celebrate peacefully, as well as to push for a thorough and rapid reform.[15]

Liberal Germans responded with anything but enthusiasm to the Social Democratic and Habsburg assault on electoral privilege. Taschek, who by this point had graduated from deputy mayor to mayor, seems to have expected a revolution to break out at any moment. Claiming to act on behalf of businessmen fearing for their property, he persuaded District Captain Křikawa to seal off the *Ringplatz/rynek* with troops on the evening of November 8, and thus to prevent another demonstration. Used for the task was a company of the 91st Infantry Regiment, whose German and Czech-speaking recruits came from the Budweis/Budějovice district. But the next evening, in a sign that Křikawa perhaps considered the show of force to have been overdone, no soldiers patrolled the streets. Instead, a single squadron stood at the ready in the courtyard of the town hall, out of sight. Furthermore, this unit was provided not by the 91st Infantry Regiment, but by the 28th—whose recruits came from Prague, and had a reputation dating back to the 1890s for having strong Czech sympathies. The squadron saw no action, because no one disturbed the peace.

Here Mayor Taschek blundered. As on the previous evening, he ordered that the soldiers downtown be served sausages and beer. He and other Germans seem to have seen a delicious irony in this gesture. Willfully blind, like Czech leaders, to the nonnational dimensions of both Social Democracy and the military, German leaders understood the food and drink at least in part as a reward to Czech soldiers for obeying their German-speaking officers, and for standing on alert to put down mostly Czech-speaking and thus mostly Czech workers. Taschek, though, had repeatedly made public his wish that German-speaking troops rather than Czech-speaking ones be stationed in town. Several of the enlisted men of the 28th Regiment had even heard a rumor that he was trying to engineer the transfer of their unit. Unlike the company of the 91st Regiment, which had accepted a meal from the mayor the evening before, the squadron of the 28th Regiment rejected the offer. Voices from the middle of the squadron, in fact, insulted Taschek, and cried that Czech soldiers would not allow themselves to be bribed by a German town hall. Czech leaders seized on the event. Local Czech newspapers published story after story, the *Beseda* held a huge meeting at which Zátka demanded Czech officers for Czech soldiers, and a throng of Czechs shouted greetings to the troops from outside the new Francis Joseph Barracks.[16]

On November 22, days before another round of Social Democratic demonstrations (in connection with the reconvening of the Austrian Parliament, to which Prime Minister Gautsch was scheduled to present his electoral reform plan), Budweis/Budějovice's town council met. In a speech, Taschek devoted little attention to the working-class demonstrators, dismissing most of them as shiftless elements and rioters. He and another Liberal German spent considerable time, though, fulminating over the behavior of the soldiers, as well as over the failure of the authorities to take strong measures. The bluster shifted attention from enfranchisement to military discipline, and masked consternation over a display of Czech consciousness and solidarity that German leaders themselves had provoked. Absent the sausages and beer (probably purchased from neither of the breweries in town), residents could have seen better that more than national conflict, class conflict had been the central issue at the beginning of the incident. The unconsumed food and drink had prompted German fear and Czech ambition to swallow up the equivalent sentiments shared by the bourgeoisie and by the working class. Unintentionally, Liberal German leaders had helped to Czechify soldiers and Social Democrats in town. The nonnational army command emerged from the Sausage Affair slightly but visibly weakened.

In social affairs, army officers already stood all but powerless. Since resigning from the *Beseda* in 1898 because of Young Czech insults, the officer corps had frequented only the *Deutsches Haus*. Brigade Commander Carl Regenspursky, the highest ranking officer in town from about 1900, had disliked the resulting appearance of national bias—which, to *Budivoj*, was no appearance at all. Thus in 1902, he had tried to create a separate casino or gathering place, neither Czech nor German, for officers. Liberal Germans, alarmed, had protested, saying they would never have dedicated municipal funds to building barracks had they known such a thing would come to pass. Taschek had refused to comply with the request for a meeting space on municipal premises. Regenspursky, apparently stalled by a lack of funds, had desisted, and the uncomfortable state of affairs had continued. Only in 1910 did Czechs, Germans, and the corps reach a compromise: a reversion to the utraquism of the 1880s and 1890s. Once again, all officers stationed in town became members of both national casinos. Belonging to neither counted no longer as a viable option.[17]

National boycotts reached new extremes. In 1903, a Czech had been able to write of the "Each to His Own" campaign that "this slogan has actually more or less been carried out in Č. Budějovice. National discipline has taken such deep root that a woman intending to buy an object unavailable in Czech stores looks around on all sides to see whether she is being observed by anyone before stepping into a German shop."[18] At first glance a pronouncement of radical success, this statement actually signals something less. In similar fashion, the publication in 1904 by the National Bohemian Forest Union (NJP) of a new directory stating the national affiliation of every business in town indicates that residents continued to have difficulty classifying some shops nationally. Between 1904 and 1906, the NJP complemented the directory (more than 5,000 copies of which were distributed in 1906 alone) with public lectures and with private meetings. At the private gatherings, calls to boycott were presumably less veiled. Czechs also created a Statistical Office and undertook a comprehensive survey of Czech family purchasing patterns, thus realizing two measures of Zátka's plan in 1892 to cut the threads making up the Czech-German cash nexus.[19]

"Remember that God created you a Czech: thou shalt not betray thy birth! [*neodrod' se!*]" So began a "List of Ten Commandments," printed in connection with a Czech festival during the summer of 1906. The list continued,

  2. We shall not give in.
  3. Czech children belong in Czech schools.
  4. Thou shalt educate thyself.
  5. Thou shalt work.
  6. Thou shalt be nobleminded.
  7. Thou shalt submit to national discipline.
  8. Thou shalt husband thy resources well.
  9. Each to His Own!
  10. Thou shalt mind thy health.[20]

Punishment for violating these commandments, particularly the seventh and the ninth, by no means remained up to a nonnational or multinational Lord in the afterlife. Rather, transgressors faced correction immediately—from a Czech court operating independently of the state, in contravention of its sovereignty, and in support of an activity ruled repeatedly by judges to violate the Fundamental Laws. Details are sketchy, probably because Czechs wished to protect the institution against hostile attention from the authorities. In 1900, Zátka had proposed creating a "national magistrates' court" to enforce the "Each to His Own" campaign. Action apparently had followed. In February 1907, the Young Czech newspaper, *Jihočeské listy*, published a brief summary of penalties that a private court, extant for some time, dealt out to Czechs seen in German businesses. The list included written reprimands, monetary fines (reaching a maximum of twenty crowns), publication of the person's name in the Czech press, and an order of complete social ostracism of the offender by Czechs.[21] At least in theory, Czechs faced a choice between boycotting and being boycotted, between doing damage to German and Budweiser commerce and having no friends.

German boycotts had less bite, for multiple reasons. Cross-class solidarities were weaker than among Czechs; Czechs by now dominated retailing in Budweis/Budějovice, except downtown and in the niche of luxury goods; Taschek, in control of town hall, had less incentive than Zátka to call into being institutions outside the legal framework; and ever more tense relations between Liberals and *völkische* made such an adventure in conspiracy unlikely to function with the smoothness necessary to avoid conviction in the courts. Germans, however, could and did inflict economic harm on their enemies. In May 1907, a cluster of Czech tenants found themselves evicted by German landlords. The Hardtmuth pencil factory, town hall, and most of the other large employers in town continued to contract whenever possible with German suppliers, to discriminate against Czech workers, and to reject the job applications of Czech managers.[22]

The Habsburg authorities did not act as vigorously as they could have against boycotters. Censors ordered newspapers confiscated, but often too late to prevent distribution. Judges imposed fines, but rarely jail sentences. By 1909, the men running the Czech private court in Budweis/Budějovice felt safe enough to stop sending out their letters of reprimand anonymously.[23] In other national matters too, imperial-royal officials acted with restraint, demonstrating a reluctance if not to enforce the law then at least to overstep it. Flying the flag of the German Empire was not illegal. Nor was demanding Czech officers for Czech soldiers, or refusing officers free use of municipal property, or declining to eat a sausage, or giving notice to tenants, or publishing business directories. National activists had considerable experience by now at testing legal limits and at packing the smallest of gestures with meaning.

New laws or decrees could have aided officials in curbing some practices. All legislation, though, required the assent of considerable numbers of nationally minded representatives—and they tended to favor curbing not the practices but the officials. In 1894 and in 1899, for example, members of the Austrian Parliament had passed bills that expanded the freedom of the press. The Badeni crisis, meanwhile, had shown on the one hand that reforms were badly needed and on the other hand that implementing them by circumventing legislators had become dangerous. To quote from a position paper concerning Bohemia that the Koerber government had prepared in 1900: "the government must join in the view that change to the legal status quo, in national matters, should not be brought about through one-sided decrees. It is to the advantage of both races to exchange for the ups and downs of debatable, contested, and cross-cutting demands a firm and secured basis in law. . . . [O]nly the constant power of the law, and not the variable power of the decree, can guarantee the peaceful and uncontested possession of national rights to the parties, and peace to the state."[24]

In the summer of 1902, *Budivoj* had assailed the head of the District Court in Budweis/Budějovice, Hugo Krabetz, for having participated, as an alderman, in Taschek's minting of new burghers. Czechs, the newspaper had claimed, did not deny anyone's right to be national; they only hated "renegades" who "stick with the Germans not out of conviction but for fat baksheesh." But Krabetz, a German who was an imperial-royal official, should have remained neutral in the national struggle. That was what Deacon Maresch/Mareš and a retired army officer on the town council had done, and supposedly what imperial-royal officials who were Czechs did more generally.[25]

Budivoj's argument hints at two factors contributing to Habsburg restraint. First, many imperial-royal officials had national sympathies. Czechs and Germans within the state apparatus may often have canceled one another out. Second, as the Czech and German dimensions to politics grew, the Habsburg one shrank increasingly to enforcing the rule of law—or to be more precise, national fairness. A crackdown on the Czech private court, in the necessary absence of a crackdown on the nonexistent German equivalent, arguably would have reflected only the historically conditioned asymmetries between the two national movements. But to Czechs, such a course of action would have seemed to reflect something else: Habsburg bias. To be sure, the more restrained course that the state took also seemed to reflect bias, against Germans. *Budivoj*'s article, though, offers indirect evidence that omission generated less resentment than did commission. In instance after instance over the years, the newspaper had criticized the Habsburg authorities for tolerating German abuses of municipal power. Now the newspaper praised those authorities in backhanded but sincere fashion, by claiming that a guiding principle of the imperial-royal civil service was to give the least possible offense to both Czechs and Germans. National fairness, when combined with restraint, did yield some sort of Habsburg legitimacy. Then again, in some contests, applying certain kinds of fairness may rule out winning, or even playing. Habsburg leaders intervened in Budweis/Budějovice less and less as contestants for power and more and more as referees—or, on the town council, as aldermen who did not vote.

The Beginnings of Institutional Reform

Late in 1906, five years after elections to the town council had come due, they could finally proceed. Both the Executive Committee of the Bohemian Diet and the Cisleithanian Supreme Administrative Court had confirmed District Captain Křikawa's cancellation of the award of burgher status to 322 men. Administrative judges had also confirmed his decision to let stand the addition of twenty-six men to the first curia. Objections to other names on the electoral rolls had succeeded in enough cases to reduce the number of voters by almost 25 percent. The number of voters, though, still exceeded the total from 1898 by about two-thirds. And despite Taschek's control of the municipal tax ledgers that often served as evidence, his Czech opponents had managed to knock several hundred of his supporters off the rolls, and to add several hundred men very likely to vote Czech.[26]

As in 1898, the Czech movement and the German movement each fielded a united slate in the third curia. Old Czechs, Young Czechs, and Czech National Socials came together, as did Liberal Germans and *völkische*. The Social Democratic Party again had no chance of getting its own candidates elected. This time, it endorsed the Czech ticket, in a protest against German fraud—as well as in an attempt at mending fences with Czechs and at gaining some say in the composition of the Czech candidate list. In order not to spark a dispute within Social Democratic ranks, though, leaders told enfranchised supporters that they stood free to vote as they saw best.

From November 6th through the 8th, as 400 soldiers occupied the *Ringplatz/rynek* with bayonets mounted, the third curia set to the solemn task of registering its collective will at the polls. Turnout, as usual, was high: about 93 percent. During the day, Zátka, Taschek, and Kohn, together with their district and ward bosses, took up posts near the voting stations. Several men, bold enough to use a ballot emblazoned with the symbol of the national movement that their employers opposed, got fired on the spot—and immediately received new jobs on the side for which they had apparently voted. Czechs carried in an invalid, complete with his bed, as well as a man who had just received extreme unction. Through the night, unofficial Czech and German sentries taken from the gymnastics clubs joined gendarmes in standing guard over the urns. Fifteen thousand people gathered on the square at one point to hear Zátka and Czech leaders from Prague speak.

On November 12, the electoral commission announced the results: the Czech slate had won, by a count of the 2,016 votes to 1,914 (amended soon thereafter to 2,012 to 1,916). Jewish voters, Czech leaders later claimed, had voted German in 178 cases and Czech in 26. The German movement had lost by a margin of less than 5 percent—more than half of which could be attributed to the decision made by the Burghers' Brewery, under Czech pressure, to drop sixty-odd employees from the electoral rolls. Despite voters' freedom to put together a ballot with twelve candidates taken from both camps, not a single German had won election in

the third curia. Czechs erupted in delirium and circled the town in a joy-
ous and pointedly peaceful victory parade. Congratulatory telegrams
flooded in from all over Bohemia, from the rest of Cisleithania, and from
abroad. The Czech pencil factory manufactured commemorative pencils.[27]
Germans, even the window repairers among them, found no cause for
celebration.

Czechs had achieved a return in town hall to the status of that of 1865—
under much more national circumstances. For the first time in more than
forty years, Liberal Germans did not control the third curia. For the first
time since 1884, Zátka could serve his town as an alderman. In a victory
speech, he made clear his understanding of Czechness as something objective, inescapable, and even biological. In one sense, he claimed, the five-
man electoral commission had had no Czech members. "But strictly speaking, there were actually three Czechs! There was Taschek, the son of a
native of Bernardice—Czech blood. There was Bitzan, the offspring of
Czech millers, and there was Watzek, whose name is also suspicious."
Taschek, supposedly, represented a completely Slavic type—although he
was infected, like all renegades, with the hereditary disease of "moral insanity." It was Taschek's fresh Czech blood that made him fit to lead the
German community. "Most of our Germans," concluded the quite
wealthy Zátka, "are degenerate. They are afflicted by the curse of
wealth."[28]

Germans, however, for all their supposed degeneracy, Czech blood, and
insanity, retained an iron grip on the remaining two-thirds of the town
council seats. Czechs, without hope of victory in the second curia, boycotted the election to it later in November. In the first curia, the few Czech
voters, together with Schweighofer's *völkisch* faction and with others, lost
to Taschek's Liberals, 53 to 106. Taschek immediately rang the bell to
start the next round: the incumbent Liberal aldermen, before stepping
down, padded their future margin of victory in the first curia by creating
an additional twenty-four honorary burghers. This time, Taschek and
Kohn paid utmost attention to all procedural rules, and disbursed 2,400
crowns from the municipal coffers for the necessary certificates and seals.
The Czech aldermen, not yet installed in office, could not register even a
minority objection to the action. Zátka, under enormous pressure from
more radical Czechs, prepared to object through demonstrations. A repetition of 1898 loomed after all.

Liberal Germans, frightened, lobbied high officials in Vienna for support—without using the 28th Infantry Regiment, presumably. Lobbying,
however, differs from the manipulation of constitutionally guaranteed
rights and of municipal privileges, which was Taschek's *forte*. As in 1902,
he received not support but the advice to start negotiating with his opponents in town for a comprehensive Czech-German settlement. Stuck be-

tween the Czech movement and the Habsburg authorities, Taschek had little choice. At the end of November, he swore before witnesses that Liberals on the town council would create no new voters through irregular means while negotiations were underway with the Czech leadership. Those negotiations started shortly thereafter—in secrecy, at Taschek's insistence.[29] The government had joined Czechs in exerting pressure through channels lacking any formal legal or institutional basis.

Publicly, Taschek signaled his intent to run town hall as he always had. The twelve Czech aldermen, however, refused to attend a single council meeting unless Taschek first granted major concessions. The tactic was a sound one, because without at least twenty-seven aldermen, the Council lacked the quorum necessary to be constituted as the new municipal government. The municipality assessed fines in an effort to coerce three or more Czechs into attending. All refused to budge. Again imperial-royal officials intervened, calling German and Czech representatives to Vienna for talks in the presence of a minister in the spring of 1907. He confronted them with the prospect of bringing down on their heads, through intransigence, the full extralegal weight of Francis Joseph's wrath—and both national sides suddenly yielded. Czech leaders, although frustrated in some of their demands, made a big step toward converting the municipality from a German institution into a binational one. The Czech aldermen won proportional representation on all town council committees, the right to nominate members to the school board, and bilingualism in all mayoral communications. Germans regained some sense of physical safety and won Czech recognition of the legitimacy of the town council. Taschek also succeeded in keeping certain terms to the agreement secret, as well as in continuing the press moratorium regarding the negotiations for a broader settlement.[30] The Habsburg Monarchy won a reprieve from rioting that, if caught up by demagogues, could have shaken the public order well beyond Budweis/Budějovice.

The electoral reform for the Austrian Parliament, meanwhile, had become reality—and the curias were no more. Henceforth, contests for almost all mandates were to be decided according to the principle of "one man, one vote," although the number of voters varied considerably from one district to another. A central Habsburg objective in the electoral reform, as in 1882 and in 1896, was to dilute the national politics of Cisleithania's primarily bourgeois parties by admixing more of the lower classes. As the new prime minister, Max Vladimir Baron von Beck, later wrote, "the emperor was the real driving element in the matter of the electoral reform, and . . . he expected as a consequence of this constitutional reform the replacement of national parties by political ones, and the gradual healing of the principal illness that ailed Austria—national conflict."[31]

One historian, Robert Kann, calls the reform of 1906–7 the most comprehensive one bearing on national conflict in the monarchy to be put into force since the Compromise of 1867.[32] Indeed, in addition to giving the votes of working-class males far more weight, the legislation redrew and shrank electoral districts throughout Cisleithania with an eye to making each district nationally—or at least linguistically—homogeneous: the new boundaries rested in large part on census data regarding the language of daily use. Architects of the reform, in other words, sought to partition the electorate ethnically, and thus to encourage voters to turn their attention from national conflict to economic and other concerns overshadowed by it. Paradoxical as this approach might sound, it made sense to Habsburg policymakers at the time—and for that matter, *mutatis mutandis*, to Social Democrats well before then, and to Bolsheviks during the 1920s and 1930s.[33] More useful here than mapping out those parallels, though, is mapping out the place of the 1907 reform within the development of Cisleithanian constitutional law.

Since 1867, the German movement had gradually shifted from pursuing the administrative and political centralization of Cisleithania to pursuing its partition or federalization into ethnic units. The Czech movement, despite continuing to understand nationhood in primarily ethnic terms, had opposed ethnic federalization, and had advocated historical federalization instead, on the basis of the Bohemian state-rights program. As the Czech movement had become reconciled to the centralist state, however, and as the descendants of the historical Bohemian "nation"—the great landowners—had faded in importance to Czech leaders, they had emphasized their historical federalism less.[34] Habsburg leaders, for their part, had pursued not so much centralization or federalization (whether historical or ethnic) as a workable solution to domestic conflicts. As those conflicts had grown more national, centralist solutions had grown less legitimate. In 1871, Francis Joseph had come to terms with the historical federalists in Bohemia—only to see that settlement vetoed by the Hungarian and German movements within the Habsburg Monarchy, as well as by the German Empire. In 1890, he and other Habsburg leaders had succeeded in switching to a mild form of ethnic federalization without alienating Old Czechs. The Young Czech Party, however, by blocking the legislation, had seized the helm of the Czech movement. In 1897, Prime Minister Badeni had pleased that movement with his decrees—but thereby had united Liberal and *völkisch* Germans in riotously successful opposition. And in 1900, the government had tacked toward the other national side again, by proposing legislation that would have made Bohemia's internal administrative boundaries coincide with its linguistic ones. "[A] linguistic partition," an official position paper had stated, "will contribute to domestic peace. Experience in numerous fields of administration . . . teaches that the separation of the national spheres is indeed the only possible form of peaceful coexistence for the two races." Young Czechs had hesitated and then, goaded by Czech National Socials, had helped to kill the bill.[35]

Unlike the four previous attempts at reconfiguring Bohemian politics since 1867, the 1906–7 electoral reform escaped veto, in large part because of key differences. One was the focus not on the Czech-German conflict but on national conflicts in Cisleithania more generally. Another was the focus not on linguistic policy or on autonomy but on elections— in other words, less on ethnic or historical-territorial nationhood than on citizenship. The redrawing of districts seemed a big step toward ethnic federalization, and thus pleased German leaders. Yet the federalization actually involved territory far less than it did voters: German representatives of the new districts would sit in the old Austrian Parliament, with no new powers and at no new threat to Bohemian state rights. The 1906–7 reform added an ethnic legitimacy to elections without reconfiguring power territorially, and thus could sail between the Scylla and the Charybdis of the Czech and German movements. Social Democratic pressure also played a role. So did arm-twisting and horse trading by the government—such that both the Upper House and the all-important Galician contingent in the Lower House voted, grudgingly, for the legislation. Most German representatives from Bohemia joined in too, once disproportionate reductions in the size of German-speaking districts had made those districts number 55 (42 percent) of the increased Bohemian total of 130, rather than an ethnically fair 48 or 49 (approximately 37 percent).[36]

In May 1907, when men across Cisleithania voted for the first time since 1848 as a single, mass electorate, the more national parties suffered relative losses. Since the elections of 1901, the number of mandates had increased more than 20 percent, to 516. But the Young Czech, Old Czech, Czech National Social, and Czech Agrarian Parties only maintained their control of 60-odd seats. And the more pragmatic, economically minded Agrarians more than quadrupled their share of that total, at the expense of the Young Czech Party from which they had seceded in 1898. German Liberals (or "Progressives"), Populists, Pan-Germans, and Independent Pan-Germans, meanwhile, lost about three dozen of their more than 110 seats. A new German Agrarian Party recovered only some. Many of the rest went to the Social Democratic Party, which fared smashingly well, despite discriminatory districting. The Marxist contingent in the Lower House mushroomed from 10 to 87 (50 in the German wing, and 24 in the Czech). The Christian Social Party, after merging with the Catholic People's Party, topped even that figure, with nearly 100. Gone, together with the curia system, were the less national great landowners.[37] But replacing them were mass parties that emphasized either Marxism or Catholicism, as well as loyalty to the Habsburgs. The national movements seemed to have consented to a reform of the Cisleithanian Parliament such that it ceased to represent feudal estate-like curias, and represented the male citizenry instead—and in the process, made that citizenry or "people" less national.

As in the past, however, the successes of the less national parties came at a price. The Czech wing of the Social Democratic Party, competing head on with Czech parties for votes, issued a manifesto making national demands. More generally, the creation of ethnically homogeneous districts discouraged nonnational or multinational political platforms. Budweis/Budějovice offers an instructive counterexample. The electoral district there was ethnically more mixed than perhaps any other in Bohemia. In the 1900 census, 60.3 percent of Budweis/Budějovice's residents had claimed Czech as their language of daily use, and 39.7 percent German. In such a context, the Czech parties faced strong incentives to join forces behind a single candidate who directed ethnic appeals at the Czech-speaking majority of the voters. The German parties faced strong incentives to field no one—and indeed did, at the same time demanding a separate, ethnic and nonterritorial district. The Social Democratic Party, finally, optimized its chances by running a less national member of its Czech wing. A more Czech candidate would have alienated German-speakers, while a member of the German wing would have alienated part of the core constituency of Czech-speaking Social Democrats—some of whom thought "Better a Czech bourgeois than a German worker." After the election, Zátka claimed that not only German workers had voted for the Social Democrat but more than 750 German bourgeois. They had broken with the Liberal and *völkisch* boycott in the belief, presumably, that "Better a Czech Social Democrat than a Czech." Zátka's man still won, by a tally of 3,315 to 1,921.[38] The more national candidate prevailed easily, and the local Czech and German wings of the Social Democratic Party moved closer together in their pursuit of power. This pattern, however, was the opposite of the larger trend.

In relations between Germans in the German Empire and Germans in Cisleithania, meanwhile, the pattern was not so much institutional reform as the creation of institutional links in the first place. Already in the 1890s, professors and other influential middle-class men in the German Empire had begun to come together in such organizations as the Pan-German League, whose stated goal was "the national consolidation of the entire German people [*Volkstum*] in Central Europe, that is, the eventual establishment of Greater Germany." In 1898, the league had published a short survey of conditions for Germans in the Bohemian lands—and had claimed that in Budweis/Budějovice, Czechs forced German children to attend Czech schools, in an "act of the most brutal sort, of mental national rape." Over the following decade or more, associations and publications in the German Empire concerned with Germans outside of it multiplied. The state's policy of noninterference in the internal affairs of the Habsburg Monarchy did not change. But some citizens of the German Empire donated money so that private German schools could be opened in Austrian communities where German-speakers were too few to qualify for state-funded education in German. In Budweis/Budějovice, increasing numbers of Germans became familiar with the German Empire—through reading, through trips to gymnastics fests and other kinds of congresses, and through encounters in town with politically engaged visitors. In what must have been a riveting experience, many residents "saw" the German Empire for the first time in 1909, on the screen of the new motion-picture theater in town.[39]

The Budweis/Budějovice Compromise

In November 1906, immediately after the Czech victory in the municipal third curia, Zátka had presented a comprehensive proposal for a political settlement in Budweis/Budějovice to Taschek. The German-Habsburg-Czech negotiations that began shortly thereafter took that proposal as a starting point, and wrought multiple changes in the details over the following seven years. Yet the essence of what gradually leaked out to the public under the name of the Budweis/Budějovice Compromise remained the same: the greatest possible separation of Czech politics from German politics in town, through their reconstitution around formal lists, or "cadastres," stating who was German and who was Czech. No such cadastre yet existed. At most, in the census, there existed language data, whose use the law prohibited except at aggregate, anonymous levels. The decision whether to legalize person-by-person use of those data or to create national cadastres in some other way had considerable implications, as will be seen. But those pale in comparison to the implications of creating national cadastres in the first place. The Budweis/Budějovice Compromise moved beyond the 1906–7 electoral reform in partitioning, or federalizing, a citizenry nationally without dividing its territory. To be sure, a far smaller territory was at stake. Yet all residents of that territory, and not only enfranchised males, were to experience a change in political status.

The potentially revolutionary nature of what might be termed national federalization of a personal (as opposed to territorial) sort probably helps to explain why Marxists counted among its strongest proponents. So do the national problems of the Austrian Social Democratic Party. Whatever the ideological and practical imperatives, Karl Renner, a German Social

Democrat in Vienna, had begun advocating such federalization for nationally mixed parts of Cisleithania in the late 1890s. Those parts included
Budweis/Budějovice. "We have two peoples in a community," he wrote
of the town in 1908,

> so we must organize the Germans and Czechs separately, each in a national com-
> munity, each of which exercises jurisdiction over its members, and in all separa-
> ble national matters administers alone. Joint matters of the territory, of course,
> can be taken care of only by a joint representative body proportionately assem-
> bled. . . . [T]here exist in Budweis a German and a Czech national community,
> and next to them a *political community* formed on the basis of proportional
> representation. No matter how surprising this form might be at first glance—is
> it not *in fact* so? Is this not the perfectly appropriate juridical expression of actual
> social and national relations in Budweis?[40]

National federalization of a personal sort did in fact promise to express
some actual relations. But it also promised to create new ones. Renner was
correct in noting of Cisleithania that

> work passbooks are scribbled full with relevant qualities of citizens such as
> "pointed nose," or "confession Roman Catholic." Every baptismal certificate
> tells us the most remarkable things about the citizen. Everything interests the
> state, and only the fact that for us [Social Democrats] is the most important—
> national affiliation—is not a juridically relevant, constituent marker of the indi-
> vidual. Which state official is German and which Czech? Certification in this
> matter is issued by—the bourgeois political party.

Yet in an aside, Renner conceded of Cisleithania's inhabitants that "very
many are amphibians, as one has called it jokingly."[41] This nod in the
direction of Budweisers and of nonnational Habsburg loyalists more generally was correct, too—and no joking matter. His characterization of personal federalization as a mere adjustment of the law to reality probably
reflects wishful national thinking, as well as an attempt at promoting enactment of the reform by downplaying its significance.

For class-based reasons explained later, Social Democrats actually opposed Zátka's proposal on important specifics. Habsburg leaders also had
reservations—yet backed the larger idea. Indeed, the Budweis/Budějovice
Compromise had company, not only in the 1906–7 electoral reform. In
1905, German-Habsburg-Czech negotiations had resulted in a national
partition of electorates in the whole of Moravia—whose population was
about 2.5 million. A similar compromise came into force in the Bukovina,
a small crownland in the east of Cisleithania, in 1910. Still another compromise, Polish-Habsburg-Ruthenian, stood on the verge of completion
in Galicia in 1914. All addressed variants on the same problem. How,
within a Habsburg framework, could one increase the national legitimacy

of the state? On the one hand, speakers of different languages were inter-mingled enough to raise serious obstacles to territorial federalization of an ethnic sort. On the other hand, in territory after territory, the weaker national movement or movements now wielded enough power to rule out a repetition of 1867, when Habsburg and Hungarian leaders had agreed on a territorial federalization of a historical sort. Together, the "little com-promises" after the turn of the century signaled hope at the highest level that the nonterritorial approach would make possible the political course represented by the failed Bohemian Compromise of 1890, as well as by additional attempts at political settlement in the past: to pursue domestic peace by turning Cisleithania, the nonnational half of the Habsburg Mon-archy, into a multinational state.

More hesitant about the Budweis/Budějovice Compromise than Habs-burg leaders were Liberal ones. Having received a second draft of Zátka's proposal after talks during 1908, Taschek failed to respond until March 1910. He seems not to have opposed the proposal in principle, however, and to have been playing only for time. In 1907, Liberal German aldermen had voted to transfer the ownership of German-language school buildings from the municipality to German associations. Czechs had challenged the legality of the act, and had triumphed in court. While Taschek delayed responding to Zátka's revised version of the Compromise, Liberal Ger-mans appealed the schools case, and lost—and then appealed and lost again. Other attempts at transferring municipal property to German asso-ciations turned out better for Taschek. He was disengaging his political machine from the municipal government, and reassembling as much of that machine as possible in less public settings.[42] He had strong incentives to carry out his retreat to a position of greater equality with Czechs no more quickly than proved absolutely necessary.

Some Czech leaders had reservations about personal federalization. But the existing political order, which promised to keep the Czech movement the local underdog for many years to come, pushed the Czech parties toward Zátka's position. He could thus keep up the pressure on his na-tional opponent. In February 1908, the Bohemian Diet seat in town, held by Liberal Germans for decades, fell to Zátka. That fall, local Czechs joined Czechs and other Slavs across Cisleithania in intimidating Germans by protesting heftily against the annexation to the Habsburg Monarchy of Bosnia and Herzegovina (administered by imperial-royal authorities since 1878, but formally still Ottoman territories). In 1910, Czech lawyers filed nearly 6,000 objections to the electoral rolls drawn up by town hall for the next municipal elections. No one in the know doubted that Liberal Germans would maintain their control of the first and second curias, or that the Czech movement would repeat its victory in the third, once all the objections had been resolved and the elections could proceed. The question, though, was whether those elections would be accompanied by Czech riots. During 1911, residents learned that the proportion of German-speakers in the 1910 census had fallen slightly, to 38.2 percent. In elections to the Austrian Parliament, the Czech movement in town increased its 1907 margin of victory over Germans and over Social Democrats—whose all-Austrian party was just splitting definitively into separate, national parties.[43]

In 1912, the Liberal German leadership shifted gears, and accelerated toward a new definition of the German community in town as a shrinking but legally constituted and protected minority. Taschek planted positive stories about the Compromise in friendly periodicals, in an effort to bring his public around to the new position. *Deutsche Erde* [*German Earth*], for example, a journal published in the German Empire, informed readers that

> in recent months, with [Taschek's] assistance, a compromise has been agreed upon with the Czechs. It will give the Germans permanent safeguards against a Czech majority, even in the event that the Germans should prove incapable of maintaining their current majority in the town council and in other autonomous bodies. The Germans of the Budweis language island are to be spared the fate of their national comrades in Prague and in Pilsen.[44]

That fall, the Czech and the German sides to the negotiations reached agreement on all points. The ironing out of technical objections by the Ministry of the Interior consumed another year. Then, in November 1913, a month after the last legal obstacles to holding municipal elections had been cleared away, the Budweis/Budějovice settlement suddenly made headlines all over Austria. Everything was set for a last major push to make the Compromise a reality.

Late in 1913, Taschek and Zátka convened separate strings of meetings in order to "sell" the Compromise in town. Czech National Socials and German *völkische* raised strong objections. So did both Social Democratic Parties. But at each meeting, which either Zátka or Taschek had choreographed carefully, the yeas prevailed. In February 1914, the town council voted unanimously in favor of the settlement—which took the form of three bills slated for passage into law by the Bohemian Diet. By May, all that remained was for the diet to vote, and for Francis Joseph to sanction the new legislation.[45]

The Czech and German cadastres at the heart of the Compromise were to comprise public bodies that, together, had all residents (as well as all firms that paid a direct state tax in town) as registered members. Each alderman was to be elected by the enfranchised members of either one cadastre or the other. Members of one cadastre, in other words, were not to be allowed to vote for candidates and members of the other cadastre. How many of the thirty-six town council seats each cadastre elected was to depend on the national ratio within the three municipal curias—after the reassignment of all burghers and honorary burghers to the curia (if any) for which they qualified on the basis only of residence and of tax payments or education. Both Czech and German leaders seem to have expected that the electoral rolls finalized in 1913 would yield a national ratio of 56:44, meaning twenty Czech aldermen and sixteen German ones. The ratio of Czechs to Germans at every rank within the municipal civil service, as well as of municipal contracts awarded to Czech or German local businesses, was to follow the national ratio within the town council. Central parts of the settlement, in other words, were to rest not on an ethnic, quantitative ratio—which the "language of daily use" data in the 1910 census placed at roughly 62:38—but on the more historical-cultural, qualitative ratio of the Czech middle and upper classes to the German ones.

According to the Compromise, municipal subsidies to private associations were to require the approval of a majority of both national factions in the town council. Each faction, though, was to be able to allocate funds from a separate budget, funded by members of the relevant cadastre through a surcharge on municipal taxes, not to exceed 10 percent. An additional surcharge was to be levied for the purpose of funding the public school system, which now was to be divided into a German and a Czech district. The municipality, finally, was to become utraquist in all its public dealings.[46] No longer were Czechs and Germans to compete in elections, in school enrollment, or in other classic venues. Nationhood in town was to comprise a pair of juridically defined, mutually exclusive, and jointly exhaustive membership groups, with membership serving as an attachment point for suffrage, taxation, and additional significant rights or obligations. Citizenship was to gain a national layer. Germanness and Czechness were to become symmetrical in their relationship to the Habsburg state.[47]

Neither national nor Habsburg leaders, however, were to be the ones deciding who belonged to which cadastre. Rather, almost all adult male residents were to make the decision for themselves, while fathers were to make the decision for their minor children, and each husband was to decide for his wife. To be sure, the decision was to be permanent, or nearly so. Only once in a lifetime, under specific circumstances (within one year of reaching legal majority or of becoming a widow, for example, or at any time, provided both cadastres consented), were residents to be able to switch from one cadastre to the other.

Only in two kinds of cases were the national movements or imperial-royal officials to have the power to assign individuals to one of the cadastres. In the first case, any resident who could be shown to have a nationality but who failed to choose a cadastre (or whose legal guardian failed to do so), was to be assigned to one by a commission. Its members were to be appointed in equal measure by the Czech and by the German aldermen. They were to determine the person's nationality through an "inquiry" [šetření], for which the Compromise specified no criteria.[48] Because individuals assigned to one of the cadastres had the right to switch to the other, however, the effect was not so much to infringe on the right of self-designation as to make the exercise of that right obligatory. No one was to be allowed to belong to neither cadastre. Very few people, furthermore, were to be allowed to belong to both: only residents who succeeded in convincing the commission that they had no nationality at all, as well as residents whose nationality was Slovene, Polish, Italian, French, or anything other than German or Czech. (The enfranchised among such people, though, were to have no choice between ballots, and were to be given only the ballot of the cadastre that commanded a majority in the relevant curia.) Soldiers on active duty, finally, in keeping with their blanket disenfranchisement, were to be *required* to belong to both cadastres—in what might be termed ascription of a negative sort.

In the second case, the state was to have the power to reassign residents who could be shown to have a nationality, but who had registered or been registered—presumably under political pressure or with plans to sow discord within enemy ranks—as members of the other national cadastre. Representatives of either cadastre were to have the right to request that the district captainship consider reassigning someone. Upon receiving such a request, imperial-royal officials were to hold a hearing, at which they would ask the person whose nationality stood under challenge whether his or her declaration had been truthful. "For purposes of cadastral registration," the Compromise stipulated, "the statement given at the hearing by the person challenged is as a rule . . . decisive." Only if the person made unclear statements, failed to appear, or lacked the right, as a dependent, to self-declaration was the district captainship to pursue the matter further:

> It is the obligation of [the district captainship] to investigate and to examine in detail the personal and family circumstances of the person challenged, and to determine his nationality on the basis of telling characteristics—for which purpose let there be taken into consideration those actions from the private, social, and public life of the person challenged that seem to give credible and genuine testimony of his national affiliation. Then the authorities will render a decision to register the person challenged in one or in both of the cadastres.

As in the first case, ethnic criteria were to be neither required nor banned. Yet in most instances, imperial-royal officials were to be prevented from using *any* criteria to overturn self-declaration. What is more, with only minor exceptions, every cadastral choice that a person made, whether for himself or for his dependents, was to become permanently immune to challenge thirty days after being registered.[49]

That the Budweis/Budějovice Compromise denied the national movements any significant control over cadastral membership contradicts their own rhetoric, yet makes considerable sense. After all, Czech and German leaders understood nationhood in varied, inconsistent, and often vague ways. Yet if Czechness and Germanness were to mesh, rather than to clash, with Cisleithanian citizenship, they had to be defined precisely, in mutually exclusive and jointly exhaustive fashion. Perhaps more striking is that the Compromise denied almost any powers of ascription to the Habsburg authorities, too. Here experiences acquired in the implementation of the Moravian Compromise of 1905 played an important role. The Moravian agreement had also created national cadastres, primarily through self-declaration. Provisions for challenging a person's cadastral choice, though, as well as the powers of imperial-royal officials to resolve such disputes, were far more broad than in the Budweis/Budějovice Compromise. The result had been an invasion of privacy that many observers found troubling. As Edmund Bernatzik, a prominent jurist, had written in 1910, a conscientious effort at objective ascription all too often involved inquiring into the books a person read, the conversations he had, and much more. "There loom trials all too reminiscent of the tribunals of the Inquisition. At stake here, after all, is the ascertainment of convictions!"[50] Habsburg leaders seem to have agreed with Bernatzik, and to have decided to reduce ascription in the Budweis/Budějovice Compromise to an absolute minimum.

Zátka agreed too, at least with his head. In an interview during the summer of 1918, he explained the Budweis/Budějovice Compromise as follows. "The basic idea was quite simply this: whoever possesses the vote or is required to attend school must declare to which nation he belongs. That, incidentally, was always a difficult question ([see] Bernatzik: *Ueber nationale Matrikeln*). It is a matter for the individual to declare to which nation he belongs." In that same interview, however, Zátka contradicted himself by calling Josef Taschek the "son of a Czech."[51] Both Anton Franz Taschek and his son Josef, despite their German convictions, counted in Zátka's heart as Czechs, on ethnic grounds.

In 1910, a draft of the Budweis/Budějovice Compromise approved by both Zátka and Taschek had proposed to make cadastral membership a function of the "language of daily use" that people declared in the census at the end of that year. The Ministry of the Interior, however, had vetoed the idea, and thereby had forced the national movements to abandon an attempt at requiring that nationality be self-declared and ethnic at the same time.[52] For children and for decisions about their schooling, meanwhile, Zátka had originally proposed a variant on the approach taken in the Moravian Compromise. After 1905, children in Moravia were generally assigned to a school system on the basis of cadastral membership. But they were also required, "as a rule," to know the language used for instruction in that system before entering it. Zátka had sought to drop the qualifying phrase "as a rule," and thus to make language, or ethnicity, trump cadastral membership in Budweis/Budějovice when the two clashed. Yet the Ministry of the Interior, moving in the opposite direction, had insisted that membership alone determine whether a child would attend a Czech-language school or a German-language one. In Moravia, experience had shown that fluency in a language was difficult to define, and that including it as a criterion opened the door to disputes that "expose the small child, completely unaccustomed to intercourse with adults, to cumbersome and repeated examinations in the presence of political representatives."[53]

By the time any child finishes a school, he or she is necessarily fluent in its language. The linking of schools to cadastres thus promised to render two already quite ethnic nationhoods still more ethnic over time. In Budweis/Budějovice, however, Habsburg leaders insisted on linking schools with cadastres in such a way that the ethnicity of a young adult would probably coincide only in the great majority of cases with his or her ethnicity as a child, while coinciding in all cases with his or her registered nationality. (Many residents, of course, were biethnic.) The Compromise promised to help make Czech and German nationhood slightly more ethnic, but in such a way that sometimes ethnicity would accommodate to nationality rather than vice versa.

Nothing in the Budweis/Budějovice Compromise prevented residents from assigning themselves and their dependents to this or that cadastre on the basis of ethnic criteria. Widespread use of ethnic criteria was even quite likely, given the history of German and Czech nationhood. Indeed, another amendment to Zátka's original proposal promised to reduce the role of financial criteria, and thus indirectly to strengthen the role of ethnic ones. In 1906, Zátka had proposed that the Czech schooling surcharge on municipal taxes be allowed to range higher than the German one. If members of the German cadastre had ended up paying a surcharge of 7 percent, for example, members of the Czech cadastre might have been required to pay as much as 9 percent. The objective was to prevent the weaker Czech tax base from causing Czech schools to have significantly less money per student. The version of the Compromise ready for ratification in 1914, however, specified that the schooling surcharge in each cadastre had to be the same. Any shortfall in the school budget of the less wealthy cadastre was to be made good by the Bohemian Diet, from its general revenues. In 1918, Zátka judged this solution superior to his own—which might have induced "a mass of people to have themselves transferred to the other cadastre, for fear of higher taxes."[54] Who had prompted this amendment remains unclear. Perhaps Czech critics of Zátka had harped on the inequality so much as to endanger the Compromise as a whole. Perhaps Zátka himself had come to have increased doubts about how steadfastly Czech many residents were.

Whoever had initiated the amendment, Habsburg leaders did not veto it. Their accommodation, rather than contradicting the anti-ascriptive and nonethnic provisions sketched out in the previous paragraphs, fits into a larger pattern. In the Budweis/Budějovice Compromise, Habsburg leaders sought to block ethnic understandings of nationhood only to the extent that such understandings seemed incompatible with the goal of reducing national strife in town by dividing politics into German and Czech spheres in legitimate, stable, and constitutional fashion. To eliminate a financial incentive to choose one cadastre over the other, for example, was to render choices more legitimate—and perhaps more ethnic. To place tight limits on straddling cadastres or switching between them, and to make school enrollment hinge not on language but on cadastral membership, was to make the cadastres more stable—and perhaps less ethnic in the short-term but more ethnic in the long. To deny the national movements any substantial role in assigning individuals to cadastres was to avoid potentially delegitimizing and destabilizing arguments between German and Czech leaders who, using different definitions of ethnicity, laid claim to one and the same residents. To deny the national movements the right to exclude anyone was to prevent Czechs and *völkische* from shoving Jews and perhaps other people into a disenfranchised pariah class, and thus to avoid a violation of the Fundamental Laws.[55]

The price that Habsburg leaders agreed to pay for the prospect of national peace in Budweis/Budějovice was high. Nonnational Cisleithania was to become binational in town, and indeed binational*izing*—in the sense of pushing residents more insistently and consistently than ever before to join one "nation" or another. The Moravian and Bukovinan Compromises, as well as the failed Bohemian Compromise of 1890, each permitted great landowners and high-ranking religious figures to stand outside and above the national camps, as powerful guardians of more-than-national interests. Such men, those three compromises stipulated, could vote on all issues in the relevant diet. A national representative, in contrast, could vote only on issues defined in advance as affecting either his "nation" or the territory as a whole. The other little compromises thus permitted a bilateral, national/more-than-national resolution of issues understood as concerning only one of the "nations," and a multilateral resolution of other issues. But in the case of Budweis/Budějovice, to have turned Church officials in town or aristocrats in the surrounding countryside into representatives of more-than-national interests on the town council would have violated the existing constitutional framework for municipal politics in all Cisleithania. And the idea of filling out the Czech-Habsburg-German triad in town with a nonnational cadastre of a mass nature—a cadastre of Budweisers, for example—met with opposition from all three parties to the negotiations. Rather, the district captain and his staff were to fill out the triad, by exercising administrative oversight over a completely nationalized municipal politics. Even the district captain himself was to be pushed to join one cadastre or the other—or to face, like everyone else, a loss of voting rights, a fine of up to 200 crowns, and/ or imprisonment for up to ten days.[56] Only members of the military were to be exempted, and indeed excluded, from the new national imperative in town. The state institution on which the enforcement of Budweis/ Budějovice's binationalization ultimately rested, in other words, was to remain nonnational. Outside town, so was the imperial-royal civil service, and for that matter, Francis Joseph.

National leaders joined Habsburg officials in placing limits on the transformation in the legitimacy of the state. At no point do Zátka and Taschek seem to have questioned the triadic nature of the negotiations over the Compromise, or to have acted as anything but loyal Cisleithanian citizens and Habsburg subjects. The two men perhaps saw advantages in preserving a Habsburg Cisleithania, umbrella-like, over the Czech and German "nations"—or lacked either the ability or the will to imagine a nationally partisan state as a replacement. Founding such a state, besides pushing Germans and Czechs farther apart, would have made national and Habsburg loyalties incompatible. The Compromise, in contrast, seemed to offer a way to separate Czechs and Germans without causing that frontal clash within many hearts.

The Compromise amounted simultaneously to a gain for nationhood (taken generically) vis-à-vis nonnational forms of legitimacy and to a loss of control over town hall for German Liberals. Yet that specifically national loss contained a smaller gain, just as the corresponding Czech gain contained a smaller loss: the use not of ethnic quantity but of historical-cultural quality in determining Czech-German ratios. Here, within a larger pattern of Zátka prevailing over Taschek, Taschek prevailed over Zátka. Or to view the matter from another perspective, the male bourgeois of both national movements prevailed, with assistance from Habsburg leaders, over women and over the lower classes. The Compromise was to split the town council electorate into German and Czech sections without enlarging it. Bourgeois Czechs, writes Pieter Judson, "who might have supported franchise reforms as the only way to gain a political majority, were effectively turned away from this strategy by [a compromise] that gave them a nationalist majority while leaving most Czechs without a vote."[57]

The Czech and German movements had agreed with Habsburg leaders to partition municipal politics nationally. As the central measure of fairness or equality, the three parties had settled on the curia system. That measure worked to the disadvantage above all of the poor and of Social Democracy, and to the advantage above all of German Liberals—whose historical-cultural understanding of nationhood the curias reflected. At the same time, both Czechs and Germans were to stand free to continue many of their ethnic practices. Cisleithanian citizenship, or membership in the Habsburg state, was to gain a national, German or Czech layer; the civic legitimacy of the Habsburg state was to become binational. Germanness and Czechness, though, were not to become civic. Rather, they were to become equidistant from the state. How well could this remarkably complex settlement have worked? On the one hand, it embodied a principle of "separate and equal." On the other hand, the Budweis/Budějovice Compromise embodied separate and only partly compatible principles—historical-cultural, ethnic, and civic—of equality. The settlement promised, in other words, to make municipal elections, schools, and commerce entirely national, but necessarily defined Czechness and Germanness in a way with which many Czechs and Germans disagreed. The Compromise was characterized by deep structural flaws that reflected the history of the German-Habsburg-Czech contest.

War

In 1914, Bohemia had no legislature to approve the Budweis/Budějovice Compromise. Crippled by the obstruction of German representatives, the diet had proven incapable of passing a budget in 1913, and had been dissolved by Francis Joseph in July. Since then, governance in the kingdom had proceeded by decree. Then fate intervened, imposing a far larger crisis atop the Bohemian one. On Sunday, 28 June 1914, a Serb fanatic assassinated Archduke Francis Ferdinand, heir to the Habsburg thrones, in the Bosnian capital of Sarajevo. News of the event reached Budweis/Budějovice that evening, while a fund-raising event was in full swing in the garden of the Czech Shareholders' Brewery. The band immediately stopped playing. A month later, in a proclamation addressed "To My peoples" [*An Meine Völker/Mým národům*], the emperor-king made public his decision to wage war on Serbia. "Criminal evil-doings reach across the border," read newspapers and placards across the Habsburg Monarchy,

> in order to unsettle the loyalty to dynasty and to fatherland of the people to whom, in paternal love, I devote My full care, as well as in order to lead the young astray and to incite them to criminal acts of madness and high treason. . . . In this grave hour, I am fully aware of the entire range of implications

of My decision, and of My responsibility before the Almighty. I have examined
and considered everything. With a clear conscience, I enter upon the course to
which duty directs Me.

To trusted advisers, Francis Joseph explained his decision in more pessi-
mistic terms: "If the Monarchy is to perish, then at least it shall perish
honorably."[58] Thus did the Great War begin.

War changed national activity in Budweis/Budějovice radically. Many
of the most energetic Czechs and Germans, young and male, departed for
the front. Strict limitations on public gatherings and on the press, as well
as a suspension of all electoral politics, tied the hands of national leaders.
The Army requisitioned both the *Beseda* and the *Deutsches Haus*.[59] The
new conditions, as well as the fog of war and postwar political upheavals
that encouraged wholesale reworkings of the past, make a reliable reconstitution of Czech and German nationhood between 1914 and 1918 hard.
One example, pursued in some detail, illustrates this point.

On April 3, 1915, when the Russian Army launched an attack near
Zborów in Galicia, many soldiers in two batallions of the 28th Infantry
Regiment surrendered without a struggle. In a highly unusual step, the
Habsburg High Command thereupon dissolved the regiment. Contributing to this decision, perhaps, was fierce sentiment against Slavs among
some Habsburg generals, who entertained the almost paranoid suspicion
that Czech and other Slavic citizens of the monarchy sympathized with
the Slavic foe, Serbia and Russia.[60] Had the "twenty-eighters," whose
involvement in Budweis/Budějovice's Sausage Affair in 1905 was discussed earlier in this chapter, in fact betrayed their country, seeing in Russia better prospects for the Czech cause?

Many Germans did interpret the incident as a nationally motivated mass
desertion. And many Czechs, especially after the war, embraced a mirror
image of the German interpretation. In 1930, a Herr Mayer, traveling
from Linz (in the Republic of Austria) to Dresden (in Germany), made
disparaging remarks about the 28th Infantry Regiment while *en route*
through Bohemia, in the Habsburg successor state of Czechoslovakia.
That country officially and systematically disparaged most aspects of the
former Habsburg Monarchy. The 28th Infantry Regiment, however, was
different. Seeing in the soldiers' supposed desertion a break with the
Habsburg past, the new state had honored the regiment by founding it
anew. Herr Mayer was hauled from the train in Prague and tossed in jail
for insulting the army of Czechoslovakia—by discussing an event that had
occurred three years before the country came into existence.[61]

In 1923, a Czech book appeared: *The Fortunes of the Good Soldier Švejk
in the World War*. Jaroslav Hašek, the author, found himself drafted not
into the 28th Infantry Regiment but into another based in Budweis/Bu-

dějovice, the 91st, at the beginning of 1915. In September, on the Russian front, he became a prisoner of war. Hašek's novel might be understood as highly mythologized autobiography. Švejk, the hero, finds himself transferred early in 1915 from a cushy posting in Prague to a unit of the 91st Regiment that is scheduled to depart soon from Budweis/Budějovice for the front. While going to great lengths to avoid appearing in town as ordered, Švejk claims—even to other Czech deserters and to Czech villagers anxious to help him hide—that he is doing his witless best to report for duty. Habsburg officers fail to see that his idiocy, unlike their own, is a mere act, and instead of having him shot, merely throw him in jail for a few days. There, protected by thick walls from all bullets, whether enemy or Habsburg, Švejk demonstrates his patriotism by bellowing the Austrian imperial anthem.

Before long, Švejk and his unit begin a long and halting journey to the Russian front. Along the way, they learn about the Russian capture of the two battalions of the 28th Regiment. Indeed, the soldiers are read official orders by Francis Joseph and by Archduke Joseph Ferdinand that, in dissolving the 28th, condemn it in wild language for Czech treachery. (Hašek, in other words, "reproduces" not the real orders but products of his national imagination.) At the end of the book, Švejk manages to get himself taken prisoner—by Hungarian-speaking Habsburg troops, which he deceives by donning a Russian uniform and by concealing his knowledge of German.[62] Hašek's message is clear: he and many other ordinary Czechs made common but atomized cause against the monarchy with the patriotic deserters of the 28th Regiment (patriotic, that is, in a future-oriented, Czechoslovak sense). He and his unspoken allies did so with such cunning, though, that the incompetent army command never noticed. That message, politically useful both to the new Czechoslovak state and to its recently Cisleithanian citizens, helps to explain the enormous and lasting popularity of *The Good Soldier Švejk* in Bohemia.

Neither Herr Mayer nor Hašek had any detailed information about what had happened near Zborów on April 3, 1915. The Army High Command, in contrast, immediately commissioned an investigation. The findings, submitted in May, did cite Czech sentiments within the regiment, but laid more blame on inexperienced officers, who had maintained scandalously lax discipline. What, then, had really happened? Many things. As a Czech (not a member of the 28th Infantry Regiment) conceded in his own postwar reminiscences, sentiments and motivations in Budweis/Budějovice had covered a wide range:

> There were many who suffered spiritually in Austrian uniform. On the other hand, there were many as well who succeeded in accommodating themselves quickly, and lent themselves quite obediently to the frightful Austrian military

machine. Indeed, they did more than was demanded of them. It came as a painful surprise when even those whom we had known before the war as defiant
Czechs turned like weathervanes in the wind.[63]

Some of the twenty-eighters who had waved a white flag on April 3 probably had done so for national and anti-Habsburg reasons. Others, though,
had probably acted in a blur of undisciplined group dynamics and terror.
Some soldiers who fell in the war no doubt died for Francis Joseph rather
than for a national cause, and others for the reverse—and still others for
both, or for neither.

Far more simple were the implications for the Czech movement of the
Habsburg Monarchy's increasingly subordinate relationship to the German Empire. Both in Galicia and in Serbia during 1915, Habsburg troops
proved unable to regain the initiative without assistance from their major
ally. The following June, a major Russian offensive made further help from
the German Empire necessary. By the end of the summer, the Habsburg
Monarchy had submitted to the creation of a joint military High Command for the Central Powers. Meanwhile, Erich von Falkenhayn, Chief of
the German General Staff, had been ousted by Paul von Hindenburg and
by Erich von Ludendorff. They quickly pushed their country far down the
path toward military dictatorship.[64] For some months, the German Empire had been pressing its ally to accept a plan for carving a pseudo-inde-
pendent Poland out of territories captured from Russia. Some strategists
thought that many men there would volunteer to fight against the Tsar
once promised even a puppet nation-state. Now Hindenburg and Ludendorff, chasing this chimera of fresh cannon fodder, all but forced the Habsburg Monarchy to accept the plan—which the Two Emperors' Manifesto
of November 5, 1916 made public. Simultaneously, however, Francis Joseph attempted to salvage a solution advanced by his own advisers: to
annex the territories to the monarchy, to combine them with Galicia into
a sort of Habsburg Poland, and to pursue a political alliance within Cisleithania with German parties—whose weight would increase through the
subtraction from Cisleithania of Galicia. As ominous as this radical course
looked from Czech perspectives, the alternative looked worse still. Hindenburg reacted to Francis Joseph's effort at bending the agreement dictated to him from abroad by hammering, in a telegram to the Chancellor
of the German Empire on November 7, for an end to the Bismarckian
policy of noninterference in the internal affairs of the Habsburg Monarchy.[65]

"The world war has prevented continued progress of the negotiations
[regarding the Budweis/Budějovice Compromise]," stated a leading
Czech newspaper in Prague on November 15. "But the pact, as far as we
know, has not become a 'wave of the past,' . . . We believe that after the

war it will resurface from the government archive."[66] The hesitant phrasing reflects how drastically expectations had changed by the tenth anniversary of Zátka's original proposal. A settlement that had promised to cushion a German loss of power and to limit a corresponding Czech gain now promised, if implemented, to cushion a *Czech* loss and to limit a *German* gain. Yet the cushion remained unchanged, while the weight had increased a thousandfold. If the Central Powers won the war, German leaders in Berlin, in Budweis/Budějovice, and elsewhere could be expected to force open a new, emphatically German epoch in Bohemian politics. Czech leaders, as long as they continued to assume that the war would indeed end in "victory," could base their very different vision of the future only on wishful "knowing" and "believing" that the Compromise, among other things, would resurface.

The spirit of the times, however, favored resurfacing far less than burying. Since the beginning of November, Francis Joseph had not been feeling well. On the 21st, after rising as usual at half past three in the morning and after spending the day working—this time with difficulty—at his desk, the 86-year-old mortal died quickly and peacefully in the evening. Emperor-king since 1848, he was the only ruler under whom the vast majority of Budweis/Budějovice's residents had ever lived. Europe lost its "last monarch of the old school," as he had once described himself to Theodore Roosevelt. In another sign that revolutionary changes were coming, the Cisleithanian prime minister, Karl Count von Stürgkh, had been assassinated precisely a month previously—by the son of Viktor Adler, the Social Democratic leader. Francis Joseph's successor, his great-nephew Charles, chose as a replacement for Stürgkh a Bohemian aristocrat who attempted to align the state apparatus with the German movement in Bohemian politics. Meanwhile, the killing on the battlefields ground on. So did the reduction of the Habsburg Monarchy to a mere satellite of the German Empire—a process evident to all by May 1918, when the new emperor-king traveled to the military headquarters of his ally in order to suffer the humiliation of a military and economic union of the two countries.[67]

More important, the entry of the United States into the war contributed mightily (more, for example, than the collapse of tsarist Russia) to deciding the outcome: not victory for the Central Powers, and not a negotiated peace, but defeat. Czech prospects suddenly shone brightly. This dynamic—a German-Czech seesaw between ambition and fear—hinged on a basic fact by 1916, regardless of which side won the war. The Habsburg leadership that, together with the German and Czech movements, framed politics in Budweis/Budějovice and in the Bohemian lands was probably going to disappear, and at the very least was going to emerge from the fighting radically weakened. Helping to fill the vacuum and to reframe

Bohemian politics would be self-serving foreign powers. Budweis/Budě-
jovice's place within European and even global political constellations was
going to shift. So was the place of Czech and German nationhood within
states.

Before the war, Zátka and Taschek had realized that defining nationhood legally in terms of individual membership could serve both national
movements in their pursuit of power within a Habsburg context—but that
a definition that denied individuals national choice could not. After the
war, Zátka and other Czech leaders came to power, in the absence of the
Habsburgs and against, rather than together with, German leaders. Bud-
weis/Budějovice became part of a state that was neither nonnational nor
evenly multinational. Rather, it was national primarily in a Czech sense,
although inhabited by many non-Czechs. In this new context, Czech leaders rejected cadastres. Riding the national seesaw upward, Czechoslovak
governments left the Budweis/Budějovice Compromise in Habsburg ar-
chives, and canceled the Moravian Compromise of 1905. Nationhood-as-
membership dropped back to the level of unsubstantiated rhetoric.

Whatever justifications for this change in course might have been used,
its underlying cause is clear: the collapse of the triadic structure to politics
in the Bohemian lands. The effect is clear, too. By refusing to anchor talk
of membership in legal code, Czech leaders gained better hopes of turning
their good luck in the war into a lasting victory in the Czech-German
struggle. They, like French leaders in Alsace-Lorraine, could now use the
vast powers of the state to persuade—or to create the appearance of having
persuaded—Germans to switch to the winning side. National cadastres,
far from promoting this process, would have hindered it. Czechoslovakia,
though, was smaller than France, and even dependent on it. Czech leaders,
in driving their end of the Bohemian national seesaw higher, rode a European trend. They also contributed, in small fashion, to the emergence of
a huge countervailing force that eventually destroyed Czechoslovakia and
much, much more: Nazi Germany.

Five

Bohemian Politics Reframed, 1918–1945

Now then, the pointer on the scales
That so carefully I held in balance
You have tipped with raw impatience.
They sway, and bloodied men fall, undead,
From both pans onto a world filled with dread.
  —*Rudolf of Habsburg, in Franz Grillparzer,* Ein
  Bruderzwist in Habsburg *(1872)*

[I]n struggles for succession, the foreigner is sum-
moned; this is how it has been in the past, and
how it must be. Either one side calls him in or the
other, or he comes of his own will, when the sides
have mauled one another to the point of collapse.
In such conflicts, the banner of St. Wenceslas
helps one not at all, because he is the saint of
both sides, and each places hope in him and in-
vokes him. He does not listen, however, and God
and all the saints turn away from such conflicts,
damning them, because these are conflicts among
brothers. When God assists the cause of right in
such conflicts, He does so through bitterness and
privation, so that we might secure the cause of
right in future from recklessness.
  —*Bolemil, in Adalbert Stifter,* Witiko *(1867)*

Between about the 1890s and the Great War, Bohemian politics had featured a triadic structure. Proportions and dimensions had shifted mark-
edly over time, and new movements phrasing their claims in terms of class,
religion, or race had emerged. Yet the Czech movement, the German
movement, and the Habsburg state had remained the principal contestants, and their power had come to be legitimized in ever more national
terms. After the Great War, the Habsburg state vanished—and the struggle for the Habsburg succession continued. In vying for control over the
state, the German and Czech movements contributed to reframing Bohemian politics dramatically, not once but four times in less than thirty years.

The first reframing, in 1918–19, might be summarized as Czech democratic dominance. The second, during the early 1930s, left Czechs in power, but saw the reopening of Bohemian politics into a triad, through the entry of a foreigner: Nazi Germany. Then came the Nazi takeover, in 1938–39. This chapter narrates those reframings, and leaves the fourth and final one, after the Second World War, for the book's conclusion.

The first two reframings were remarkably peaceful, and the last two shockingly bloody. Throughout, contexts became ever less local and ever more global, and Czechness and Germanness continued to change. Now, though, the political spectrum within each national movement narrowed, in a reversal of the trend before 1914. By 1940, "German" had "Nazi" as its functional equivalent in Budweis/Budějovice. "Czech," in contrast, came to imply an antifascist and even leftist stance. A century ago, when the German and Czech movements had first emerged in town, "German" had perhaps implied a position more to the Left and "Czech" a position more to the Right. Yet the two national trajectories comprised not so much intersecting opposites as a double strand twisted by historical asymmetries. And after 1918, the Habsburg state, which had played a role in creating those asymmetries, held them in balance no more.

A Czech State

By 1918, food shortages and political ferment gripped the Habsburg Monarchy. In January, in Budweis/Budějovice, Social Democrats staged a demonstration at which speakers demanded, in both German and Czech, peace, food, and self-determination. In February 1918, a local gathering of bourgeois Czechs passed a resolution stating that Bohemia's Germans qualified only for minority rights in a future democratic state dominated by Czechs. And in May, Emperor-King Charles issued a decree providing for the division of Bohemia into twelve new administrative units beginning in 1919. The Ministry of the Interior drew up the boundaries so as to make each unit overwhelmingly monolingual and thus, according to the dominant conception, nationally homogeneous. Budweis/Budějovice and its surroundings, though, were to comprise a binational unit, with Czechs separated from Germans not territorially but personally, through cadastres. The Habsburg leadership was abandoning its pursuit of consensus and attempting to impose a national settlement on the town. That settlement, furthermore, now formed part of a larger solution to German-Czech conflict. In Budweis/Budějovice and elsewhere, Czech leaders organized rallies to protest against that solution, which violated the Bohemian state-rights program.[1]

In September, the military situation worsened dramatically for the German Empire and for its Habsburg satellite. On political fronts, Czech preparations for the Habsburg succession in the Bohemian lands were already quite advanced. A small cohort of Czech leaders, active in exile since 1914, had succeeded in winning recognition from the monarchy's enemies of a provisional government for "Czechoslovakia." The new word denoted a nation-state for Czechs, Slovaks, and Ruthenes, to be assembled from the Bohemian lands and from Northern Hungary. In Budweis/Budějovice, German leaders, quiet since early in the war, responded to the erosion of their prospects by turning confrontational. At a town council meeting on September 12, the publisher of the *Budweiser Kreisblatt* introduced a resolution condemning Austria's enemies. Responding to a query, he made clear that he meant, among others, Czechs. For the first time in years, Czech and German aldermen voted against each other as blocs.[2]

On October 16, as the war lurched to an end, the emperor-king issued a manifesto proclaiming a national federalization of an ethnic, territorial sort for the whole of the monarchy. Two days later, the *Budweiser Zeitung* printed an editorial that ignored the manifesto, and centered instead on the Czechoslovak state, whose founding now seemed certain. Round about that state, the editorial read, "will stand the German one; opposite the white, red, and blue border markers will be black, red, and gold ones. And here it will be German! . . . [I]n German Austria, to which today's German Bohemia will belong, a complete purge of the Czechs will be carried out. No Czech will have the right to use his language in any way here. The Czech state will be surrounded as by a Chinese wall." Budweis/Budějovice, then, would belong not to Czechoslovakia but to a hostile German Austrian state—whose relationship to the German Empire the editorial left unclear. On October 21, when German leaders in Vienna proclaimed an "independent German Austrian state," they left that relationship unclear too, but claimed sovereignty over all German areas—whatever that meant—of Habsburg Austria.[3]

A week later, on the morning of October 28, word rapidly spread in town that the monarchy had sued for peace and that Czechs in Prague had just proclaimed the Czechoslovak Republic. Local Czech leaders swung into action. Within an hour, more than 5,000 people had flocked to the *Ringplatz/rynek* (renamed Francis Joseph Square in 1915), drawn by orators and by Czech songs. The crowd watched the torching of several Austrian and German flags and the hanging of the Czech white, red, and blue from Town Hall, as well as the tearing down of a double-headed imperial-royal eagle bolted to the facade of the post office. The emblem of the now deposed Habsburgs inflicted a deep wound in the hand of its attacker. Many Czechs then set off on a hunt for more symbols to destroy. The memorial to Emperor Joseph II that Germans had unveiled with considerable fanfare thirty-five years previously, as well as many German-language signs, did not survive the night.[4]

The Czech press, even while expressing understanding for such vandalism, condemned it. "We Czechs," *Jihočeské listy* declared on the last day of October, "are not going to follow our enemies in violence. We will show that we stand morally and culturally higher than they." Violence, of course, lies in the very nature of power—which Czech leaders were seizing. But they succeeded in focusing their followers' physical attacks on public symbols and in sparing private property and people. The self-inflicted injury at the post office may count as the bloodiest in town. Giving backbone to newspapers' calls for restraint and for order were *Sokol* gymnasts, who temporarily replaced the suspect police force. Indeed, throughout the Bohemian lands, the *Sokol* set to transforming itself into the disciplined core of a new Czechoslovak army.[5]

On October 29, negotiations commenced regarding the takeover of power indoors as well. Zátka headed a newly established Czech National Committee, composed of representatives from the major Czech parties. The German majority on the town council, led by Mayor Taschek, resisted the demand that it surrender immediately the reins of municipal power. Zátka, perhaps, would have liked to appeal to his national opponent's reason. Another Czech, though, flung open a window of Town Hall that looked onto Francis Joseph Square, and told Taschek that "10,000 Czechs are waiting for your decision under the windows." Indeed, an enormous crowd stood below—as in 1898—ready to take action. Taschek and his associates, cowed, set to negotiating the particulars of their new minority status. Outside, the Czech civilians joined soldiers in swearing an oath of loyalty to Czechoslovakia. Those freshly minted citizens then learned from Zátka that the German aldermen had agreed to resign. "České Budějovice is in Czech hands!" he declared. The sentence, because of the twin meaning of "*české*," resonated in Czech with an untranslatable ineluctability. Speeches followed, as did more attacks on German-language shop signs.[6]

That day's issue of the *Budweiser Zeitung* featured an editorial, "What will become of us?" In it, the *völkisch*-leaning owner of the newspaper conceded that the town was likely to end up in Czechoslovakia, and urged Germans to remain calm. The Czech population, he wrote,

> As regards political discipline, is far above us, and has far more trust in its leaders than do we Germans in ours. Although national hatred . . . today remains still quite strong, the Czechs will not allow themselves to descend into acts of violence if they are not provoked. But what will there be in future to provoke them? The administration will lie in their hands. . . . Politically, . . . they will be in charge, and have no occasion to complain of oppression by Germans. And if we are reasonable enough and know what we are entitled to demand as a minority, then national hatred . . . will lose its edge.

Some Czechs, the author objected, were harassing people in the street for speaking German. He did not acknowledge that his own newspaper had recently served notice that the German successor state to the Habsburg Monarchy would harass inhabitants for speaking Czech. Rather, in a more subtle threat, he now observed that educated Czechs knew that it made no sense to demand linguistic rights for Czech residents of Vienna while denying those rights to Germans in Czechoslovakia. Elsewhere in the same issue, an article detailing the destruction of the preceding twenty-four hours concluded with the comment that "the Germans cannot be done away with through these Czech demonstrations."[7]

If German leaders in town were beginning to resign themselves to inclusion in Czechoslovakia, German leaders elsewhere were not. Late in October and early in November, a bloc of Bohemian Germans in the prewar Austrian Parliament proclaimed solidly German-speaking parts of the Bohemian lands to belong to German Austria. In the north, two provisional provinces—bordering on the German Empire, and cut off from their new mother country by large Czech-speaking areas—came into tenuous being. And just to the south of Budweis/Budějovice, German leaders created a "Bohemian Forest District" and proclaimed its annexation to German Austria's neighboring province of Upper Austria. The Austrian Provisional National Assembly supported those steps in a note to the American president, Woodrow Wilson. But in a shift highly relevant to Budweis/Budějovice, the note clarified the Austrian position of October 21 and claimed the right of national self-determination only for German-speaking majorities in contiguous areas. This new position dovetailed with an emergent American inclination to draw some new borders in Central Europe on the basis of prewar census data or of plebiscites—in other words, in quantitative, ethnic, and even democratic fashion. The ninth of the Fourteen Points that Wilson had made public in January 1918, in fact, had signaled an American rejection of Italy's claim (backed by France and Great Britain) to swaths of Habsburg territory where Italian-speakers formed only a small minority: "A readjustment of the frontiers of Italy should be effected along clearly recognizable lines of nationality."[8]

In Budweis/Budějovice, the purge of things German became more systematic. Francis Joseph Square became Freedom Square, with the commemorated freedom being obviously neither German nor Habsburg. A street named after Anton von Schmerling, an Austrian statesman of the 1860s, became Žižka Street, in honor of a Hussite military hero. Elsewhere, the name of the German Emperor yielded to that of Wilson—on whom Czechs, even more than Germans, pinned great hopes. After all, the tenth of his Fourteen Points stated, "The peoples of Austria-Hungary . . . should be accorded the freest opportunity of autonomous development."[9]

On November 7, Czech became the official language of the municipality. Czech leaders in Budweis/Budějovice thus showed themselves equal to German ones in changing course quickly. As recently as October 31, *Jihočeské listy* had pledged that Czechs would exact no revenge for past injustices. On the basis of the new ordinance (which did set a policy of bilingualism in certain circumstances), municipal employees set to work finishing the job started by private individuals, and removed all German-language signs from public buildings. The *Budweiser Zeitung*, employing a language of rights and reason all too alien to its pages until very recently, as well as all too reminiscent of Czech editorials before October 28, commented that "in the state of Austria, the Czechs were always against a state language and demanded complete equality, but now they are implementing their state language resolutely, without regard for German fellow residents. This can awaken no enthusiasm in German Bohemia for annexation to the Czechoslovak state." In the same issue, the newspaper reported that the night watchman downtown had received an order to break with the long-standing tradition of crying out "Praised be Jesus Christ in all eternity" in German on the quarter hour. Later in the month, the watchman (or a successor) took up the cry again—in Czech.[10]

Policemen also resumed work, relieving the non-salaried *Sokol*. Now, however, they sported republican caps, not spiked helmets. On November 9, members of the police force joined other municipal employees in swearing an oath of allegiance to Czechoslovakia. Zátka, as head of an administrative commission of eight Czechs and four Germans that had replaced the town council, made a speech. No one, he declared, stood under any obligation to change his or her nationality. Renegades would meet only with contempt among Czechs. Now only talent, diligence, and character would count in town hall. Municipal employees, the new administration declared separately, stood free to continue participating in German clubs and sending their children to German schools. In 1919, though, a publication of the *Böhmerwaldbund* claimed that some German civil servants, after swearing allegiance to Czechoslovakia, had been stripped of their posts or transferred to completely Czech-speaking districts.[11]

Many policemen transferred their children to Czech schools. These "renegades," as well as others, did meet with contempt. It came more from the German side, though, and failed to halt them. In January 1919, the *Budweiser Zeitung* wrote,

> With the state upheaval, many also-Germans [*Auchdeutsche*] have simply gone back on their word, falling over themselves in their haste to present themselves to the Czechs in the most favorable possible light. . . . [F]or the sake of a small advantage, they would even become Hottentots, and as Chinese grow themselves a pigtail. . . . We see that many also-Germans and no-Germans [*Nein-*

deutsche] have taken their children (about 800) out of German schools and sent them to Czech ones, and that many earlier also-Germans have resigned from German associations. In short, they are wherever they gain an advantage.

Czech newspapers also wrote about side-switching, but often deflected attention away from Christians by focusing on Jews. The abandonment of a German Liberal stance by the rabbi in town, for example, received more coverage than did the abandonment of a Habsburg one by the bishop. The difference probably owed something not only to the different faiths of the switchers but to the nonnational nature of the bishop's earlier allegiance. When the Czech Catholic newspaper in town did address side-switching squarely, on November 11, the rhetoric was not one of renegades but of "artificial Germans" rescued from oppression and temptation:

> Since the 28th of last month, our nation has gained a million Czechs. Czechs of various towns ruled by the notorious Tittas, Tascheks, and their like—who before the war pursued the very profitable trade of Germanizing and of representing a tinseled Germandom—have now come to their senses. With the bullies pushed aside, these people flock to the Czech standard. Germanization has ended, and of artificial Germans there are becoming Czechs. The next census will tell us how many Czechs multiplied the "German" nation.[12]

Underlying such rhetoric was an ethnic understanding of nationhood. Yet a historical, Bohemian state-rights understanding underlay Czech territorial claims, at least in the western half of the new state. In mid-November, Czech leaders in Prague issued a provisional Czechoslovak constitution and created a Revolutionary National Assembly, thereby sweeping aside the Cisleithanian Fundamental Laws, the Austrian Parliament, and the crownland diets. That assembly, not one of whose appointed delegates was German, asserted jurisdiction over the whole of the Bohemian lands—including their rim, whose population of more than three million had figured in the 1910 census as more than 90 percent German-speaking. At the same time, the Revolutionary National Assembly asserted jurisdiction over much of Northern Hungary, thereby violating the historical integrity of that kingdom. Included were large areas where the majority of the population spoke Slovak. Also included, though, were areas where the majority spoke Hungarian, such that the Czech or Czechoslovak claims had neither a historical nor an ethnic basis. The *Budweiser Zeitung* pointed out the contradictions to its readers.[13]

Almost simultaneously, the Austrian Provisional National Assembly proclaimed a Republic of German Austria, and then declared that Republic a part of the German Republic that had been proclaimed days previously in Berlin. The Provisional National Assembly also repeated the Austrian claim to German-speaking parts of Bohemia and Moravia. When the clash between the Czech historical-territorial position in the Bohemian lands and the Austrian or German ethnic-territorial position came to a head in December, the outcome reflected realities of power. Encountering almost no resistance, Czech army units disbanded the Bohemian Forest District and additional would-be provincial administrations. Forced as well by the *Entente* to stop the rush toward *Anschluss*, or Austrian annexation to Germany, German leaders transferred their fading hopes to the possibility of redrawing state borders later, through *Entente*-backed plebiscites.[14] France and Great Britain, however, had a higher priority: to make their relationship with Czechoslovakia one that spared, rather than cost, them resources in a long-term effort to prevent another war with Germany. The German and Austrian republics were to be kept down, Czechoslovakia up, and the *Entente* powers (as well as Bolshevism) out of Central Europe.

In the second half of December, the leader of the Czechoslovak movement abroad, Tomáš G. Masaryk, returned to Bohemia. On his way to Prague, he stopped briefly in Budweis/Budějovice, where a huge crowd of Czechs hailed him as the new President of the Czechoslovak Republic—a position bestowed on him by the Revolutionary National Assembly. Masaryk then resumed his journey, and two days later addressed the assembly:

> With regard to Germans in our territories, our program has long been known: the area settled by Germans is our area, and will remain so. We erected our state [in ancient times], we maintained it, and now we build it anew. . . . I repeat: we created our state. Thereby is determined the state-rights position of our Germans, who came to the country originally as emigrants and colonists.

The very next day, Masaryk stated to German leaders: "Be assured that the Germans of our renewed state will enjoy full equality."[15] His "we," it should be noted, did not include the great landowners, whose power had long been shriveling and whose estates were soon to become the principal target of a nationally motivated land reform. The historical continuity that Masaryk asserted between Czechoslovakia and the pre-Habsburg Bohemian state rested on little more than the use by medieval Bohemian kings of an early version of the Czech language, and the refusal by modern Czech leaders to distinguish in their version between "Bohemian" and "Czech."

In Masaryk's words may be glimpsed the new, post-Habsburg structure to national politics in the Bohemian lands: a vertical line whose upper end amounted to a fusion of two vertices to the prewar triad. The Habsburg state, or at least parts of it, was to become national in a Czech sense, "our state." Yet the historical strand (both territorial and cultural) to Czechness was not to be converted into a civic one. To be sure, all longtime residents of the Bohemian lands (and for that matter, of a newly invented Slovakia) were to become citizens of the new, Czech state, and to enjoy "full equality." Not all citizens, though, were to be understood by that state as Czechs. Only ethnic Czechs were. And they were to enjoy *more* equality.[16] They were to play an unequal role in writing the law, first by excluding German representatives from the National Assembly and then by resorting to more subtle methods that allowed Czech leaders, in the name of an ethnic majority and in accordance with democratic procedures, to outvote German leaders on key issues. Even as the Czech movement realized—and indeed, overrealized—its historical state-rights program, the ethnic strand to Czechness remained dominant. The state became Czech, but Czechness did not gain a civic strand.

Czech State, German Minority

As the dust settled in the New Year, many Czech associations in town stirred for the first time since 1914. They failed, however, to regain the role that they had played under the Habsburgs. The School Foundation reconstituted itself as a mere memory of what it had been, and disbanded in 1925. By that point, almost all the Czech private schools had become public. Czechs no longer had any incentive to maintain from their own pockets an educational system conceived in response to the challenges of another era. A brochure published in 1927 by a student association, in explaining why it had not resumed its sponsorship of Czech lectures and libraries in nationally fluid parts of Southern Bohemia, cut to the heart of the matter: "It was expected that the Czechoslovak state itself would take up the issue of the organization [of such activities]."[17]

On the German side, the revival of associations proved stronger and longer lasting. A national movement long accustomed to relying on public bodies for funding and guidance now had to cultivate in members a greater willingness to make personal sacrifices for the cause. The Veterans' Association and additional German-dominated clubs found themselves evicted from their rent-free quarters in municipal buildings. German schools had to contend with authorities who, rather than providing moral and material backing as in the old days, devoted considerable energy to investigating whether any Czech children required rescuing from the already half-emptied classrooms.[18] Not only had many individuals in Budweis/Budějovice switched national sides, but the national movements themselves had switched places in town hall—and the Habsburg state no longer existed to restrain the dominant of the two.

In June 1919, Czechoslovakia's citizens voted for the first time, in municipal elections. New legislation had introduced proportional representation and party candidate lists, had eliminated electoral distinctions of sex and wealth, and had permitted (indeed, required) all adult citizens to vote. In Budweis/Budějovice, where the last town council had been elected in 1906, this democratization had national implications. The Czech parties, sure of a large majority, ignored Zátka's calls to continue the prewar tradition of intranational harmony at the polls, and ran separate campaigns. (The Young Czech Party, in an apt change of name, became the Nationally Democratic Party.) The German parties, moving in the opposite direction, formed an umbrella Unity Party that fielded equal numbers of Liberal, *völkisch*, and Christian Social candidates, plus a single token Jew. The Jewish electorate, like Zátka (and Taschek, for that matter, who did not even seek office), no longer stood near the center of the political landscape. Nor, because of the principle of "one person, one vote," did Germans. The Unity Party captured only six seats, and the German Social Democratic Party two, while five Czech parties (with the National Socials at the front and Zátka's old-fashioned National Council at the rear) took the remaining thirty-four. Even if one factors in the roughly 500 Germans who had chosen Austrian citizenship over Czechoslovak and had thus lost the right to vote, the results signaled a change in the Czech:German ratio to about 80:20.[19]

Later that summer came the peace treaties. The one signed at St. Germain on September 10 confirmed that Czechoslovakia's borders contained the whole of the Bohemian lands. German protests were muted, perhaps because of how German demonstrations had ended in March. In several towns, Czech troops and gendarmes had opened fire, killing more than fifty people. Small consolation to German leaders was that the Treaty of St. Germain obliged Czechoslovakia to incorporate provisions for protecting national minorities into its legal code.[20]

Those provisions, in fact, became a part of the Czechoslovak constitution. "We, the Czechoslovak nation," began the preamble, "desiring to consolidate the perfect unity of our people, . . . to contribute to the common welfare of all citizens of this State and to secure the blessings of freedom to coming generations, have in our National Assembly this 29th day of February 1920 adopted the following constitution." All citizens, the sixth and final section declared, "shall be in all respects equal before the law and shall enjoy equal civic and political rights whatever be their race, their language, or their religion." In private and business intercourse, as well as in religious matters, in the press, and in public assemblies, all citizens stood free to use any language they chose. In communities where a "considerable fraction" of citizens belonged to a national minority, public schools were obliged to offer "a due opportunity" for instruction in the appropriate language. "Every manner whatsoever of forcible denationalisation is prohibited." Yet a language law promulgated on the same day required courts and other state institutions to use a language other than Czech or Slovak only in districts where at least 20 percent of citizens had claimed that language in the most recent census. The "Czechoslovak" language, in contrast, had to be accepted by all public bodies, could be made a compulsory subject of instruction in any public school, and counted as the "state, official language of the Republic." National questions aside, the constitution generally followed established West European models. But when one legal expert claimed, "We endeavored to remove from it everything reminiscent of the [Habsburg Monarchy]," he exaggerated. The president, for example, possessed the power to appoint ministers, to dissolve the National Assembly, and to make key personnel decisions in the ministries of Defense and of Foreign Affairs—much as Francis Joseph had done, to Czech dismay, during his reign.[21]

In Budweis/Budějovice that year, the authorities sometimes acted less to enforce the law than to place limits on Czech violations of it. At the beginning of February, a Bohemian German leader, Rudolf Lodgman von Auen, visited town to give a speech in the *Deutsches Haus*. Offended by his previous criticisms of the new state, several hundred Czech National Socials invaded the building and provoked a riot. A few Germans, including Leopold Schweighofer, who was an alderman, were bloodied. The police force (some of whose members, presumably, had served loyally under Schweighofer's old intranational nemesis, Taschek) quickly restored order, but did so in large part by siding with the Czechs, none of whom was arrested. In March, the Ministry of the Interior, acting several weeks *before* the enactment of legislation aimed at bringing place names "into harmony with the history and external relations of the Czechoslovak nation," issued a decree making *Böhmisch/České* an obligatory part of Budweis/Budějovice's name. Only in April did Germans gain representation in the National Assembly, to which the first elections were now held. In town, 80 percent of voters cast ballots for Czech parties, 18 percent for German ones, and just under 2 percent for a Jewish coalition.[22]

That fall, anti-German demonstrations erupted across Bohemia. In Budweis/Budějovice, the Czech press had been voicing frustration for some time over the reappearance of German-language shop signs and over the seeming slowness with which the new state was sweeping away remnants of the old. On November 18 and 19, not so much a riot as a systematic purge occurred. A large crowd advanced through the streets, stopping at public institutions and at private residences. The mass of men confiscated portraits of members of the Habsburg and Hohenzollern dynasties, busts of Bismarck, German-language signs, and similar items by the dozen, then made a huge bonfire of them on Freedom Square. Again, there were no arrests. Indeed, the new district captain and a gendarme accompanied the lawbreakers, simultaneously legitimizing and curbing their actions. This time, there were no injuries, perhaps because Germans had learned that resistance ensured only increased damage and danger.[23]

After 1920, such crude methods almost disappeared. Underpinning the new calm, like the excesses before it, was a preponderance of Czech force, tempered by residual German strength. Another moderating factor was the long-standing Czech reliance on ethnic, quantitative, and even democratic rhetoric. Given ethnic ratios in the Bohemian lands and the strength of the ethnic strand to Czechness, universal suffrage usually produced content that was Czech enough for most Czech purposes. And when it was not, solutions far less disruptive than bonfires could be found. As late as 1927, government officials were appointing all members of district and provincial assemblies, although the law required elections. And in 1921, a majority in the National Assembly imposed a Finance Commission on all municipalities. The commission, at least half of whose members were appointed by the state administration, had the very broad power to suspend any town council decision "of a financial character." Such measures counteracted the class implications of democratization, and reinforced the national ones. Wealthy and well-connected strata gained a near-veto over the tax-and-spend inclinations of the Left, which had profited so much from the award of an equal vote to all adult citizens as to win about one-half of town council and parliamentary seats. More important, perhaps, is that Czech leaders added to the majoritarian control that they exercised over the country as a whole (through such institutions as the National Assembly) a way to exercise control over local government in German areas. Czech leaders centralized their state, denying German opponents refuge in federalist structures, more successfully than German Liberal leaders had centralized the Habsburg state during the 1860s and 1870s. Town halls lost their importance as sites where the Czech-German struggle unfolded. Perhaps in recognition of the shift, Zátka resigned his town council seat in 1920.[24]

In February 1921, Czechoslovakia carried out its first census. Those polled had to answer separate questions about citizenship and about "nationality (mother tongue)." Anyone who claimed more than one nationality or none at all was to be instructed by the census commissioner that nationality meant, as a rule, a "racial belonging, whose principal external marker is the mother tongue." Should the person persist, he or she was to be assigned to a nationality. Even a person who claimed a single nationality from the start could face assignment to another—although regulations required written consent and provided for punishment of commissioners who abused their power. In effect, individuals were required to choose one nationality for which they had ethnic evidence. The Czechoslovak census discarded the Habsburg practice of polling "language of daily use," but continued the practice of asking nothing about command of a second language. In a rich irony, Czechs could assert their Czechness through the census little better than before the war, because officials corrected all claims of "Czech" nationality to "Czechoslovak." The category, which corresponded to a full-blown ideology of "Czechoslovakism," helped to paper over the inconvenient fact that ethnic Germans in the Slavic state numbered too many: only about 50 percent less than ethnic Czechs, and about 50 percent *more* than ethnic Slovaks.[25]

When published, first in April 1921 as preliminary data and then in 1924 as official totals, the census results showed significant Czech gains. In Czechoslovakia as a whole, Czechs, bolstered by nearly two million Slovaks, could claim to outnumber 3.2 million Germans (more than 93 percent of whom lived in the Bohemian lands) by nearly three to one. In the Bohemian lands, where people claiming Czech as their language of daily use in the 1910 Habsburg census had made up 64 percent of the citizenry, those now listed under the Czechoslovak nationality made up nearly 69 percent. Despite the war, the Czech population had increased by about 325,000. The German population in the Bohemian lands, in contrast, had decreased by about 420,000, even if one counts the 88,000 Germans who did not become citizens of Czechoslovakia. And in Budweis/Budějovice, approximately 35,800 Czechs or Czechoslovaks now faced only 7,415 Germans. The third-largest nationality in town, with 212 adherents, was the Jewish one, officially interpreted in Czechoslovakia as a "national group that has lost its language."[26] Since the last Habsburg census, the Czech or Czech-speaking population in town had increased by 8,500 (more than a third), the German or German-speaking population had decreased by 9,500 (more than half), and the national ratio had shifted from 62:38 to 81:17.

Official Czechoslovak explanations of these changes coincided with the explanation offered already in 1918 by the Czech Catholic newspaper in Budweis/Budějovice. Artificial Germans had returned to the native Czech fold, now that Czechoslovakia had given them "the freedom to claim their nationality." This reading, like its German counterpart involving "also-Germans," avoided confronting the possibility that as many as one-fifth of all town residents had been genuinely German before the war, and had become genuinely Czech after it. Then again, the Czechoslovak census was no system of cadastres, and institutionalized nationhood only weakly. To make public an individual's responses to the census questionnaire was illegal. The nationality that a person had claimed did not appear on his or her school transcript, municipal employment contract, voter's registration card, passport, or any other state document. By imposing such limits, the new state made its own goal of favoring one "nation" more difficult to realize. Why? One explanation is that Czech leaders seem to have assumed that state officials would be able to determine whether any person was Czech quite easily, through a short conversation that amounted to a test of whether the person spoke Czech as a native. For certain strata of the population, though, that assumption broke down—and those strata were perhaps nowhere more broad than in Budweis/Budějovice.[27]

Even in aggregate, anonymous form, the claims of nationality registered in the census had considerable political impact. Because Germans in Budweis/Budějovice had fallen below 20 percent of the population, they lost the right to communicate with state officials in German. Disappointment among Germans was keen. It was also probably inevitable. One of the postwar mayors hinted in 1928 that had the proportion of Germans in town seemed likely to exceed 20 percent in the 1921 census, Czech leaders probably would have taken action to push the figure below the legal trigger point. One way to do that would have been to extend the municipal boundaries to include surrounding suburbs—as had been done elsewhere. When the Czech majority on the town council voted on July 2, 1921 to make the municipal administration monolingual through and through, Schweighofer protested. In reply, Czech aldermen recited German injustices from the past. *Jihočeské listy* commented that "July 2 confirmed the old truth that *everything founded on lies and violence, with time, is overthrown! České Budějovice is Czech!*"[28]

Such confrontations helped to give meaning to the new category of Bohemian or "Sudeten" Germans. (Czechs, in an echo of the *böhmisch/ tschechisch* debate, tended to take offense at the term, which derived from the Sudeten Mountains in the solidly German-speaking North). Institutional links between Germans in Bohemia and Germans in Moravia grew stronger, while institutional links between Germans in the Bohemian lands and Germans elsewhere in the now defunct Cisleithania grew weaker. Yet the relationship between the Czechoslovak state and its German citizens was at root negative. And even as institutional links to Germans in the Austrian duchies became a part of the past, emotional links to those Germans—and to the Germans of Germany—gained new consistency and focus.

During the first half of the 1920s, Lodgman, the German whose visit had helped spark a riot in Budweis/Budějovice, exploited his parliamentary immunity to make openly seditious declarations in the name of "Sudeten" Germans. Both in town and in the Bohemian lands as a whole, his German National Party (of which Schweighofer was a local leader), together with the more marginal German National Socialist Workers' Party (which predated Adolf Hitler's National Socialist German Workers' Party in Germany) won a larger share of the German vote than had the *völkische* under the Habsburgs. Radicalism, however, undermined the "unity" tack first tried in the municipal elections of 1919. German Liberals, Christian Socials, and others ran on separate, more conciliatory platforms in elections to the National Assembly, and together with Social Democrats, captured three-fourths of the German vote throughout the 1920s. A contributing factor here was the spectacle of hyperinflation next door in 1923, when Germany's government, in a revolutionary attempt at halting its war reparations payments, rendered worthless the life savings of millions of citizens. Czechoslovak Germans could find a silver lining to having ended up in a Czech but "victor" state. Three years later, two German parties became a part of the governing coalition in Czechoslovakia. Soon the German Social Democratic Party joined the coalition too. Their "activism," as opposed to the truculence of Lodgman, resulted in small but concrete political gains.[29]

Meanwhile, Germans were losing demographic ground. In Budweis/ Budějovice, the results of municipal elections in 1927 dictated that the German presence on the town council shrink, from eight seats to seven. And the second Czechoslovak census, in December 1930, recorded an increase of 700 Czechoslovaks but a decrease of 300 Germans—such that the German minority in town fell to only 15.5 percent. In the country as a whole, the number of Germans increased slightly. That of Czechoslovaks, however, increased more, such that Germans fell from 23.36 percent to 22.32 percent of the citizenry. Because the new postwar national order rested on ethnic demography, these declines mattered. To quote a pamphlet commissioned by all the German parties and entitled *Rights and Obligations of All Persons of German Nationality (Mother Tongue) in the 1930 Census,* "In the age of democratism [*Demokratismus*], the effect of the number plays . . . no small role."[30]

The 1930 tally, in fact, probably concealed how many Germans were in the process of becoming Czechs. New census guidelines, issued in the summer, had redefined nationality in a much more ascriptive sense. "As a rule," they read, "nationality will be registered on the basis of mother tongue. A nationality other than that to which the mother tongue testifies may be registered only if the person polled speaks his mother tongue neither in his family nor in his household, and has complete mastery of the language of the nationality in question. Jews, however, may always claim the Jewish nationality." Census commissioners who complied with this directive quite likely prevented some former Germans who voted Czech and sent their children to Czech schools from boosting still higher the Czech gains since 1921. One result, at least in the short to medium term, was to make both the census results and the Czechoslovak state as a whole more legitimate to Germans, by undercutting any charges that it was distorting data to Czech advantage and denationalizing Germans.[31]

Yet in the long term, a more legitimate Czechoslovak state threatened the German cause in the Bohemian lands. The German pamphlet cited earlier had provided readers with arguments, derived from court decisions, to use against hostile census officials. Someone from a nationally mixed marriage could have a Czech mother but the German mother tongue and thus the German nationality, because

> by mother tongue, the language of the mother is not always to be understood. Understood, rather, is the language in which the person in question was 'primarily' raised at home and in school, and in which he prefers to feel, to think, and to read and write outside the workplace. It is, so to speak, the language that he can show to be his own, and the language of his nation [*Volk*], to which he belongs on the basis of upbringing, family tradition, birth, or conviction.[32]

But as new generations of children in unmixed, German families learned Czech at native or near-native levels in Czechoslovak schools (much as many children of Czech-speaking parents had acquired German in Habsburg schools), more people could be expected to use such arguments in national reverse. And the state, in agreeing to count those people as Czechoslovaks, would violate neither its own laws nor the Czech understanding of ethnicity that underlay them. To the contrary, the state would complete that ethnicity with ascriptive confirmation.

Even over several decades, the bulk of Czechoslovakia's Germans were probably going to remain Germans, just as Germanness was probably going to remain at odds with Czechness. Germany and Soviet Russia, on the other hand, could not be expected to remain in their immediate postwar state of prostration. Yet Czech leaders made quite different assumptions during the 1920s. In 1928, a Czech iconoclast asked "if it is appropriate [*vhodné*] to join Czechs and Slovaks into one nation, a political nation, then why not be consistent, and join into one political nation the entire population of Czechoslovakia?" To the extent that a Czech answer existed, it amounted to hoping that gradually, the piecemeal measures born to the union of a predominantly ethnic Czechness with a predominantly democratic statehood would induce large numbers of Germans to join the Czechoslovak "nation" (although doing so required checking one's Germanness at the door), and would persuade remaining Germans to be loyal citizens. Even as Czechness remained ethnic and deeply anti-German, Germanness in Czechoslovakia was to become civic or at least pro-Czech. No new course was needed, only patience with the old. As President Masaryk claimed to tell himself almost daily at the end of the 1920s, "Thirty more years of peaceful, rational, efficient progress and the country will be secure."[33]

Czech State, German Minority, and Germany

By the time of the 1930 census, the Depression had hit Budweis/Budějovice and the whole of Central Europe. For a time, the slump was less pronounced than in Germany. Yet Germans in Czechoslovakia had reason to believe that they were shouldering more than their fair share of economic misfortune within the country. In the public sector, Czech job applicants had been favored over German ones for a decade. In the private sector, and especially in those branches where the concentration of Germans was most disproportionate, work dried up. And at the intersection of the two sectors, German businessmen had difficulty winning contracts to supply the army or to build roads or government buildings, because the state favored businesses owned and staffed by Czechs.[34]

During the early 1930s, thanks in great measure to the Depression and to how Adolf Hitler and other politicians in Germany reacted to it, a revolution occurred in relations among Czechoslovakia, Germany, and their inhabitants. In Germany, what Rogers Brubaker calls a German "homeland nationalism"—a perception of Germany as the mother state to all ethnic Germans—took hold, to some degree in official policies but even more so in civil society. In Czechoslovakia, within the German "minority nationalism," reciprocal sentiments surged. Czechoslovakia's German National Socialist or Nazi Party, for example, saw its members double in number between 1930 and 1932, less because of its own actions than because of those of the Nazi Party in Germany. What is more, the new members were much less willing than the old ones to accept the Czechoslovak state. After Hitler became the Chancellor of Germany and seized power, early in 1933, he actually dictated that the Foreign Office exercise greater restraint regarding Czechoslovakia than had recently been the case. Yet his Nazi Party program of 1920, whose first two points demanded "the union of all Germans in a Greater Germany on the basis of the right of national self-determination" and the revocation of the Versailles and St. Germain peace treaties, remained unchanged. Before the war, the second German Empire, or Reich, had followed a Bismarckian, Prussian policy of leaving Bohemian Germans to their own fate. For the time being, the new Third Reich did not break with that policy. But the political forces potentially unleashed by rupturing with it mushroomed.[35]

These developments amounted to a restoration of a triadic structure to national conflict in the Bohemian lands. Unlike the prewar triad of two nonstate national movements and one nonnational or multinational state, though, the new triad comprised a national movement in control of the state to which the Bohemian lands belonged, a national movement understood as an ethnic minority within that state, and a second state to which that minority might be construed, ethnically, as belonging. The Czech-German conflict came to involve, at least potentially, considerable conflict between two states. Or to use the relevant but rather confusing English-language term, the Czech-German conflict became internationalized. Brubaker argues, in fact, in his 1996 book *Nationalism Reframed*, that multiple national conflicts in Central Europe became structurally similar during the interwar era by centering increasingly on a two-state, triadic dynamic. A corollary to this reframing is that local actors could have less affect on the course of events. At the end of the Great War, the room for maneuver of national leaders in Budweis/Budějovice had shrunk, through a nationalization and centralization of the state. Now, as Czech-German conflict gained an interstate dimension, that room shrank further.[36]

In the fall of 1933, the authorities prepared to outlaw the German National and Nazi Parties in Czechoslovakia. The parties dissolved themselves first, though, and several leaders fled to Germany. Konrad Henlein, a *völkisch* German (and gymnast) less of a radical pan-German sort than of a more traditional Bohemian one, exploited the moment to found a new movement, the Sudeten German Homeland Front. It quickly gained many adherents, not only from the ranks of the now prohibited radical parties. The Homeland Front's program, which was vague, and Henlein's charisma, which was lacking, do not explain such success. Important, rather, were the radicalization of Bohemian Germans (who now watched as Germany's economy improved, and as Hitler claimed credit), the Front's newness and position as the least conservative German party permitted by the authorities, and its very name—which signaled an ambition to overcome party-political divisions among Germans. In the short term, the largely inadvertent result of Henlein's success was not to overcome those divisions but to build them into a single organization, and thereby to help destabilize the postwar structure to German politics in Bohemia.[37]

Budweis/Budějovice gained a chapter to the Homeland Front in the summer of 1934. Its leader was Hans Westen, a factory owner and former member of the German National Party. As Henlein embraced symbols strikingly similar to those used by Hitler's Nazis, yet publicly rejected pan-Germanism and courted conservative members (both German and Czech) of the Czechoslovak government, Westen and his associates kept very busy in town. Much worked in their favor: unemployment hit new highs and a state-appointed commissioner took over the municipal government, which had been lamed by a budget crisis and by vicious intra-Czech feuding of the sort that August Zátka had labored so long to avoid. Indeed, his death in January 1935 confirmed that an era of local Czech unity had ended. Shortly before parliamentary, provincial, and district council elections scheduled for May, the authorities decided to let the Homeland Front field candidates, on the condition that it change its name to the Sudeten

German Party. Covertly, Nazi Germany provided some funds, although not enough to shape either the party's program or the election results decisively.[38]

Those results stunned pundits. In Budweis/Budějovice, the Sudeten German Party received votes from more than 2,000 men and women, or nearly 60 percent of the German electorate. In the country as a whole, the Party fared still better, with almost 1,250,000 votes or about 66 percent. These percentages, to be sure, are somewhat inflated, because some voters for the Communist Party of Czechoslovakia (KPTsch/KSČ)—the sole nonnational or multinational party—were German at least in an ethnic sense. During the 1920s, the Communist Party had enjoyed significant backing among Czechoslovakia's national minorities, and had functioned as a catch-all protest party, regularly receiving more than 10 percent of the overall vote. But in the Bohemian lands and in urban areas, the party had done less well. And since 1929, crackdowns by the authorities as well as factional struggles (triggered by developments in the Soviet Union, where Bolsheviks increasingly presumed to dictate policy to Communists abroad) had taken a toll. The Communist share of the vote in Budweis/Budějovice, only 4.5 percent in 1929, sank to 3.9 percent in 1935. Whether Westen, Henlein, and their party captured the handful of votes that the Communist Party lost is difficult to say. What is certain is that the Sudeten German Party captured many more votes from the German "activist" parties—and claimed after the elections to speak on behalf of all Germans in Czechoslovakia.[39] The Liberal wing to the German movement had been all but eliminated by the *völkisch* one.

In the spring of 1936, just after Hitler remilitarized the Rhineland and just before he began intervening in the Spanish Civil War, the Czechoslovak National Assembly passed a "Law for the Defense of the State." One result was the assignment of sweeping powers to the military within a new 25-kilometer border zone—including not only Budweis/Budějovice but the homes of more than 90 percent of Bohemia's ethnic Germans. Covert Nazi funding of the Sudeten German Party swelled into a torrent, and contributed to a dramatic erosion of the more traditionalist faction within the party leadership.[40] Hitler had broken with Bismarck.

In December, elections to the town council in Budweis/Budějovice brought to an end two years of governance by the state commissioner. German Liberals failed to field a slate. Henlein visited town during the campaign and gave a speech in the *Deutsches Haus*. The *Budweiser Zeitung*, calling on its readers to vote for his party, wrote that "Election-making is census-taking [*Wahltag ist Zahltag*]!" The outcome, though, was mixed. On the one hand, the Sudeten German Party scored another electoral victory (2,447 votes, more than 65 percent of the German total). On the other hand, Germans suffered a demographic setback. Approximately

3,800 residents had cast a ballot for a German party in 1931, while about 3,700 did so in 1936, even though the electorate had grown. Westen and four other Sudeten Germans took up seats on the town council, next to a German Christian Social representative who had been elected with 808 votes (21.5 percent). The German Social Democratic Party, having fallen short of winning a seat, consigned its 475 votes (13 percent) not to another German party but to the Czech Social Democrats. Incensed over the resulting reduction in the German contingent from seven to six aldermen, the *Budweiser Zeitung* questioned whether "the German Social Democrats and their hangers-on" (in context, a transparent allusion to Jews) had a right to call themselves Germans.[41] The would-be leaders of a national minority, as it shrank, sought salvation in still further shrinkage. They denied the Germanness of German-speaking opponents and of German-speakers targeted for discrimination under Hitler's Nuremberg Laws, enacted in Germany the previous year.

Local leaders of the parties now set to cobbling together a workable majority—and had difficulty doing so, because of irreconcilable differences between the Czech Left and the Czech Right. Here Westen and the Sudeten German Party demonstrated their flexibility and joined with the German Christian Social alderman in entertaining coalition offers. In 1931, the *Budweiser Zeitung* had claimed that "the Germans in the municipality are the pointer on the scales in important decisions"—thus applying to Germans a term that had tended to be used before the war of Budweis/Budějovice's Jews. Now Germans, or at least many non-Jewish ones, indeed did tip the balance. In January 1937, the six German aldermen forged an agreement with Czech National Socials, Catholics, and rightists (the "National Union," headed by Vlastislav Zátka, a son of August). In return for supporting those three Czech parties, which commanded twenty-two of the forty-two Council votes, the German leaders gained a pledge that German interests would be taken into consideration "according to the national ratio in Budweis."[42] The hiring and contracting practices of town hall were to change.

Days later, the German activist parties submitted a memorandum to the Czechoslovak government calling for similar changes in policy toward the German minority across the country. The cabinet, which had invited the memorandum in an effort to shore up those parties against the Sudeten German onslaught, responded quickly by clearing the way for a proportionally more fair allocation to Germans of state aid, contracts, and jobs. Henlein, though, countered the Czech concessions by demanding more: extensive territorial autonomy for the "Sudetenland," and personal autonomy for Germans who lived elsewhere in Czechoslovakia. Sudeten Germans in the National Assembly followed up in April by proposing new legislation. For the purpose, supposedly, of bringing about national equality and self-rule, national cadastres were to be created, each a public body with very broad powers. All citizens were to have the right and obligation to join the cadastre associated with their mother tongue, except in cases that roughly paralleled the exceptions specified in the census guidelines issued in 1930. This borrowing, far from signaling a Sudeten German willingness to let Jewish or bilingual individuals decide on their nationality for themselves, amounted to a sloppy effort at finding a basis in Czechoslovak law for keeping the German cadastre free of Jews.[43] Thanks in great measure to Nazi pressure from abroad, *völkisch* politics had fused in ominous ways with the constitutional tradition of the Bohemian, Moravian, and Budweis/Budějovice Compromises.

In November 1937, as contradictions between the Sudeten German cadastre proposal and a Czech counterproposal remained unresolved, Hitler ordered his generals to prepare plans for destroying the Czechoslovak and Austrian republics. The following January, Budweis/Budějovice gained a "Czech-German Club." *Jihočeské listy* explained that the Czechs involved in founding the club saw in the fact that two-thirds of Germans backed the Sudeten German Party an indication of errors in Czechoslovakia's policy toward its national minorities. Reporting on a meeting of the club in the *Deutsches Haus* on March 12, the Czech newspaper emphasized that both Czechs and Germans had filled the building and that they had concluded the evening by singing the Czechoslovak anthem. But that anthem, unlike the Habsburg one, had no German-language version. The *Budweiser Zeitung* ridiculed the claims of harmony, and noted that the Sudeten German aldermen had boycotted the event.[44]

Also on March 12, Germany's army, or *Wehrmacht*, occupied Austria. The next day, Hitler folded the entire country (including his hometown of Braunau, a few dozen miles from Budweis/Budějovice) into the Third Reich. France and Great Britain did not act. Now the Bohemian lands had Germany as a neighbor not only to the North and West, but to the South as well. On March 17, a Sudeten German leader, Ernst Kundt, visited town and made abundantly clear his opinion that the era of Czech dominance in Bohemia was coming to a close. As the *Anschluss* of Austria awaited full analysis by Czech diplomats and generals, all German members of the cabinet resigned, and two of the activist parties dissolved themselves into the Sudeten German Party. In Budweis/Budějovice, that party announced that two other activist parties, the German Liberals and the German Social Democrats, "through their behavior, have placed themselves offsides once and for all, and we no longer regard them as belonging to the Sudeten German national group [*Volksgruppe*]." Officials carried out an air raid blackout drill. In Berlin, Hitler told Henlein in a secret meeting, "We must always demand so much [of the Czechs] that we can never be satisfied."[45]

On Hitler's birthday, April 20, Westen's son threw himself into a dispute on Masaryk Square (as Freedom Square had been renamed in 1934) between a group of Czechs and a man from Germany driving an automobile that sported a Nazi banner. A brawl started, and the young Westen received such a thrashing that he required medical attention. German fascists quite likely had hoped for violence in reaction to the swastika. Certainly they engaged in conscious provocation in May, when they promenaded around the square repeatedly in German folk costume. Some Czechs took the bait, spitting on or throwing ink at women in dirndls, and even roughing up what the *Budweiser Zeitung* described disingenuously as "harmless German passersby." On May 13, 14, and 15, crowds demonstrated outside the *Deutsches Haus* and elsewhere, singing Czech songs and even hurling stones. The police, displaying a resolve to maintain order that had been lacking during the excesses of 1920, intervened. Times had changed, and with them, methods. Yet the goal remained national. In order to deny credibility to any Nazi claims of an anti-German reign of terror, which Hitler could have used as a pretext for war, the Czech authorities set policemen on Czech demonstrators.[46]

On May 20, believing that Germany was shifting troops toward the border, the Czechoslovak Army mobilized. For the first time since 1866, residents of Budweis/Budějovice were called up for possible action against soldiers commanded from Berlin. Many Germans failed to answer the summons. Hitler humiliated Czechoslovakia, furthermore, by convincing Great Britain and France (an ally of Czechoslovakia) that Germany was blameless. Days later, in municipal elections held almost everywhere but in Budweis/Budějovice, the Sudeten German Party captured at least 85 percent of the German vote, in part by exploiting Czech restraint in areas near the border in order to terrorize Germans. In town, the purchase of gas masks became obligatory, and the Sudeten German Party concluded a new recruitment drive, claiming a total of nearly 2,000 members. The *Budweiser Zeitung* objected stridently to Czech efforts at blocking the transfer of children to German schools—suddenly an ominously urgent issue.[47]

Henlein, meanwhile, at a Sudeten German Party congress on April 23–24, had presented a stunning series of demands, centered on national cadastres. Over the spring and summer, he made sure not to alienate British and French diplomats and mediators, while the Czechoslovak government made concession after concession in the direction of his "Eight Points." By early September, Henlein found himself in the awkward position of having prevailed on all counts. Czech leaders, backed against a wall, agreed to grant fascists far more power within Czechoslovakia than Hungarian leaders had gained within the Habsburg Monarchy in 1867 or than Czech and German leaders had stood on the verge of gaining within town in 1914. In a sign, though, that one or both of the parties negotiated in bad faith, the agreement did not specify how the national cadastres were to be constituted—who would belong to which one. This pivotal matter, in fact, found mention only in a single sentence toward the end of the nearly 3,000-word document: "The nationality of every citizen will be attested by national registers."[48]

In mid-September, as Hitler fulminated publicly against Czechoslovakia, Sudeten Germans staged an amateurish uprising, which the Czechoslovak Army quelled quickly and with minimal bloodshed. In Budweis/Budějovice, Czechs, German Social Democrats, and Communists held an enormous rally in support of the republic. War seemed imminent. Then Great Britain and France, anxious to avoid war with Germany at almost any cost to Czechoslovakia, presented an ultimatum: Czechoslovakia must surrender its predominantly German areas to Germany, or consider the alliance with France null and void. Over the following ten days, the Czechoslovak government resigned, the Czechoslovak Army mobilized a second time, Hitler increased his demands in an attempt to unleash a European war after all, and French and British leaders caved in yet again. Edvard Beneš, who had succeeded Masaryk as president in 1935, declared, "I will not drive the nation to the slaughterhouse for this," and prevailed against his General Staff. The British prime minister, Neville Chamberlain, hailed the settlement, reached in Munich, as meaning "peace in our time."[49]

To this day, the term "Munich" is synonymous, for good reason, with appeasement and dishonor. Yet the Munich *Diktat* of September 29–30, which shifted Germany's border within a few miles of Budweis/Budějovice, served national justice far better than the post-1918 settlement had—for what national justice is worth. With only minor exceptions, the new state boundary followed the ethnic one. (For the redrawing, Hitler had ruled out the use of nationality data from the Czechoslovak censuses—but allowed "language of daily use" data from the 1910 Habsburg census. The *Diktat* also provided for plebiscites in some areas, but a less than impartial International Commission decided in October to avoid the embarrassment of a vote.) Czechoslovak census results from 1930, when projected onto the new map, yielded an estimate that more than 730,000 Czechs had found themselves made residents of the Third Reich. So too, though, had more than 2,800,000 Germans. Nearly four times as many individuals won the right of national self-determination as lost it. In those parts of the Bohemian lands that remained within the Slavic nation-state, non-Czechs fell from more than one-third to less than one-twentieth of the population. Once stripped of the "Sudetenland" as defined at Munich, in fact, the Bohemian lands counted as one of the most ethnically homogeneous zones in Europe.[50] Such numbers perhaps help to explain why Beneš decided against war.

In 1848, Czech leaders had entertained the idea of an ethnic federalization of Bohemia. Later, the Czech position had switched, and then hardened so much as to render moot a switch by German leaders (at first *völkisch* and then Liberal, too) in the opposite direction. Now Sudeten German advocates of ethnic, territorial division—not within a single state but between two states—had found such powerful external backing as to overwhelm Czech opposition. Indeed, the disproportion was so great as to raise a question. What, besides the Great Powers and the risk of contradicting the rhetoric of national self-determination, prevented Nazi Germany from seizing the whole of the Bohemian lands? Beneš, discredited, went into exile; the Czech party system disintegrated; and a right-wing government courted Berlin. After an amnesty in November, Westen and other Nazi sympathizers who had fled to Germany in September returned home—and redoubled their seditious activities. Kundt, the Sudeten German leader, visited Budweis/Budějovice again. He urged Sudeten Germans to "stick it out" and not to emigrate to the Reich during this "time between." *Jihočeské listy* asked "between what?"[51]

As Czech-German battle lines hardened, some loyalties softened. Or as George Kennan, the American diplomat, noted of another town in the Bohemian lands, "It became difficult to tell where Czech left off and German began." In August 1938, Westen's chapter of the Sudeten German Party had written dismissively about side-switching:

> In earlier times, people would quip: "In Southern Bohemia there are Germans, Czechs, and Budweisers." That, thank God, has ended. Here too, there are now only Germans and Czechs. And should a few "Budweisers" still exist, then we can say without hesitation that they should switch over to the other side. There is no place for them in our ranks.

In September, *Jihočeské listy* had written sarcastically of Budweisers who "have always held two irons in the fire" and now were contributing to a mood of defeatism among Czechs. But by the end of the year, the newspaper was far less confident about people "neither fish nor fowl." Objecting to the transfer of Czech children to German schools, *Jihočeské listy* denied rumors that the Nazi Party (which had just absorbed the Sudeten German one) had a million Reichsmarks to hand out in town.[52]

In January 1939, Josef Taschek died. The *Budweiser Zeitung* treated the Liberal leader only slightly better dead than it recently had alive. But in a report about a ceremony at which Westen inducted new members into the Nazi Party, the newspaper boasted that "in recent weeks our Germandom has quadrupled." Nazis who had recently been Czechs, apparently, counted as more German than did longtime German Liberals. Participants

in the ceremony, meanwhile, by swearing allegiance to Hitler, to homeland, and to National Socialism, raised a fundamental question. Days before, Kundt had spoken in the National Assembly on behalf of Nazis in
Czecho-Slovakia (as the rump state had been renamed, with the hyphen
serving as a sop to Slovaks demanding autonomy or more). He had proclaimed the loyalty of those Germans to the country—provided that it
recognized them as members of Hitler's movement.[53] But how could individuals serve both German "nation" and Czech state, now that the two
stood so radically at odds?

Citizen, Subject, Jew

Nazi Germany resolved the dilemma by obliterating the Czech state. On
March 14, Hitler ordered Dr. Emil Hácha, Beneš's successor as president,
to Berlin. There, in the middle of the night, Hitler presented stark facts.
Slovak leaders, with German encouragement, were proclaiming a Slovak
Republic. Germany's armed forces would begin occupying the rest of the
country at dawn. If Hácha did not cooperate, the army would exercise no
restraint, and the air force would rain bombs on Prague. When Hácha
fainted, Nazis revived him, and had a doctor administer injections. The
broken man signed the papers placed before him. The occupation commenced the next morning, with hardly a shot fired. In Prague, on the
sixteenth, Hitler established a Protectorate of Bohemia and Moravia (not
including the Sudetenland) as a supposedly autonomous unit within his
Reich. Legal experts, in drafting the necessary decree, used as a model a
treaty imposed by France on the Tunisian bey in 1881. The preamble,
which Hitler wrote himself, opened with the claim that the Bohemian
lands had belonged to the living space [Lebensraum] of the German nation
for a millennium.[54] The Third Empire or Reich was restoring the boundaries of the first, Holy Roman one. France and Great Britain finally acted—
by guaranteeing the independence of Poland.

"We are free!" the Budweiser Zeitung rejoiced. "Our fate is united with
the fate of the Greater German Empire for all time." In Budweis/Budějo-
vice, Westen and his comrades in arms, together with the foreigner they
had helped summon, quickly reframed politics. Town hall changed hands.
So did churches, schools, the press, and every other public institution.
Even traffic was gleichgeschaltet, or put into gear with Nazism. Drivers of
the several hundred automobiles in town, accustomed to keeping to the
left, had to switch to the right. Masaryk Square became Adolf Hitler
Square. The mayor and other leading Czechs (as well as Communists and
German Social Democrats) ended up not in comfortable retirement, as

Taschek had after 1918, but in concentration camps. Now it was for Czechs that "nation" and state stood at irreconcilable odds.[55]

Bohemian Germans, however, played only minor roles in that state. Henlein remained a public figure. And Karl Hermann Frank, a Sudeten German radical, became Deputy to the Reich Protector—Konstantin Baron von Neurath, an old-school diplomat whom Hitler had used as his Minister of Foreign Affairs until 1938. Yet those men had limited say (more, to be sure, than President Hácha and his Czech-staffed Protectorate government) in the formulation of policy. Key agents, rather, were Hitler and top officials in Berlin. They knew and cared to know little about the Bohemian lands, but understood very well that Nazi Germany had gained control for the first time over a sizable, compactly settled, ethnically non-German population. Very quickly, those new overlords reframed the national politics of Bohemia into a vertical line, with Germans on top. Unlike the Czech line of the 1920s, the new line was a fascist one. National democracy yielded to dictatorship. The Enlightenment ideal of equality before just laws yielded to inequality before laws imposed by *force majeure*. And the primarily ethnic categories of German and Czech became redistributed across three "racial" statuses anchored in law: Reich citizen, Protectorate subject, and Jew.

Hitler's decree created, in effect, unequal national cadastres. Slated to become full citizens of the Reich were all German inhabitants of the Protectorate. Neither the decree nor any other part of Nazi law, however, defined "German" clearly. Only the Nuremberg Laws of 1935 had made an initial attempt, in a negative way, by defining as Jewish (and thus non-German and ineligible for Reich citizenship) anyone with three or four grandparents who had belonged to a Jewish religious community. The decree of March 1939, for that matter, left Jews unmentioned, and used the word "Czech" only once. Non-Germans, referred to as the Protectorate's "remaining inhabitants," became not Reich citizens but "Protectorate subjects." Reich citizens were bound by Reich law, even within the Protectorate. They could not have sexual contact, for example, with any Jew. Protectorate subjects, in contrast, were bound by Protectorate law, which derived from Czechoslovak antecedents. Perhaps because Nazis accepted the Czech myth that Czech soldiers had betrayed the Habsburg Monarchy en masse during the Great War, Protectorate subjects were exempted from military service. Jewish Protectorate subjects, meanwhile, were defined formally, using Nuremberg criteria, only in the summer— for the purpose of stripping Jews of certain possessions. From the start of the occupation, though, ad hoc discrimination against Jews was harsh.[56]

The decree, besides failing to define terms clearly, made no provision for individuals to change statuses, or cadastres. Membership was to be permanent, and transmitted genetically. One implication was that the need for a question about Germanness in future censuses all but disappeared—much as the need for elections had disappeared already. Reich citizens, or Germans, had only one political party, while Protectorate subjects had none. Indeed, the National Assembly had been abolished. In April 1939, when Hitler appointed Westen to the German Parliament (itself a mere sham), the *Budweiser Zeitung* trumpeted that at last, ninety-one years after the convening of the Frankfurt Parliament in 1848, Germans in town had a representative in the *Reichstag*. Westen's appointment, the newspaper noted, would be confirmed later through an election. It was never held.[57]

Although the decree distinguished the statuses of Reich citizen and of non-Jewish Protectorate subject clearly from one another, it did not dictate much social distance between them. In August, the press in Budweis/Budějovice reported that marriage between Reich citizens or "German-blooded individuals" and "persons of alien blood, such as Jews, gypsies, coloreds, and mixed breeds" was forbidden. Missing was any mention of non-Jewish subjects or of Czechs. To be sure, German women married to a Protectorate subject were denied Reich citizenship. But this exclusion fit with a long-standing, pre-Nazi legal tradition of deriving a woman's citizenship from that of her husband. And the exclusion was later reversed, in June 1941—shortly after a confidential decree required "the Czech party" to a German-Czech marriage to meet vaguely defined racial and political criteria. From the fall of 1939, all Germans and non-Germans were required to carry new identification papers at all times. But associations permitted by the state stood under no obligation to have only Germans or only non-Germans as members.[58]

Only two weeks after the issuance of the decree, meanwhile, the Reich Ministry of the Interior had issued a confidential follow-up decree that defined "German"—and thus, by exclusion, "Czech" as well. "Whoever professes himself to be a member of the German nation is a member of the German nation," read the second paragraph, "provided that this profession [*Bekenntnis*] is confirmed by certain facts, such as language, upbringing, culture, etc. Persons of alien blood, particularly Jews, are never Germans. . . . Because professing to be a member of the German nation is of vital significance, even someone who is partly or completely of another race [*Stamm*]—Czech, Slovak, Ukrainian, Hungarian, or Polish, for example—can be considered a German."[59] Days later, the *Budweiser Zeitung* ran several stories with headlines such as "We Reject Forceful Germanization of Non-German National Groups," and "We Will Not Germanize!"

At the base of this antiethnic definition of nationhood was a racist anti-Semitism. The European nations, the authoritative Nazi commentary to the Nuremberg Laws stated, all derived from six ancient races (Nordic,

Phalic, Dinaric, Western, Eastern, and East Baltic). Germans, Danes, Poles, and all other native Europeans—as opposed to members of the inferior Jewish race—were of "cognate blood." That technical term had recently replaced "Aryan descent," which was now declared "partially misleading since it derives from linguistic (and not racial) science."[60] Nazis emphatically rejected ethnicity: a German-speaking Jew was no German. In place of ethnicity, they embraced "race," or the religious affiliation of a person's grandparents. For a small minority in the Protectorate, that definition eliminated choice. Whatever their "profession," or national consciousness, the state classified them as Jews. For a majority, however, the Nazi definition created choice. They could remain Czech, or become German—even if supporting evidence of an ethnic sort was weak. Nazis signaled that they were shutting the door to Germandom, but defined it in such a way as to let racially superior (meaning non-Jewish and Nazi-minded) speakers of Czech slip inside. The historical-cultural strand to German nationhood at last gained constitutional expression, not as elitist, meritocratic liberalism but as populist, racist fascism.

On April 26, the *Budweiser Zeitung* reported that the Nazi Party had stopped admitting new members, but "enrollments in the National Cadastre are still being accepted. . . . No one should be left out!" A subsequent issue alerted readers to a deadline of May 31. No mention was made of National Solidarity [*Národní souručenství*], a "movement" that President Hácha had launched already in March. It supposedly lacked any political program, yet replaced all Czech parties, much as the Nazi Party had replaced German ones. Probably by no coincidence, the *Budweiser Zeitung*'s cry that no German should be left out came in the midst of a week-long drive by National Solidarity to recruit members. It sought, in fact, to enroll every Czech adult male in the Protectorate. Shortly after the drive, National Solidarity managed to publish the results in the Czech-language press. In the Protectorate as a whole, 2,079,185 men, supposedly 98.5 percent of eligible Czechs, had signed up. In Budweis/Budějovice, where Vlastislav Zátka headed the movement, 10,504, or 97.9 percent, had done so.[61]

What was old about this "national plebiscite," as National Solidarity termed the exercise, was the assumption that all Czechs in fact could be counted, because Czechness was defined not so much subjectively, by consciousness, as objectively, by language. New, and inspired by the Nazi cadastres, was the attempt to register all Czechs, everywhere, by name—not just in small territories, as in August Zátka's proposal for a Budweis/Budějovice Compromise, and not anonymously, as in nationally polarized elections and in the Czechoslovak censuses. But the assumption was false, and the attempt no less fact-making (as opposed to fact-finding) than the Nazi one. Even if National Solidarity succeeded at counting biethnic individuals consistently, it could not have accurately counted "Czechs" who failed to enroll. In a few towns with a sizable German minority, local leaders of National Solidarity reported results over 100 percent, probably in an attempt to embarrass the enemy by showing that some monoethnic Germans preferred Czechness to Nazism. (Unquantifiable numbers of Social Democrats and draft dodgers who spoke no Czech no doubt really did sign up, and not only in those towns.) The Nazi reaction proved so sharp, though, that the Czech movement revised its claims. When a second drive followed at the end of May, aimed at seventeen- to twenty-four-year-olds of both sexes, National Solidarity reported quantitatively similar but politically less provocative results.[62]

National Solidarity's aim was not to make Czechs out of Germans. Rather, it sought to prevent the state from making Germans out of Czechs—to dissuade Czechs from applying for Reich citizenship. And the effort succeeded. That is the inference one must draw from the Nazi failure to counter the numbers of National Solidarity with other numbers during the summer of 1939, as well as from subsequent, confidential Nazi data discussed later. The Czech movement, although newly stateless, turned out to have much of what a Nazi police report called "national discipline"—adherents who kept the ranks firm, in part through economic and social boycotts of the sort that Habsburg authorities had found impossible to stop.[63]

One price to National Solidarity's success was the formal exclusion of Jews from the Czech "nation." That does not seem to have been the original plan. In May, National Solidarity proposed to the Protectorate government that it deny many rights to Jewish subjects—but make public its definition of a Jew (i.e., a member of a Jewish religious community) before January 1, 1940, the date when the classification would go into effect. By hinging on a date in the future, the seemingly ascriptive definition actually would have enabled individuals to classify themselves as they liked. Nazi officials, though, killed the idea. The Protectorate government, whose members worked closely with the leaders of National Solidarity, could only drag out discussions with Reich officials. In April 1940, a Protectorate decree came into force that defined Jews in Nuremberg fashion, and prohibited Jewish doctors from practicing medicine on non-Jewish Protectorate subjects. By that point, a ban by National Solidarity on social contact between members and Jews had already contributed to making Czechness officially anti-Semitic, and thus closer to Nazi Germanness. Yet unofficially, many Czechs took a different tack, and made small gestures of kindness to Jews. This was not because Czech anti-Semitism had disappeared but because Nazis had reframed it as contradicting, and no longer complementing, Czech hostility toward Germans.[64]

On June 3 and 4, immediately after the closing of the German cadastre, Budweis/Budějovice hosted a huge Nazi rally. Deputy Protector Frank,

Figure 6. Budweis/Budějovice Town Hall, April 1939. Concealed inside the swastika-covered column in the center is the statue of August Zátka erected in 1936. Nazi authorities removed it in the summer. Courtesy of the State Regional Archive in České Budějovice.

in a speech on Adolf Hitler Square, delivered a warning. The recruitment success of National Solidarity, he declared, only made the Protectorate government more answerable for Czech deeds, and more obligated to re-educate the Czech "nation." Frank also dismissed census data. "Budweis was German, and remains so." His statement, and the rally as a whole, hinted at a recent Nazi decision to make German showcases of a few towns in the Protectorate that had sizable German minorities.[65] His statement also reflected the Nazi rejection of ethnicity, in the classification not only of individuals but of territories as well.

A high Nazi priority was getting Czech-staffed factories to make significant and reliable contributions to Germany's war machine. Extremes that could have provoked Czechs into collective and disruptive action were avoided. Already in March, an eleven-ton statue of August Zátka, installed on Masaryk Square by Czechs in 1936, had been encased in a wooden box. Covered with swastikas, that box had then obstructed views at the Nazi rally in June. In July and August, after subtle but unmistakable displays of anti-Nazi sentiment by many individual Czechs before the monument, as well as before a plaque to Masaryk on Town Hall, both symbols were carted away. Nazi officials claimed, though, to be motivated by purely aesthetic considerations, and drew a contrast to how Czechs had treated Germans and their symbols in 1920. When German was placed over Czech in schools, on street signs, and even at the Burghers' Brewery (now purged of Jewish owners and headed once again by Schweighofer), Nazis claimed to be implementing a just policy, for which they revived the Habsburg term "utraquism."[66]

On September 1, Nazi Germany triggered off the Second World War by invading Poland and dividing up the country with the Soviet Union. Parts of the Nazi half had once belonged to the Holy Roman Empire—and were incorporated directly into the Third Reich, in keeping with a historical-territorial understanding of Germanness. Other parts, however, had not, and had no significant German-speaking population. For those additions to Hitler's Greater Germany, the only national justification was one of German superiority. During September, in a measure designed to bolster German superiority on the battlefield, the Nazi state created a path to Reich citizenship from Protectorate subjecthood. A decree allowed non-Jewish men to volunteer for the *Wehrmacht* and to petition as soldiers for naturalization. Otherwise, switching cadastres remained legally impossible. Material incentives for Czechs to think about becoming Germans multiplied, yet figured much less as a Germanization strategy than as byproducts of measures aimed simply at winning the war. In August, a labor obligation was instituted for young Czech men. And over the following months, even as the state carefully maintained Czech salaries and calories (rationing started in October), the supposed autonomy of the Protectorate grew ever less territorial, ever more personal, and ever more negative. More and more, in other words, the "rights" of Protectorate subjects amounted to exclusion from a growing range of German privileges—themselves only partial compensation for the military draft and for shrinking supplies and security. Harsh crackdowns on Czech demonstrators, meanwhile, tore the velvet from the Nazi fist and spurred hatred, which some Czechs concealed behind obedient smiles. Life imitated the fictive tactics of the good soldier Švejk during the First World War.[67]

In March 1940, Budweis/Budějovice celebrated the first anniversary of its *Heimkehr*, or "return home," to Germany. "Yes, Budweis is German again," the *Budweiser Zeitung* commented. "The town has come home to the Reich, and now Budweis is once again 'the always loyal.'" In December, the newspaper had indicated one way that residents might go about taking up anew the German loyalty that they supposedly had always had. According to a small notice, a Nazi official in the Sudetenland who was a native of town had changed his surname from Wlček (meaning "young wolf" in Czech) to Wölfel (meaning the same in German). Confidential Nazi numbers, though, signal that if the man switched national sides during the first year of the Protectorate, he was a rare specimen. According

to the 1930 Czechoslovak census, 235,000 Germans had lived in the territory that later became the Protectorate. Yet according to a Nazi report in
March 1940, only 189,000 of the Reich citizens in the Protectorate were
not recent arrivals. (Many of the missing Germans no doubt were soldiers,
posted elsewhere in Europe.) The size of the shortfall suggests that former
Czechs probably made up only a small fraction of the Protectorate's German minority. That minority, furthermore, was quite small: less than 3
percent. One hundred and eighty-nine thousand native Germans faced
7,250,000 Protectorate subjects, of whom 90,000 were classified as Jewish—10,000 against their will.[68]

After the war, the Czech press in Budweis/Budějovice reported that the
night watchman downtown had switched from the Czech to the German
side at some point during 1940. Confidential Nazi data complement this
anecdotal case, and indicate that between March 1940 and December
1941, at least 80,000 subjects, or about 1 percent of the population, became Reich citizens. Postwar Czech sources and wartime Nazi ones agree
that many of the converts were criminals, political extremists, or people
willing to do almost anything for a small gain.[69] Otherwise, much remains
unclear: how the Nazi state circumvented its own legal obstacles to turning
subjects into citizens, how much Germany's lightning conquest of France
in the spring of 1940 (a huge blow to Czech morale) affected side-switching in the Protectorate, and how many subjects became citizens after 1941.
Censorship, propaganda, Švejkian dissembling, and wartime chaos have
muddied the waters, as have postwar taboos and the national assumptions
of historians.[70]

Quite clear, though, is that side-switching in Budweis/Budějovice far
outstripped the Protectorate average, both during the Nazi occupation
and immediately after it. In 1946, a Czech newspaper reported that in the
district containing the town and its surroundings, 12,560 Czechs had
taken up Reich citizenship, and now were trying—in a fashion described
in the conclusion—to switch sides again.[71] The 1930 census had recorded
nearly 110,000 Czechs and slightly more than 12,000 Germans in the
district. Thus 11 percent of Czechs had become Germans under the Nazis,
as opposed to approximately 2 percent in the Bohemian lands as a whole.
Converts to Germannness who died before 1946, or who lived but did
not attempt to convert back to Czechness, no doubt push the percentage
higher. For Budweis/Budějovice proper, the conservative rate of 11 percent yields an estimate of 4,000 converts.

Some of the converts, as will be seen, spoke hardly any German. But
the high rate of bilingualism in town must underpin any explanation of
why disproportionately high numbers of people switched sides in Bud-
weis/Budějovice. Then again, even in town, the number of converts seems
to have fallen well below Nazi expectations. During the first two years of

the Protectorate, the Nazi state succeeded in reframing Bohemian politics through three hierarchically arranged statuses: Reich citizen, Protectorate subject, and Jew. The Czech movement, however, succeeded in preventing Nazis from using the first two statuses in order to bring about a significant shift in the definition and demographics of German and Czech nationhood. Despite the intentions of Nazi leaders, their "races" translated in practice into little more than particularly anti-Semitic versions of the primarily ethnic German and Czech "nations" in the Bohemian lands.

Madness

In June 1941, Hitler's armies invaded the Soviet Union. In the longer term, this megalomaniacal act increased the likelihood of Germany's defeat. In the Bohemian lands, the attack also eventually helped the Communist movement, which the Nazi-Soviet Pact of August 1939 had demoralized, as well as discredited among Czechs. But in the shorter term, residents of the Protectorate had little to celebrate. To the contrary. In September, Hitler replaced Reich Protector von Neurath with SS *Obergruppenführer* Reinhard Heydrich, a man notorious even among Nazis for his viciousness. Heydrich, who added the post to his others, played a crucial role over the following months in organizing the mass murder of Nazi-defined Jews from across Europe. In Budweis/Budějovice, the order for deportation came in April 1942. A train carried nearly a thousand residents to Theresienstadt/Terezín, a garrison town north of Prague that the Nazi regime had converted into a holding pen for Jews and for political prisoners. Most of the passengers were kept there only briefly, and then shipped onward to newly established death camps in the former Poland. Almost no one survived. Elsewhere in the Bohemian lands, people defined as Jews by the Nuremberg Laws suffered the same fate.[72]

Even before assuming command of the Protectorate, Heydrich had helped to formulate a policy for altering radically the German-Czech balance of the Protectorate's non-Jewish population. During the second half of 1940, he had participated in discussions with Hitler, von Neurath, and Frank. All had agreed that Czechs had to disappear from the Bohemian lands. But even Frank, a Bohemian German steeped in a *völkisch*, ethnic tradition, had come around to the position that perhaps 50 percent of Czechs were racially fit—and thus suited not for expulsion or extermination but for "national mutation" [*Umvolkung*]. Nazi leaders, meanwhile, had continued to assign high priority to maintaining economic production. Unlike Jews, Czechs were not to be eliminated immediately, at all costs. Nazi subordinates had elaborated plans, but had not implemented them.[73] Postponement had allowed the regime to remain blind to how detached from political realities its racial criteria and assimilation strategies, if not its capacity for genocide, were.

Now, a year later, Heydrich began to try to turn theory into practice. At least some work on the "farsighted, final task" of Germanizing the Bohemian lands, he told leading Nazis at a strictly confidential meeting in October 1941, could be undertaken without endangering the "short-term, wartime task" of maintaining peace so that the Czech worker "places his manpower fully in the service of the German war effort." Work could begin, quietly, on an "overview of which people in this space are Germanizable," on a "national and racial sounding of the entire population." Individuals ranked high in terms of both race and conviction would be Germanized, and individuals ranked low would be deported: "There is much room in the East." The regime would prevent people of bad race but good conviction from having children, but would not antagonize them. People of good race but bad conviction, finally, would be reeducated in completely German surroundings or, failing that, would be shot—"because I cannot resettle them, as over there in the East they would form a leading stratum directed against us."[74]

Heydrich proposed, in effect, to replace the pseudo-ascriptive cadastres of citizen and subject with new, genuinely ascriptive cadastres that were nonethnic. Race, conviction, and an assigned yield of approximately 50 percent Germans, though, provided a far less objective foundation than did the religious affiliation of grandparents. In March 1942, in connection with receiving a new identity card, all Protectorate residents born in certain years were required to provide answers to a series of racial and political questions. In April, supposedly as part of a tuberculosis prevention program, the first of five mobile squads armed with x-ray machines began to screen Czech schoolchildren.

Upon succeeding von Neurath, Heydrich had ordered an intense burst of police repression in the Protectorate. This increased use of a "stick," he deluded himself, went hand in hand with increased use of a "carrot." He increased the fat ration for Czech workers and talked about encouraging nonnational, local patriotic sentiment in Czechs by indulging their interest in sport and by depicting St. Wenceslas as a leader who "realized that the Czech nation can live only in harmony with the German [living] space."[75] With little more than fat, football, and St. Wenceslas, nearly a century of nationalization was to be undone. Soon Budweisers were to walk the earth again—and this time around, were to turn into Germans in far greater numbers. In the meantime, carefully administered doses of terror gave Heydrich the "peace" that he and the Third Reich wanted.

That peace worried Beneš, the former Czechoslovak president, who led a government-in-exile in London. Having learned between 1914 and 1918 just how dramatically political fortunes could change as a result of

war, he did not lose hope. Indeed, he aspired to regain the whole of the
Bohemian lands for the Czech movement, and even hoped to make the
Sudetenland genuinely Czech for the first time—in part by having a million or more Germans expelled from it. But the British Foreign Office,
embarrassed by its role in the Munich debacle, had treated Beneš and his
fellow refugees shabbily, and had refused to grant their government-in-
exile full recognition until July 1941. Even then, Great Britain had refused to commit itself to reestablishing Czechoslovakia in its pre-Munich
boundaries. That Czech-staffed factories were doing an exemplary job of
meeting Nazi orders undermined Beneš's already weak position. Applying
his considerable intelligence to the problem, he decided to have Heydrich
assassinated. Resistance leaders in the Protectorate, when consulted,
begged Beneš to cancel the plan, fearing monstrous reprisals. But the mission—assigned to a symbolically balanced squad of Czech, Slovak, and
Ruthenian paratroopers dropped into Bohemia—proceeded as Beneš had
planned. Heydrich, badly wounded in an ambush near the Prague Castle
late in May, died early in June.[76]

The Third Reich responded just as Czech Resistance leaders had feared.
In Budweis/Budějovice, for weeks, newspapers published lists of Czechs,
some from town, made into examples (and martyrs) before firing squads.
The town synagogue was dynamited and the Jewish cemetery razed. The
authorities, who had canceled the word *Böhmisch* before Budweis in official
use of the town's name earlier in the occupation, now completed their
reversal of Czechoslovak legislation by canceling the *České* before Budějovice. Across the Protectorate, a wave of arrests hit the Czech Resistance so
hard that it never recovered. With great publicity, Nazi forces executed
the nearly 200 men in a village called Lidice, deported its women to
camps, gassed those children deemed racially inferior, and put up the rest
for adoption by Germans. Altogether, perhaps 2,000 Czechs and 1,000
Jews lost their lives.[77]

"It's awful what they are doing," Beneš told his inner circle when the
first reports about Lidice reached London, "but politically this has brought
us one certainty: no situation can now arise in which Czechoslovakia would
not conduct itself as a recognized state with a right to independence." And
indeed, as the British press reverberated with denunciations of the atrocities
in the Protectorate, the Czechoslovak government-in-exile at last won nul-
lification of Munich. Approval followed in 1943 from Great Britain and
from the Soviet Union, as well as from the United States (now one of the
Allies), for Beneš's expulsion plans.[78] During and after the First World War,
the Czech leadership had succeeded in exploiting the collapse of the 28th
Infantry Regiment at the eastern front to crack an image of Czech sympa-
thy for the Habsburgs. Now a single Czech leader who commanded nearly
no material resources in the Bohemian lands had succeeded in shattering

an image of Czech collaboration with the Nazis, by cold-bloodedly harnessing the enemy's power and evil. For that matter, he had harnessed the even greater power of the Allies—already applied to destroying Nazism, and thus Nazi plans for making the Bohemian lands completely German—to his plans for making those lands completely Czech. In the Protectorate, when the reprisals ended, the racial screening begun by Heydrich did not resume.

At the beginning of 1943, Soviet troops finished battering entire German armies into oblivion at Stalingrad and took up a long and bloody advance in the direction of Berlin. By the fall of 1944, Budweis/Budějovice presented a pathetic, even desperate sight. Group after group of German-speaking peasants from points farther East, fleeing the Red Army, crowded the streets with carts piled high with personal effects. (After the war, one German who had lived in town at the time wrote indignantly that "the Czechs took in hardly a single refugee.") Both Czech and German residents perhaps found their own privation made more bearable through comparison with these caravans of misery, but faced new reductions in rations, the suspension of school in December due to a lack of coal, and a deep and growing uncertainty over how and when the end to Nazi rule would come. In March 1945, Allied bombers targeted Budweis/Budějovice for the first time. More than 150 people died. The *Budweiser Zeitung*, its printing shop damaged, had to abandon the Gothic letters with which it had affirmed its Germanness for decades. In April, unending columns of the retreating German Army poured through town.[79]

On May 5, as Germany's unconditional surrender became imminent, members of a new Czech Revolutionary National Committee marched to Town Hall. The Nazi-appointed mayoral commissioner attempted that day to take flight, but got nowhere because his car broke down. Frantic, he put a pistol to his head, and transported himself instantly to the side of Hitler—who had recently chosen the same "hero's death." For the living, there followed several days of great confusion and danger. Czech fighters avoided confrontation with German soldiers, but hunted German civilians. Narratives that place the body count in the thousands defy credibility, but without doubt, Nazi rule in town sank from the rising surface of time to the sounds of looting, beating, raping, and killing. The Red Army, after its arrival on the 9th, engaged in the same activities, displaying less national bias in its selection of victims.[80] German fortunes in town had never been lower, in part because one foreigner, Nazi Germany, had ended up summoning another, Soviet Russia. It now helped decide the final phase of the struggle for the Habsburg succession in the Bohemian lands.

Conclusion _____

Budweis Buried, 1945–1948

Farewells, farewells, how difficult they are
oh, how it pains the heart
when must part
the Czech/Bohemian land from Germany.

When we said farewell, both of us wept,
the Germans shedding
tears of bitter sorrow,
the Czechs of heartfelt joy.

You or I must die, not the both of us,
whoever wins shall be lord
and sing to the other amen,
then bury him.
    —*Karel Havlíček Borovský (1848), cited in*
Jihočech, *29 June 1945*

In May 1945, the shooting in Budweis/Budějovice and in the Bohemian lands stopped, and a final phase in a century-long struggle began. The Czech movement had prevailed, and now set to "burying" its German opponent—if not literally, then more nearly so than Karel Havlíček Borovský, a Czech journalist, could have imagined when he composed the above poem, less about Czechs and Germans than about the Bohemian lands and a Greater Germany, in 1848. Federalization, both territorial and personal, as well as centralization, both democratic and dictatorial, had been tried as solutions to Czech-German conflict. So too, from September 1938 until March 1939, had a partition of the Bohemian lands between two nation-states. Now a different solution was to be tried, with the backing of the Allies. A reestablished Czech state, containing the whole of the Bohemian lands, was going to expel the vast majority of Germans, forever.

Little debate arose over this solution among Czechs. Nor did Czech leaders allow any discussion with Germans. Debate did arise among Czechs, however, on how to define nationhood. How should one determine who was Czech and who was German, who could stay and who had to leave, who sang amen and who was buried? Clearly one needed laws— if not in order to contain more than one "nation" within a single state, as had been the case previously, then at least in order to compile a one-time list of expellees. Should those laws center on ethnicity, though, or on loyalty to the state, even during a six-year occupation and war when the state in question had not existed? Czech leaders had long emphasized ethnicity. Some leaders, though, incensed by former Czechs who had claimed Reich citizenship during the occupation and now were attempting to become Czechs once again, sought to exclude such turncoats by creating, retroactively, a civic strand to Czechness. Divisions within the Czech elite, as well as popular resistance to the effort at redefinition, condemned it to failure.

By expelling the German population, Czech leaders rendered Bohemian politics completely Czech: not a Czech-Habsburg-German triad, and not a Czech-German line, but a Czech point. Total national unity and security, those leaders seem to have thought, were at last within reach. To some extent, they were right. Yet at the same time, the Bohemian framework to politics shrank in significance. Major decisions concerning the Bohemian lands were now made from without, with little input from within. Czechoslovakia became part of a new Communist bloc in a global Cold War.

Once a German, Always a German

In Budweis/Budějovice, Czech leaders turned public life inside out with dramatic speed and force. Down came the swastika from above Town Hall. Out front on the square, Masaryk's name reclaimed its prewar place from the name of Hitler. Inside, Czechs seized all municipal posts, dumping the previous officeholders onto the street, into detention camps, or in some cases into graves. The Nazi regime had destroyed associations and representative bodies, so these the Revolutionary National Committee could not recapture for Czechs. But in the hunger, relief, and anxiety-filled weeks that followed the end of the war, the niceties of parliamentary procedure and club gatherings would not have counted for much in any case. Many Germans had to perform forced labor, wear an identifying armband, and make do with rations not larger, as previously, but smaller than those granted Czechs.[1]

Early in April 1945, in the eastern Slovak town of Košice, a government headed by Beneš had reconstituted itself on Czechoslovak soil. In a reflection of Soviet influence and of the blighting effect of Nazi Germany's defeat on rightist politics, the government included only centrist and left-wing elements: the Catholic People's Party, the National Socials, the Social Democrats, and the Communists in the Bohemian lands, and the Communists in Slovakia. Together, those parties formed a National Front united around a program of radical social and economic reforms. Not only

German parties but also conservative ones contradicted the Slavic national and revolutionary spirit of the times—and thus were outlawed.[2]

In Budweis/Budějovice, the *Deutsches Haus* gained a new, Czech name: *Stalinův dům*, or Stalin House. Pan-Slavic sentiments perhaps encouraged this exaggerated embrace of Czechoslovakia's new neighbor—new because it had annexed intermediate territories formerly part of Poland, and exaggerated because Stalin had signaled his less-than-friendly intentions by annexing Czechoslovakia's own easternmost province of Subcarpathian Ruthenia. Hard geopolitical facts help explain the Czech insistence on friendship with the Soviets: the Red Army had liberated and now occupied far more of Czechoslovakia than did British or American troops. Friendship was better than the alternative. The "Munich syndrome" also played a role in the repudiation of the Western course steered between the wars by the First Republic. As Beneš's *chef de cabinet* in the government-in-exile had remarked already in 1943, some Czech politicians "cannot even swallow a spoonful of soup without crying 'Munich' if they think the British did not put enough salt into it."[3]

Germany, however, figured in the calculations of Beneš and of other Czechs more than the Soviet Union or Great Britain. And behind Germany loomed the central issue of nationhood. Czech leaders, convinced that their "nation" had barely escaped annihilation, ranked questions of Communism or capitalism, East or West lower than the question of how to protect Czechs against a renewed German onslaught in the future. Across the permitted political spectrum, consensus ruled at the end of the war regarding the answer: to expel Germans from Czechoslovakia.[4] In Budweis/Budějovice, Czechs would not simply restore the adjective *České* to the name of the town. They would also remove the noun *Budweis*, and together with the German word, the people who used it. Yet Czech consensus on expulsion was one thing, and Allied consent another. Beneš's government-in-exile had worked hard at laying the diplomatic foundations for the deportation of large numbers of Germans from Czechoslovakia. British and American objections of both a humanitarian and a practical nature, however, had hindered the effort. They had also helped, by contrasting with Soviet willingness, to confirm the leftward and eastward drift of Czech politics.[5]

In April 1945, the National Front, lacking international clearance for a program of wholesale expulsion, had pledged at Košice to rid Czechoslovakia merely of war criminals and Nazis. During May, June, and July, as such clearance grew increasingly likely, the government expanded radically the projected scope of what it termed euphemistically a "transfer" [*odsun*] of Germans. Spurring this escalation were ad hoc and often quite violent attempts (which the National Front permitted and even covertly encouraged) by Czechs at expelling Germans from the country.[6] Indeed, the

Figure 7. Townspeople greet the Red Army in Budweis/Budějovice's central square, May 1945. Courtesy of the State Regional Archive in České Budějovice.

parties of the National Front competed with one another over the emotionally charged issue. "[W]e will purify Prague and the border districts [of Germans]," the Communist Minister of Education proclaimed on May 29, "and we are in a position to do so, because we have a great helper in doing this—the Red Army. Not every army would have helped us in doing this. . . . We must say 'Yes' or 'No.' We must decide either for the East or the West." The minister did not mention that his party had opposed the idea of expulsion until fairly late in the war.[7]

In Budweis/Budějovice, *Jihočech*, the Social Democratic newspaper, repeatedly criticized the American army that summer for its mild treatment of Germans in its small Czechoslovak occupation zone a few kilometers to the south. *Jihočech* also regularly praised the Red Army, albeit in oddly abstract terms that hinted perhaps at dismay over the concrete comportment (including the raping of Czech women) of units stationed in town. By August, Social Democrats were demanding that even Germans who had remained loyal to Czechoslovakia through the war be expelled. To be sure, the leadership of the Social Democratic Party was riddled with Communist fellow travelers. The leaderships of the National Social and People's Parties, in contrast, were not. Yet the local chapter of the People's Party if anything outdid its competitors to the Left in assailing everything

German. "Experience with the Germans," the party newspaper claimed in July, "has shown that our coexistence with them within the framework of one state is impossible. 'Our' Germans waited for the decisive moment to stab us in the back! We shall be masters in our own house. The verdict on Germans: leave *our* land, where there is no place for traitors!"[8] The four Czech parties, in an emergent bidding war for votes and power, denominated at least some of their calls in the common currency of plans for expelling Germans.

Not only expulsion plans but also German property, separated from its owners, emerged in 1945 as an important medium of exchange between the Czech population and the parties of the National Front. On May 19, in Presidential Decree No. 5, Beneš had ordered that all property belonging to individuals or organizations considered unreliable in their loyalty to the state [*státně nespolehlivý*] be placed under Czechoslovak custody. Further decrees in June and October, widely anticipated, converted the sequestration into outright confiscation. Some of the assets under question had belonged to Czechs or Jews before 1939—and in some cases reverted to them. "Unreliable," according both to the May decree and its successors, meant fascists, collaborators with occupying forces, Germans, and Hungarians (who were resident with few exceptions in Slovakia, and for that reason are not discussed here).[9] Presidential Decree No. 5 thus established separate legal standards for Germans and for Czechs. Germans, unless exempted individually as proven antifascists, stood condemned as a group to the loss of the right to own property. Related decrees negated additional fundamental rights, again on the basis of the principle of collective guilt. By July, 800 Germans in town were confined in a camp. Surrounded with a fence and policed by armed guards, the camp featured a gate inscribed with the Czech words "An eye for an eye, a tooth for a tooth!" Czechs, on the other hand, unless charged as individuals for specific acts, were absolved en masse of responsibility for what had happened under the Nazi regime. Indeed, in May, the government retroactively legalized many acts, including rape and murder, if they had been committed by Czechs against Germans or Nazi collaborators. And in December, the government retroactively legalized such acts again, up to October 28, 1945.[10]

Presidential Decree No. 5 also authorized "reliable" Czechs to serve as National Administrators of sequestered German property. Some Czechs in Budweis/Budějovice threw themselves into an orgy of state-sanctioned expropriation. They "administered" and eventually came to own apartments, houses, and small businesses. Even pianos, furniture, and jewelry changed hands, although usually through unauthorized initiatives best termed theft and robbery. Both the Commission for National Administration and the Section for the Securing of German Property in town hall seem to have paid close attention not only to the Czechness but to the party affiliation of applicants for the position of National Administrator. At least part of the new, postwar politics in town thus rested quite literally on a spoils system. Officials belonging to the Communist Party, whose leaders stood on good terms with Soviet troops and dominated the ministries most directly involved in confiscation and in law enforcement, seem to have succeeded in steering more assets to followers than did officials belonging to the other parties. The number of Communists in the Bohemian lands ballooned from 27,000 in May 1945 to slightly more than a million a year later.[11]

But who exactly *were* Germans? Presidential Decree No. 5 explicitly defined them, and thus, implicitly, Czechs as well. "As persons of the German or Hungarian nationality," read Paragraph 6, "are to be considered persons who in any census since 1929 claimed the German or Hungarian nationality, or who became members of national groups, formations, or political parties gathering [*sdružujících*] persons of German or Hungarian nationality."[12] This was a quite broad definition of Germanness. Even Jews who had survived the death camps could be, and were, classified as Germans on the basis of Decree No. 5. (They could petition, however, for exemption from discriminatory measures.) And as the Social Democratic newspaper in Budweis/Budějovice, *Jihočech*, explained to its readers later in the year, referring specifically to the May decree, "in the determination of nationality, neither mother tongue nor culture are decisive from the legal perspective."[13] Or to be more precise, mother tongue was not decisive in the determination of *German* nationality. In the determination of Czech nationality, on the other hand, ethnicity counted as a necessary but no longer sufficient condition. One also had to have shunned German organizations during the Nazi occupation—to have remained a loyal citizen of Czechoslovakia even after its destruction. In negative and retroactive fashion, Czechness had officially gained a civic strand.

What is also striking about Decree No. 5 is that it defined nationhood as a set of membership groups, or cadastres, and reserved for the state the right of determining, on the basis of objective criteria, who belonged to which one. The Nazi regime had done much the same in defining a Jewish "people." In practice, however, if not in theory, that regime had left others, especially Czechs, considerable leeway to decide on their nationality or race themselves. The interwar Czechoslovak state had created ascriptive, ethnic, but anonymous cadastres, in the census. Otherwise, citizens had been classified nationally only in informal and ad hoc fashion, and whatever their nationality, had enjoyed a fairly broad complement of constitutional rights. The Habsburg state, finally, in the "little compromises" before the First World War, had insisted on keeping ascription to a minimum

in the determination of cadastre membership. For the first time in Bohemian history, ascription was to play the central role. And by no coincidence, nationality now counted as an attachment point for fundamental
rights—indeed, for the very status of citizenship. To be sure, the reference
in Decree No. 5 to the 1930 Czechoslovak census was probably disingenu-
ous, or at least unrealistic. On the whole, officials do not seem to have
searched the results in order to ferret out candidates for expulsion. But
membership lists of many German organizations under the Protectorate
were readily available and exploited systematically.[14]

Within six weeks of the issuance of Decree No. 5, approximately 4,000
residents of Budweis/Budějovice filed a petition for exemption from measures against Germans. Very few were Jewish. Did those petitioners come
from the ranks of the Czechs who had become Germans during the war
(who, as was argued in the previous chapter, numbered at least 4,000, or
approximately 11 percent of the population)? Were they converts, in other
words, now attempting to cross back from the German side? Or were the
4,000 petitioners what might be termed "constant" Germans, who hoped
for admission to the purgatory-like status of unpunished German on the
basis of antifascist activity? The local press provided no details. Whatever
the case, the petitioners met with hostility from the municipal commission
that evaluated their cases—perhaps because all its members had served
time under the Nazi regime as political prisoners. Working quickly, the
commission rejected all but thirty-four, or 1 percent, of the petitions by
the end of June.[15] Both Decree No. 5 and official interpretations of it in
town added up to an uncompromising stance: once a German, always a
German.

That stance, however, did not meet with unanimous Czech approval.
Hlas lidu, the newspaper of the People's Party, reacted cautiously to news
of the nearly blanket rejection. Several thousand people, an editorial noted,
had attended a recent program in the municipal stadium concerning exemption from measures against Germans. Applauding members of the
commission for adopting a hard line in hard times, *Hlas lidu* simultaneously sounded a note of concern: "We must not allow ourselves to make
Czechs out of Germans, but then again, we must not allow ourselves to
make Germans out of Czechs. Many mixed marriages as well, and especially the children from those marriages, must be examined very carefully,
so that we do not commit any injustice." In the same issue, the newspaper
announced that the Commission for National Administration in town had
decided to require not only Germans but their Czech relatives ("in direct
lines of descent to the fourth degree and in secondary lines to the second
degree"[16]) to file a list of everything they owned. Relatives, it seems, were
passing one another assets across the national divide in order to keep them

within the family. How clear or deep can that divide have been if such transfers, by their size and numbers, had provoked so strong a countermeasure? How would Czechs react when not the property of relatives but the relatives themselves faced "transfer," as Germans, out of Czechoslovakia?

Once a Czech, Always a Czech

On August 2, 1945, outside Berlin, Prime Minister Clement Attlee of Great Britain, President Harry Truman of the United States, and Generalissimo Joseph Vissarionovich Stalin of the Soviet Union signed a protocol containing formal Allied approval for the expulsion of Germans from three countries: Czechoslovakia, Hungary, and Poland. Contained in the protocol were standards for the humane treatment of expellees, as well as a variety of technical stipulations. Only in January 1946, after the standards and stipulations had all been met, did the trains begin to roll. But in the central question of how many Germans Czechoslovakia expelled, the Allies set no limit. Stalin deserves considerable credit for this outcome, as Communists made certain the Czech population knew.[17]

Also on August 2, President Beneš signed a decree, No. 33, stripping Czechoslovakia's Germans (and Hungarians) of their citizenship and thus of their right to live in the country. Exempted were individuals able to demonstrate that they had remained loyal to the Czechoslovak Republic, had never committed an offense against Czechs or Slovaks, and either had participated actively in the struggle for Czech and Slovak liberation or had suffered under fascism. In rare cases, German or Hungarian members of occupations whose skills the Czechoslovak state required could remain in the country, too, as laborers without political rights. In Budweis/Budějovice, thousands of residents celebrated the twin tidings of August 2 at a demonstration and beer fest three days later. A band played the Czechoslovak and Soviet anthems. "The President's decree," commented *Hlas lidu*, "changes our state into a nation-state."[18]

Decree No. 33, even as it paved the way for the expulsion of Germans, changed the definition of them. Some individuals defined by Decree No. 5 as Germans gained access to the Czech side, via two bridges. First, anyone who had officially claimed the Czech or Slovak nationality during the "period of heightened danger to the Republic" (defined in open-ended fashion as the period since May 1938) now counted as a Slav—even if he or she had been German or Hungarian during the early to mid-1930s. Second, to cite a handbook written for municipal officials in 1946 by a chief technical adviser to the Ministry of the Interior, "Czechs, Slovaks, and members of other Slavic nations who registered themselves as Germans or Hungarians during the period of heightened danger to the Re-

public, having been compelled to do so under duress or under circumstances worthy of special consideration, are not viewed as Germans or
Hungarians, should the Ministry of the Interior approve a certificate concerning their national reliability—issued by the District National Committee having jurisdiction, after a review of the facts of the case."[19]
Czechoslovakia, on the same day that it received clearance from the Allies
to expel its Germans, moved the legal boundary between Czechness and
Germanness. Turncoats prevented from becoming Czech again in May
and June could now have another try, under more favorable circumstances. The state now accepted the argument that some of those turncoats, by becoming Germans, had preserved themselves physically for the
Czech cause at a later date—or had saved their children from starvation
or from adoption by real Germans.[20]

Decree No. 33 compressed the number of Germans in Czechoslovakia
and expanded the number of Czechs. It also served as a lens focusing the
fate of Germans on expulsion, and as a prism refracting the fates of Czechs
across a broader spectrum. The lens, after August, saw much use but little
change. The prism remained a work in progress. Decrees and directives
issued during the second half of 1945 and even in 1946 differentiated
more finely among Czechs. Now that the Czech "nation" and state were
going to include individuals of lesser character or loyalty, punishment had
to be devised for them.

Already in the summer of 1945, the so-called Large Decree (No. 16)
had established a system of People's Courts to judge Czechs, Germans,
and others for a wide range of crimes specific to the Nazi occupation.
Now, in the fall, the Small Decree (No. 138) supplemented the Large
by establishing Penal Adjudication Commissions to punish Czechs and
Slovaks for "offenses against national honor." Among these offenses were
"the claiming of German or Hungarian nationality, should it not already
have had as a consequence the loss of Czechoslovak citizenship," excessive
social contact with Germans, unnecessarily eager cooperation with authorities or slavish obedience to employers, and additional interactions
with the enemy. Such acts, it should be noted, continued to be offenses
well into 1946. Indeed, in October 1945, a decree by the Ministry of the
Interior prohibited any further marriages between a Czech and a German.[21]

"In České Budějovice there perhaps does not exist a German who has
not submitted . . . an application for the acknowledgment of loyalty [to
Czechoslovakia]," wrote *Hlas lidu* in mid-September. Several months
later, *Jihočeská pravda*, the organ of the Communist Party in town, used
sarcasm to make much the same point, printing a front-page article head-
lined "Adolf Hitler Petitions for Exemption from Measures against Germans." Both newspapers exaggerated grossly. By early October, petitions

for the reinstatement of Czechoslovak citizenship totaled approximately 4,000—the same as the number of petitions in May and June. Again, the press failed to report how many were constant Germans, seeking recognition as antifascists, and how many were turncoats, seeking recognition of duress. Indeed, the petition process for both was the same.[22]

Circumstantial evidence, however, indicates that a majority of the petitioners were turncoats. Late in September 1945, *Jihočech* explained to its readers that there existed many kinds of Germans, including "Czech traitors" who had sought material advantage during the occupation. Such cases, the Social Democratic newspaper continued, defied easy analysis. Many traitors had pulled their families along with them, including children who had remained Czech in their hearts. As those minors had matured and the draft age had fallen, "cases could also occur in which Czechs, without becoming traitors, became members of the *Wehrmacht*, and today perhaps are in prisoner-of-war camps without hope of being able to return to the center of their nation." Early in December, *Jihočech* and other newspapers in town began publishing the names of petitioners and urged readers to report immediately any wartime incidents that might call into doubt the validity of any particular petitioner's sworn statement. The great majority of those names, which appeared in issue after issue, were either Czech or nationally ambivalent, but spelled in Czech fashion.[23] One implication is that most of the petitioners were turncoats, and not Germans seeking classification as antifascists. Another is that newspaper editors, censors, and the reading public in Budweis/Budějovice tended to agree that the turncoats indeed were Czechs—provided that their behavior during the occupation had remained within certain limits.

A third implication is that hundreds and even thousands of constant Germans in town—whose numbers in 1945 are unclear—did not attempt to regain their Czechoslovak citizenship on the basis of antifascist activity. Some constant Germans, of course, did. Very few met with success: eventually only ninety-eight in the Budweis/Budějovice District, or less than one-tenth of one percent of the German population that had been registered in the 1930 Czechoslovak census. Some members of that very small minority, furthermore, joined other constant Germans during 1946 and 1947 in leaving their homeland for an unknown destination in a devastated Germany that many had never before seen. Czech officials and politicians favored and even promoted emigration by German antifascists, permitting them to take more than the 1,000 Reichsmarks and 100 kilograms of personal effects set as a limit for expellees.[24]

Most petitioners in Budweis/Budějovice for the reinstatement of Czechoslovak citizenship did not receive any response from the authorities for months. Even turncoats who did win early, positive adjudication of their cases generally failed thereby to regain their freedom. They could exit the system of camps that by early October 1945 held almost all Germans as they awaited expulsion or trial—but only in order to enter a parallel system of camps holding Czechs as they awaited trial or a disciplinary hearing for offenses against national honor. There some turncoats languished, in part because of administrative confusion and a huge backlog of cases. The Penal Adjudication Commission in town, dedicated to passing judgment on delinquent Czechs, held its first hearing only in March 1946. The People's Court, meanwhile, with jurisdiction over both Czechs and Germans charged with graver crimes, commenced operation already at the beginning of September, but adjudicated only ninety-three cases by January and fewer than 400 during its first seven months. It also assigned higher priority to Germans than to Czechs, trying the accused in a national ratio at first higher than 3:1, and about half that by March.[25]

The option for the Czechoslovak state of expelling Germans helps explain why Germans placed on trial in Budweis/Budějovice generally received stiffer sentences than did Czechs. People's Court officials seem to have focused, particularly during 1945, on the more serious German criminals. Their incarceration in small numbers could satisfy Justice, at least symbolically, and thereby render unnecessary a transfer of every last German scoundrel to prison—a policy that would have raised awkward questions about who was left over for transfer to Germany. Also playing a role in the sentencing differential was the screening process by which turncoats became Czechs again. The more serious a person's offenses during the war, the less likely his or her release from Germanness. Jan Ebert, for example, tried in September 1945 by the People's Court, could easily have been classified as a Czech: "Ebert testified to the court that his father had been neither a Czech nor a German, and that he himself had been first a Czech, then a German, and that the same was true for his family [*a jeho rodina rovněž tak*]. He had completed only three grades of elementary school, but with the Germans was able to occupy the position of shop foreman." Accused, however, of joining a Nazi paramilitary unit, of threatening Czech laborers under his supervision, and of forcing an accelerated work pace, Ebert figured in the docket as a person "now of the German nationality [*nyní německé národnosti*]"—and received a sentence of twenty years at hard labor.[26]

As passions ignited during the war cooled, both the People's Court and the Penal Adjudication Commission handed out shorter sentences. Time was on the wrongdoer's side. Reminted Czechs in town, by floating for months in administrative limbo, perhaps ended up sentenced to shorter terms than did people tried with greater dispatch—more likely Germans. Straightforward national bias affected outcomes as well. Two sets of spouses, each tried as a couple during October 1945 for the same crime, denouncing a Czech to the Nazi authorities, straddled the national divide.

Pavla Reiss had become a German during the war, while her husband's application for the same status had been denied. Sofie Albrecht, always a German, had been joined as such after 1939 by her husband, Jan, previously a Czech. More German than the males, the females received far harsher sentences—although in nationally homogeneous cases, the People's Court seems to have discriminated against men.[27]

Late in January 1946, the actual removal of Germans from Czechoslovakia got under way. Soon several trains a day were leaving for occupied Germany, each carrying approximately 1,200 expellees. In Budweis/Budějovice, the press suddenly raised the question of what to do with turncoats whose petitions for the reinstatement of Czechoslovak citizenship had been denied. "Caution . . . is in order," wrote *Jihočech*, the Social Democratic newspaper, on February 8, "so that in cases where lapses [*poklesky*] occurred among Czechs (and they really did occur), persons of Czech origins are not transferred. We all have an obligation to punish strictly, but we have no right to punish with transfer." On the same day, *Jihočeská pravda*, commenting in the name of the Communist Party, objected that many of those scheduled for deportation were "in fact Czechs," people knowing not a word of the German language. Such turncoats, furthermore, had children. The authors of the commentary wrote that everything in them rebelled at the thought of "Czech blood and Czech children" serving to compensate, through expulsion to Germany, for losses that Germans had incurred in a war of aggression. Calling for solutions that would save "indisputably Czech blood" for the Czech "nation" and also meet the requirements of justice, *Jihočeská pravda* concluded that "there is a need for fitting and individual punishment."[28]

Less than two weeks later, *Jihočeská pravda* reported that a number of women who had claimed the German nationality during the war but spoke no German had recently been pulled off a train in town by the authorities, moments before the train departed for Germany. Those authorities belonged to the Ministry of the Interior, which the Communist Party dominated. In a sign of disagreement among Communist leaders, however, the author of the article went on to contradict the party line. He stressed that the quality of Czechs mattered more than their quantity, and criticized the Czech National Social and Social Democratic Parties for recently declaring their opposition to the expulsion of turncoats who spoke no German.[29] Now that expulsion was actually under way, Czech leaders committed to defining Czechness not only ethnically but civically as well—even in the attenuated fashion laid down by Decree No. 33—became fewer.

Not in all cases did the two Czech understandings of nationhood clash. Late in March 1946, *Jihočeská pravda* reported that the commission had restored Czechoslovak citizenship to nearly one thousand people in Budweis/Budějovice and in the rest of Budweis/Budějovice District. Seventy were Germans with special occupational skills required by the Czechoslovak state, and thirty made up the first contingent of Germans reinstated as Czechoslovak citizens on the basis of antifascist activity. A further 115 were either German minors having a Czech father or German women having a Czech husband—treated as less responsible for their actions during the war than were adult males. The remaining 752 petitioners succeeded in persuading the commission that they had claimed German nationality under duress or had been registered as a German without their knowledge, usually by a German husband who was now dead, in flight, or in captivity outside Czechoslovakia.[30]

Jihočeská pravda did not report in March how many petitions the commission had denied and how many still awaited adjudication. Nor did that newspaper or any other indicate how thoroughly employees of the Ministry of the Interior were combing deportation lists and trains for native speakers of Czech. Unclear as well is whether Allied authorities in occupied Germany, confronted with expellees who spoke no German, applied pressure on Czechoslovakia to change its definition of nationhood. Clear, though, is that the exclusively ethnic faction within the Czech leadership succeeded in identifying many Czech-speakers slated for deportation and in placing them at the end of the line. By July 1946, camps in and around Budweis/Budějovice contained approximately 1,300 turncoats. Some had been denied Czechoslovak citizenship, and some were still awaiting adjudication of their cases.[31]

"Significant Changes in the Transfer of Germans," a front-page headline in *Jihočeská pravda* announced on July 4. "Persons of German nationality but Czech origins will not be transferred." The article that followed reported on a new ordinance by the Ministry of the Interior that overturned the provisions of Decree No. 33 regarding Czechness, Czechoslovak citizenship, and the reacquisition of them by turncoats. Henceforth, people who had claimed the Czechoslovak nationality in the 1930 census, who spoke Czech as a mother tongue, or who had attended Czech schools (local conditions permitting) were not to be expelled, even if their petition for the reinstatement of Czechoslovak citizenship had been denied. Turncoats now faced only trial, not expulsion.[32]

By October 1946, when the Allied occupation authorities suspended population movements until spring, the great bulk of Czechoslovakia's German population was starting a new life in a new land. They were joined the following year by almost all remaining Germans. One of the exceptions was Leopold Schweighofer, the firebrand who had led the *völkisch* revolt against Taschek at the turn of the century. Old and broken, he died in a camp outside Budweis/Budějovice while awaiting deportation. Another exception was Schweighofer's successor as the local leader of the more ethnic wing to the German movement, Hans Westen. He was hanged in February 1947, one of more than seventy people from town executed for their crimes. That spring, the Passion Plays started up again in Höritz/Hořice—or rather, in Hořice, because the overwhelmingly German-speaking population of the village had been expelled, and replaced by a Czech-speaking one. The Czechoslovak Settlement Office, in fact, had selected new inhabitants with an eye to their suitability as actors in the rewritten, now supposedly Slavic plays. In Budějovice's cemeteries, German-language inscriptions on tombstones were removed.[33]

Since the end of the war, the line drawn by the Czechoslovak state between Bohemia's two "nations" had shifted. "Once a German, always a German," with Germanness understood either in ethnic or in civic terms, had yielded to "Once a Czech, always a Czech," with the ethnic strand to both Czechness and Germanness once again dominant. Czech leaders, divided among themselves and to some extent pressed by the public that they supposedly led, had dropped loyalty to the state from the definition of Czechness. At the same time, through the expulsion of almost all Germans, residents of the Bohemian lands had come to be Czechs almost without exception. The long-standing tension between the ethnic and the historical-territorial strands to Czechness had been resolved. The members of a single, ethnically national cadastre had come to make up the whole of the citizenry in the Bohemian lands. Czechness had not gained a civic strand, yet Czechoslovak citizenship had become national, in a Czech sense.

Czech—and Communist—Budějovice

The parties of the National Front, and especially the Communist Party, were intent not only on expelling the German population but also on expropriating Czech capitalists—whether or not that was the Czech popular will. In 1945, President Beneš issued a number of decrees providing for takeover by the state of key industries and of large corporations. Because Germans had already been stripped of their assets, the businessowners and shareholders affected in the Bohemian lands were primarily Czechs. What is more, Beneš issued the most important of those decrees just before a "Provisional National Assembly" convened in November, even though its members would probably have been willing to lend legitimacy to the measures by voting to enact them as laws. The members, after all, had appeared on a single National Front ticket and had merely been confirmed by public acclaim, rather than elected. Seven months later, when citizens of the reestablished state finally had the chance to vote for representatives, parties outside the National Front remained banned. A new suffrage law, furthermore, disenfranchised not only all Germans but also any Czech formally accused of offenses against national honor—a provision that Communists exploited by unleashing a small avalanche of false denunciations against members of the National Social and People's Parties.[34] German Liberals had employed similar tactics against Czech voters in Budweis/Budějovice before the First World War. Now, though, those denied the vote had no right of appeal. They were also disenfranchised by members of the same national camp—to the extent that Communists were Czech.

The Communist Party fared very well in the parliamentary elections of May 1946, capturing a plurality, 40 percent, in the Bohemian lands. In Budějovice, the National Social Party emerged the frontrunner, with 35 percent. Communists came in a strong second, though, with 30 percent. They also exercised powerful control, behind the scenes, over leaders of the Social Democratic Party, which tallied 12 percent in town and 15.5 percent overall. For that matter, the Communist Party had numbers on its side of an extra-electoral and extra-Czech sort: the many soldiers of the Red Army. By then it had withdrawn from Czechoslovakia, but remained within striking distance. After the elections, the head of the Communist Party became prime minister, replacing a pro-Communist Social Democrat. But in Budějovice, the local results led the parties of the National Front to make a National Social, Alois Neuman, the new mayor. He had been the mayor in March 1939, and had displayed considerable courage during the first days of the Nazi occupation—enough to end up in Buchenwald, the concentration camp. When he returned, in 1945, he apparently changed the spelling of his name, from the more German "Neumann."[35]

Over the following year, tensions within the National Front grew. Not for nothing did Winston Churchill speak in March 1946 of an "Iron Curtain" descending across Europe. In town, Communists failed in a bid to have a food processing factory owned by the Zátka family expropriated. They succeeded, though, in the case of the Czech Shareholders' Brewery. Its owners, *Jihočeská pravda* stated in January 1947, should consider it an honor, and not a punishment, to hand the business over to the "nation." That spring, as the hundredth anniversary of August Zátka's birth approached, the newspaper hailed him and his struggle against German capital, and then attacked his children for exploiting their own people.[36]

In May 1947, the People's Courts disbanded, and the Penal Adjudication Commissions surrendered their remaining cases to regular district courts. Weeks later, Czechoslovakia sent a delegation to talks in Paris concerning American economic aid, or the Marshall Plan—and then abruptly withdrew, having been all but ordered to do so by Stalin. At the end of the summer, the parties of the National Front formally renewed their coalition agreement. *Jihočech*, though, noted that differences had grown dangerous. The warning signaled that the local Social Democrats who controlled the newspaper sided with a growing faction opposed to the Social Democratic Party's leadership in Prague, which was slavishly pro-Communist. The local chapter of the National Social Party, in contrast, proved friendly to Communists, and thereby bucked its own Prague headquarters, which was anti-Communist. The National Social leader in Budějovice, Mayor Neuman, added his party to the "socialist bloc" of the National Front in town hall that fall. Meanwhile, growing talk of holding the first genuine municipal elections since before the war heightened tensions within the National Front. As Joseph Rothschild has observed of several postwar governments in East Central Europe, "It is a truism of political science that an oversize multiparty coalition, in which some members are arithmetically and politically superfluous, will be subject to strains as each member maneuvers to avoid being targeted as redundant and to remain among the surviving partners."[37]

The Communist Party had arguably taken a less hard-line stance on the expulsion than had other members of the National Front. Now, though, Communist leaders worked to stake out a position as the most anti-German of the Czech parties. The few remaining Germans in the country, *Jihočeská pravda* complained repeatedly during the fall, were being treated too gently. Early in November, the newspaper published a cartoon showing the Marshall Plan, backed by tanks in Germany, threatening Czechoslovakia. The same issue gave front-page coverage to a speech by the Minister of Information, a leader of the Communist Party: "We must realize that we do not live between West and East," he was quoted as saying,

> but between Germany, which the Western capitalists are attempting to put back on its feet, and the Soviet Union, which showed with deeds how it understands the freedom and independence of small nations. . . . A firm and indivisible alliance with the Soviet Union secures us against the possibility that Germans should ever lay hand on Czech or Slovak territory. It secures us further against the possibility that even a single German transferred beyond the borders of our fatherland will ever return to the Sudetens and here prepare our end.

A century previously, Franz Schuselka, the German liberal from town, had posed much the same stark choice: "German or Russian?" Habsburg leaders, though, had refused to accept the dichotomy and had prevailed. František Palacký, for that matter, the Czech leader, had also refused to accept the dichotomy, and had proposed instead a multinational, federalized Habsburg Monarchy. Now their successor, Beneš, could propose only a nationally purged and centralized Czechoslovakia—too small to withstand any serious challenges to its sovereignty by Russia's successor, the Soviet Union. As Palacký had written in 1848, "Imagine Austria dissolved into a mass of small and still smaller republics. What a welcome foundation for a Russian universal monarchy!"[38]

In December 1947, the Minister of Justice, a National Social, proposed to close out all remaining cases concerning offenses against national honor. The Communist Party reacted vehemently. It called for a reexamination of all acquittals, and went on to urge a purge of supposedly fascist elements from the army and civil service. A month later, the minister, Prokop Drtina, presented shocking news to the National Assembly. In September, crudely constructed bombs had been mailed to him and to the Foreign Minister—Jan Masaryk, the son of the first Czechoslovak president. Now investigators had learned that behind that assassination attempt had been high-ranking Communists.[39]

In February 1948, the Minister of the Interior, a Communist, dismissed half a dozen of the few remaining non-Communist police chiefs in Prague. Instructed by a majority of the ministers to reverse himself, he simply stopped attending cabinet meetings, claiming to be ill. His superior in the Communist Party, the prime minister, refused comment. National Social and People's Party ministers, together with colleagues belonging to the Slovak Democratic Party, decided to trigger a cabinet crisis by submitting their resignations to President Beneš. They failed, however, to consult with him in advance. Nor did they consult with the Social Democratic Party, whose anti-Communist wing had recently seized control of the top party positions, and whose ministers stood in a position to give either side in the government the majority. The Communist Party, meanwhile, mobilized its rank and file, applying intense pressure on Beneš and on the Social Democratic ministers from the streets. On February 25, Beneš surprised the anti-Communists by accepting their resignations. The Social Democrats remained in the cabinet with the Communists, and were soon joined by new appointees. Security personnel across the country began rounding up those anti-Communist leaders who had not gone into hiding or fled the country. Jan Masaryk fell or was pushed from a window in the Prague Castle, and died. Drtina attempted suicide in the same way, but survived, paralyzed—and was imprisoned.

In April, in the midst of many arrests, came a reconvening of the People's Courts and Penal Adjudication Commissions. At the end of May came elections to the National Assembly. Voting, supposedly, was secret and free. The National Front, however, permitted no choice. "A United Candidate List—For a United Nation," read one headline in Budějovice. "Whoever Loves the Republic Will Vote For It," read another. Simultaneously, the regime celebrated the hundredth anniversary of the abolition of serfdom. By then, the new regime had disbanded or subordinated not only all non-Communist newspapers but all manner of non-Communist associations as well—including the *Beseda* and the *Sokol*. It had also begun to expropriate all businesses with as few as fifty employees, even while making much ado about finally granting full ownership over formerly German assets to National Administrators. In July, shortly after the holdings of the Czech branch to the Schwarzenberg family had been confiscated and shortly before the Zátka factory was expropriated, too, *Jihočeská pravda* informed readers of a plan to construct a dam, the largest in the country, in the Bohemian Forest along the Austrian border. Readers did not need to be told that this part of the Iron Curtain would become easier to patrol, and that formerly German-speaking ghost villages would disappear under water. In town, the former Hardtmuth pencil factory and its Czech equivalent were merged into a single "national enterprise." (Already before the Communist seizure of power, the same had been done with the Burghers' Brewery and with the Czech Shareholders' Brewery.) At least part of the Zátka family fled into exile, ending up in Canada. Yet again, the central square was renamed: Masaryk, too bourgeois, yielded to Žižka, the Hussite warrior.[40]

At the end of February, when the Communist Party had rounded up leaders of the non-Communist parties, it had not needed to search for Mayor Neuman. He had found them. Already on February 27, a heavily censored issue of *Jihočech* had reported that he was heading a new Action Committee for the whole of the National Social Party. The Communist leadership had decided to maintain the National Front as a fiction—as a front of another kind—and to use Neuman to that end. His reward for eviscerating his own party was leadership of it, as well as a minor cabinet post. The new head of the Secretariat of the People's Party, who became the Minister of Health, was another member of the Budějovice Town Council: Josef Plojhar, a priest. Upon returning from the Nazi concentration camp in Dachau at the end of the war, supposedly, Plojhar had administered the German deacon in town a beating. The same source also claims that Plojhar had been a German for some time during the 1920s or 1930s. Certainly he played a significant role during the first years of Communist rule in repressing both political Catholicism and the Church more generally.[41] Budějovice, "the always loyal," could claim the unusual distinction of being home to two of the most prominent turncoats in the now completely Czech Bohemian lands.

Unlike earlier turncoats, Neuman and Plojhar switched only political parties, not "nations." Here the case of Beneš, better documented than the others, offers insight. He did not offer his services to the new regime. But he did not oppose it either. Indeed, he failed to resign his position as president for more than three months after the Communist seizure of power. Why? His personal secretary and legal adviser from 1939 until 1945, who found refuge in the United States, offers an answer based both on first-hand knowledge and on research. After the Communist seizure of power, "Czechoslovakia continued to exist as the country of the Czechs and Slovaks, retained its statehood, and did not confront the danger of national extinction." Such thinking was common even among the most anti-Communist of Czechs. In the early 1950s, another emigré carried out research in Vienna among Czechs who had recently escaped from Czechoslovakia. His conclusions, published in 1953, were that Czechs would welcome an invading American army with open arms. Large-scale desertion from the Czechoslovak military—national legends about the 28th Infantry Regiment in 1915 leap to mind—could be expected. Yet if liberation from Communist rule were to come thanks not to American soldiers but to German ones, Czechs in their great majority could be expected to side in battle with the Soviets.[42]

By 1945, Czech leaders of the left, right, and center had concluded that their state could not afford to grant its Germans their nationhood, citizenship, or even the basic right of residence. István Bibó, a scholar in Hungary, captured the heart of the matter in 1946:

> Czechoslovakia . . . no longer expects democracy to forge unity from its multi-lingual country. . . . But while previously the antidemocratic consequences of such disillusionment consisted of settling into a policy of petty linguistic oppression and denationalization of the relative country's minorities, . . . Czechoslovakia has gone beyond this and has unfurled a program of deporting all the non-Slavic minorities. This is insane, but there is method to it; the Czechs want democracy for themselves and peace for their country from the nationalities. At the same time, they want to keep their territory intact; in other words, they want everything at once. Behind this greed stands not the realization of power but fear that feeds on the catastrophe through which the Czechs have lived.

The democracy to which Bibó referred, of course, was a limited one, even for Czechs: thus the suffrage restrictions imposed by the National Front, as well as its prohibition of any sort of parliamentary opposition.[43] And yet, the Czech leadership could persuade itself in 1945 that it had won everything, at a relatively low price (except to Czechoslovakia's Germans): not only some sort of democracy but also national security and state sovereignty within pre-Munich boundaries.

In 1948, Czech elites drew a further, more painful conclusion from their experiences. Czechs, given the new bipolarity of Europe, could preserve their national security in the future only by compromising their state sovereignty and by surrendering their already compromised democracy. In 1938, Beneš had refused to "drive the nation to the slaughterhouse" over the Munich settlement. A decade later, he again refused to fight, in part because his country and his "nation" again faced a vastly more powerful opponent. It was wiser, Beneš seems to have reasoned on both occasions, to submit and thus to live for battle on another day, with better odds. But in 1948, Beneš and many other Czech leaders did not project onto the Communist future the attempts at annihilating the Czech "nation" that they found in the recent Nazi past. (Had Beneš expected those attempts in 1938, he would presumably have chosen war; he understood his submission to the Munich *Diktat* as a Czech *escape* from the slaughter-house.) In a Communist future, Beneš, Neuman, Plojhar, and many other Czechs saw safety from Germans.

Czech leaders concluded an agreement with the Soviet Union that mer-its comparison with the Compromise of 1867 between Hungarian leaders and the Habsburg state. In both cases, leaders of a national movement negotiated with leaders of a state over the heads of national opponents, and succeeded in gaining considerable powers within a historically defined territory. Habsburg and Soviet leaders, for their part, gained national le-gitimacy for their rule there, without sharing control over the army or over foreign policy. Yet the Hungarian-Habsburg case took federalist and constitutional form, while the Czech-Soviet one took the form of one state granting a formally sovereign satellite limited room for maneuver on the basis of unwritten and imprecise rules. Hungarian leaders exploited the Compromise in order to suppress domestic national opponents. Hun-garian nationhood, though, became more civic, such that many ethnic Germans, Slovaks, and others became Hungarians with the passage of time. ("All citizens of Hungary," to cite Hungary's Nationalities Law of 1868, ". . . form, in the political sense, one nation—the indivisible and united Hungarian nation, of which every citizen of the homeland, regard-less of nationality, is a member with equal rights."[44]) Czech leaders, in contrast, saw in the Soviet Union a guarantee that national opponents, defined ethnically and expelled from Czechoslovakia, would never return. Czech-German relations ceased to be demographically fluid, and became an interstate matter—with the principal German state on the other side of what soon became a Cold War. In 1949, a new citizenship law made naturalization contingent on little more than residence in Czechoslovakia for five years. The "ethnic cleansing" of the Bohemian lands had made the explicit use of ethnic criteria unnecessary.[45]

The Czech-Soviet "compromise," finally, was no compromise at all. Rather, it was a *Diktat* imposed by a state far more powerful than the Habsburg one. At the same time, the Soviet Union was less interested in Czech-German conflict than had been Nazi Germany—and thus more flexible in accommodating the position of one of the contestants. Some historians argue that "The expulsion of the Sudeten population was the first, and perhaps the most decisive step towards complete Communist rule." They miss the point. Expulsion or no expulsion, the Soviet Union would have turned Czechoslovakia into a satellite.[46] The most decisive step toward complete Communist rule was the Soviet victory against Nazi Ger-many. Yet expulsion had its Soviet uses. It made the takeover of Czechoslo-vakia nationally more legitimate. Underpinning Communist rule in Czechoslovakia was not only Soviet military might but Czech nationhood.

A Contest for the Habsburg Succession

Between 1848 and 1948, Bohemian politics changed dramatically. Habsburg loyalties and legitimacies, once dominant, disappeared. Nationhood, once peripheral, became institutionalized and central. Indeed, the right of residence and in some cases even life itself came to hinge on the national affiliation that individuals succeeded in claiming. Budweis/Budějovice, a town inhabited by Budweisers, became České Budějovice, a town inhabited by Czechs and purged of both Germans and Jews. Bohemian politics, including even Communism, became Czech—and has remained Czech to this day.

Czechness and Germanness themselves also changed. Always linked but at first quite different, they became more similar. Germanness, which for a time featured a strong civic strand, became primarily ethnic, like Czechness—even as German and Czech understandings of ethnicity continued to differ. Both nationhoods also became far more populist, far more inclusive of the lower classes. Germanness, though, retained a historical-cultural, qualitative strand, such that Bohemian Germans increasingly understood themselves as an ethnic minority that was entitled by its superiority to privileges vis-à-vis the Czech majority. Czechness, on the other hand, dropped the historical-cultural strand (and with it, the Bohemian nobility) fairly early, and retained instead a historical-territorial one. During the 1920s, that Czech ethnic and historical-territorial combination translated into majoritarian, democratic dominance over the whole of the Bohemian lands, including the ethnically German rim. And after the Second World War, that combination found expression through the expulsion of Germans.

Over the course of a century, the relationship between nationhood and the state changed, too. After recovering from near-collapse in 1848, the Habsburg state suppressed both national movements in the Bohemian lands for a decade. Then, during the 1860s, military defeats and fiscal crises spelled an end to neo-absolutist rule and a beginning to a protracted struggle over the internal configuration—centralist or federalist—of the Habsburg state. Germanness and Czechness became ever more important within that struggle. In 1867 came a major victory for centralists and for German Liberals. They succeeded in implementing their vision of the Habsburg state within Cisleithania, as well as in filling important government positions. In 1871, federalists and Czechs nearly brought about a reversal. Thereafter, and especially after the replacement of a German Liberal government with Taaffe's Iron Ring in 1879, the two nationhoods gradually became equidistant from the Habsburg state. The failed Bohemian Compromise in 1890, the Moravian Compromise in 1905, and the almost implemented Budweis/Budějovice Compromise in 1914 pointed the way to an integration of Czechness and Germanness into constitutional structures. The Habsburg state became multinational, in complex ways intended to reconcile both German and Czech understandings of nationhood, as well as both centralist and federalist stances. But that fragile experiment, as well as the whole of the Habsburg state, collapsed during the First World War. After 1918, one national movement or the other enjoyed a privileged relationship with the state. Czechoslovakia demanded loyalty of Bohemian Germans, yet treated them in ways that contributed to a reorientation of Germanness in the Bohemian lands toward Nazi Germany. That state, after obliterating Czechoslovakia, treated Czechs far worse—and Jews worst of all. Czechoslovakia, when reestablished, sought to eliminate its relationship with Bohemian Germans altogether.

Through all this change, at least two features to Bohemian politics remained relatively constant. First, definitions of "German" and of "Czech" tended to be imprecise and contradictory. A significant minority of Budweis/Budějovice's unusually bilingual population took advantage of the resulting ambiguity in order to switch to the more powerful national side, in some cases more than once. Some residents probably figured as Germans before the First World War, as Czechs after it, as Germans during the Nazi occupation, and as Czechs again beginning in 1945. Second, the state played an important role, although one that varied over time: nonnational, multinational, Czech, German-fascist, and Czech-Communist. At the end of this narrative, the point should seem obvious. Yet as was explained at the beginning, political contestants and historians have neglected the Habsburg state or have misinterpreted it in national fashion. They have interpreted Bohemian politics as an essentially static contest between ethnic Germans and Czechs, rather than as a much more complex and dynamic contest for the Habsburg succession, for a redefinition of the very nature of politics. Political contestants and historians have focused on the Czechs and Germans who succeeded Budweisers and other Habsburg loyalists, and have neglected those loyalists, their state, and its attempt to survive by supplementing traditional, nonnational forms of legitimacy with civic and multinational ones. Such neglect is in error, because that state continued to make up a vital part of Bohemian politics until 1918. In order to understand the central change in that politics between 1848 and 1948—its nationalization—historians must pull the Habsburg state into their narratives and push supposedly ancient ethnic groups out.

What did the nonnational and multinational roles of the Habsburg state in Bohemian politics yield? On the one hand, the Habsburg state long helped to maintain the peace in the Bohemian lands. "The town of Budweis," wrote Ernst Franz Richter at some point before his death in 1870, "possesses the noble appellation of *the always loyal* [*die allezeit getreue*], and may bear it with good justification, for since coming into being, the town has remained invariably loyal and constant to its rightful ruler. The storms of nearly six centuries have succeeded in shaking neither the [Catholic] faith of the town nor its loyalty."[47] And indeed, residents—whether Budweiser, Czech, or German—did remain loyal to the same rightful ruler until the end of the First World War. On the other hand, the decades-long Habsburg peace allowed the German and Czech movements to grow remarkably strong, in balanced but asymmetrical fashion. The violence that they wreaked during and after the Second World War could thus be all the greater.

Robert Scheu, the German, Social Democratic journalist from Vienna who visited Budweis/Budějovice during the summer of 1918, concluded his account with solemn words:

> As a German, one can understand only with difficulty that it is not a joy for the members of a small nation to be able to participate in our cultural community. The more genuine the lament, the more painful our surprise. But we must give up the mental habit of considering the other nations insincere when they declare that we cannot fill them with happiness. That is the first and most important step toward understanding things as they are. When I left Budweis, I had learned at least this. A heartrending education, this traveling between two races which, bound by fate to a life together, understand one another so badly.[48]

This book has sought to understand the "heartrending education" that Scheu and many others received in Budweis/Budějovice. To understand, though, is not to agree. As the expulsion of 1945–47 shows, Scheu was mistaken about the future. Germans and Czechs were not bound to a life together. An impersonal "fate," furthermore, played no role in that outcome. Czechs, Germans, Nazi Germany, and the Allies did. More important, Scheu and many others were mistaken about the past. An impersonal "fate" had not created the Czech and German "races," ethnic groups, or "nations" long ago. Rather, men and women had created those imagined communities, through the contest for the Habsburg succession that was Bohemian politics since 1848. We must give up the mental habit of assuming "nations," and of ignoring nonnational kinds of politics. We must stop thinking ahistorically. That is an important step toward understanding things as they are and were.

Notes

Introduction
Budweisers into Czechs and Germans

1. See Karl Kratochwil and Alois Meerwald, eds., *Heimatbuch der Berg- und Kreisstadt Böhmisch-Budweis mit einer Sammlung von alten und neueren Sagen* (Böhmisch-Budweis: Kratochwil, 1930), pp. 429–30; *Budweiser Zeitung*, 13 August 1938, p. 10; and Bohumír Janoušek, *Město na soutoku: Vyprávnění o historii Českých Budějovic* (Č. Budějovice: Nový život, 1964–66), p. 223.

2. *Budweiser Wochenblatt*, 10 August 1861, pp. 4–5, 7–8; see also 5 October 1861, p. 3. Regarding the mayor, see Leopold M. Zeithammer, *České Budějovice a okolí. Přírodní, národohospodářské, kulturní a národnostní poměry, dějiny jakož i staré stavitelské a jiné památky* (Č. Budějovice: nákladem vlastním, 1904), p. 248; Kratochwil and Meerwald, *Heimatbuch*, p. 428; "Klavík," in *Ottův slovník naučný*, vol. 14 (Prague: J. Otto, 1899), p. 322; and "Klavík," in Leo Santifaller, ed., *Österreichisches biographisches Lexikon 1815–1950*, vol. 3 (Graz-Köln: H. Böhlau, 1965), p. 373.

3. *Budweiser Wochenblatt*, 6 April 1861, p. 4; 26 October 1861, p. 4; 23 November 1861, pp. 5–6; and 7 December 1861, p. 4; and *Budweiser Kreisblatt*, 29 November 1862, pp. 1–2.

4. *Budweiser Wochenblatt*, 7 December 1861, p. 6.

5. *Budivoj*, 28 August 1870, p. 1; Rudolf Strnad, *Dr. A. Zátka* (Č. Budějovice: Odbor NJP / K. Fiala, 1927), p. 17. See, however, the description of Haug in 1918 by a Czech leader, August Zátka, as a "mixture of German and Slav," in Robert Scheu, *Wanderungen durch Böhmen am Vorabend der Revolution* (Vienna and Leipzig: Strache 1919), p. 28.

6. *Budivoj*, 21 September 1865, p. 3. See also sources cited in chapter 1.

7. *Budweiser Wochenblatt*, 2 March 1861, Extrablatt.

8. *Anzeiger aus dem südlichen Böhmen*, 14 March 1863, p. 3; see also "Der deutsche Renegat," 26 November 1862, p. 3, for an article that disparages someone—Ottokar Haug?—who "according to what his interests recommend or demand is today a German, tomorrow a Czech." See also *Budivoj*, 22 June 1865, p. 1; Zeithammer, *České Budějovice*, p. 106; *Jihočeské listy*, 17 September 1938, p. 3, and 21 September 1938, p. 2, as well as the multiple examples given later in this study.

9. W. Wonesch, *Deutsche Liedertafel in Budweis 1856–1926. Ein geschichtlicher Rückblick* (B. Budweis: 1926), p. 6; Vojtěch J. Pucherna, *Paměti Besedy česko-budějovické 1862–1902* (Č. Budějovice: Přibyl, 1903), pp. 2–6; Strnad, *Dr. A. Zátka*, p. 12; and *Budweiser Kreisblatt*, 10 May 1862, p. 4, 17 May 1862, p. 3, and 4 June 1862, p. 1.

10. *Anzeiger aus dem südlichen Böhmen*, 6 December 1862, p. 2, and 15 July 1863, p. 2.

11. Joseph Roth, "The Bust of the Emperor," in *Hotel Savoy* (London: Chatto and Windus, 1986), pp. 182–83; and *The Emperor's Tomb* (Woodstock, NY: Overlook, 1984), pp. 38–39. For discussions of parallels to Budweisers elsewhere in Bohemia, including brewery shareholders (*Brauberechtigte*) and Bohemians, see Scheu, *Wanderungen*, p. 94; Gary Cohen, *The Politics of Ethnic Survival: Germans in Prague, 1861–1914* (Princeton: Princeton University Press, 1981), chap. 1; and Jiří Kořalka, *Tschechen im Habsburgerreich und in Europa 1815–1914* (Munich: Oldenbourg, 1991), pp. 54, 63. For nuanced contributions to the literature concerning local or provincial patriotism, see Robert Kann, *Dynasty, Politics and Culture: Selected Essays* (Boulder, Colo.: Social Science Monographs, 1991); and Miroslav Hroch, *V národním zájmu* (Praha: Lidové noviny, 1999), pp. 23–30.

12. Eugen Weber, *Peasants into Frenchmen: The Modernization of Rural France, 1870–1914* (Stanford: Stanford University Press, 1976).

13. Arthur Haas, "Metternich and the Slavs," in *Austrian History Yearbook*, vols. 4–5 (1968–69): 120–49, esp. p. 121.

14. See, for example, Benedict R. Anderson, *Imagined Communities: Reflections on the Origin and Spread of Nationalism* (London: Verso, 1983); and Ernest Gellner, *Nations and Nationalism* (Ithaca: Cornell University Press, 1983).

15. See, in addition to works listed in the notes that follow, Friedrich Prinz, *Geschichte Böhmens 1848–1948* (Gütersloh: Langen Müller, 1988); Jan Křen, *Konfliktní společenství* (Toronto: 68 Publishers, 1989) [German translation 1996]; Mark Cornwall, "The Struggle on the Czech-German Language Border, 1880–1940," *English History Review* 109 (September 1994): 914–51; Marcela Efmertová, *České země v letech 1848–1918* (Prague: Libri, 1998); and Karl Bahm, "Beyond the Bourgeoisie: Rethinking Nation, Culture, and Modernity in Nineteenth-Century Central Europe," *Austrian History Yearbook* 29, part 1 (1998): 19–36.

16. Jörg Hoensch, *Geschichte Böhmens* (Munich: Beck, 1987), p. 322; and Zdeněk Kárník, ed., *Sborník k problematice multietnicity: České země jako multietnická společnost: Češi, Němci a Židé ve společenském životě českých zemí 1848–1918* (Prague: Univerzita Karlova, 1996), p. 6. For additional examples, see Arthur May, *The Hapsburg Monarchy 1867–1914* (Cambridge: Harvard University Press, 1951), p. 24; Robert Kann, *A History of the Habsburg Empire, 1526–1918* (Berkeley: University of California Press, 1974), p. 379; István Deák, *The Lawful Revolution. Louis Kossuth and the Hungarians, 1848–1849* (New York: Columbia University Press, 1979), pp. xvii–xviii, 140–41; Imre Gonda and Emil Niederhauser, *A Habsburgok* (Budapest: Gondolat, 1987), p. 167; Prinz, *Geschichte Böhmens*, pp. 62–63; Kořalka, *Tschechen*, pp. 125, 157, 184; Hugh L. Agnew, *Origins of the Czech National Renascence* (Pittsburgh: University of Pittsburgh Press, 1993), p. 254; Arnošt Klima, "The Czechs," in *The National Question in Europe in Historical Context*, ed. Mikuláš Teich and Roy Porter (Cambridge: Cambridge University Press, 1993), pp. 228–47, especially 232–34; Vasilij Melik, "The Representation of Germans, Italians and Slovenes in Ljubljana, Trieste, Maribor and Other Neighboring Towns from 1848 until the Second World War," in Geoffrey Alderman, ed., *Governments, Ethnic Groups and Political Representation*, ed. Geoffrey Alderman (New York: New York University Press, 1993), pp. 123–66, especially 129; Jiří Kořalka, "Nationality Representation in Bohemia, Moravia and Austrian Silesia, 1848–

1914," in Alderman, *Governments, Ethnic Groups*, pp. 85–122, esp. 85–91; Peter Sugar, "External and Domestic Roots of Eastern European Nationalism," in *Nationalism in Eastern Europe*, 2nd edition, ed. Peter Sugar and Ivo Lederer (Seattle: University of Washington Press, 1994), pp. 3–54, esp. 38; Steven Beller, *Francis Joseph* (New York: Longman, 1996), pp. 36–42; and Hroch, *V národním zájmu*, pp. 7–37.

17. Fritz Mauthner, *Erinnerungen* (Munich: Georg Müller, 1918), p. 79. The reference is to Monsieur Jourdain, in *The Would-Be Gentleman*.

18. François Furet, *Interpreting the French Revolution* (New York: Cambridge University Press, 1981), p. 10; and Daniel Gordon, "The Great Enlightenment Massacre," in *The Darnton Debate. Books and Revolution in the Eighteenth Century*, ed. Haydn Mason (Oxford: Voltaire Foundation, 1998), pp. 129–56, esp. 131. See also Rogers Brubaker, *Nationalism Reframed: Nationhood and the National Question in the New Europe* (New York: Cambridge University Press, 1996), esp. p. 15, for a discussion of analysis vs. practice, a distinction that Brubaker borrows from Pierre Bourdieu.

19. See Vladimír Macura, *Znamení zrodu. České národní obrození jako kulturní typ*, 2nd edition (Prague: H&H, 1995), esp. pp. 13–132, 192–97.

20. Christoph Stölzl, "Zur Geschichte der böhmischen Juden in der Epoche des modernen Nationalismus," *Bohemia* 14 (1973): 179–221, esp. pp. 183–95; Kořalka, "Nationality Representation," pp. 87–89; Zeithammer, *České Budějovice*, pp. 108–9; Ernst Franz Richter, *Kurzgefaßte Geschichte der k. befreiten allezeit getreuen Berg- und Kreisstadt Böhmisch-Budweis* (Budweis: F. Zdarssa, n.d. [1859?]), pp. 71–72; and Karl Adalbert Sedlmeyer, ed., *Budweis. Budweiser und Stritschitzer Sprachinsel* (Miesbach: Verlag Bergemann & Mayr, 1979), pp. 163–65, 173–76.

21. Brubaker, *Nationalism Reframed*, pp. 13–16. See also Anderson, *Imagined Communities*, 2nd edition (New York: Verso, 1991), pp. 6–7; Etienne Balibar, "The Nation Form: History and Ideology," in *Becoming National: A Reader*, ed. Geoff Eley and Ronald Suny (New York: Oxford University Press, 1996), pp. 132–49, esp. 138–140, 149; and Rogers Brubaker and Frederick Cooper, "Beyond 'Identity,'" *Theory and Society* 29 (February 2000): 1–47.

22. See Richard Plaschka, *Von Palacký bis Pekař: Geschichtswissenschaft und Nationalbewußtsein bei den Tschechen* (Graz: Böhlau, 1955); Joseph Zacek, *Palacký: The Historian as Scholar and Nationalist* (The Hague: Mouton, 1970); Andrew Lass, "Romantic Documents and Political Monuments: The Meaning-Fulfillment of History in 19th-Century Czech Nationalism," *American Ethnologist* 15, no. 3 (August 1988): 456–71; Dennis Deletant and Harry Hanak, eds., *Historians as Nation-Builders. Central and South-East Europe* (London: Macmillan, 1988); Jiří Kořalka, *František Palacký* (Prague: Argo, 1998); Anderson, *Imagined Communities*, pp. 187–206; and Prasenjit Duara, *Rescuing History from the Nation: Questioning Narratives of Modern China* (Chicago: University of Chicago Press, 1995).

23. Regarding the highly politicized prehistory of the term "ethnic," before its adoption and adaptation by specialists in Habsburg Central Europe, see Marco Heinz, *Ethnizität und ethnische Identität. Eine Begriffsgeschichte* (Bonn: Holos, 1993); David Hollinger, *Postethnic America. Beyond Multiculturalism* (New York: Basic Books, 1995), esp. chap. 3; Marcus Banks, *Ethnicity: Anthropological Con-*

structions (London: Routledge, 1996); and Matthew Jacobson, *Whiteness of a Different Color. European Immigrants and the Alchemy of Race* (Cambridge: Harvard University Press, 1998). And for a more detailed version of the argument given here, see Jeremy King, "The Nationalization of East Central Europe: Ethnicism, Ethnicity, and Beyond," in *Staging the Past: The Politics of Commemoration in Habsburg Central Europe, 1848 to the Present,* ed. Nancy Wingfield and Maria Bucur (West Lafayette: Purdue University Press, 2001), pp. 112–52.

24. Gary Cohen counts among the first historians of Habsburg Central Europe to engage seriously with the social scientific literature concerning ethnicity. He also counts, together with Miroslav Hroch, as one of the pioneering social historians of German and Czech nationhood. See Cohen, *The Politics of Ethnic Survival;* and Miroslav Hroch, *Die Vorkämpfer der nationalen Bewegung bei den kleinen Völkern Europas* (Prague: Univerzita Karlova, 1968). See also Geoff Eley, "Nationalism and Social History," *Social History* 6, no. 1 (January 1981): 83–107; István Deák, *Beyond Nationalism: A Social and Political History of the Habsburg Officer Corps, 1848–1918* (New York: Oxford University Press, 1990); and Andreas Moritsch, ed., *Vom Ethnos zur Nationalität* (Munich: Oldenbourg, 1991).

25. An outstanding synthesis of German-Czech conflict before 1918 that succeeds at not taking national sides is Křen, *Konfliktní společenství.*

26. See Cohen, *Politics of Ethnic Survival;* Macura, *Znamení zrodu* [1st edition 1983]; Andrew Lass, "Romantic Documents;" Andrew Lass, "What Keeps the Czech Folk 'Alive'?" *Dialectical Anthropology,* 14 (1989): 7–19; Peter Bugge, "Czech Nation-Building, National Self-Perception and Politics 1780–1914," Ph.D. diss., University of Aarhus, Denmark, 1994; and Vladimír Macura, *Český sen* (Prague: Lidové noviny, 1998). Innovative recent work by Bohemian historians includes Jiří Rak, *Bývali Čechové: české historické mýty a stereotypy* (Jinočany: H&H, 1994); and Robert Luft, "Nationale Utraquisten in Böhmen," in *Allemands, Juifs et Tchèques à Prague / Deutsche, Juden und Tschechen in Prag 1890–1924,* ed. Maurice Godé, Jacques Le Rider, and François Mayer (Montpellier: Université Paul-Valéry-Montpellier III, 1996), pp. 37–51. Miroslav Hroch, in his recent study *V národním zájmu* (1999), makes no mention of Cohen, and titles the first chapter "From Ethnic Group to National Movement."

27. Rudolf Hermann von Herrnritt, *Nationalität und Recht* (Vienna: Manz, 1899), pp. 43–49, 136.

28. For useful discussions of "aristocratic nationalism," see Peter Sugar and Ivo Lederer, eds., *Nationalism in Eastern Europe* (Seattle: University of Washington Press, 1969), pp. 48–49, 259–309.

29. Kořalka, *Tschechen,* esp. pp. 23–75; and Pieter Judson, *Exclusive Revolutionaries. Liberal Politics, Social Experience, and National Identity in the Austrian Empire, 1848–1914* (Ann Arbor: University of Michigan Press, 1996).

30. István Deák, "Comments," in *Austrian History Yearbook,* 3, part 1 (1967): 303–7; Péter Hanák, "Polgárosodás és asszimiláció Magyarországon a XIX. században," *Történelmi szemle,* no. 4 (1974): 513–36; Péter Hanák, ed., *Magyarország története 1890–1918* (Budapest: Akadémiai kiadó, 1978), especially chapter 5; Deák, *The Lawful Revolution;* Andrew Janos, *The Politics of Backwardness in Hungary 1825–1945* (Princeton: Princeton University Press, 1982); and Katherine Verdery, *Transylvanian Villagers* (Berkeley: University of California Press, 1983). See

also Jeremy King, "Austria vs. Hungary: Nationhood, Statehood, and Violence since 1867," in *Nationalitätenkonflikte im 20. Jahrhundert. Ursachen von interethnischer Gewalt im europäischen Vergleich*, ed. Philipp Ther and Holm Sundhaussen (Berlin: Harrassowitz, 2002), pp. 163–82.

31. Verdery, *Transylvanian Villagers*; Moritsch, *Vom Ethnos*; Celia Applegate, *A Nation of Provincials: The German Idea of Heimat* (Berkeley: University of California Press, 1990); and Alon Confino, *The Nation as a Local Metaphor: Württemberg, Imperial Germany, and National Memory, 1871–1918* (Chapel Hill: University of North Carolina Press, 1997). See also William Hubbard, *Auf dem Weg zur Großstadt. Eine Sozialgeschichte der Stadt Graz 1850–1914* (Munich: Oldenbourg, 1984).

32. Andreas Kappeler, *Russland als Vielvölkerreich* (Munich: Beck, 1992); Yuri Slezkine, "The USSR as a Communal Apartment, or How a Socialist State Promoted Ethnic Particularism," *Slavic Review* 53, no. 2 (Summer 1994): 414–52; Brubaker, *Nationalism Reframed*, chap. 2; Karen Barkey and Mark von Hagen, eds., *After Empire. Multiethnic Societies and Nation-Building* (Boulder, Colo.: Westview, 1997); Francine Hirsch, "Empire of Nations: Colonial Technologies and the Making of the Soviet Union, 1917–1939," Ph.D. diss., Princeton University, 1998; Terry Martin, *Affirmative Action Empire: Nations and Nationalism in the Soviet Union, 1923–1939* (Ithaca: Cornell University Press, 2001); Robert Geraci, *Window on the East: National and Imperial Identities in Late Tsarist Russia* (Ithaca: Cornell University Press, 2001); and Ronald Grigor Suny and Terry Martin, eds., *A State of Nations: Empire and Nation Making in the Age of Lenin and Stalin* (New York: Oxford University Press, 2001).

33. Maurice Agulhon, *The Republic in the Village: The People of the Var from the French Revolution to the Second Republic* (New York: Cambridge University Press, 1982) [French edition 1970]; Peter Sahlins, *Boundaries: The Making of France and Spain in the Pyrenées* (Berkeley: University of California Press, 1989); Caroline Ford, *Creating the Nation in Provincial France: Religion and Political Identity in Brittany* (Princeton: Princeton University Press, 1993).

34. A. G. Przedak, *Geschichte des deutschen Zeitschriftenwesens in Böhmen* (Heidelberg: Carl Winter, 1904), pp. 205–6; Heinrich Rauchberg, *Der nationale Besitzstand in Böhmen* (Leipzig: Duncker und Humblot, 1905), p. 441; Franz Storch, "Preßrecht," in *Österreichisches Staatswörterbuch. Handbuch des gesamten österreichischen öffentlichen Rechtes*, vol. 3, ed. Ernst Mischler and Josef Ulbrich (Vienna: A. Holder, 1907), pp. 973–83; František Roubík, *Časopisectvo v Čechách v letech 1848–1862* (Prague: Duch Novin, 1930), pp. 185–86; František Roubík, *Bibliografie časopisectva v Čechách z let 1863–1895* (Prague: Česká akademie věd a umění, 1936), pp. vii–xv, 305; and Bruce Garver, *The Young Czech Party 1874–1901 and the Emergence of a Multi-Party System* (New Haven: Yale University Press, 1978), pp. 46–49.

35. See Jeremy King, review of Hugh Agnew, *Origins of the Czech National Renascence* (Pittsburgh: Pittsburgh University Press, 1993), *Nationalities Papers* 14, no. 4 (December 1996): 748–50.

36. See Max Weber, "Politics as Vocation," in *From Max Weber: Essays in Sociology*, ed. H. H. Gerth and C. Wright Mills (New York: Oxford University Press, 1946), p. 78; Rogers Brubaker, *Citizenship and Nationhood in France and Ger-*

many (Cambridge: Harvard University Press), pp. 21–31; and Gianfranco Poggi, *The State: Its Nature, Development and Prospects* (Stanford: Stanford University Press, 1990), pp. 3–33.

37. Scheu, *Wanderungen*, pp. 5–8, 19–22.

38. Norbert Frýd, *Vzorek bez ceny a Pan biskup* (Prague: Československý spisovatel, 1966); and Norbert Frýd, *Hedvábné starosti aneb: Uprostřed posledních sto let* (Prague: Československý spisovatel, 1968). For a survey of fiction and memoirs concerning Budweis/Budějovice, see Vladimír Novotný and Robert Sak, "literatura," in Jiří Kopáček, ed., *Encyklopedie Českých Budějovic* (České Budějovice: Nebe, 1998), pp. 242–44; and Jan Mareš, "paměti," in Kopáček, *Encyklopedie*, p. 344. The best historical studies of Budweis/Budějovice include Zeithammer, *České Budějovice*; Strnad, *Dr. A. Zátka*; Kratochwil and Meerwald, *Heimatbuch*; Janoušek, *Město na soutoku*; František Rada, *Když se psalo c.k. Ze života Č. Budějovic na počátku století* (České Budějovice: Nakladatelství Č. Budějovice, 1966); František Rada, *Když se psalo T.G.M. České Budějovice v prvním desetiletí republiky* (České Budějovice: Růže, 1970); Sedlmeyer, *Budweis*; Jiří Chvojka, *Město pod černou věží* (České Budějovice: Actys, 1992); and Miloslav Pecha, *Státní převrat v říjnu 1918 v Českých Budějovicích* (České Budějovice: Gabreta, 1999).

Chapter One
Politics in Flux, 1848–1871

1. Rauchberg, *Der nationale Besitzstand*, p. 32; see also pp. 49–51.

2. Richter, *Kurzgefaßte Geschichte*, pp. 48–53, 271; and Ferdinand Böhm, ed., *České Budějovice* (Č. Budějovice: Obchodní organisátor, 1928), pp. 11–12.

3. Strnad, *Dr. A. Zátka*, p. 3–8; Rudolf Strnad, ed., *Padesát let odboru Národní jednoty pošumavské v Č. Budějovicích. 1884–1934* (Č. Budějovice: NJP, 1934), pp. 24–25; Zeithammer, *České Budějovice*, p. 108; Böhm, *České Budějovice*, p. 14; Sedlmeyer, *Budweis*, p. 4; and Johann Gottfried Sommer, *Das Königreich Böhmen: statistisch-topographisch dargestellt*, vol. 9: *Budweiser Kreis* (Prague: F. Ehrlich, 1841), p. 3. More generally, see Mack Walker, *German Home Towns: Community, State, and General Estate, 1648–1871* (Ithaca: Cornell University Press, 1971).

4. Theodor Žákavec, *Lanna* (Prague: 1936), pp. 24, 92; Miloš Vondruška, ed., *Jihočeská technická práce* (Č. Budějovice: Odbor spolku čs. inženýrů v Č. Budějovicích, 1938), pp. 29, 172–74; and Sedlmeyer, *Budweis*, p. 81.

5. Zeithammer, *České Budějovice*, pp. 108–9.

6. Macura, *Znamení zrodu*, p. 6. See also Karl W. Deutsch, *Nationalism and Social Communication* (New York: John Wiley, 1953), esp. pp. 25–30, 60–65; Gellner, *Nations and Nationalism* (Ithaca: Cornell University Press, 1983), esp. pp. 32–50; Anderson, *Imagined Communities*, 2nd edition, esp. pp. 24–46, 67–82; Verdery, *Transylvanian Villagers*; Hroch, *Die Vorkämpfer*; Miroslav Hroch, *Na prahu národní existence* (Prague: Mladá fronta, 1999); and Bugge, *Czech Nation-Building*, pp. 16–37.

7. Johann Georg Kohl, *Hundert Tage auf Reisen in den österreichischen Staaten*, vol. 1, *Reise in Böhmen* (Dresden and Leipzig: Arnold, 1842), pp. 328–29. Used here is the English translation provided in Johann Georg Kohl, *Austria* (London: Chapman and Hall, 1844), pp. 72–73. See also *Germanisirung oder Czechisirung?*

Ein Beitrag zur Nationalitätenfrage in Böhmen (Leipzig and Heidelberg: C. F. Winter, 1861), p. 17; Götz Fehr, *Fernkurs in Böhmisch* (Hamburg: Hoffmann und Campe, 1977), entire; *Jihočeské listy,* 21 September 1938, p. 2; and David Laitin, *Language Repertoires and State Construction in Africa* (New York: Cambridge University Press, 1992), pp. 3–9.

8. Kohl, *Hundert Tage,* vol. 1, *Reise,* pp. 328–29. This passage does not appear in the English edition, which is abridged.

9. See Rita Krueger, "From Empire to Nation: The Aristocracy and the Formation of Modern Society in Bohemia, 1770–1848," Ph.D. diss., Harvard University, 1997, chapter 1; as well as Verdery, *Transylvanian Villagers,* pp. 115–18; and Anderson, *Imagined Communities,* 2nd edition, pp. 6–7.

10. Kohl, *Austria,* pp. 62–63. See also Judson, *Exclusive Revolutionaries,* entire.

11. Karl Freiherr von Czoernig, *Ethnographie der österreichischen Monarchie,* vol. 1 (Vienna: k.k. Direction der administrativen Statistik/k.k. Hof- und Staatsdruckerei, 1857), pp. v–xiii, 40–41; and Benedict R. Anderson, *The Spectre of Comparisons. Nationalism, Southeast Asia and the World* (New York: Verso, 1998), p. 36.

12. von Czoernig, *Ethnographie,* pp. 74–80. Von Czoernig counted Jews as a separate, "Asiatic" *Sprachstamm,* or linguistic race—regardless of what they spoke. See also Křoalka, *Tschechen,* pp. 23–75, 133–38.

13. Josef Jireček, *Národopisný přehled Králowstwí českého roku 1850* (Prague: W Komissí kněhkupectwí Řiwnáčowa, 1850), pp. 3–4, 10, 23. See also von Czoernig, *Ethnographie,* pp. viii–x, 33.

14. "Jireček," in *Ottův slovník naučný,* 13: 542–46.

15. Krueger, From Empire to Nation; Rak, *Bývali Čechové,* Chapter 4; and Bugge, *Czech Nation-Building,* pp. 16–37.

16. See Křen, *Konfliktní společenství,* pp. 34–45; Gary Cohen, "The German Minority of Prague, 1850–1918," in *Ethnic Identity in Urban Europe (Comparative Studies on Governments and Non-Dominant Ethnic Groups in Europe, 1850–1940),* vol. 8, ed. Max Engman (New York: NYU Press, 1992), pp. 267–90, esp. 269–70; Bugge, *Czech Nation-Building,* pp. 24, 49; Anderson, *Imagined Communities,* 2nd edition, p. 78; Josef Pfitzner, *Das Erwachen der Sudetendeutschen im Spiegel ihres Schrifttums bis zum Jahre 1848* (Augsburg: Stauda, 1926); Eugen Lemberg, *Grundlagen des nationalen Erwachens in Böhmen, geistesgeschichtliche Studie am Lebensgang Josef Georg Meinerts (1773–1844)* (Reichenberg: Stiepel, 1932); and Wolfgang Menzel, *Die nationale Entwicklung in Böhmen, Mähren und Schlesien. Von der Aufklärung bis zur Revolution 1848* (Nuremberg: Preussler, 1985).

17. Kohl, *Austria,* pp. 61–63; Křoalka, *Tschechen,* p. 76; Hana Housková, "Česká studentská knihovna a její přínos ke vzniku národního vědomí v Č. Budějovicích," in *Minulost a současnost Č. Budějovic. Studie a materiály I* (Č. Budějovice: MNV, 1969), pp. 75–85, esp. 76–78; and *Jihočeské listy,* 3 December 1938, p. 3.

18. Macura, *Znamení zrodu,* pp. 36–37. See also Bugge, *Czech Nation-Building,* p. 28.

19. For a superb summary, see Josef Ulbrich, "Böhmen," in *Österreichisches Staatswörterbuch,* vol. 1, ed. Ernst Mischler and Josef Ulbrich (Vienna: A. Holder, 1905), pp. 530–611, esp. 539–43.

20. It should be conceded that in the Czech case (and in the Hungarian case as well, both in 1848 and after 1867), "the state" was in fact only an autonomous unit within the Habsburg Monarchy.

21. *Der Löwe*, 22 April 1848, p. 4; 29 April 1848, pp. 11, 14; 6 May 1848, pp. 17–18, 21–23; Kratochwil and Meerwald, *Heimatbuch*, pp. 367–96; Janoušek, *Město na soutoku*, pp. 201–10; Anna Bajerová, *Z české revoluce r. 1848* (Prague: Topič, 1919), pp. 16–18, 58–62; Chvojka, *Město*, pp. 122–24; and Judson, *Exclusive Revolutionaries*, p. 42.

22. Kratochwil and Meerwald, *Heimatbuch*, pp. 10; *Germanisirung oder Czechisirung?*, p. 53; Kořalka, *Tschechen*, pp. 19, 64–71; and *Der Löwe*, 6 May 1848, pp. 17–18.

23. Bajerová, *Z české revoluce*, pp. 16–18, 58–62; Kratochwil and Meerwald, *Heimatbuch*, pp. 403–10; and *Der Löwe*, 27 May 1848, pp. 44, 47–48.

24. *Der Löwe*, 20 May 1848, p. 36; 3 June 1848, pp. 51–52, 54–55; and 10 June 1848, p. 57; Pucherna, *Paměti Besedy*, p. 2; Chvojka, *Město*, pp. 122–24; and Bajerová, *Z české revoluce*, pp. 16–18, 58–62.

25. *Der Löwe*, 8 July 1848, pp. 89–90; and 29 July 1848, pp. 113–15; Richter, *Kurzgefaßte Geschichte*, p. 63; Janoušek, *Město na soutoku*, pp. 202–11; and Bugge, *Czech Nation-Building*, pp. 60–79.

26. *Der Bürgerfreund*, 22 November 1848, pp. 2–3.

27. Palacký's letter is reproduced in Menzel, *Die nationale Entwicklung*, pp. 206–10. For an English translation, see Charles Jelavich and Barbara Jelavich, eds., *The Habsburg Monarchy: Toward a Multinational Empire or National States?* (New York: Rinehart, 1959), pp. 18–22.

28. Bugge, *Czech Nation-Building*, pp. 79–88; Ulbrich, "Böhmen," pp. 544–45; Robert Kann, *The Multinational Empire. Nationalism and National Reform in the Habsburg Monarchy 1848–1918*, vol. 2 (New York: Octagon, 1970), pp. 21–39; and Kořalka, *Tschechen*, pp. 175–200.

29. *Der Löwe*, 23 July, 1848, p. 111. See also *Der Löwe*, 6 May 1848, pp. 21–22; and 27 May 1848, pp. 47–48; Franz Schuselka, *Deutsch oder Russisch? Die Lebensfrage Oesterreichs* (Vienna: Jasper, Hügel und Manz, 1849); Sedlmeyer, *Budweis*, p. 561; and Zeithammer, *České Budějovice*, pp. 246–47. "Slav(e)" is an attempt at translating *Slave*, a combination of the German words for "Slav" (*Slawe*) and for "slave" (*Sklave*).

30. *Der Bürgerfreund*, 2 December, 1848, pp. 1–2; and 6 December, 1848, pp. 1–2.

31. Kořalka, "Nationality Representation," p. 93.

32. Hagen Schulze, *The Course of German Nationalism* (Cambridge: Cambridge University Press, 1991), p. 140. I have corrected grammatical errors in the translation.

33. Ulbrich, "Böhmen," pp. 545–46; Kořalka, "Nationality Representation," p. 94; Bugge, *Czech Nation-Building*, pp. 84–87; Judson, *Exclusive Revolutionaries*, pp. 54–55; Max Kulisch, "Gemeinden: Gemeindewahlen," in Mischler and Ulbrich, *Österreichisches Staatswörterbuch*, 2:335–47, especially 335–37; and Eugene Anderson and Pauline Anderson, *Political Institutions and Social Change in Continental Europe in the Nineteenth Century* (Berkeley: University of California Press, 1967), chap. 8.

34. Christoph Stölzl, *Die Ära Bach in Böhmen* (Munich: Oldenbourg, 1971).

35. *Der Bürgerfreund*, 22 November 1848, pp. 2–3; and *Der konstitutionelle Staatsbürger*, 8 March 1849, p. 4; and 15 March 1849, p. 3.

36. See Judson, *Exclusive Revolutionaries*, pp. 70–87.

37. Kořalka, *Tschechen*, pp. 142–45; Garver, *Young Czech Party*, pp. 24–25; D. Rauter, *Österreichisches Staats-Lexikon* (Vienna: Perles, 1885), pp. 35–36, 95–98; "Čechy," in *Ottův slovník naučný*, 6:1–572, esp. 565; *Österreichische National-Encyklopädie*, vol. 1 (Vienna: Beck'sche Universitäts-Buchhandlung, 1835), p. 430; and Judson, *Exclusive Revolutionaries*, pp. 11–13. Rounding out the Bohemian Diet were the Archbishop, three bishops, and the rector of the university in Prague.

38. The quotation is from *Budweiser Wochenblatt*, 23 February, 1861, pp. 2–3; see also 15 December 1860, pp. 1–2, and 2 March 1861, p. 4; and Kulisch, "Gemeinden: Gemeindewahlen," pp. 335–47. The only women allowed to vote in Budweis/Budějovice did so in their capacity as the widow of a burgher—through a proxy.

39. *Budweiser Wochenblatt*, 2 March 1861, pp. 4, Extrablatt; as well as 22 December 1860, p. 3; 26 January 1861, p. 7; 23 February 1861, pp. 1–3; 9 March 1861, p. 10; and 23 March 1861, p. 4; as well as Judson, *Exclusive Revolutionaries*, p. 87.

40. *Budweiser Wochenblatt*, 23 March, 1861, p. 4; and 6 April 1861, p. 4; and the Stenographic protocols of the Bohemian Diet, which may be found at http://www.psp.cz/cgi-bin/win/eknih/1861skc/stenprot/010schuz/s010005.htm.

41. *Der Reichsrath. Biographische Skizzen der Mitglieder des Herren- und Abgeordnetenhauses des österreichischen Reichsrathes*, vol. 1 (Vienna: Fr. Förster und Brüder, 1861), pp. 12–55; and personal communication from Robert Sak.

42. Judson, *Exclusive Revolutionaries*, pp. 92, 103, and also 58–64, 88–103; as well as Pieter Judson, "'Whether Race or Conviction Should Be the Standard': National Identity and Liberal Politics in Nineteenth-Century Austria," *Austrian History Yearbook* 22 (1991):76–95, esp. 81–84; and von Herrnritt, *Nationalität und Recht*, pp. 43–44, 129–37.

43. *Anzeiger aus dem südlichen Böhmen*, 19 February 1862, p. 2; and *Budweiser Wochenblatt*, 11 May 1861, p. 4.

44. *Budivoj*, 13 October 1864, p. 3; 10 November 1864, p. 3; 17 November 1864, pp. 1–3; and *Anzeiger aus dem südlichen Böhmen*, 28 March 1863, p. 3; 11 May 1864, pp. 2–3; 2 July 1864, p. 1; 16 July 1864, p. 3; 9 July 1864, p. 4; and 14 September 1864, p. 3.

45. *Budweiser Wochenblatt*, 21 July 1860, p. 4; *Anzeiger aus dem südlichen Böhmen*, 15 July 1863, p. 2 and 7 September 1864, p. 1; *Budivoj*, 1 September 1864, p. 1; 22 September 1864, pp. 1–2; 17 November 1864, pp. 1–3; 15 January 1865, p. 3; 1 June 1865, p. 3; 8 June 1865, pp. 1–3; and 11 June 1865, pp. 3–4; and Zeithammer, *České Budějovice*, p. 117.

46. *Budivoj*, 15 June 1865, p. 3; 18 June 1865, p.3; 22 June 1865, pp. 1–3; 29 June 1865, p. 3; 13 July 1865, pp. 2–3; and 16 July 1865, p. 1.

47. See Judson, *Exclusive Revolutionaries*, pp. 103–9.

48. *Budivoj*, 24 March 1867, p. 2; Bugge, *Czech Nation-Building*, pp. 113–15; and Judson, *Exclusive Revolutionaries*, pp. 109–14.

49. *Budivoj*, 19 May 1867, p. 1.

50. von Herrnritt, *Nationalität und Recht*, pp. 48–56; Rauter, *Österreichisches Staats-Lexikon*, pp. 124–26; Bugge, *Czech Nation-Building*, p. 115; Alfred Fischel, "Nationalitäten," in Mischler and Ulbrich, *Österreichisches Staatswörterbuch*, 3:676–702, esp. 690; and Judson, *Exclusive Revolutionaries*, pp. 118–29.

51. *Budivoj*, 30 June 1867, pp. 1–3; and 7 July 1867, pp. 1–3. Richter's quotation from *Anzeiger* appears in *Budivoj*, 11 July 1867, p. 1. Pucherna, *Paměti Besedy*, p. 18; *Matice školská v Čes. Budějovicích. Její vzor a její pokračovatelé* (Č. Budějovice: Matice školská / K. Fiala, 1925), pp. 4–5.

52. *Budivoj*, 28 September 1865, p. 1.

53. Zeithammer, *České Budějovice*, p. 118; and Pucherna, *Paměti Besedy*, pp. 22–23.

54. Judson, *Exclusive Revolutionaries*, pp. 135–37; Ulbrich, "Böhmen," pp. 549–50; Bugge, *Czech Nation-Building*, pp. 116, 132; Kořalka, *Tschechen*, pp. 73, 98–99, 108; and Gustav Kolmer, *Parlament und Verfassung in Österreich*, vol. 1: *1848–1869* (Graz: Akademische Druck- und Verlagsanstalt, 1972), pp. 347–50. Regarding the term *českoslovanský*, see also Kořalka, *Tschechen*, pp. 57–75.

55. Strnad, *Dr. A. Zátka*, p. 15; *Budweiser Kreisblatt*, 4 October 1871, p. 2; *Budivoj*, 9 November 1871, p. 1; and Böhm, *České Budějovice*, p. 21.

56. *Budivoj*, 6 June 1869, p. 1; and 11 July 1869, p. 3.

57. *Budivoj*, 31 July 1870, p. 3; 11 August 1870, p. 1; 14 August 1870, p. 1; 25 August 1870, pp. 1–2; and 28 August 1870, p. 1; Strnad, *Dr. A. Zátka*, p. 17; and Rudolf Strnad, ed., *Projevy a řeči dra. Augusta Zátky* (Č. Budějovice: Odbor NJP, 1935), pp. 7–8.

58. *Budivoj*, 18 September 1870, p. 3; and 29 September 1870, p. 1; and Pucherna, *Paměti Besedy*, p. 28.

59. *Budivoj*, 13 October 1870, p. 1; Strnad, *Dr. A. Zátka*, p. 18; and Strnad, *Projevy a řeči*, p. 8.

60. *Budivoj*, 6 November 1870, p. 3; and 10 November 1870, pp. 1–3; and *Budweiser Kreisblatt*, 22 March 1871, p. 2.

61. Rauter, *Österreichisches Staats-Lexikon*, pp. 71–77; Ulbrich, "Böhmen," pp. 551–56; and Bugge, *Czech Nation-Building*, pp. 119–20.

62. *Budweiser Kreisblatt*, 26 August 1871, p. 2; 9 September 1871, p. 2; and 13 September 1871, p. 2; and *Budivoj*, 7 September 1871, p. 1.

63. *Budweiser Kreisblatt*, 16 September 1871, p. 2; 20 September 1871, p. 1; 27 September 1871, p. 2; 4 October 1871, pp. 2–3; and 16 December 1871, p. 1; *Budivoj*, 21 September 1871, p. 1; Fischel, "Nationalitäten," p. 692; Strnad, *Dr. A. Zátka*, p. 24; and Pucherna, *Paměti Besedy*, p. 32.

64. *Budivoj*, 21 April 1872, p. 2.

65. *Budivoj*, 3 September 1871, p. 1; 5 November 1871, p. 1; and 12 November 1871, p. 3.

66. See Hillel Kieval, *The Making of Czech Jewry: National Conflict and Jewish Society in Bohemia, 1870–1918* (New York: Oxford University Press, 1988), pp. 5–10; Ruth Kestenberg-Gladstein, "The Jews between Czechs and Germans in the Historic Lands, 1848–1918," in *The Jews of Czechoslovakia*, vol. 1 (Philadelphia: Jewish Publication Society of America, 1968), pp. 27–31; as well as *Anzeiger aus*

dem südlichen Böhmen, 9 January 1864, p. 2; Richter, *Kurzgefasste Geschichte*, pp. 71–72; and Sedlmeyer, *Budweis*, pp. 163–65.

67. *Budivoj*, 14 December 1871, p. 1.

68. *Budivoj*, 17 December 1871, p. 2; and 21 December 1871, pp. 1, 3.

69. *Budivoj*, 13 October 1864, p. 3.

Chapter Two
A More Broad and National Politics, 1871–1890

1. *Budivoj*, 14 April 1867, p. 1. See also Strnad, *Padesát let odboru*, p. 25.

2. Jiří Klabouch, *Die Gemeindeselbstverwaltung in Österreich, 1848–1918* (Munich: Oldenbourg, 1968), esp. pp. 93–95; Garver, *Young Czech*, pp. 88–98; Josef Redlich, *Das Wesen der österreichischen Kommunal-Verfassung* (Leipzig: Duncker & Humblot, 1910), esp. pp. 61–62, 67; Gerald Stourzh, "Problems of Conflict Resolution in a Multi-Ethnic State: Lessons from the Austrian Historical Experience, 1848–1918," in *State and Nation in Multi-ethnic Societies*, ed. Uri Ra'anan (New York: Manchester University Press, 1991), p. 74; and Ronald Smelser, "German-Czech Relations in Bohemian Frontier Towns: The Industrialization and Urbanization Process," in *Studies in East European Social History*, vol. 2, ed. Keith Hitchins (Leiden: E. J. Brill, 1981), pp. 62–87, esp. 71–73.

3. *Budivoj*, 4 February 1869, p. 4. See also 24 July 1870, p. 3.

4. See, for example, *Budivoj*, 29 August 1869, p. 3; and 21 August 1870, p. 2; and Johannes Zemmrich, *Sprachgrenze und Deutschtum in Böhmen* (Braunschweig: Vieweg und Sohn, 1902), p. 102.

5. Jiří Klabouch, "Die Lokalverwaltung in Cisleithanien," in *Die Habsburgermonarchie 1848–918*, vol. 2: *Verwaltung und Rechtswesen*, ed. Adam Wandruszka and Peter Urbanitsch (Vienna: Österreichische Akademie der Wissenschaften, 1975), pp. 270–305, esp. p. 287; and Garver, *Young Czech*, pp. 36–37.

6. See František Hlíza, ed., *Sedmdesát let trvání továrny na tabák v Čes. Budějovicích. 1872–1947* (Č. Budějovice: Společenské knihtiskárny, 1947); and Wilibald Böhm and Emmerich Zdiarsky, *Die Stadt Budweis. Eine Orts- und Volkskunde* (Budweis: Selbstverlag, 1904), p. 55.

7. *Matice*, pp. 7–11; and Strnad, *Dr. A. Zátka*, p. 20.

8. Neruda, "Eklogy," pp. 228–29.

9. In 1871–72, the *Liedertafel* had 247 members, and the *Turnverein* 140. Pucherna, *Paměti Besedy*, pp. 34, 148; *Festschrift der Deutschen Liedertafel in Budweis anläßlich ihrer 50 jähr. Bestandsfeier* (Budweis: Selbstverlag, 1906), pp. 38–39; *Budweiser Kreisblatt*, 29 January 1873, p. 2; and 12 February 1873, p. 2; and *Bericht des Deutschen Turnvereines in Budweis. Herausgegeben aus Anlaß des 50 jährigen Vereinsbestandes mit besonderer Berücksichtigung der letzten 10 Vereinsjahre* (Budweis: A. Pokorný, 1912), pp. 63–69.

10. *Budweiser Kreisblatt*, 15 February 1873, p. 7.

11. *Budweiser Kreisblatt*, 19 February 1873, p. 1; 14 May 1873, pp. 1–2; and 24 May 1873, p. 2.

12. *Budweiser Kreisblatt*, 29 January 1873, p. 2; 24 May 1873, p. 2; and 31 May 1873, pp. 1–2.

13. *Budweiser Kreisblatt*, 29 January 1873, p. 2; 19 February 1873, p. 2; and 9 April 1873, p. 2; Kratochwil and Meerwald, *Heimatbuch*, p. 451; Strnad, *Dr. A. Zátka*, pp. 27–28; William Jenks, *The Austrian Electoral Reform of 1907* (New York: Columbia University Press, 1950), p. 15; Bugge, *Czech Nation-Building*, pp. 138–39; and Rauter, *Österreichisches Staats-Lexikon*, p. 230.

14. *Bericht*, pp. 13–15; Strnad, *Dr. A. Zátka*, p. 26; Zeithammer, *České Budějovice*, p. 124–26; and *Matice*, pp. 5–6, 13.

15. *Statuten des Militär-Veteranen-Vereines zu Budweis* (Budweis: Josef Watzl, n.d. [1872?]), p. 3; Pucherna, *Paměti Besedy*, p. 38; Deák, *Beyond Nationalism*, pp. 98–99; and Johann Christoph Allmayer-Beck, "Die bewaffnete Macht in Staat und Gesellschaft," in Wandruszka and Urbanitsch, *Die Habsburgermonarchie 1848–1918*, 5:1–141, esp. 82–83, 98.

16. *Anzeiger aus dem südlichen Böhmen*, 9 March 1864, p. 2; 2 July 1864, p. 1; and 6 July 1864, p. 3; *Budivoj*, 17 November 1864, pp. 1–3; and 15 January 1888, p. 2; and Böhm, *České Budějovice*, p. 97.

17. *Budweiser Kreisblatt*, 24 May 1879, pp. 1–2; and 28 May 1879, p. 3; *Budivoj*, 25 May 1879, pp. 2, 3; and 28 May 1879, p. 3; Žákavec, *Lanna*, pp. 57, 65; and Zeithammer, *České Budějovice*, p. 127.

18. *Budweiser Kreisblatt*, 28 May 1879, p. 3; C. A. Macartney, *The Habsburg Empire, 1790–1918* (New York: MacMillan, 1969), p. 609; and Judson, *Exclusive*, p. 184.

19. Josef Penížek, ed., *Politické úvahy Gustava Eima* (Prague: J. Otto, 1898), pp. 280–81. Regarding Eim, see Garver, *Young Czech*, pp. 106–7; and Křen, *Konfliktní společenství*, p. 250.

20. Křen, *Konfliktní společenství*, p. 221; and F. R. Bridge, *From Sadowa to Sarajevo: The Foreign Policy of Austria-Hungary, 1866–1914* (London: Routledge and Kegan Paul), pp. 104–7.

21. Ulbrich, "Böhmen," pp. 556–61; Garver, *Young Czech*, p. 84; Berthold Sutter, *Die Badenischen Sprachenverordnungen von 1897* (Graz and Cologne: Böhlau, 1960), 1:83–87; Robert A. Kann, *The Multinational Empire. Nationalism and National Reform in the Habsburg Monarchy 1848–1918* (New York: Octagon, 1970), 1:198–201, 406; and Theodor Veiter, "Die Sudetenländer," in *Das Nationalitätenrecht des alten Österreich*, ed. Karl Gottfried Hugelmann (Vienna and Leipzig: Wilhelm Braumüller, 1934), p. 418.

22. *Budweiser Kreisblatt*, 5 June 1880, p. 3; Strnad, *Dr. A. Zátka*, pp. 27–28; and Kratochwil and Meerwald, *Heimatbuch*, pp. 483–84.

23. *Budweiser Kreisblatt*, 18 September 1880, p. 4; and Kratochwil and Meerwald, *Heimatbuch*, p. 484.

24. See *Matice*, p. 8; and Bugge, *Czech Nation-Building*, p. 165. Regarding the German School Association, which should not be confused with an identically named organization in the German Empire, see Judson, *Exclusive Revolutionaries*, pp. 207–15.

25. Adolf Ficker, *Vorträge über die Vornahme der Volkszählung in Österreich* (Vienna: k.k. Hof- und Staatsdruckerei, 1870), pp. 87, 89–90. The same statements appear in Ficker, *Die Völkerstämme der österreichisch-ungarischen Monarchie, ihre Gebiete, Gränzen und Inseln. Historisch, geographisch, statistisch dargestellt* (Vienna: k.k. Hof- und Staatsdruckerei, 1869), p. 34; also pp. 30–33. Regarding Ficker and

his understanding of "nationality," see Emil Brix, *Die Umgangssprache in Altöster-reich zwischen Agitation und Assimilation* (Vienna: Böhlau, 1982), esp. pp. 72–73, 93–94. For another semi-official explanation of "nationality," see Leopold Neumann, "Die Bevölkerung Oesterreich's. Ethnographische und confessionelle Verhältnisse," in *Statistisch-Administrative Vorträge auf Veranstaltung der k.k. Statistischen Central-Commission* (Wien: k.k. Hof- und Staatsdruckerei, 1867), pp. 53–68.

26. Ficker, *Vorträge*, pp. 87, 89–90; Ficker, *Völkerstämme*, pp. 30–33, 34; and Brix, *Umgangssprache*, pp. 47–49, 77–96. Rogers Brubaker has pointed recently toward the pitfalls of understanding nationhood as a universally distributed, individual attribute. See especially *Nationalism Reframed*, pp. 13–18; and Brubaker and Cooper, "Beyond 'Identity,'" entire. For additional examples in recent scholarship, see Charles Tilly, "A Bridge Halfway: Responding to Brubaker," *Contention* 4, no. 1 (Fall 1994): 15–19, esp. 16; Craig Calhoun, "Nationalism and Ethnicity," *Annual Review of Sociology* 19 (1993): pp. 211–39; and Anderson, *Spectre of Comparisons*, pp. 35–45.

27. Ficker, *Völkerstämme*, p. 34; Brix, *Umgangssprache*, pp. 98–105; and Wilhelm Hecke, "Volksvermehrung, Binnenwanderung und Umgangssprache in den österreichischen Alpenländern und Südländern," *Statistische Monatschrift*, Neue Folge, 18 (1913): 323–92, esp. 391.

28. Brix, *Umgangssprache*, 72–109; Edmund Bernatzik, *Über nationale Matriken: Inaugurationsrede* (Vienna: Manz, 1910), pp. 29–30; and Adam Müller-Guttenbrunn, *Deutsche Sorgen in Ungarn* (Vienna: Strache, 1918), p. 160.

29. Ficker notes that cooperation by Habsburg statisticians with statisticians from other "German" states was particularly close. This is significant, because in Prussia, the equation of language with "nationality" during the 1860s by statisticians was strong. See Ficker, *Vorträge*, pp. 26–27, 67; as well as Richard Böckh, "Die statistische Bedeutung der Volkssprache als Kennzeichen der Nationalität," in *Zeitschrift für Völkerpsychologie und Sprachwissenschaft*, vol. 4 (Berlin: 1866), pp. 259–402, esp. 300; Ernst Mischler, "Volkszählung," in Mischler and Ulbrich, eds., *Österreichisches Staatswörterbuch*, 4: 848–52, esp. 849; Stourzh, "Problems of Conflict Resolution," p. 72; and Laitin, *Language Repertoires*, pp. 4–5. The Habsburg wish to avoid recognizing the existence of a Jewish language, emphasized by Brix, helps to explain only the establishing of a set list of languages that census respondents could claim to use—not the requirement that every respondent choose one and only one language from the list. See Brix, *Umgangssprache*, pp. 77–96.

30. *Budweiser Kreisblatt*, 18 December 1880, pp. 1–2.

31. *Budweiser Kreisblatt*, 22 December 1880, p. 3; as well as Brix, *Umgangssprache*, p. 254.

32. *Budweiser Kreisblatt*, 24 December 1880, p. 9; 8 January 1881, p. 3; and 12 January 1881, pp. 4–5; Brix, *Umgangssprache*, p. 255; and *Budweiser Kreisblatt*, 15 November 1884, p. 4.

33. *Budivoj*, 14 December 1890, p. 1; Strnad, *Dr. A. Zátka*, p. 28; and *České Budějovice. Krása našeho domova* (Č. Budějovice, 1926), p. 5. See also Zemmrich, *Sprachgrenze*, p. 102.

34. All figures cited include military personnel. See Sedlmeyer, *Budweis*, pp. 163–65; and Zeithammer, *České Budějovice*, pp. 108, 128–29. See also Brix, *Um-*

gangssprache, p. 65; and Alfred Bohmann, *Bevölkerungsbewegungen in Böhmen 1847–1947* (Munich: Colegium Carolinum, 1958), pp. 55–56. See also Donald L. Horowitz, *Ethnic Groups in Conflict* (Berkeley: University of California Press), p. 194; Eric J. Hobsbawm, *Nations and Nationalism since 1780* (Cambridge: Cambridge University Press, 1990), pp. 97–100; and Anderson, *Imagined Communities*, 2nd edition, pp. 164–70.

35. Cited in Brix, *Umgangssprache*, pp. 413–14, and p. 112; see also Anderson, *Spectre of Comparisons*, pp. 35–45, regarding what he labels "bound seriality."

36. Strnad, *Dr. A. Zátka*, pp. 27–29; Pucherna, *Paměti Besedy*, p. 56; Zeithammer, *České Budějovice*, p. 129; *Budivoj*, 20 June 1869, p. 1; Kratochwil and Meerwald, *Heimatbuch*, p. 484; and *Budweiser Kreisblatt*, 12 January 1884, p. 3; 16 July 1884, pp. 2–3; 19 July 1884, p. 2; and 13 August 1884, p. 2. Von Jungmann/ z Jungmannů continued to speak up on behalf of Czechs; see *Budweiser Kreisblatt*, 15 November 1884, p. 4; and *Budivoj*, 30 September 1888, p. 5.

37. *Jihočeský kalendář. Schematismus a adresář na rok 1901* (Č. Budějovice: Družstvo vydavatelské a nakladatelské, n.d. [1900?]), p. 87. See also Garver, *Young Czech*, p. 124; and Ulbrich, "Böhmen," p. 561.

38. Maysl, *Obchodní*, pp. 47–50, 74–79, 95–97; *Matice*, p. 55; Pucherna, *Paměti Besedy*, p. 63; Kratochwil and Meerwald, *Heimatbuch*, p. 486; *Budivoj*, 20 June 1902, pp. 1–2; and Strnad, *Dr. A. Zátka*, p. 30.

39. Strnad, *Dr. A. Zátka*, p. 31; Strnad, *Projevy*, p. 8; and Pucherna, *Paměti Besedy*, pp. 62, 71–74.

40. Sedlmeyer, *Budweis*, pp. 269–70, 564–65; and Kratochwil and Meerwald, *Heimatbuch*, pp. 486–87.

41. Strnad, *Projevy*, pp. 135, 152; Strnad, *Dr. A. Zátka*, p. 5; *Budivoj*, 9 January 1898, p. 3; and 28 January 1902, p. 1; *Stráž lidu*, 27 November 1903, p. 6; Scheu, *Wanderung*, pp. 27–28; and *Naše svoboda*, 7 December 1946, p. 2. On pictures of Francis Joseph, present in nearly every office, barracks, classroom, and business (including even brothels), see Helmut Niederle, *"Es war sehr schön, es hat mich sehr gefreut* (Vienna: Oesterreichischer Bundesverlag, 1987), p. 172; and Joseph Roth, *The Radetzky March* (Woodstock, N.Y.: Overlook, 1974), pp. 67, 73, and 97–98.

42. *Budweiser Kreisblatt*, 2 February 1881, pp. 1–2; Strnad, *Projevy*, p. 76; and Judson, "'Whether Race,'" pp. 76–95.

43. *Festschrift*, pp. 23–24; *Bericht*, pp. 17–18; *Budivoj*, 2 February 1888, p. 2; *Budweiser Kreisblatt*, 2 July 1884, p. 1; and 4 October 1884, p. 3; Wonesch, *Deutsche Liedertafel*, p. 7; Pucherna, *Paměti Besedy*, p. 63; Zeithammer, *České Budějovice*, pp. 133, 159; and Judson, *Exclusive Revolutionaries*, p. 205.

44. *Budweiser Kreisblatt*, 29 October 1884, pp. 1–2; *Budivoj*, 13 May 1888, p. 3; *Jihočeské listy*, 13 November 1918, p. 2; Sutter, *Badenischen*, 1:12; Sedlmeyer, *Budweis*, p. 380; and Nancy Wingfield, "Statues of Emperor Joseph II as Sites of German Identity," in *Staging the Past: The Politics of Commemoration in Habsburg Central Europe, 1848 to the Present*, ed. Nancy Wingfield and Maria Bucur (West Lafayette: Purdue University Press, 2001), pp. 178–205.

45. *Budweiser Kreisblatt*, 20 February 1884, pp. 1–2; and 29 March 1884, p. 1. See also *1884–1934. Fünfzig Jahre Deutscher Böhmerwaldbund* (Budweis: Deutscher Böhmerwaldbund / Felix Zdarssa, 1934), p. 3; Sedlmeyer, *Budweis*, pp. 380–83; and Macura, *Český sen*.

46. See Judson, *Exclusive Revolutionaries*, pp. 207–17; Sedlmeyer, *Budweis*, p. 381; *Budweiser Kreisblatt*, 22 March 1884, p. 4; 29 March 1884, p. 3; 15 October 1884, p. 2; and 22 October 1884, p. 3; Günter Schödl, "Varianten deutscher Nationalpolitik vor 1918. Zur politischen Organisation und Programmbildung deutscher Minderheiten in Ost- und Südosteuropa," in *Südostdeutsches Archiv* 22–23 (1979–80), pp. 109–12; and Stanley Kimball, *Czech Nationalism: A Study of the National Theatre Movement, 1845–83* (Urbana: University of Illinois Press, 1967), pp. 33–40, 59, 76–78, 124–30, 135–43.

47. *Festschrift*, pp. 38–39, 106–8; Pucherna, *Paměti Besedy*, pp. 53, 71, 89, 148–49; *Sedlmeyer, Budweis*, p. 381; *Bericht*, pp. 14, 63–69; and Böhm, *České Budějovice*, p. 81.

48. Zeithammer, *České Budějovice*, p. 138; Rudolf Strnad, *1884–1924. Čtyřicet let činnosti odboru Národní jednoty pošumavské v Č. Budějovicích* (Č. Budějovice: Odbor NJP, 1924), p. 9; Strnad, *Projevy*, pp. 51, 86–87; *Budweiser Kreisblatt*, 5 and 12 April 1884, both p. 3; and 25 June 1884, p. 3; Pucherna, *Paměti Besedy*, p. 99; *Jihočeské listy*, 9 February 1907, p. 2; and *Budivoj*, 29 July 1888, p. 2; as well as 14 November 1913, p. 2.

49. The text of Zátka's speech may be found in Strnad, *Projevy*, pp. 17–20. See also Pucherna, *Paměti Besedy*, pp. 56–57, 67; and *Budweiser Kreisblatt*, 28 June 1884, p. 1; 2 July 1884, pp. 1, 3; and 22 November 1884, p. 3.

50. Pucherna, *Paměti Besedy*, pp. 67, 150–51; Strnad, *Dr. A. Zátka*, pp. 35–36; *Matice*, pp. 19–23, 54; and Zeithammer, *České Budějovice*, pp. 133–34.

51. *Budweiser Kreisblatt*, 29 November 1884, p. 2; and 3 December 1884, p. 1; Strnad, *Dr. A. Zátka*, p. 35; Kratochwil and Meerwald, *Heimatbuch*, p. 188; and Arthur Skedl, ed., *Der politische Nachlass des Grafen Eduard Taaffe* (Vienna: Rikola, 1922), pp. 464–66.

52. *Budweiser Kreisblatt*, 20 December 1884, pp. 3–4; *Budweiser Bote*, 2 January 1886, p. 1; Strnad, *Projevy*, p. 60; *Budivoj*, 6 November 1890, pp. 1–2; and Pucherna, *Paměti Besedy*, p. 84.

53. See William Jenks, *Austria under the Iron Ring 1879–1893* (Charlottesville: University Press of Virginia, 1965), esp. pp. 104–21; Stanislaus Ritter von Starzyński, "Wahlen: Reichsrathswahlen," in Mischler and Ulbrich, eds., *Österreichisches Staatswörterbuch*, 4: 871–94, esp. 877; Peter Pulzer, *The Rise of Political Anti-Semitism in Germany and Austria* (New York: Wiley, 1964), pp. 210–11; John W. Boyer, *Political Radicalism in Late Imperial Vienna: Origins of the Christian Social Movement, 1848–1897* (Chicago: University of Chicago Press, 1981), p. 64; Judson, *Exclusive Revolutionaries*, p. 198; Maysl, *Obchodní*, p. 80; *Budivoj*, 16 February 1888, p. 2; and Strnad, *Dr. A. Zátka*, pp. 35–36. The number of those enfranchised, as opposed to those who actually voted, ranges somewhat higher. The percentages given for 1885 and 1887 are slightly high, because I have used the 1880 census figures as the denominator in all calculations, although the population of Budweis/Budějovice grew by nearly 20 percent between 1880 and 1890.

54. Skedl, *Der politische Nachlass des Grafen Eduard Taaffe*, p. 7; Mommsen, *Sozialdemokratie*, pp. 128–54; Zdeněk Šolle, *Dělnické hnutí v Českých zemích koncem minulého století* (Prague: Rovnost, 1951), pp. 68–78; Friedrich Tezner, "Vereinsrecht," in Mischler and Ulbrich, *Österreichisches Staatswörterbuch*, 4:712–

22; and Tezner, "Versammlungsrecht," in Mischler and Ulbrich, *Österreichisches Staatswörterbuch*, 4:746–53.

55. Strnad, *Dr. A. Zátka*, pp. 36, 40–41; Strnad, *Projevy*, p. 18; Zeithammer, *České Budějovice*, pp. 124, 138; Kratochwil and Meerwald, *Heimatbuch*, p. 488; *Budivoj*, 9 February 1888, p. 2; 1 April 1888, p. 1; 17 June 1888, pp. 1–2; 7 October 1888, p. 1; 14 October 1888, p. 2; and 5 January 1890, p. 1; Ulbrich, "Böhmen," p. 561; Garver, *Young Czech*, pp. 123–25; and Gary Steenson, *After Marx, Before Lenin: Marxism and Socialist Working-class Parties in Europe, 1884–1914* (Pittsburgh: University of Pittsburgh Press, 1991), p. 172. This paragraph and the several that follow are also based on the following studies: Carl Schorske, *Fin-de-siècle Vienna: Politics and Culture* (New York: Vintage, 1981), esp. chap. 3; Pulzer, *Rise of Political*, chaps. 15–17; Cohen, *Politics*, chaps. 4 and 5; Boyer, *Political Radicalism*, chap. 2; and Judson, *Exclusive Revolutionaries*, chaps. 7 and 8.

56. *Budweiser Kreisblatt*, 2 July 1884, p. 3; and 20 August 1884, p. 3; *1884–1934. Fünfzig Jahre*, p. 3; *Budweiser Bote*, 7 July 1886, pp. 2–3; *Budivoj*, 12 August 1888, p. 2; 26 October 1890, p. 2; 1 January 1898, p. 1; and 2 September 1902, p. 2; *Bericht*, pp. 18–21; Strnad, *Projevy*, pp. 53–54; Judson, *Exclusive Revolutionaries*, pp. 236–39; and Prinz, *Geschichte Böhmens*, p. 291.

57. Raimund Friedrich Kaindl, *Der Völkerkampf und Sprachenstreit in Böhmen im Spiegel der zeitgenössischen Quellen* (Vienna and Leipzig: Braumüller, 1927), p. 47; Kořalka, *Tschechen im Habsburgerreich*, pp. 126–138; Judson, *Exclusive Revolutionaries*, pp. 202–4; Schorske, *Fin-de-siècle*, pp. 125–29; May, *Habsburg*, pp. 434–37; Brix, *Umgangssprache*, p. 436; Urbanitsch, "Die Deutschen," pp. 33–35; and *Budivoj*, 7 October 1888, p. 1.

58. *Budivoj*, 13 May 1888, p. 3; Scheu, *Wanderungen*, p. 27; and Cohen, *Politics*, p. 282.

59. Garver, *Young Czech*, pp. 60–83, 123–28, 230; and Kořalka, *Tschechen im Habsburgerreich*, pp. 26–75. See also Horowitz, *Ethnic Groups*, p. 32, where the author argues that national conflict, under certain circumstances, "goes hand in hand with conservative politics."

60. Strnad, *Dr. A. Zátka*, p. 77. See also Pecha, *Státní převrat v říjnu 1918 v Českých Budějovicích*, p. 24. I thank Dr. Pecha for his assistance in tracking down Taaffe's statement.

61. Brix, *Umgangssprache*, pp. 84–85; and Judson, *Exclusive Revolutionaries*, pp. 107, 269–70.

62. *Budivoj*, 25 October 1888, p. 2. See also Hubka, *Naše menšiny a smíšené kraje na českém jihu* (Prague: Samostatnost, 1899), p. 258.

63. The quotation comes from [Jan Palacký], *Böhmische Skizzen, 1860. Von einem Landeskind* (Leitomischl: Anton Augusta, 1860), p. 38. See also Deák, *Beyond Nationalism*, p. 4; Pucherna, *Paměti Besedy*, pp. 59, 110–12; and *Budweiser Kreisblatt*, 6 December 1884, p. 2. *Pero* (1922), Josef Holeček's autobiographical novel, contains pertinent remarks concerning army officers and the importance to the *Beseda* in Pisek/Písek (located not far from Budweis/Budějovice) of gaining them as members. See esp. p. 195.

NOTES TO CHAPTER THREE

64. *Budweiser Bote*, 7 July 1886, p. 4; *Budweiser Kreisblatt*, 9 July 1884, p. 3; Zeithammer, *České Budějovice*, p. 136; Sedlmeyer, *Budweis*, p. 490; and Kopáček, *Encyklopedie*, p. 74.

65. Carol Krinsky, *Synagogues of Europe* (New York: Architectural History Foundation, 1985), pp. 165–66; and Frýd, *Vzorek bez ceny a pan biskup*, pp. 117–18. See also Rada, *Když se psalo T.G.M. České Budějovice v prvním desetiletí republiky*, p. 162.

66. Both quotations come from *Budivoj*, 16 September 1888, p. 1. See also Zemmrich, *Sprachgrenze*, pp. 12–13; Garver, *Young Czech*, pp. 64, 123; Hubka, *Naše menšiny*, p. 204; *Budweiser Kreisblatt*, 28 May 1884, p. 3; and Pucherna, *Paměti Besedy*, p. 164.

67. Chvojka, *Město*, p. 148.

Chapter Three
Free-for-All, 1890–1902

1. For a persuasive study of how intranational debate can lead to a deepening of national sentiments, see Katherine Verdery, *National Ideology under Socialism. Identity and Cultural Politics in Ceausescu's Romania* (Berkeley: University of California Press, 1991). See also Horowitz, *Ethnic Groups*, pp. 333–58, for an explanation of why such debate, when it occurs within a political system that includes more than one national movement, tends to drive them apart.

2. The following paragraphs are based on Gustav Kolmer, *Parlament und Verfassung in Österreich*, vol. 4 (Vienna: k.u.k. Hof-Buchdruckerei, 1907), pp. 398–426; Max Menger, *Der böhmische Ausgleich* (Stuttgart: Cotta, 1891); Ulbrich, "Böhmen," pp. 561–63; Garver, *Young Czech*, pp. 146–49, 347, 435–36; Kořalka, *Tschechen*, pp. 152–57; Judson, *Exclusive Revolutionaries*, pp. 246–49; and Kann, *Multinational Empire*, 1:201–2.

3. The quotations come from *Budivoj*, 26 October 1890, p. 2; and Strnad, *Projevy*, p. 65. See also *Budivoj*, 16 November 1890, p. 2; 27 November 1890, p. 1; and 19 January 1898, p. 1.

4. *Budivoj*, 18 December 1890, p. 1; 9 November 1890, p. 1; 11 December 1890, pp. 1–2; and 25 December 1890, p. 1.

5. The quotation comes from Pucherna, *Paměti Besedy*, p. 89. Regarding the Czech private census, see *Budivoj*, 23 November 1890, p. 2; 7 December 1890, p. 2; and 14 December 1890, p. 1; Strnad, *Projevy*, p. 50; and Strnad, *Dr. A. Zátka*, pp. 41–42.

6. Strnad, *Projevy*, p. 45; *Budivoj*, 23 November 1890, p. 2; 7 December 1890, p. 2; 11 December 1890, p. 2; 14 December 1890, p. 1; and 18 December 1890, p. 2.

7. Austria, k.k. statistische Central-Commission, *Österreichisches Städtebuch. Statistische Berichte der grösseren österreichischen Städte*, vol. 4 (Vienna: k.k. Hof-und Staatsdruckerei, 1891), pp. xxii–xxvi; Hubka, *Naše menšiny*, p. 200; Zemmrich, *Sprachgrenze*, p. 74; and Zeithammer, *České Budějovice*, p. 106. In religious terms, about 27,300 Catholics shared the town in 1890 with approximately 1,100 Jews and 130 Protestants. Discrepancies between the official total of Czech- and

German-speakers (28,227) and the Czech total of Czechs and Germans (26,862) also stemmed from difficulties for Czechs in carrying out their survey with precision in working-class areas on the outskirts of town. See Strnad, *Projevy*, pp. 44, 50, 86.

8. *Českobudějovické listy*, 27 August 1892, pp. 1–2; and 3 September 1892, pp. 2–3; and Strnad, *Dr. A. Zátka*, pp. 44–49.

9. The text of Zátka's speech may be found in Strnad, *Projevy*, pp. 48–52. See also pp. 43, 46, 57; Strnad, *Dr. A. Zátka*, pp. 43–44; and Zeithammer, *České Budějovice*, p. 163.

10. *Českobudějovické listy*, 16 July 1892, pp. 1–2; *Budivoj*, 28 October 1902, pp. 1–3; *Jihočeský kalendář*, p. 85; Strnad, *Projevy*, pp. 53–54; and Strnad, *Dr. A. Zátka*, pp. 45–46. Founding members of the breakaway, Old Czech *Sokol* (called *Sokol Tyrš*) numbered 73. See Zeithammer, *České Budějovice*, p. 164.

11. The quotation comes from Smitka, *Státní převrat v Čes. Budějovicích a jihočeské sokolstvo* (Č. Budějovice: K. Fiala, 1928), p. 15. See also Böhm, *České Budějovice*, p. 81.

12. *Bericht des Deutschen*, pp. 31–32, 63–65. Members of the original *Turnverein* numbered 227 shortly before the split, 230 immediately after it, and 265 in 1902. See also Judson, "'Whether Race or Conviction Should Be the Standard,'" entire.

13. *Budweiser Zeitung*, 3 September 1895, p. 2; *Budweiser Kreisblatt*, 4 September 1895, p. 1; *Budivoj*, 5 September 1895, p. 1; and Vlastimil Kolda, "K výročí návštěvy císaře Františka Josefa I. v Českých Budějovicích," in *Jihočeský sborník historický* 64 (1995): 189–95.

14. Regarding the Austrian Social Democratic Party between its founding in 1888–89 and the mid-1890s, see Mommsen, *Sozialdemokratie*, pp. 155–234; Šolle, *Dělnické hnutí*, pp. 103–200; Kořalka, *Tschechen*, pp. 201–57, esp. 231; Jan Galandauer, *Od Hainfeldu ke vzniku KSČ* (Prague: Svoboda, 1986), pp. 15–56; and Manfred Steger, "Viktor Adler and Austrian Social Democracy, 1889–1914," in *Vienna: The World of Yesterday, 1889–1914*, ed. Stephen Bronner and F. Peter Wagner (New Jersey: Humanities Press, 1997), pp. 204–20.

15. This paragraph and the several that follow are based on Jean-Paul Bled, *Franz Joseph* (Oxford: Blackwell, 1992), pp. 262–65; Macartney, *Habsburg Empire*, pp. 659–62; Prinz, *Geschichte Böhmens*, pp. 170–75, William Jenks, *Austrian Electoral*, pp. 21–22; May, *Hapsburg Monarchy*, pp. 322–45; Boyer, *Political Radicalism*, p. 322; Mommsen, *Sozialdemokratie*, pp. 170–75; and Judson, *Exclusive Revolutionaries*, pp. 248–51.

16. Chvojka, *Město*, pp. 147–50; Pecha, *Státní převrat*, pp. 35–37; and Janoušek, *Město*, pp. 238–56.

17. Mommsen, *Sozialdemokratie*, pp. 172–79, 195–98; Šolle, *Dělnické hnutí*, pp. 194–98; Galandauer, *Od Hainfeldu*, p. 28; and Garver, *Young Czech*, pp. 165, 181–85.

18. Cited in Mommsen, *Sozialdemokratie*, pp. 118–19, also p. 161; as well as Steger, "Viktor Adler," esp. pp. 205–7.

19. Cited both in Mommsen, *Sozialdemokratie*, pp. 121–22; and in Steger, "Viktor Adler," p. 214. See also Roman Szporluk, *Communism and Nationalism: Karl Marx vs. Friedrich List* (New York: Oxford University Press, 1988), pp. 172–

74; Mommsen, *Sozialdemokratie*, pp. 10, 66, 118–20, 142; and Kann, *Multinational Empire*, 1:106.

20. See Steenson, *After Marx*, p. 172; Garver, *Young Czech*, pp. 226, 349; Jenks, *Austrian Electoral*, pp. 22–25; and Boyer, *Political Radicalism*, pp. 322–23.

21. Garver, *Young Czech*, pp. 349–51; Macartney, *Habsburg Empire*, p. 663; Galandauer, *Od Hainfeldu*, pp. 57–60; and Mommsen, *Sozialdemokratie*, p. 167.

22. Strnad, *Dr. A. Zátka*, pp. 50–52; *Budivoj*, 1 January 1898, p. 1; Kratochwil and Meerwald, *Heimatbuch*, pp. 492–93; Pucherna, *Paměti*, p. 108; Pecha, *Státní převrat*, pp. 27–29; Garver, *Young Czech*, pp. 236, 350; and Hubka, *Naše menšiny*, p. 202.

23. Galandauer, *Od Hainfeldu*, pp. 128–30; and Garver, *Young Czech*, p. 230.

24. Galandauer, *Od Hainfeldu*, pp. 61–64; Mommsen, *Sozialdemokratie*, pp. 206–9; and Šolle, *Dělnické hnutí*, p. 242. Regarding the Badeni language ordinances, see Sutter, *Badenischen*, 1:230–42, 273–77; Ulbrich, "Böhmen," pp. 563–65; and Kann, *Multinational Empire*, 1:202–5.

25. Garver, *Young Czech*, pp. 237–44; Bohuslav Šantrůček, *Václav Klofáč* (Prague: Mladé Proudy, 1928); Steenson, *After Marx*, pp. 185, 199; Šolle, *Dělnické hnutí*, pp. 233–41; Kořalka, *Tschechen*, p. 208; and Mommsen, *Sozialdemokratie*, pp. 228–29.

26. Strnad, *Dr. A. Zátka*, p. 52; *Jihočeský dělník*, 28 May 1898, p. 3; and Rauter, *Österreichisches*, p. 143.

27. *Budivoj*, 1 January 1898, p. 1.

28. Kann, *Multinational Empire*, 2:345; *Jihočeský dělník*, 24 December 1897, p. 1; 31 December 1897, p. 4; and 14 January 1898, p. 4; 22 April 1898, p. 3; and 14 May 1898, p. 2; Janoušek, *Město*, pp. 248–60, 282–85; Zeithammer, *České Budějovice*, pp. 166–67; and Pecha, *Státní převrat*, pp. 27–29.

29. The quotation comes from *Volksblatt für Stadt und Land*, 23 May 1896, p. 3. See also *Jihočeský dělník*, 24 December 1897, p. 1; Andrew Whiteside, *Austrian National Socialism before 1918* (The Hague: Martinus Nijhoff, 1962), pp. 1–2, 86–90; Pulzer, *Rise of Political*, pp. 199–210; Joseph Zacek, "Czechoslovak Fascisms," in Peter Sugar, ed., *Native Fascism in the Successor States, 1918–1945* (Santa Barbara: ABC-Clio, 1971), pp. 56–62; Garver, *Young Czech*, pp. 283–94; Kořalka and Crampton, "Die Tschechen," p. 514; Boyer, *Political Radicalism*; John Boyer, *Culture and Political Crisis in Vienna: Christian Socialism in Power, 1897–1918* (Chicago: University of Chicago Press, 1995); and Kann, *Multinational Empire*, 2:208–13.

30. See Bugge, *Czech Nation-Building*, p. 316.

31. Cited in Garver, *Young Czech*, p. 252, also pp. 245–57; and Sutter, *Badenischen*, 2: esp. p. 104.

32. Mark Twain [Samuel Clemens], "Stirring Times in Austria," in *The Complete Essays of Mark Twain* (Garden City: Doubleday, 1963), pp. 208–35, esp. 235. Twain's account, although entertaining, suffers from factual flaws (not reproduced here) and from a bias against Czechs.

33. *Budweiser Zeitung*, 3 January 1896, pp. 3, 5; and 7 January 1898, p. 6; and *Budivoj*, 1 January 1898, p. 1.

34. Strnad, *Dr. A. Zátka*, p. 50; *Budivoj*, 6 January 1898, p. 1; and 19 January 1898, pp. 1–2; and *Budweiser Zeitung*, 11 January 1898, p. 1; and 14 January 1898, p. 8.

35. *Jihočeský dělník*, 14 January 1898, p. 2; *Budivoj*, 9 January 1898, pp. 1–2, 5; and 19 January 1898, pp. 1–2; and *Budweiser Zeitung*, 11 January 1898, p. 5. The edited text of Schwarzenberg's speech, printed by *Budivoj* on 9 January 1898, pp. 1–2, contains no such statement.

36. Hubka, *Naše menšiny*, p. 199; *Budivoj*, 16 January 1898, p. 5; 19 January 1898, pp. 1–2, 3; 23 January 1898, pp. 1–3; 27 January 1898, p. 2; 30 January 1898, p. 1; and 2 February 1898, p. 2; Strnad, *Dr. A. Zátka*, pp. 55–56; *Budweiser Zeitung*, 18 January 1898, pp. 5–6; and 21 January 1898, pp. 3, 4; and *Jihočeský dělník*, 29 January 1898, pp. 1–2.

37. *Budivoj*, 16 January 1898, p. 1; 19 January 1898, pp. 1–2; 23 January 1898, pp. 1–2, 3; 27 January 1898, p. 1; and 30 January 1898, p. 2; and *Budweiser Zeitung*, 25 January 1898, pp. 1–2, 4–6, 8.

38. *Budivoj*, 23 January 1898, pp. 1–2, 3; and 19 January 1898, pp. 1–2; and *Budweiser Zeitung*, 25 January 1898, pp. 1–2.

39. *Jihočeský dělník*, 12 February 1898, p. 3; *Budivoj*, 23 January 1898, pp. 1–3; and 27 January 1898, pp. 1–2, 4; *Budweiser Zeitung*, 21 January 1898, p. 6; 25 January 1898, pp. 1–6; and *Stráž lidu*, 14 June 1901, p. 5.

40. *Budweiser Zeitung*, 25 January 1898, pp. 3–4, 7–8, 18; and *Budivoj*, 23 January pp. 1–3; and 27 January 1898, pp. 2, 4.

41. The Christian Social Party also endorsed the Whitsun Program, but in lukewarm fashion. F. R. Bridge, *From Sadowa to Sarajevo*, pp. 252–53; Zemmrich, *Sprachgrenze*, pp. 107–9; Sutter, *Badenischen*, 2:461; Kann, *Multinational Empire*, 1:104–5, as well as 2:155–57, 208–19; Mommsen, *Sozialdemokratie*, pp. 8, 171, and 295; Galandauer, *Od Hainfeldu*, pp. 112–16; Boyer, *Culture and Political Crisis*, pp. 39–43; and Klemens von Klemperer, *Ignaz Seipel. Christian Statesman in a Time of Crisis* (Princeton: Princeton University Press, 1972), pp. 22–25, 61–63. The Whitsun Program is reproduced in Ulbrich, "Böhmen," p. 568; and the relevant passages from the Social Democratic Program of 1899 in Rudolf Sieghart, *Die letzten Jahrzehnte einer Grossmacht* (Berlin: Ullstein, 1932), p. 431.

42. William Johnston, *The Austrian Mind. An Intellectual and Social History, 1848–1938* (Berkeley: University of California Press, 1972), pp. 175–76; and Bled, *Franz Joseph*, pp. 300–302.

43. *Mitteilungen des Deutschen Böhmerwaldbundes*, no. 44 (1901), p. 5. Cited on pp. 404–5 in Pieter Judson, "Frontiers, Islands, Forests, Stones: Mapping the Geography of a German Identity in the Habsburg Monarchy, 1848–1900," in *The Geography of Identity*, ed. Patricia Yaeger (Ann Arbor: University of Michigan Press, 1996), pp. 382–406. All figures cited include military personnel. Sources disagree slightly, especially with regard to the Czech private census. See Rauchberg, *Der nationale Besitzstand*, pp. 16–17; Zeithammer, *České Budějovice*, p. 106; Strnad, *Projevy*, p. 107; Sedlmeyer, *Budweis*, pp. 163–65; Karel Vondráček, *1884–1934. 50 let Národní jednoty pošumavské* (Prague: NJP, 1934), p. 109; Brix, *Umgangssprache*, pp. 266–70, 294; and *Pamětní list jubilejní matiční slavnosti v Českých Budějovicích, 28. a 29. června 1908* (Budějovice: 1908), p. 6.

44. Václav Kudrnáč, *Úplný adresář hejtmanství Česko-Budějovického. Soudní okresy: Č. Budějovický, Hlubocký, Lišovský, Trho-Svinenský* (Turnov: Kudrnáč. n.d. [1904?]), p. 35, 131–36; *Jihočeský kalendář*, pp. 11–12; Böhm and Zdiarsky, *Stadt Budweis*, p. 7; Rada, *Když se psalo c.k.*, p. 111; *Jihočeský dělník*, 24 December 1897, p. 4; and 31 December 1897, p. 4; and Kořalka, *Tschechen*, p. 208.

45. *Budivoj*, 16 October 1890, p. 4; 6 January 1898, p. 1; 23; January 1898, pp. 1–3; and 29 November 1901, p. 2.

46. Strnad, *Dr. A. Zátka*, pp. 37, 54, 60; *Budivoj*, 30 September 1888, p. 5; 5 September 1902, p. 1; and 19 September 1902, p. 1; *Matice*, p. 45; Böhm, *České Budějovice*, p. 17; and Pucherna, *Paměti Besedy*, p. 138.

47. Only 25 of 336 Jewish voters voted for Czech candidates in elections at the turn of the century. *Deutsche Volkswehr*, 28 October 1897, p. 5; *Budivoj*, 20 June 1902, pp. 1–2; and *Budweiser Zeitung*, 11 January 1898, p. 5. See also Kieval, *Making of Czech Jewry*, p. 61; and Christoph Stölzl, *Kafkas böses Böhmen. Zur Sozialgeschichte eines Prager Juden* (Munich: Edition Text & Kritik, 1975), p. 50.

48. See Alon Rachamimov, "Diaspora Nationalism's Pyrrhic Victory: The Controversy Regarding the Electoral Reform of 1909 in Bukovina," in *State and Nation Building in East Central Europe: Contemporary Perspectives*, ed. John Micgiel (New York: Columbia University Institute on East Central Europe, 1996), pp. 1–16.

49. *Budivoj*, 30 January 1898, p. 2; Pucherna, *Paměti Besedy*, pp. 110–11; and Strnad, *Projevy*, p. 117.

50. *Budweiser Zeitung*, 1 February 1898, p. 3. See also Deák, *Beyond Nationalism*, p. 68; and Allmayer-Beck, "Die bewaffnete Macht," 5:86.

51. Smaller Czech enterprises included a flag factory, founded in 1887. See *Budivoj*, 6 November 1890, pp. 1–2; Strnad, *Dr. A. Zátka*, p. 36; Strnad, *Projevy*, p. 19; Janoušek, *Město*, pp. 229–34; Zeithammer, *České Budějovice*, p. 172; *Jihočeský kalendář*, pp. 87–88; Böhm, *České Budějovice*, p. 181; and Rada, *Když se psalo c.k.*, p. 9.

52. Strnad, *Projevy*, pp. 75, 117; Scheu, *Wanderungen*, pp. 19–20, 27; Miroslav Burian, ed., *Město České Budějovice* (Č. Budějovice: Městská rada, n.d. [1938?]), pp. 58–62; Sedlmeyer, *Budweis*, pp. 265–69; and Zemmrich, *Sprachgrenze*, p. 76.

53. See *Budweiser Bote*, 18 September 1886, p. 4; as well as *Budivoj*, 16 February 1888, p. 2; 22 July 1902, p. 2; and 29 July 1902, p. 1; and *Budweiser Zeitung*, 25 November 1905, p. 5.

54. *Budweiser Zeitung*, 14 January 1898, p. 2, and 18 January 1898, pp. 5–6. See also Strnad, *Projevy*, pp. 116–17; as well as Sedlmeyer, *Budweis*, p. 209.

55. *Budivoj*, 13 January 1898, pp. 1, 2; and 11 February 1913, p. 2; Hubka, *Naše menšiny*, pp. 202–3; Sedlmeyer, *Budweis*, p. 383; Strnad, *Projevy*, pp. 75–76, 116; and Leopold Schweighofer, *Die allgemeinen Verhältnisse im Bürgerlichen Bräuhaus in Budweis (Rede)* (Budweis: A. Blaha, 1900), p. 38.

56. Zeithammer, *České Budějovice*, p. 174; Böhm and Zdiarsky, *Stadt Budweis*, pp. 66–67; and *Jihočeský kalendář*, pp. 87–88. Zátka, in a speech on 29 December 1900, gave the slightly higher figure of 728. In 1909, the putative Czech municipal tax burden increased further, to 44.5%. See Strnad, *Projevy*, pp. 87, 122–23, 149; as well as *Budivoj*, 14 February 1902, p. 1; and *Pamětní list*, p. 4. Germans put up

fierce resistance in the Association of Barbers and Hairdressers, to no avail. See *Budivoj*, 26 March 1902, p. 2.

57. Janoušek, *Město*, pp. 286–90; Pecha, *Státní převrat*, pp. 36–37; and Karel Pletzer and Oldřich Šeda, *Měšťanské i městské pivovarství a dvě stě let Prvního česko-budějovického pivovaru Samson* (České Budějovice: Jihočeské pivovary, 1995), p. 74.

58. *Budivoj*, 21 December 1871, pp. 2–3; and Strnad, *Dr. A. Zátka*, p. 21. Regarding the Burghers' Brewery more generally, see Reinhold Huyer, *Geschichte des Bräuwesens in Budweis* (Budweis: Selbstverlag des Bräuausschusses, 1895); and Oldřich Šeda, "Kalendárium vývoje českého a amerického piva 'Budweiser,'" in Jihočeské muzeum, *Průvodce po budějovických hostincích a kapitoly z jihočeské pivní historie* (České Budějovice: Jihočeské muzeum, 1999), pp. 140–65. For perceptive remarks about the similarly structured Burghers' Brewery in Pilsen/Plzeň, see Scheu, *Wanderungen*, pp. 78, 94.

59. Sedlmeyer, *Budweis*, p. 300; Pucherna, *Paměti Besedy*, pp. 57–59; *Budweiser Kreisblatt*, 27 August 1884, p. 3; *Budivoj*, 26 January 1888, p. 2; and 13 January 1898, p. 2; Pletzer and Šeda, *Měšťanské*, pp. 57–62; Šeda, "Kalendárium," pp. 148–50; and Ivo Hajn, "Obchodní politika Českého akciového pivovaru v Českých Budějovicích v období před první světovou válkou," in Jihočeské muzeum, *Průvodce*, pp. 130–33.

60. Pucherna, *Paměti Besedy*, pp. 89, 139; Antonín Hubka, ed., *Čes. Budějovice. Pamětní list slavnosti Praha—Čes. Budějovicům konané ve dnech 29., 30. června a 1. července 1906 v Praze* (Č. Budějovice: Slavnostní výbor, 1906), pp. 17–18; Strnad, *Dr. A. Zátka*, p. 36; *Budivoj*, 8 August 1902, p. 2; and 12 December 1902, p. 2; and Pletzer and Šeda, *Měšťanské*, p. 69.

61. František Richtr, "Minulost pivovarství v jižních Čechách a v Č. Budějovicích," in *Kvasný průmysl* 16, no. 6 (1970): 129–33; *Budivoj*, 25 November 1902, p. 2; and Šeda, "Kalendárium," p. 150.

62. Pucherna, *Paměti Besedy*, p. 101; *Jihočeský kalendář*, p. 88; Richtr, "Minulost," pp. 129–33; *Budivoj*, 3 October 1902, p. 2; Hajn, "Obchodní," p. 132; Kopáček, *Encyklopedie*, p. 147; and Strnad, *Dr. A. Zátka*, p. 56.

63. *Südböhmische Volkszeitung*, 7 May 1933, p. 5; and Hajn, "Obchodní," p. 130.

64. Schweighofer, *Die allgemeinen*, pp. 1–25; and Pletzer and Šeda, *Měšťanské*, p. 69.

65. Schweighofer, *Die allgemeinen*, pp. 37–38. Two years later, Zátka echoed Schweighofer in a speech, stating to supporters that "If we were to achieve victory [in Budějovice], it would possess not only national significance but an important material aspect as well—from which our shopkeepers and tradesmen would gain the most. Should the town and everything connected to it (the District Assembly, the bank, the Burghers' Brewery—assuming it continues to exist) fall to us, then there would open up for our people a hundred springs that thus far have served only Germans." See *Budivoj*, 28 October 1902, pp. 1–3; as well as *Budweiser Zeitung*, 21 January 1898, p. 3; and Strnad, *Dr. A. Zátka*, p. 64.

66. Böhm, *České Budějovice*, p. 38; and Zemmrich, *Sprachgrenze*, p. 75.

67. *Budivoj,* 4 February 1902, p. 2; and 4 March 1902, p. 3; see also 8 November 1901, p. 3; 22 November 1901, p. 2; and 14 January 1902, p. 1.
68. Schweighofer, *Die allgemeinen,* p. 10; *Gradaus!,* 17 November 1901, p. 3; and *Budivoj,* 18 February 1902, p. 4; and 8 April 1902, p. 2.
69. Pletzer and Šeda, *Měšťanské,* pp. 69, 73; and *Deutsche Volkswehr,* 1 March 1902, p. 4.
70. Judson, *Exclusive Revolutionaries,* esp. pp. 1–5, 267–72.

Chapter Four
Toward a Multinational State, 1902–1918

1. Fr. Vodňanský, *Náš zápas o III. sbor* (Č. Budějovice: K. Stieflmaier, 1906), p. 7; Ludwig Spiegel, "Heimatrecht," in Mischler and Ulbrich, *Österreichisches Staatswörterbuch,* 2:809–43, esp. 816–17; Rauter, *Österreichisches Staats-Lexikon,* pp. 95, 125; Redlich, *Wesen,* p. 53; and Hugo Weiss, *Das Heimatrecht nach der Heimatgesetznovelle von 1896* (Vienna: Manz, 1906): 73–77. In 1902, the number of individuals to gain hometown status in Budweis/Budějovice receded to approximately 400. See *Österreichisches Städtebuch* 10 (1904): 506–7; and Wilhelm Hecke, "Volksvermehrung, Binnenwanderung und Umgangssprache in den nördlichen Ländern Österreichs," *Statistische Monatschrift,* Neue Folge, 19 (1914): 653–723, esp. 681.
2. Hecke, "Volksvermehrung" (1914): 678–79; *Sborník vydaný v 45. výročí založení Národní jednoty pošumavské. Deset let národní práce v jižních Čechách po převratu* (Prague: NJP, 1930), pp. 1–2; and Strnad, *Projevy,* p. 103.
3. *Budivoj,* 29 November 1901, p. 2; 3 December 1901, p. 2; 10 December 1901, p. 2; 21 January 1902, p. 2; 4 February 1902, p. 5; 14 February 1902, p. 4; 18 February 1902, p. 2; 7 March 1902, p. 2; and 23 December 1902, p. 2; *Gradaus!,* 3 November 1901, p. 2; Strnad, *Projevy,* pp. 94–95; and Zeithammer, *České Budějovice,* p. 149.
4. *Budivoj,* 8 November 1901, p. 3; 29 November 1901, p. 2; 10 December 1901, p. 2; 14 February 1902, pp. 1–3; and 25 February 1902, p. 1; Strnad, *Dr. A. Zátka,* pp. 62; and Strnad, *Projevy,* p. 95.
5. Vodňanský, *Náš zápas,* pp. 7–8; and *Budivoj,* 21 January 1902, p. 2; and 23 May 1902, p. 1.
6. The quotations comes from *Gradaus!,* 2 February 1902, p. 1; and *Deutsche Volkswehr,* 1 February 1902, p. 4. See also *Deutsche Volkswehr,* 8 February 1902, pp. 1–2; *Budivoj,* 24 December 1901, p. 2; 31 December 1901, p. 2; 3 January 1902, p. 1; 7 January 1902, p. 2; 28 January 1902, pp. 1, 2; and 4 February 1902, pp. 1–2; *Gradaus!,* 9 February 1902, p. 2; Strnad, *Projevy,* pp. 94–95; and Kopáček, *Encyklopedie,* pp. 74–75. National parties had already manufactured burghers for electoral purposes in Moravia. See *Deutsche Volkswehr,* 22 February 1902, pp. 3–4; and Zeithammer, *České Budějovice,* p. 149.
7. In May 1902, Taschek had Rabbi Wunder made an honorary burgher. *Budivoj,* 4 February 1902, pp. 1–2; 14 February 1902, pp. 1, 3; 30 May 1902, p. 3.
8. Mayor Kneissl, in fact, retired in November 1903 and was replaced by Taschek. *Budivoj,* 31 January 1902, p. 2; 14 February 1902, p. 3; 18 February 1902, p. 3;

28 February 1902, p. 2; 7 March 1902, p. 2; and 30 May 1902, p. 2; and *Bericht des deutschen Turnvereines*, p. 37. Křikawa, born in 1851, had some relatives who spelled their surname in more Czech fashion: Křikava. See *Budweiser Zeitung*, 13 August 1932, pp. 5, 16; and *Českobudějovické listy*, 20 March 1996, p. 11.

9. *Budivoj*, 28 January 1902, p. 1; 4 February 1902, pp. 1–2, 5; 7 February 1902, pp. 1, 6; 11 February 1902, p. 3; 14 February 1902, pp. 1–3; 18 February 1902, p. 4; 25 February 1902, p. 2; 28 February 1902, pp. 1–2, 3; 4 March 1902, p. 4; and 11 April 1902, pp. 1–3; *Deutsche Volkswehr*, 22 February 1902, pp. 3–4; and 1 March 1902, pp. 3–4; *Gradaus!*, 16 February 1902, p. 4; and Rada, *Když se psalo c.k.*, p. 31. Zátka's speech of 3 February is reproduced in Strnad, *Projevy*, pp. 94–95.

10. *Budivoj*, 28 January, p. 2; 4 February, pp. 2, 5; 11 February, p. 2; 14 February, pp. 1–3, 4; 18 February, p. 2; 25 February, p. 2; 28 February, p. 1; 7 March, p. 2; 21 March, pp. 1–2; 28 March, p. 2; 2 April, p. 1; 8 April, p. 2; 11 April, p. 4; 15 April, p. 1; 22 April, p. 3; 29 April, p. 1; 2 May, p. 1; 21 May, p. 2; and 23 December, p. 2 (all in 1902); Strnad, *Dr. A. Zátka*, pp. 62–63; Vodňanský, *Náš zápas*, pp. 8–11; and Zeithammer, *České Budějovice*, pp. 149–50.

11. Strnad, *Projevy*, p. 116; Strnad, *Dr. A. Zátka*, p. 63; p. 7; and *Budivoj*, 7 March 1902, p. 2; and 25 April 1902, p. 1.

12. The quotation from *Jihočeský dělník* appears in *Budivoj*, 21 March 1902, p. 5. See also 14 March 1902, p. 2; and 1 September 1895, p. 3.

13. *Budivoj*, 20 June 1902, pp. 1–2. See also *Budivoj*, 28 January 1902, p. 2; 7 February 1902, p. 5; 11 February 1902, p. 2; 21 October 1902, p. 2; and 28 October 1902, pp. 1–3; Rada, *Když se psalo c.k.*, p. 30; Strnad, *Dr. A. Zátka*, pp. 64–65; Strnad, *Projevy*, p. 110; and Janoušek, *Město na soutoku*, p. 272.

14. *Bericht des deutschen Turnvereines*, p. 36. See also *Upomínka na slet sokolstva Č Budějovicich 1903. Program slavnosti a pokyny* (Č Budějovice: J. Přibyl, 1903), entire; Böhm, *České Budějovice*, p. 82; Smitka, *Státní převrat*, p. 20; *Budivoj*, 4 July 1902, p. 2; and Rada, *Když se psalo c.k.*, p. 117.

15. Galandauer, *Od Hainfeldu*, pp. 69–74; and Jenks, *Austrian Electoral*, pp. 32–45, 211. Both Young Czech and Czech National Socialist deputies in the Austrian Parliament had just proposed universal suffrage. But those parties did not join the Social Democratic one in organizing wave after wave of demonstrations.

16. *Budweiser Zeitung*, 15 November 1905, pp. 5–6; 18 November 1905, p. 5; 22 November 1905, pp. 5–6; and 25 November 1905, pp. 3–5; *Deutsche Volkswehr*, 9 December 1905, p. 1; *Naše svoboda*, 20 November 1946, p. 3; Strnad, *Projevy*, pp. 114, 171–72; Janoušek, *Město na soutoku*, pp. 299–300; Allmayer-Beck, "Die bewaffnete Macht," p. 116; and Deák, *Beyond Nationalism*, p. 66.

17. Karel Fenzl, *Paměti Besedy česko-budějovické 1902–1912* (Č. Budějovice: Beseda č. Budějovická, 1913), pp. 49, 55, 88–93; Strnad, *Projevy*, p. 117; and *Budivoj*, 3 January 1902, p. 2; and 10 January 1902, p. 2. I thank István Deák for providing me with information regarding Regenspursky from *Kais. König. Militär-Schematismus für 1880* (Vienna, 1879), p. 158.

18. Zeithammer, *České Budějovice*, p. 188. See also Hubka, *Čes. Budějovice*, p. 44; Strnad, *Projevy*, pp. 86–87; *Stráž lidu*, 20 October 1899, p. 3; 5 December 1902, pp. 5, 6; and 27 November 1903, pp. 1, 3; and *Budivoj*, 30 September 1902, pp. 1–2.

19. Kudrnáč, *Úplný adresář*, entire; Strnad, *1884–1924. Čtyřicet let*, pp. 16–17; Strnad, *Projevy*, pp. 109, 133–36; *Südböhmische Volkszeitung*, 26 February 1905, pp. 1–2; and *Jihočeské listy*, 28 January 1907, p. 1; 2 February 1907, p. 1; 4 February 1907, p. 1; and 9 February 1907, p. 2. For a fictional account from a *völkisch* perspective of a boycott during this period in town, written with the radicalizing hindsight of the 1930s, see Jaksch, *Alle Wasser*, p. 40.

20. Hubka, *Čes. Budějovice*, pp. 26–28.

21. Strnad, *Projevy*, pp. 86, 150; and *Jihočeské listy*, 16 February 1907, p. 2. See also *Jihočeské listy*, 20 March 1907, p. 1.

22. *Jihočeské listy*, 28 January 1907, p. 3; 9 February 1907, p. 2; 4 May 1907, p. 1; and 8 May 1907, p. 2.

23. Strnad, *Projevy*, pp. 86, 150; *Jihočeské listy*, 9 February 1907, p. 2; *Budivoj*, 14 November 1913, p. 2; and, more generally, Garver, *Young Czech*, pp. 47–49, 102–8; and Mommsen, *Sozialdemokratie*, pp. 24–25.

24. Ulbrich, "Böhmen," p. 574. See also Storch, "Preßrecht," pp. 974–82.

25. *Budivoj*, 28 January 1902, p. 2; 8 April 1902, p. 3; and 3 June 1902, p. 2. See also Judson, "'Whether Race or Conviction Should Be the Standard,'" entire.

26. Strnad, *Projevy*, pp. 110–23; Zeithammer, *České Budějovice*, pp. 149–50; Vodňanský, *Náš zápas*, pp. 10–11; Rada, *Když se psalo c.k.*, pp. 29–30; and *Budivoj*, 28 January 1902, p. 3; 31 January 1902, p. 2; 8 April 1902, p. 2; and 15 April 1902, p. 1.

27. Strnad, *Projevy*, pp. 127–28; Strnad, *Dr. A. Zátka*, pp. 69–72; Kratochwil and Meerwald, *Heimatbuch*, pp. 494–96; *Naše svoboda*, 27 November 1946, p. 3; and 7 December 1946, p. 2; and Vodňanský, *Náš zápas*, pp. 12, 57.

28. *Naše svoboda*, 7 December 1946, p. 2

29. Strnad, *Projevy*, pp. 134–36; and Strnad, *Dr. A. Zátka*, p. 73.

30. *Jihočeské listy*, 9 January 1907, p. 1; 19 January 1907, p. 1; and 25 May 1907, p. 1; Strnad, *Projevy*, pp. 134–39; Strnad, *Dr. A. Zátka*, pp. 72–73; and Macartney, *Habsburg Empire*, p. 762.

31. Max Vladimir Freiherr von Beck, "Der Kaiser und die Wahlreform," in *Erinnerungen an Franz Joseph I*, ed. Eduard Ritter von Steinitz (Berlin: Verlag für Kulturpolitik, 1931), pp. 197–224, esp. 223. See also Kann, *Multinational Empire*, 2:220, 360–62; Jenks, *Austrian Electoral*, entire; Steenson, *After Marx*, p. 179; and Bled, *Franz Joseph*, pp. 272–75.

32. Kann, *Multinational Empire*, 2:220.

33. Regarding Austrian Social Democratic proposals during the 1870s for a "national articulation" of the working-class movement, see especially Křalka, *Tschechen*, pp. 248–49. The rapidly growing literature concerning early Soviet nationalities policy includes Ronald Suny, *The Revenge of the Past: Nationalism, Revolution, and the Collapse of the Soviet Union* (Stanford: Stanford University Press, 1993); Slezkine, "The USSR as a Communal Apartment;" Martin, *Affirmative Action Empire*; Brubaker, *Nationalism Reframed*, esp. chap. 2; and Hirsch, "Empire of Nations."

34. Kaindl, *Völkerkampf*, pp. 48–50, 52–53; Sieghart, *Die letzten Jahrzehnte*, p. 422; and Křalka, *Tschechen*, pp. 146–52. See also von Herrnritt, *Nationalität*, pp. 43–49.

238

NOTES TO CHAPTER FOUR

35. Ulbrich, "Böhmen," p. 575, and pp. 580–82; Kaindl, *Völkerkampf*, pp. 61–64; and Jenks, *Austrian Electoral*, p. 36.

36. Jenks, *Austrian Electoral*, pp. 54–64,144–68; and Kořalka, *Tschechen*, pp. 166–68.

37. Jenks, *Austrian Electoral*, pp. 179–91, 215; Macartney, *Habsburg Empire*, p. 794; Kann, *Multinational Empire*, 2:225; Garver, *Young Czech*, pp. 288–95; and Prinz, *Geschichte Böhmens*, pp. 186–88.

38. *Jihočeské listy*, 24 April 1907, p. 2; 30 April 1907, p. 1; 13 May 1907, p. 1; 15 May 1907, pp. 1, 2; and 18 May 1907, p. 2; Strnad, *Dr. A. Zátka*, pp. 61, 75; Strnad, *Projevy*, pp. 140, 144; and Kratochwil and Meerwald, *Heimatbuch*, pp. 494–96. See also Horowitz, *Ethnic Groups*, pp. 291–348.

39. The quotations come from Brubaker, *Nationalism Reframed*, p. 116; and from Karl Türk, *Böhmen, Mähren und Schlesien* [*Der Kampf um das Deutschtum*, 6. Heft] (Munich: Lehmann, 1898), p. 60. See also Zemmrich, *Sprachgrenze*, pp. vi, 72–76, 114; and Sedlmeyer, *Budweis*, p. 348. *Deutsche Arbeit*, published in Prague and sold both in the Habsburg Monarchy and in the German Empire, featured a special "Budweis Issue" in 1905: see vol. 4, no. 9, especially p. 562. More generally, see the following journals: *Mitteilungen des Deutschen Böhmerwaldbundes, Das Deutschtum im Ausland* (expanded version from 1901, new series from 1909); *Deutsche Erde*, esp. vol. 4 (1905), pp. 185–86; *Der getreue Eckart* (from 1902); and *Mitteilungen des Vereins Südmark* (from 1905).

40. Karl Renner, *Der nationale Streit um die Aemter und die Sozialdemokratie* (Vienna: Vorwärts, 1908), p. 14. See also Renner, *Der deutsche Arbeiter und der Nationalismus* (Vienna: Brand, 1910), p. 63; as well as Renner [Rudolf Springer], *Der Kampf der Oesterreichischen Nationen um den Staat* (Leipzig and Vienna: Deuticke, 1902), entire; Otto Bauer, *Die Nationalitätenfrage und die Sozialdemokratie* (Vienna: Brand, 1907); Mommsen, "Otto Bauer, Karl Renner und die sozialdemokratische Nationalitätenpolitik in Österreich 1905–1914," in Mommsen, *Arbeiterbewegung und nationale Frage* (Göttingen: Vandenhoeck und Ruprecht, 1979), pp. 195–217; Mommsen, *Sozialdemokratie*, p. 295; Gerald Stourzh, "Die Gleichberechtigung der Volksstämme als Verfassungsprinzip 1848–1918," in Wandruszka and Urbanitsch, *Die Habsburgermonarchie* 3:975–1206, esp. 1169–71, 1188; Kann, *Multinational Empire*, 2:157–61, 349; and Anton Pelinka, *Karl Renner zur Einführung* (Hamburg: Junius Verlag, 1989), pp. 18–21.

41. Renner, *Der nationale Streit*, pp. 14–15.

42. Strnad, *Projevy*, pp. 148–55; Kratochwil and Meerwald, *Heimatbuch*, pp. 497–98; *Jihohočeské listy*, 8 May 1907, p. 2; and *Budivoj*, 4 February 1913, p. 3; 14 February 1913, p. 1; 18 February 1913, p. 2; 22 April 1913, pp. 1–2; 6 May 1913, p. 2; and 8 July 1913, p. 3.

43. Pucherna, *Paměti Besedy*, p. 139; *Jihočeské listy*, 28 January 1907, p. 1; and 11 May 1907, p. 3; *Budivoj*, 31 January 1913, pp. 1–2; Kratochwil and Meerwald, *Heimatbuch*, p. 496; Böhm, *České Budějovice*, p. 30; Strnad, *Dr. A. Zátka*, pp. 74–80; Strnad, *Projevy*, pp. 144–57; Strnad, *Padesát let odboru*, p. 98; Sedlmeyer, *Budweis*, pp. 163–65; and Emil Brix, "Der böhmische Ausgleich in Budweis," *Österreichische Osthefte* 24, no. 2 (1982): 225–48, esp. 228–30. The 1910 census registered approximately 16,900 speakers of German and 27,300 speakers of Czech. These figures represent increases since 1900 of about 11 percent and 12

percent respectively. Catholics numbered approximately 42,500, Protestants 315, and Jews 1,640.

44. Johannes Zemmrich, "Josef Taschek," *Deutsche Erde* 11 (1912): p. 61.

45. Strnad, *Dr. A. Zátka,* pp. 80–85; Brix, "Der böhmische Ausgleich," pp. 237–38; Pecha, *Státní převrat,* pp. 42–45; Karel Kazbunda, *Otázka česko-německá v předvečer velké války* (Prague: Univerzita Karlova, 1995), pp. 336–39, 369–70; Janoušek, *Město na soutoku,* p. 309; and Kratochwil and Meerwald, *Heimatbuch,* p. 497.

46. Dr. Rohmeder, "Der Budweiser Ausgleich," *Das Deutschtum im Ausland,* 19 (1914): pp. 87–88; Strnad, *Projevy,* p. 149; Strnad, *Dr. A. Zátka,* pp. 80–85; Brix, "Der böhmische Ausgleich," pp. 232–39; Pecha, *Státní převrat,* pp. 43–44; and Stourzh, "Die Gleichberechtigung," p. 1190. These two paragraphs and the half-dozen paragraphs that follow are based in part on a close reading of the thirty-three-page text of the Compromise. Its Czech-language version, printed without title in 1913 or 1914 by the Společenská tiskárna in Budějovice, was made available to me by Jan Mareš of the Státní vědecká knihovna in town.

47. See Bernatzik, *Über nationale Matriken,* p. 4; Stourzh, "Die Gleichberechtigung," p. 1179; Herrnritt, *Nationalität,* pp. 16–22, 76–82, 137–39; Anderson, *Spectre of Comparisons,* pp. 29–45; and Brubaker, *Citizenship and Nationhood,* pp. 21–34.

48. Compromise text, p. 3, §4.

49. Compromise text, pp. 4–7 (§5–8).

50. Bernatzik, *Über nationale Matriken,* pp. 29–30; and Stourzh, "Die Gleichberechtigung," pp. 1184–86.

51. Scheu, *Wanderungen,* pp. 28, 30. See also Bernatzik, *Über nationale Matriken.*

52. Brix, "Der böhmische Ausgleich," pp. 234–35. "Language of daily use" data from the census, however, were to have served as the basis for the Polish and Ruthenian cadastres on the verge of implementation through the Galician Compromise in 1914. See Stourzh, "Die Gleichberechtigung," pp. 1182–86, 1194–97; and Brix, *Umgangssprache,* pp. 43, 66.

53. The quotation comes from Brix, "Der böhmische Ausgleich," p. 236. Zátka seems to have worked at obscuring to the Czech public the nonethnic implications of the decision made by the Ministry of the Interior; see Brix, "Der böhmische Ausgleich," p. 237. See also Stourzh, "Die Gleichberechtigung," pp. 1175–76.

54. The quotation comes from Scheu, *Wanderungen,* p. 33. See also Brix, "Der böhmische Ausgleich," pp. 232–39.

55. In 1909, within the framework of the Bukovinan Compromise, the government had vetoed the creation of a Jewish national cadastre—whether based on self-designation or on ascription. To relate political rights in any way to religion, the Ministry of the Interior had decided, would constitute a violation of the rights guaranteed every Cisleithanian citizen in the Fundamental Laws. Stourzh, "Die Gleichberechtigung," pp. 1192–93; and Rachamimov, "Diaspora," pp. 6–11.

56. Horst Glassl, *Der mährische Ausgleich* (Munich: Fides-Verlagsgesellschaft, 1967), entire; Johanna Spunda, "Die verlorenen Inseln. Ein Beitrag zur Erforschung der nationalen Auseinandersetzung und Umvolkung in Mittelmähren," *Bohemia* 2 (1961): 357–413 and 3 (1962): 273–359, esp. 365–66; Robert Luft, "Die Mittelpartei des mährischen Grossgrundbesitzes 1879 bis 1918. Zur Prob-

lematik des Ausgleichs in Mähren und Böhmen," in *Die Chance der Verständigung: Absichten und Ansätze zu übernationaler Zusammenarbeit in den böhmischen Ländern 1848-1918*, ed. Ferdinand Seibt (Munich: Oldenbourg, 1987), pp. 187–244. Sieghart, *Die letzten Jahrzehnte*, pp. 424–26; Kořalka, *Tschechen*, pp. 160–64; Stourzh, "Die Gleichberechtigung," pp. 1180–83, 1192–98; Rachamimov, "Diaspora," p. 6; Stanislaus Ritter von Starzyński, "Eine neue Konstruktion der Minoritätenvertretung," in *Österreichische Zeitschrift für öffentliches Recht*, 3 (1918): 419–33; Garver, *Young Czechs*, pp. 147–48; and Compromise text, pp. 7–8, §9. In 1915, the governor of Bohemia proposed assigning all imperial-royal civil servants in town to both cadastres. The implications of such an amendment to the Compromise, which German and Czech leaders joined in opposing, would have been considerable, because about 150 imperial-royal civil servants were entitled to vote in either the second or the first municipal curia—whose members numbered only in the low hundreds. See Brix, "Der böhmische Ausgleich," pp. 239–40, 247–48.

57. Judson, *Exclusive Revolutionaries*, p. 264. The town council electorate, in fact, was to shrink slightly, through the elimination of poor or nonresident men among the number of burghers and honorary burghers that Taschek had manufactured in 1902 and 1906. See also Kořalka, *Tschechen*, pp. 162–63, 173; and Stourzh, "Die Gleichberechtigung," pp. 1180–81.

58. *Jihočeské listy*, 1 August 1914, p. 1; and Franz Conrad Graf von Hötzendorf, *Aus meiner Dienstzeit, 1906–1918*, vol. 4 (Vienna: Rikola, 1923), p. 162. See also Böhm, *České Budějovice*, p. 82; Kazbunda, *Otázka*, entire; and Pecha, *Státní převrat*, p. 47.

59. *Sborník vydaný*, p. 4; Sedlmeyer, *Budweis*, p. 397; *Slavnostní list Budivoje S.A.J. 1877–1927* (Č. Budějovice: Budivoj S.A.J. / K. Fiala, 1927), pp. 14, 25–26; Rada, *Když se psalo T.G.M.*, pp. 6–41; Pecha, *Státní převrat*, pp. 50–69; Strnad, *Dr. A. Zátka*, pp. 85–88; and Strnad, *1884–1924. Čtyřicet let*, p. 21.

60. Richard Plaschka, "Zur Vorgeschichte des Überganges von Einheiten des Infanterieregiments Nr. 28 an der russischen Front 1915," in *Österreich und Europa. Festgabe für Hugo Hantsch zum 70. Geburtstag*, Universität Wien, Institut für österreichische Geschichtsforschung (Graz: Styria, 1965), pp. 455–64; Karel Pichlík, Vlastimil Vávra, and Jaroslav Křížek, *Červeno bílá a rudá* (Prague: Naše vojsko, 1967), pp. 34–37; and Rudolf Jeřábek, "The Eastern Front 1914–1918," in *The Last Years of Austria-Hungary*, ed. Mark Cornwall (Exeter: University of Exeter Press, 1990), pp. 101–16, esp. 108–9. Francis Joseph, it should be noted, had the regiment reconstituted in December 1915.

61. Personal communication from Erwin Schmidl; *Bohemia*, 20 September 1930, p. 1; and 23 September 1930, p. 6. I thank Nancy Wingfield for providing me with these materials. See also Plaschka, "Vorgeschichte," p. 464.

62. Jaroslav Hašek, *The Good Soldier: Švejk* (New York: Ungar, 1962), pp. 197–257, 343–44, 447–48.

63. Smitka, *Státní převrat*, p. 28; and Plaschka, "Vorgeschichte," pp. 460–63. See also Alon Rachamimov, "Imperial Loyalties and Private Concerns: Nation, Class, and State in the Correspondence of Austro-Hungarian POWs in Russia, 1916–1918," *Austrian History Yearbook*, 31 (2000): pp. 87–105.

64. Jeřábek, "The Eastern Front," pp. 108–11; Mark Cornwall, "The Dissolution of Austria-Hungary," in Cornwall, *Last Years*, pp. 117–42, esp. 124–25; Gordon Craig, *Germany, 1866–1945* (New York: Oxford University Press, 1978), pp. 349, 371–76; and Zbynek Zeman, *The Breakup of the Habsburg Empire, 1914–1918* (New York: Oxford University Press, 1961), pp. 100–111.

65. Cited in Zeman, *Breakup*, p. 110.

66. *Národní listy*, 15 November 1916, pp. 2–3. Cited in Pecha, *Státní převrat*, p. 57.

67. Bled, *Franz Joseph*, p. 321; Zeman, *Breakup*, pp. 152–62; and Ernst Birke, "Der Erste Weltkrieg und die Gründung der Tschechoslowakei 1914–1919," in *Handbuch der Geschichte der böhmischen Länder*, vol. 3, ed. Karl Bosl (Stuttgart: Hirsemann, 1968), pp. 274–446, esp. 318–29.

Chapter Five
Bohemian Politics Reframed, 1918–1945

1. Rada, *Když se psalo T.G.M.*, pp. 15–16, 44; *Budweiser Zeitung*, 25 January 1918, p. 4; *Hlas lidu*, 24 January 1918, p. 1; *Jihočeské listy*, 2 October 1918, p. 2; Zdeněk Tobolka, *Politické dějiny československého národa od r. 1848 až do dnešní doby*, vol. 4: *1914–1918* (Prague: Čsl. Kompas, 1937), pp. 313–24; and Birke, "Der Erste Weltkrieg," pp. 325–27.

2. *Jihočeské listy*, 14 September 1918, pp. 1, 2.

3. *Budweiser Zeitung*, 18 October 1918, pp. 1–2; Rada, *Když se psalo T.G.M.*, p. 51; Johann Wolfgang Brügel, *Tschechen und Deutsche 1918–1938* (Munich: Nymphenburger, 1967), pp. 48, 69; and Ladislav Lipscher, *Verfassung und politische Verwaltung in der Tschechoslowakei: 1918–1939* (Munich: Oldenbourg, 1979), p. 32.

4. Smitka, *Státní převrat*, pp. 37–45; *Jihočeské listy*, 31 October 1918, p. 1; *Budweiser Zeitung*, 29 October 1918, p. 3; and Rada, *Když se psalo T.G.M.*, pp. 52–56.

5. *Jihočeské listy*, 31 October, 1918, p. 4; 9 November 1918, pp. 1–2; 13 November 1918, p. 2; and 20 November 1918, p. 2; *Budweiser Zeitung*, 29 October 1918, p. 3; and 8 November 1918, p. 4; *Budweiser Kreisblatt*, 31 October 1918, p. 2; and 6 November 1918, p. 3; Rada, *Když se psalo T.G.M.*, pp. 56–60; *Mitteilungen des Deutschen Böhmerwaldbundes*, no. 62 (December 1919): insert, pp. 1–4; and Smitka, *Státní převrat*, pp. 52–53.

6. Smitka, *Státní převrat*, pp. 41–45; *Budweiser Kreisblatt*, 31 October 1918, pp. 1, 2; Rada, *Když se psalo T.G.M.*, pp. 62–63; Kratochwil and Meerwald, *Heimatbuch*, pp. 501–6; and *Mitteilungen*, no. 62 (December 1919): insert, p. 1.

7. *Budweiser Zeitung*, 29 October 1918, pp. 1, 3.

8. Brügel, *Tschechen und Deutsche*, pp. 48–49, 69; Joseph Rothschild, *East Central Europe between the Two World Wars* (Seattle: University of Washington Press, 1974), pp. 78–79; and Thomas Paterson, ed., *Major Problems in American Foreign Policy. Documents and Essays*, vol. 2, *Since 1914* (Lexington, Mass.: Heath, 1978), p. 65.

9. *Budweiser Zeitung*, 8 November 1918, p. 5; and 12 November 1918, p. 5; Sedlmeyer, *Budweis*, p. 484; Paterson, *Major Problems*, pp. 64–65; and Arthur

Link, ed., *The Papers of Woodrow Wilson*, vol. 45 (Princeton: Princeton University Press, 1984), p. 463.

10. *Budweiser Kreisblatt*, 9 November 1918, p. 2; and 28 December 1918, p. 3; *Budweiser Zeitung*, 5 November 1918, p. 4; and 26 November 1918, p. 4; *Jihočeské listy*, 31 October 1918, p. 1; and *Hlas lidu*, 11 November 1918, p. 2. See also Rada, *Když se psalo T.G.M.*, text accompanying picture of the Black Tower, between pp. 96 and 97.

11. *Mitteilungen*, no. 62 (December 1919), insert, pp. 1–4; *Hlas lidu*, 11 November 1918, p. 2; *Budweiser Kreisblatt*, 13 November 1918, p. 3; *Jihočeské listy*, 13 November 1918, p. 2; and 4 December 1918, p. 1 *Budweiser Zeitung*, 15 November 1918, p. 5; and 6 January 1940, pp. 8–9; and Böhm, *České Budějovice*, p. 42.

12. The quotations come from *Budweiser Zeitung*, 14 January 1919, pp. 4–5; and *Hlas lidu*, 11 November 1918, p. 3. See also *Budweiser Zeitung*, 8 November 1918, p. 5; 12 November 1918, p. 1; 22 November 1918, p. 4; 26 November 1918, p. 4; and 15 October 1927, pp. 2–3; *Mitteilungen*, no. 62 (December 1919), insert, pp. 3–4; *Jihočeské listy*, 9 November 1918, p. 2; and 23 November 1918, pp. 1–2; *Hlas lidu*, 18 November 1918, p. 2; Rada, *Když se psalo T.G.M.*, p. 146; and Oskar Rabinowicz, "České Budějovice," in *Encyclopedia Judaica*, vol. 5 (Jerusalem: Macmillan, 1971), p. 315. Wenzel Titta was a prominent figure in the Pan-German League in the north of Bohemia.

13. *Budweiser Zeitung*, 8 November, 1918, p. 1; and István Bibó, "A kelet-európai kisállamok nyomorúsága," in *Válogatott tanulmányok*, vol. 2 (Budapest: Magvető, 1986), p. 202.

14. Brügel, *Tschechen und Deutsche*, pp. 59–69; Lipscher, *Verfassung*, pp. 20–24, 32–35; Rothschild, *East Central Europe*, p. 79; Victor Mamatey, "The Establishment of the Republic," in *A History of the Czechoslovak Republic, 1918–1948*, ed. Victor Mamatey and Radomír Luža (Princeton: Princeton University Press, 1973), pp. 3–38, esp. 28–30; and Rada, *Když se psalo c.k.*, p. 66.

15. *Budweiser Kreisblatt*, 21 December 1918, p. 2; and 28 December 1918, p. 3; Ferdinand Peroutka, *Budování státu*, vol. 1 (Prague: Lidové noviny, 1991), pp. 304–5; and Brügel, *Tschechen und Deutsche*, pp. 43–45.

16. See Alicia Cozine, "A Member of the State: Citizenship Law and Its Application in Czechoslovakia, 1918–1938," Ph.D. diss., University of Chicago, 1996, pp. 32–58.

17. *Slavnostní list*, pp. 29, 34; *Sborník*, p. 4; *Matice*, pp. 20, 62; Karel Fenzl, *Beseda česko-budějovická v letech 1923–1932. K sedmdesátiletému trvání* (Č. Budějovice: Společenská tiskárna, 1933), pp. 11, 12, 35; and Böhm, *České Budějovice*, pp. 61, 89.

18. *Budweiser Zeitung*, 31 January 1919, p. 4; and 7 March 1919, p. 5; *Mitteilungen*, No. 62 (December 1919): insert, p. 5; and Sedlmeyer, *Budweis*, p. 488.

19. *Budweiser Zeitung*, 30 May 1919, p. 3; and 3 June 1919, p. 4; *Jihočeské listy*, 28 May 1919, p. 1; 11 June 1919, pp. 1, 2; 14 June 1919, p. 2; and 18 June 1919, p. 1; *Mitteilungen*, no. 62 (December 1919): insert, pp. 3–4; Kratochwil and Meerwald, *Heimatbuch*, pp. 508–9; Strnad, *Dr. A. Zátka*, p. 89; and Rada, *Když se psalo T.G.M.*, p. 70.

20. Brügel, *Tschechen und Deutsche*, pp. 75–109, 120–42; František Weyr, "Menšiny," in *Slovník veřejného práva Československého*, vol. 2, ed. Emil Hácha, Jiří Hoetzel, František Weyr, and Karel Laštovka (Brno: Polygrafia, 1932), pp. 570–78, esp. 576.

21. Jiří Hoetzl and Václav Joachim, eds., *The Constitution of the Czechoslovak Republic* (Prague: L'Effort de la Tchéchoslovaquie, 1920), pp. 19, 44–50; Emil Sobota, *Republika národní či národnostní?* (Prague: Čin, 1929), entire; Václav Beneš, "Czechoslovak Democracy and Its Problems 1918–1920," in Mamatey and Luža, *A History of the Czechoslovak Republic*, pp. 39–98, esp. 96; Prinz, *Geschichte Böhmens*, pp. 395–96; and Peter Bugge, "Czech Democracy 1918–1938—Paragon or Parody?" in *Phasen und Formen der Transformation in der Tschechoslowakei. Vorträge der Tagung des Collegium Carolinum in Bad Wiessee vom 23. bis 26 November 2000*, ed. Christiane Brenner (Munich: Oldenbourg, forthcoming).

22. *Budweiser Zeitung*, 7 February 1920, pp. 2–3; and 17 November 1920, p. 5; Böhm, *České Budějovice*, p. 17; Czechoslovak Republic, *Sbírka zákonů a nařízení státu československého*, 30 April 1920, pp. 595–96; and 29 January 1921, p. 33; Brügel, *Tschechen und Deutsche*, pp. 150–51; and Czechoslovak Republic, Státní úřad statistický, *Les élections à l'assemblée nationale en Avril 1920 et les élections communales en Bohême, Moravie et Silésie en Juin 1919* (Prague: Bursík et Kohout, 1922), pp. 62–63.

23. *Budweiser Zeitung*, 24 November 1920, pp. 1, 4–5; and 27 November 1920, pp. 5–6; Sedlmeyer, *Budweis*, p. 495; Rada, *Když se psalo T.G.M.*, pp. 77–81; and Stölzl, *Kafkas*, p. 99.

24. Karel Laštovka, "Dějiny organisace politické správy v Československé republice," in Hácha et al. *Slovník veřejného práva*, 1:345–60, esp. 360; Václav Kural, "Češi a Němci v čs. státě 1918–1948," in *Kapitoly z dějin Střední Evropy. Češi a Němci*, ed. Rudolf Kučera (Munich: Tschechischer Nationalausschuß, 1989), pp. 188–230, esp. 201; Lipscher, *Verfassung*, pp. 88–89; Christoph Boyer, *Nationale Kontrahenten oder Partner?* (Munich: Oldenbourg, 1999), p. 272; and Jiří Hoetzel, "Samospráva. B. Územní samospráva. I. Obce," in Hácha et al. *Slovník veřejného práva*, 4:2–9; the quotation is from p. 9. See also Bugge, "Czech Democracy"; and Jeremy King, "Austria vs. Hungary."

25. Czechoslovak Republic, Státní úřad statistický, *Die Volkszählung in der Čechoslovakischen Republik vom 15. Februar 1921*, vol. 1 (Prague: Bursík und Kohout, 1924), pp. 9*–14*, 64*–66*; and Bohmann, *Bevölkerungsbewegungen*, pp. 57–61.

26. Robert Kollar, "Sčítání lidu," in Hácha et al. *Slovník veřejného práva*, 4:186; *Jihočech*, 25 April 1921, p. 1; Sedlmeyer, *Budweis*, pp. 163–65; and Czechoslovak Republic, Státní úřad statistický, *Die Volkszählung*, pp. 65*–66*, 73*–79*, 44, 116. In 1924, the figures for Budweis/Budějovice were amended to 35,577 and 7,006. Civilians having Czechoslovak citizenship divided into approximately 35,000 Catholics, 1,400 Jews, 1,900 without confession, 900 Protestants, and 4,500 who had joined the new Czechoslovak Church—an anti-Catholic, anti-Habsburg, and anti-German Christian denomination launched with support from the state in 1920 and in many ways strikingly similar to the *Los von Rom* movement of *völkische* at the turn of the century.

NOTES TO CHAPTER FIVE

27. Czechoslovak Republic, Státní úřad statistický, *Die Volkszählung*, p. 75*; and Boyer, *Nationale Kontrahenten*, pp. 4–5, 393–94. See also Eugen Lemberg, *Lebensbilder zur Geschichte der böhmischen Länder*, vol. 5, *Ein Leben in Grenzzonen und Ambivalenzen* (Munich: Oldenbourg, 1986); and Czechoslovak Republic, *Sammlung der Gesetze und Verordnungen des čechoslovakischen Staates*, 5 November 1920, p. 1736.

28. Böhm, *České Budějovice*, pp. 17, 30, 33; Czechoslovak Republic, Státní úřad statistický, *Les élections*, p. 120; Richard Engelmann, "Österreichs städtische Wohnplätze mit mehr als 25,000 Einwohnern Ende 1910, ihr Wachstum seit 1869 und die konfessionelle und sprachliche Zusammensetzung ihrer Bevölkerung 1880–1910," in *Statistische Monatschrift*, Neue Folge, 19 (1914): 413–510, esp. 449; "Budějovice," in *Ottův slovník naučný nové doby*, vol. 1, no. 2, pp. 778–79; *Budweiser Zeitung*, 5 July 1939, p. 1; Bohmann, *Bevölkerungsbewegungen*, pp. 59–60; Emanuel Rádl, *Válka Čechů s Němci* (Prague: Čin, 1928), pp. 193–98; Václav Ambrož, *Z minulosti Českých Budějovic. Příručka k vlastivědě* (Č. Budějovice: Karel Ausobský, 1933), p. 85; Karel Fenzl, *Beseda česko-budějovická v letech 1913–1922. K šedesátiletému trvání* (Č. Budějovice: K. Fiala, 1923), p. 13; and *Jihočeské listy*, 9 July 1921, p. 2.

29. Brügel, *Tschechen und Deutsche*, pp. 150–97; Rothschild, *East Central Europe*, pp. 109–13; Stephan Horak, ed., *Eastern European National Minorities 1919–1980. A Handbook* (Littleton, Colo.: Libraries Unlimited, 1985), p. 115; and Fenzl, *Beseda česko-budějovická v letech 1923–1932*, pp. 11, 20, 28, 35.

30. Deutschpolitisches Arbeitsamt in der Tschechoslowakischen Republik, *Rechte und Pflichten aller Personen deutscher Nationalität (Muttersprache) bei der Volkszählung 1930* (Prague: Deutschpolitisches Arbeitsamt, 1930), p. 4; Rothschild, *East Central Europe*, p. 89; Czechoslovak Republic, Státní úřad statistický, *Sčítání lidu v Republice Československé ze dne 1. prosince 1930*, vol. 1 (Prague: Bursík a Kohout, 1934), pp. 26, 82; *Südböhmische Volkszeitung*, 3 September 1933, p. 6; *Jihočeské listy*, 15 September 1934, p. 1; Burian, *Město*, p. 34; Kratochwil and Meerwald, *Heimatbuch*, p. 510; and Sedlmeyer, *Budweis*, pp. 163–65.

31. Czechoslovak Republic, *Sammlung der Gesetze*, 30 June, 1930, pp. 495–97; Kollar, "Sčítání lidu," p. 186; and Bohmann, *Bevölkerungsbewegungen*, pp. 57–63. The new guidelines also banned private censuses.

32. Deutschpolitisches Arbeitsamt, *Rechte und Pflichten*, p. 37; and Kollar, "Sčítání lidu," p. 186.

33. Rádl, *Válka*, p. 143; and Karel Čapek, *Talks with T. G. Masaryk*, trans. Michael Henry Heim (North Haven, Conn.: Catbird, 1995), p. 244.

34. Jiří Korostenski, *Příspěvek k historii KSČ v letech 1928–1938 na Českobudějovicku* (České Budějovice: KSČ, 1981), p. 68; *Budweiser Zeitung*, 7 February 1934, p. 6; Edvard Beneš, *The Problems of Czechoslovakia* (Prague: Orbis, 1936), pp. 18–19; Prinz, *Geschichte Böhmens*, p. 401; Rothschild, *East Central Europe*, pp. 123–24; Radomír Luža, *The Transfer of the Sudeten Germans: A Study of Czech-German Relations, 1933–62* (New York: New York University Press, 1964), pp. 42–45; Alfred Bohmann, *Das Sudetendeutschtum in Zahlen* (Munich: Sudetendeutscher Rat, 1959), pp. 56–60, 98–101; and F. Gregory Campbell, *Confrontation in Central Europe: Weimar Germany and Czechoslovakia* (Chicago: University of Chicago Press, 1975), pp. 82–84, 230–31, 258–59.

35. Brubaker, *Nationalism Reframed*, pp. 107–47; Campbell, *Confrontation*, chap. 5; Ronald Smelser, *The Sudeten Problem 1933–1938. Volkstumspolitik and the Formulation of Nazi Foreign Policy* (Middletown, Conn.: Wesleyan University Press, 1975), esp. chaps. 1–3; and Lothar Gall, ed., *Fragen an die deutsche Geschichte* (Bonn: Deutscher Bundestag, 1981), p. 316.

36. Brubaker, *Nationalism Reframed*, esp. pp. 4–6; and King, "Austria vs. Hungary."

37. Smelser, *Sudeten Problem*, pp. 50–102; Campbell, *Confrontation*, pp. 260–64; *Südböhmische Volkszeitung*, 8 October 1933, pp. 1, 13; 22 October 1933, p. 1; and 19 November 1933, p. 1; and *Jihočeské listy*, 20 January 1934, p. 1.

38. Smelser, *Sudeten Problem*, pp. 100–119; *Budweiser Zeitung*, 4 August 1934, p. 13; 31 October 1934, p. 7; and 10 November 1934, p. 8; *Südböhmische Volkszeitung*, 27 January 1935, p. 1; and 31 March 1935, p. 3; and *Jihočech*, 25 July 1935, p. 1. On Westen, see *Budweiser Zeitung*, 29 April 1939, p. 9; Burian, *Město*, p. 62; and Sedlmeyer, *Budweis*, pp. 265–69, 568–69.

39. Brügel, *Tschechen und Deutsche*, pp. 265–67; Smelser, *Sudeten Problem*, pp. 100–19; Luža, *Transfer*, pp. 76–81; Rothschild, *East Central Europe*, pp. 109–26; *Jihočech*, 20 May 1935, p. 1; and 23 May 1935, pp. 1, 2; *Südböhmische Volkszeitung*, 27 January 1935, p. 1; Korostenski, *Příspěvek*, pp. 14–20, 49–66; and Miloslav Pecha, Stanislav Šmíd, and Václav Vondra, *Protifašistický odboj 1938–1945 na Českobudějovicku* (Č. Budějovice: Okresní národní výbor Č. Budějovice, 1986), p. 21.

40. Boyer, *Nationale Kontrahenten*, p. 368; Luža, *Transfer*, p. 88; Lipscher, *Verfassung*, pp. 159–61; and Smelser, *Sudeten Problem*, pp. 143–65.

41. The quotations come from *Budweiser Zeitung*, 2 December 1936, pp. 1–2; and 9 December 1936, p. 1. See also 14 November, 1925, p. 5; 2 December 1936, p. 6; 5 December 1936, pp. 3, 7; and 3 April 1937, p. 1; as well as Burian, *Město*, p. 38. Czech parties received 81.44 percent of the vote, German parties 14.95 percent, and the Communist Party 3.61 percent.

42. The quotations come from *Budweiser Zeitung*, 23 September 1931, p. 4; and 27 January 1937, pp. 6–7. See also 12 December 1936, p. 8; 13 February 1937, p. 5; and Burian, *Město*, p. 37. In the opposition were five Czech Tradesmen [*Živnostenská strana*], four Czech Social Democrats, two Communists, and three more Czechs, each representing a different party (Republican, Houseowners', and Civic Non-political).

43. *Budweiser Zeitung*, 24 February 1937, p. 1; and 20 March 1937, pp. 12–13; Lipscher, *Verfassung*, pp. 170–75; Luža, *Transfer*, pp. 96–102; Brügel, *Tschechen und Deutsche*, pp. 308–18; and Jiří Hájek, *Setkání a střety* (Köln: INDEX, 1983), p. 97.

44. *Jihočeské listy*, 12 January 1938, p. 2; 19 January 1938, p. 2; 9 March 1938, p. 1; and 16 March 1938, pp. 1, 2; and *Budweiser Zeitung*, 12 January 1938, p. 8; 12 March 1938, p. 6; and 16 March 1938, p. 10.

45. The quotations come from *Budweiser Zeitung*, 30 March 1938, p. 11; and Luža, *Transfer*, p. 114 . See also *Jihočeské listy*, 30 March 1938, p. 1; *Südböhmische Volkszeitung*, 27 March 1938, p. 1; and 3 April 1938, p. 1; *Budweiser Zeitung*, 19 March 1938, p. 9; 26 March 1938, pp. 1, 2; and 30 March 1938, pp. 7, 9–10; and Rothschild, *East Central Europe*, p. 129.

46. *Jihočeské listy*, 16 May 1934, p. 1; 14 May 1938, p. 2; 18 May 1938, p. 2; and 21 May 1938, p. 1; and *Budweiser Zeitung*, 23 April 1938, p. 8; 14 May 1938, pp. 8, 10; and 18 May 1938, pp. 8–9.

47. *Budweiser Zeitung*, 4 June 1938, p. 8; 11 June 1938, p. 8; 25 June 1938, p. 7; and 16 July 1938, p. 7; Kural, "Češi a Němci," pp. 211–13; Luža, *Transfer*, pp. 121–30.

48. Monica Curtis, ed., *Documents on International Affairs 1938*, vol. 2 (London: Oxford University Press, 1943), pp. 178–84; Brügel, *Tschechen und Deutsche*, pp. 419–64; and Kural, "Češi a Němci," p. 214.

49. Libuše Otáhalová and Milada Červinková, eds., *Dokumenty z historie čs. politiky 1939–1943* (Prague: Academia, 1966), p. 348; and Hubert Ripka, *East and West* (London: Lincolns-Praeger, 1944), pp. 129–32. See also István [Stephen] Borsody, *The Tragedy of Central Europe* (New Haven: Yale Concilium on International and Area Studies, 1980), p. 76.

50. Bibó, "A kelet-európai kisállamok," esp. pp. 204, 207; Curtis, *Documents*, pp. 359–60; Gerhard Jacoby, *Racial State. The German Nationalities Policy in the Protectorate of Bohemia-Moravia* (New York: Institute of Jewish Affairs, 1944), pp. 11–17; Brügel, *Tschechen und Deutsche*, p. 506; Luža, *Transfer*, pp. 163, 187; Hubert Ripka, *Československo v nové Evropě* (London: Lincolns-Praeger, 1945), p. 66; John W. Wheeler-Bennett, *Munich: Prologue to Tragedy* (New York: Viking, 1948), pp. 192–94; and *Jihočeské listy*, 24 September 1938, pp. 1, 2; 28 September 1938, pp. 1, 3; and 14 December 1938, p. 3. The figures of 2,800,000 Germans and 730,000 Czechs, based on the 1930 census, come from Bohmann, *Sudetendeutschtum*, pp. 122–23; and from Jacoby, *Racial State*, p. 309, who cites *Central European Observer*, 16 December 1938, p. 392. Vojtěch Mastný, in *The Czechs under Nazi Rule* (New York: Columbia University Press, 1971), p. 24, uses figures of 3,500,000 and 600,000. See also *Za obnovu státu Čechů a Slováků 1938–1945* (Prague: Státní pedagogické nakladatelství, 1992), p. 50; and Bohmann, *Bevölkerungsbewegungen*, p. 227.

51. *Jihočeské listy*, 17 September 1938, p. 3; 26 November 1938, p. 1; and 7 December 1938, pp. 1, 2; *Budweiser Zeitung*, 2 July 1938, p. 10; and 3 December 1938, p. 1; and Theodore Procházka, *The Second Republic: The Disintegration of Post-Munich Czechoslovakia* (Boulder, Colo.: East European Monographs, 1981), p. 92.

52. George Kennan, *From Prague after Munich. Diplomatic Papers 1938–1940* (Princeton: Princeton University Press, 1968), p. 134; *Budweiser Zeitung*, 13 August 1938, p. 10; and *Jihočeské listy*, 17 September 1938, p. 3; 21 September 1938, p. 2; 17 December 1938, p. 1; and 21 December 1938, p. 2.

53. *Budweiser Zeitung*, 24 December 1938, p. 5; and 1 February 1939, p. 6; *Jihočeské listy*, 14 December 1938, p. 1; 17 December 1938, p. 1; and 31 December 1938, p. 2; Luža, *Transfer*, p. 158; and Sedlmeyer, *Budweis*, p. 199.

54. Luža, *Transfer*, p. 173; Mastný, *Czechs*, pp. 36, 164, 197–98; Jacoby, *Racial State*, pp. 19–50; Emil Sobota, *Co to byl protektorát?* (Prague: Kvasnička a Hampl, 1946), pp. 29–43; Detlef Brandes, *Die Tschechen unter deutschem Protektorat*, vol. 1 (Munich: Oldenbourg, 1969), pp. 20–21; and Helma Kaden, ed., *Die faschistische Okkupationspolitik in Österreich und der Tschechoslowakei (1938–1945)* (Berlin: Deutscher Verlag der Wissenschaften, 1988), pp. 103–6.

55. *Budweiser Zeitung*, 16 March 1939, pp. 1–3; 5 April 1939, p. 8; 29 April 1939, p. 7; 10 June 1939, p. 8; 15 July 1939, p. 7; and 19 August 1939, p. 8; and *Hlas lidu*, 10 October 1945, p. 1.

56. *Budweiser Zeitung*, 24 June 1939, p. 1; and 20 September 1939, p. 10; Rudolf Beyer, ed., *Die Nürnberger Gesetze* (Leipzig: Reclam, 1938), pp. 23–53; Mastný, *Czechs*, p. 53; Sobota, *Co to byl*, p. 122; Detlef Brandes, *Die Tschechen unter deutschem Protektorat*, vol. 2 (1975), p. 36; Jacoby, *Racial State*, pp. 73–86, 108–12, 310; and Kaden, *Die faschistische Okkupationspolitik*, pp. 103–6.

57. Jacoby, *Racial State*, pp. 130–37; Sobota, *Co to byl*, p. 60; *Budweiser Zeitung*, 29 April 1939, pp. 7, 9; and Brandes, *Tschechen*, 1:160.

58. *Budweiser Zeitung*, 5 August 1939, pp. 5–6; 9 August 1939, p. 7; 4 November 1939, p. 14; and 15 November 1939, p. 8; Sobota, *Co to byl*, pp. 130–31; Jacoby, *Racial State*, p. 81; Brandes, *Tschechen*, 1:38, 161; and Kaden, *Die faschistische Okkupationspolitik*, pp. 167–68.

59. "Deutscher Volkszugehöriger ist, wer sich selbst als Angehöriger des deutschen Volkes bekennt, insofern . . ." Cited in Brandes, *Tschechen*, 1:160. See also *Budweiser Zeitung*, 1 April 1939, p. 3; and 5 April 1939, p. 1; Jacoby, *Racial State*, pp. 80–81; and Sobota, *Co to byl*, pp. 128–30.

60. Jacoby, *Racial State*, pp. 78–80.

61. *Budweiser Zeitung*, 26 April 1939, p. 8; and 17 May 1939, p. 8; Sobota, *Co to byl*, pp. 57–60; Jacoby, *Racial State*, pp. 136–43; Brandes, *Tschechen*, 1:41–44, 104; Tomáš Pasák, *Pod ochranou Říše* (Prague: Práh, 1998), pp. 58–64, 97; and Leoš Nikrmajer, "Vznik Národního souručenství v Českých Budějovicích a jeho činnost do vypuknutí druhé světové války," *Jihočeský sborník historický* 65 (1996): 106–11.

62. Nikrmajer, "Vznik," p. 107; and Kennan, *From Prague*, pp. 157–58. National Solidarity conducted a drive to recruit adult females only in 1940.

63. Brandes, *Tschechen*, 1:41; *Budweiser Zeitung*, 17 June 1939, pp. 7–8; Sobota, *Co to byl*, p. 126; and *Sbírka zákonů a nařízení Protektorátu Čechy a Morava*, 18 January 1940, p. 19.

64. Brandes, *Tschechen*, 1:41–45, 117–18; Sobota, *Co to byl*, pp. 126, 151–58; *Budweiser Zeitung*, 2 August 1939, p. 5; and 20 September 1939, p. 10; Jacoby, *Racial State*, pp. 139–43; Pasák, *Pod ochranou*, pp. 59, 124–26; Kennan, *From Prague*, p. 189; and *Sbírka zákonů a nařízení Protektorátu Čechy a Morava*, 24 April 1940, pp. 337–42.

65. *Budweiser Zeitung*, 7 June 1939, pp. 1–2; and 5 July 1939, p. 1; Brandes, *Tschechen*, 1:46; Nikrmajer, "Vznik," pp. 112–13; Kennan, *From Prague*, pp. 133–34, 180–81; and Pasák, *Pod ochranou*, pp. 144–47.

66. *Budweiser Zeitung*, 5 April 1939, p. 8; 29 April 1939, p. 7; 6 May 1939, pp. 5, 6; 17 June 1939, p. 7; 24 June 1939, p. 6; 5 July 1939, p. 6; 15 July 1939, p. 7; 22 July 1939, p. 9; 19 August 1939, p. 8; 23 August 1939, p. 4; 4 November 1939, p. 14; 6 January 1940, pp. 8–9; and 2 April 1941, p. 8; Brandes, *Tschechen*, 1:124–25; and Daniel Kovář, "Likvidace českobudějovických pomníků v letech okupace," *Jihočeský sborník historický* 68 (1999): 199–215.

67. Jacoby, *Racial State*, pp. 81–82; Sobota, *Co to byl*, pp. 127–37; Mastný, *Czechs*, pp. 70–85; *Budweiser Zeitung*, 4 October 1939, p. 11; Brandes, *Tschechen*, p. 40; and Kennan, *From Prague*, pp. 117, 209.

68. *Budweiser Zeitung,* 2 December 1939, p. 7; 16 March 1940, pp. 10–11; and 23 March 1940, p. 9; *Jihočech,* 19 October 1945, p. 2; Pecha, Šmíd, and Vondra, *Protifašistický,* p. 52; Brandes, *Tschechen,* 1:160; Jacoby, *Racial State,* p. 310; Miroslav Kárný, Jaroslava Milotová, and Margita Kárná, eds., *Deutsche Politik im "Protektorat Böhmen und Mähren" unter Reinhard Heydrich 1941–1942* (Berlin: Metropol, 1997), pp. 122–27; Bohmann, *Sudetendeutschtum,* p. 194; and Sobota, *Co to byl,* p. 89.

69. Brandes, *Tschechen,* 1:160, 236–39; *Jihočeská pravda,* 8 February 1946, pp. 1–2; Kárný et al., *Deutsche Politik,* pp. 209–12; Václav Král, ed., *Die Deutschen in der Tschechoslowakei 1933–1947* (Prague: Československá akademie věd, 1964), pp. 409–10; and Benjamin Frommer, "Retribution against Nazi Collaborators in Postwar Czechoslovakia," Ph.D. diss., Harvard University, 1999, p. 210. Please consult as well relevant footnotes in the next chapter.

70. Historians in Germany have paid little attention to the Protectorate in recent years, while historians in the Czech Republic have continued to assume national categories, rather than to tackle the task of tracing their historical development. See, for example, Václav Král, *Pravda o okupaci* (Prague: Naše vojsko, 1962); Pasák, *Pod ochranou;* Jan Gebhart and Jan Kuklík, *Dramatické i všední dny protektorátu* (Prague: Themis, 1996); Jiří Doležal, *Česká kultura za protektorátu: školství, písemnictví, kinematografie* (Prague: Národní filmový archiv, 1996); and Václav Kural, *Vlastenci proti okupaci. Ústřední vedení odboje domácího 1940–1943* (Prague: Univerzita Karlova, Ústav mezinárodních vztahů, 1997). See, however, Chad Bryant, "Making the Czechs German: Ethnic Politics and Nazi Policy in the Protectorate of Bohemia and Moravia, 1939–1945," Ph.D. diss., University of California, Berkeley, forthcoming.

71. Bohmann, *Bevölkerungsbewegungen,* p. 162; *Jihočeská pravda,* 4 July 1945, p. 2; and 29 August 1946, p. 2; and Frommer, "Retribution," pp. 210, 258. For the whole of the Bohemian lands, the figure that corresponds to 12,560 is 143,000. The "Czechoslovak" population of Budweis/Budějovice District thus had made up one sixty-sixth of the all-Bohemian total (7.3 million) in the 1930 census, but one-eleventh of all would-be double converts. (In the Sudetenland, already during 1938 and 1939, probably more than 100,000 Czechs had exchanged their Czechoslovak citizenship for Reich citizenship. But because expropriation, as well as expulsion to Czecho-Slovakia or to the Protectorate, had hung as a threat in the air, comparison with the Protectorate is difficult.)

72. *Sbírka zákonů a nařízení Protektorátu Čechy a Morava,* 1942, pp. 565–70; Jacoby, *Racial State,* p. 90; and Sobota, *Co to byl,* pp. 157–60.

73. Brandes, *Tschechen,* 1:124–37, 209–11, 236–38; Václav Král, *Lesson from History. Documents concerning Nazi Policies for Germanisation and Extermination in Czechoslovakia* (Prague: Orbis, 1961), pp. 47–142; and Král, *Die Deutschen in der Tschechoslowakei,* pp. 412–28.

74. The quotations are from Kárný et al., *Deutsche Politik,* pp. 115, 118–19; see also pp. 154–55, 272; and Brandes, *Tschechen,* 1:236–38.

75. Kárný et al., *Deutsche Politik,* p. 117; and Brandes, *Tschechen,* 1:211–14.

76. Mastný, *Czechs,* pp. 99–101, 160–63, 181–221; Luža, *Transfer,* pp. 229–30; Joseph Zacek, "Nationalism in Czechoslovakia," in *Nationalism in Eastern Europe,* ed. Peter Sugar and Ivo Lederer (Seattle: University of Washington Press,

1969), pp. 166–206, esp. 197–98; Václav Černý, *Pláč koruny české* (London: Roz-mluvy-Svědectví, 1985), pp. 339–51; Edward Táborský, *President Edvard Beneš: Between East and West 1938–1948* (Stanford: Hoover Institution Press, 1981), pp. 36–41; Táborský, "Politics in Exile, 1939–1945," in Mamatey and Luža, *A History of the Czechoslovak Republic*, pp. 322–42; Otáhalová and Červinková, *Dokumenty*, pp. 248–55; Hájek, *Setkání a střety*, pp. 117–18.

77. Luža, *Transfer*, pp. 210–11, 235–37; Mastný, *Czechs*, pp. 207–23; *Bud-weiser Zeitung*, 18 March 1939, p. 5; 2 June 1942 through 3 July 1942; *Budějo-vické listy*, 29 July 1942, p. 2; and *Hlas lidu*, 29 August 1945, p. 1.

78. Otáhalová and Červinková, *Dokumenty*, p. 274; Táborský, *President Edvard Beneš*, pp. 42–43, 125–26, 156–62; Callum MacDonald, *The Killing of SS Ober-gruppenführer Reinhard Heydrich* (New York: Free Press, 1989), pp. 199–204; and Wenzel Jaksch, *Europe's Road to Potsdam* (New York: Praeger, 1963), pp. 371–73.

79. Sedlmeyer, *Budweis*, pp. 504–8; *Budweiser Zeitung*, 10 October 1944, p. 5; 20 October 1944, p. 6; 27 October 1944, p. 5; 23 January 1945, p. 5; 20 March 1945, p. 6; 27 March 1945, p. 1; 30 March 1945, pp. 1, 2, and 4; and 6 April 1945, p. 3.

80. *Budweiser Zeitung*, 2 May 1945, p. 1; Pecha, Šmíd, and Vondra, *Protifaši-stický*, pp. 163ff; *Hlas lidu*, 18 July 1945, p. 3; and Sedlmeyer, *Budweis*, pp. 504–19.

Conclusion
Budweis Buried, 1945–1948

1. Sedlmeyer, *Budweis*, pp. 507–8, 511, 518–19; Pecha, Šmíd, and Vondra, *Pro-tifašistický*, p. 167; *Jihočeská pravda*, 13 June 1945, p. 2; 16 May 1946, p. 4; and 28 May 1946, p. 2; *Hlas lidu*, 15 June 1945, pp. 1–2; *Jihočech*, 5 October 1945, p. 2; Jiří Petráš, "Konec soužití Čechů a Němců v Českých Budějovicích," *Jihočeský sborník historický* 66–67 (1997–98): 147–72, esp. 150–55; and Luža, *Transfer*, pp. 269–70.

2. Beneš, formerly a National Social, belonged to no party as postwar president of Czechoslovakia. Luža, *Transfer*, pp. 255–56, 276; Paul E. Zinner, *Communist Strategy and Tactics in Czechoslovakia 1918–1948* (New York: Praeger, 1963), pp. 91–93, 111, 179; and Táborský, *President Edvard Beneš*, pp. 207–9. See also *Hlas lidu*, 7 June 1945, pp. 5, 6.

3. Cited in Vojtěch Mastný, *Russia's Road to the Cold War* (New York: Colum-bia University Press, 1979), p. 135. See also *Jihočeská pravda*, 6 June 1945, p. 3.

4. Luža, *Transfer*, pp. 221, 261, 320; Martin Myant, *Socialism and Democracy in Czechoslovakia, 1945–1948* (Cambridge: Cambridge University Press, 1981), p. 66; Karel Veselý-Štainer, *Cestou národního odboje. Bojový vývoj domácího odbojového hnutí v letech 1938–45* (Prague: Sfinx, 1947), pp. 160, 214; and Jon Bloomfield, *Passive Revolution: Politics and the Czechoslovak Working Class, 1945–1948* (New York: St. Martin's Press, 1979), pp. 62–64.

5. Luža, *Transfer*, pp. 246–51, 272–73, 277–78; Jaksch, *Europe's Road*, pp. 397–401, 459–60; Otáhalová and Červinková, *Dokumenty*, pp. 750–51; and Wal-ter Ullmann, *The United States in Prague, 1945–1948* (Boulder, Colo.: East Euro-pean Quarterly, 1978), p. 60.

6. Luža, *Transfer*, pp. 268–72; Kurt Glaser, *Czecho-Slovakia. A Critical History* (Caldwell, Idaho: Caxton Printers, 1961), p. 117; Jaksch, *Europe's Road*, p. 423; Elizabeth Wiskemann, *Germany's Eastern Neighbors* (London: Oxford University Press, 1956), p. 105; and Frommer, "Retribution," pp. 17–19.

7. Ygael Gluckstein, *Stalin's Satellites in Europe* (Boston: Beacon Press, 1952), p. 189. See also Černý, *Pláč*, pp. 193–96.

8. The quotation comes from *Hlas lidu*, 18 July 1945, p. 1. See also *Jihočech*, 7 June 1945, p. 1; 15 June 1945, pp. 1–2; 29 June 1945, p. 3; 4 July 1945, p. 2; and 10 August 1945, p. 1; *Hlas lidu*, 27 June 1945, p. 1; 4 July 1945, pp. 2–3; 11 July 1945, pp. 1–2; 25 July 1945, p. 1; 14 August 1945, p. 2; and 17 October 1945, p. 1; Sedlmeyer, *Budweis*, p. 513; Ludvík Němec, "Solution of the Minorities Problem," in Mamatey and Luža, *A History of the Czechoslovak Republic*, pp. 416–21; Ullmann, *The United States*, pp. 60–65; Myant, *Socialism*, pp. 64–66; and Libuše Hanušová, *Co s nimi?* (Prague: Rebec, 1946), p. 47.

9. Jaroslav Fusek, *Osvědčení o státní a národní spolehlivosti* (Brno: Zář, 1946), pp. 8–12; *Jihočech*, 19 April 1946, p. 4; Němec, "Solution," p. 420; Zinner, *Communist Strategy*, p. 107; and Glaser, *Czecho-Slovakia*, p. 135.

10. *Hlas lidu*, 11 July 1945, pp. 1–2; and Frommer, "Retribution," pp. 164–65. On the issue of collective guilt and Beneš's embrace of it in a speech at Lidice on June 10, see Jaroslav Stránský, *Odsun Němců z ČSR z hlediska národního a mezinárodního* (London: Ústav Dr. Edvarda Beneše, 1953), 2:60. See also Stránský's commentary on that speech in a letter to Václav Beneš, dated 30 March 1954, located in the Smutný papers, Bakhmeteff Archive, Rare Book and Manuscript Library, Columbia University, Box 22, Folder 4. See also Hanušová, *Co s nimi?*, p. 35.

11. *Hlas lidu*, 4 July 1945, p. 2; 11 July 1945, p. 2; 18 July 1945, p. 3; 25 July 1945, p. 4; 1 August 1945, p. 3; 14 August 1945, p. 5; 29 August 1945, p. 2; 19 September 1945, p. 5; 26 September 1945, p. 2; 5 December 1945, p. 1; and 19 December 1945, p. 4; *Jihočech*, 12 October 1945, p. 3; 31 October 1945, p. 1; 4 January 1946, p. 5; 19 April 1946, pp. 3, 4; 26 April 1946, p. 3; 14 June 1946, p. 4; 15 November 1946, p. 2; 13 June 1947, p. 2; and 12 March 1948, p. 2; *Jihočeská pravda*, 6 June 1945, p. 4; 13 June 1945, p. 3; 22 March 1946, p. 3; 24 October 1946, p. 2; and 24 April 1947, p. 5; Gluckstein, *Stalin's Satellites*, pp. 190–91; Zinner, *Communist Strategy*, pp. 124, 138–39; Hájek, *Setkání a střety*, p. 136; Josef Korbel, *The Communist Subversion of Czechoslovakia 1938–1948* (Princeton: Princeton University Press, 1959), pp. 131, 138; and Korbel, *Twentieth Century Czechoslovakia* (New York: Columbia University Press, 1977), p. 220. *Jihočech*, reporting in January of 1946 on a forthcoming decree that would regulate the transfer to Czechs of ownership of small and medium-sized businesses (perhaps residential buildings as well) confiscated from Germans and collaborators, expressed hope that there would be no repetition of "the fever that we experienced already in the course of the staffing of these firms with National Administrators" (see 11 January 1946, p. 2). In February 1947, the former director of the Section for the Securing of German Property, a Communist, was arrested after the police found many valuable items, acquired illegally from Germans, in his apartment. See *Jihočech*, 28 February 1947, p. 3; and *Jihočeská pravda*, 6 March 1947, p. 1.

12. Fusek, *Osvědčení*, p. 9.

13. *Jihočech*, 5 October 1945, p. 2.
14. See, for example, Frommer, "Retribution," p. 214.
15. *Jihočeská pravda*, 20 June 1945, pp. 1, 4.
16. *Hlas lidu*, 27 June 1945, pp. 3, 4.
17. Géza Paikert, *The German Exodus* (The Hague: M. Nijhoff, 1962), pp. 8–9; Luža, *Transfer*, pp. 278–79; and Ullmann, *The United States*, pp. 64–72.
18. *Hlas lidu*, 8 August 1945, p. 2; and 14 August 1945, p. 2; *Jihočech*, 10 August 1945, p. 1; 20 September 1945, p. 2; and 5 October 1945, p. 2; Fusek, *Osvědčení*, p. 11; and Josef Mucha and Karel Petrželka, *O některých problémech národnostně smíšených manželství* (Prague: Svoboda, 1946), p. 7.
19. Fusek, *Osvědčení*, p. 11. See also Mucha and Petrželka, *O některých problémech*, p. 8.
20. See the case of Fr. Špát, discussed in *Jihočech*, 28 September 1945, p. 2.
21. Fusek, *Osvědčení*, pp. 10, 12–15; the direct quotations come from p. 13. See also Mucha and Petrželka, *O některých problémech*, pp. 14–15; and Frommer, "Retribution," pp. 193–207.
22. *Hlas lidu*, 12 September 1945, p. 3; and 3 October, 1945, p. 3; *Jihočeská pravda*, 8 February 1946, pp. 1–2; 15 February 1946, p. 1; 22 February 1946, p. 1; 13 June 1946, p. 3; and 14 August 1946, p. 5; and *Jihočech*, 5 October, 1945, p. 3; and 6 September 1946, p. 3.
23. The quotation is from *Jihočech*, 28 September 1945, p. 2. See also 31 August 1945, p. 2; 7 December 1945, p. 2; 14 December 1945, p. 2; 21 December 1945, p. 4; and 4 January 1946, p. 2; *Hlas lidu*, 17 October 1945, p. 3; and 5 December 1945, p. 3; *Jihočeská pravda*, 31 October 1945, p. 2; 4 January 1946, p. 2; and 25 January 1946, p. 2; and *Svoboda*, 3 March 1948, p. 5. The practice of publishing such lists continued at least until the fall of 1946; see *Jihočeská pravda*, 10 October 1946, p. 5; and 14 November 1946, p. 2.
24. Petráš, "Konec soužití," pp. 156–57; Luža, *Transfer*, pp. 284–90; Wiskemann, *Germany's Eastern Neighbors*, p. 106; Stránský, *Odsun*, 2:36; *Jihočech*, 8 February 1946, p. 1; and *Svoboda*, 3 March 1948, p. 5. A memorandum circulated within the Czechoslovak government-in-exile during 1944, marked "Secret," reads "Obstacles will not be placed in the way of voluntary emigration by innocent members of the German minority." See Smutný papers, Bakhmeteff Archive, Rare Book and Manuscript Library, Columbia University, Box 22, Folder 1.
25. *Jihočech*, 28 September 1945, p. 2; and 5 October 1945, p. 2; and *Jihočeská pravda*, 11 January 1946, p. 1; 25 January 1946, p. 3; 1 March 1946, p. 3; 8 March 1946, p. 3; 15 March 1946, p. 1; and 22 March 1946, p. 3.
26. *Hlas lidu*, 12 September 1945, p. 1; and Frommer, "Retribution," pp. 241–85.
27. *Jihočech*, 5 October 1945, p. 1; and 19 October 1945, p. 2; and Frommer, "Retribution," pp. 184–87, 217, 225. The assertions in this paragraph rest on a comparison of multiple cases, including the following: *Hlas lidu*, 5 September 1945, p. 1 (Hlaváč); *Jihočech*, 28 September 1945, pp. 2 (Turek, Špát, Chalupa) and 3 (Bejwel); 5 October 1945, p. 1 (Duchek); 31 October 1945, p. 2 (Růžička, Borovková); 14 December 1945, p. 2 (Jirovský, Samohejlová, Dušek and Dušková); 2 August 1946, p. 2 (Hrdina); 22 November 1946, p. 4 (Drahorád); and 25 July 1947, p. 2 (Weis); and *Jihočeská pravda*, 15 March 1946, p. 1 (Antoš,

Oswald); and 19 December 1946, p. 2 (Nečásek). More generally, see *Jihočeská pravda*, 8 February 1946, p. 2; 22 February 1946, p. 1; and 29 March 1946, p. 2; *Jihočech*, 9 May 1947, p. 4; and *Svoboda*, 3 March 1948, p. 5.

28. *Jihočech*, 8 February 1946, p. 1; and *Jihočeská pravda*, 8 February 1946, pp. 1–2.

29. *Jihočeská pravda*, 22 February 1946, p. 1.

30. *Jihočeská pravda*, 29 March 1946, p. 2; as well as 13 June 1946, p. 3.

31. *Jihočeská pravda*, 4 July 1946, p. 1.

32. Ibid.

33. *Jihočech*, 11 January 1946, p. 2; and 4 April 1947, p. 1; *Jihočeská pravda*, 29 May 1947, p. 4; Frommer, "Retribution," p. 258; and Sedlmeyer, *Budweis*, pp. 267, 510, 569.

34. *Jihočech*, 10 October 1945, p. 1; 19 October 1945, p. 3; and 27 September 1946, p. 4; *Hlas lidu*, 12 September 1945, p. 1; and 26 September 1945, p. 2; *Jihočeská pravda*, 10 October 1945, p. 1; and 25 April 1946, p. 3; *Dějiny Československa v datech* (Prague: Svoboda, 1968), p. 365; and Frommer, "Retribution," pp. 193, 234–35.

35. Frommer, "Retribution," pp. 234–35; *Jihočeská pravda*, 28 May 1946, p. 1; 11 July 1946, p. 1; *Svoboda*, 3 March 1948, pp. 1, 2; and *Jihočech*, 28 June 1946, p. 5.

36. *Jihočeská pravda*, 9 January 1947, p. 3; 20 February 1947, p. 1; 12 June 1947, p. 2; and 14 August 1947, p. 1; and *Jihočech*, 14 February 1947, p. 1.

37. *Jihočech*, 9 May 1947, p. 4; 26 September 1947, pp. 1, 2; and 10 October 1947, p. 1; and Joseph Rothschild, *Return to Diversity. The Political History of East Central Europe since World War II*, 2nd edition (New York: Oxford University Press, 1993), pp. 93, 122–23.

38. *Jihočeská pravda*, 6 November 1947, pp. 1, 2. See also 11 September 1947, pp. 3, 4; 16 October 1947, p. 1; and 23 October 1947, p. 3; *Jihočech*, 5 December 1947, p. 1; and Menzel, *Die nationale Entwicklung*, p. 210.

39. *Jihočeská pravda*, 24 December 1947, p. 1; and Frommer, "Retribution," pp. 340–51. Jan Masaryk, like Beneš, had no party affiliation.

40. *Jihočeská pravda*, 4 March 1948, p. 1; 1 April 1948, p. 5; 8 July 1948, p. 1; and 22 July 1948, p. 3; *Svoboda*, 3 March 1948, pp. 1, 2; *Jihočech*, 25 March 1948, p. 1; 14 May 1948, pp. 1, 2; 21 May 1948, p. 1; and 28 May 1948, pp. 1, 3; Kopáček, *Encyklopedie*, pp. 281, 379; and personal communication from Jan Mareš.

41. The source referred to is Sedlmeyer, *Budweis*, p. 513. See also *Jihočech*, 27 February 1948, p. 1; *Jihočeská pravda*, 4 March 1948, p. 1; *Svoboda*, 3 March 1948, pp. 1, 2; and 24 March 1948, p. 1; and Kopáček, *Encyklopedie*, p. 368.

42. Táborský, *President Edvard Beneš*, pp. 224, 240, 253–54; and Luža, *Odsun*, pp. 49–52. See also Jaksch, *Europe's Road*, pp. 358–59.

43. Bibó, "A kelet-európai kisállamok nyomorúsága," p. 208. See also Rothschild, *Return to Diversity*, p. 123.

44. Cited in Béla Bellér, *A magyarországi németek rövid története* (Budapest: Magvető, 1981), pp.102–3.

45. Cozine, "A Member of the State," pp. 217–18.

46. Paikert, *The German Exodus*, p. 17. See also Stránský, *Odsun*, 2:34; Zinner, *Communist Strategy*, pp. 110, 138; Rudolf Kučera, "Komentář," *Střední Evropa 7*, no. 20 (1991): pp. 4–10, esp. 8; and Frommer, "Retribution," pp. 277–85.

47. Ernst Franz Richter, *Südböhmische Sagen und Geschichten. Mit einer kurzgefassten Geschichte der k.k. Berg-Kreisstadt Böhmisch-Budweis* (Korneuburg: Kühkopf, 1881), p. 48. See also Sedlmeyer, *Budweis*, pp. v, 4.

48. Scheu, *Wanderungen*, p. 36.

Selected Bibliography

Contemporary Periodicals

Anzeiger aus dem südlichen Böhmen
Budějovické listy
Budivoj
Budweiser Bote
Budweiser Kreisblatt
Budweiser Wochenblatt
Budweiser Zeitung
Der Bürgerfreund
Česko-budějovické listy
Deutsche Erde
Deutsche Volkswehr
Das Deutschtum im Ausland
Gradaus!
Hlas lidu
Jihočech
Jihočeská jednota
Jihočeská pravda
Jihočeské listy
Jihočeský dělník
Der konstitutionelle Staatsbürger
Der Löwe
Mitteilungen des Deutschen Böhmerwaldbundes
Naše svoboda
Sammlung der Gesetze und Verordnungen des čechoslovakischen Staates
Sbírka zákonů a nařízení Protektorátu Čechy a Morava
Sbírka zákonů a nařízení státu československého
Stráž lidu
Südböhmische Volkszeitung
Svoboda
Volksblatt für Stadt und Land

Other Primary Materials

1884–1934. Fünfzig Jahre Deutscher Böhmerwaldbund. Budweis: Deutscher Böhmerwaldbund / Felix Zdarssa, 1934.

Ambrož, Václav. *Z minulosti Českých Budějovic. Příručka k vlastivědě o Č. Budějovicích.* Č. Budějovice: Karel Ausobský, 1933.

Beck, Max Vladimir Freiherr von. "Der Kaiser und die Wahlreform." In *Erinnerungen an Franz Joseph I.* Edited by Eduard Ritter von Steinitz. Berlin: Verlag für Kulturpolitik, 1931, pp. 197–224.

Beneš, Edvard. *Paměti: Od Mnichova k nové válce a novému vítězství.* Prague: Orbis, 1947.

———. *The Problems of Czechoslovakia.* Prague: Orbis, 1936.

Beneš, Vojta. *The Vanguard of the "Drang nach Osten."* Chicago: Czechoslovak National Council of America, 1943.

Bericht des Deutschen Turnvereines in Budweis. Herausgegeben aus Anlaß des 50 jährigen Vereinsbestandes mit besonderer Berücksichtigung der letzten 10 Vereinsjahre. Budweis: A. Pokorný, 1912.

Bernatzik, Edmund. *Über nationale Matriken: Inaugurationsrede.* Vienna: Manz, 1910.

Böhm, Wilibald, and Emmerich Zdiarsky. *Die Stadt Budweis. Eine Orts- und Volkskunde.* Budweis: Selbstverlag, 1904.

Burian, Miroslav, ed. *Město České Budějovice.* Č. Budějovice: Městská rada, n.d. [1938?].

Černý, Václav. *Pláč koruny české.* London: Rozmluvy-Svědectví, 1985.

České Budějovice. Krása našeho domova. Č. Budějovice, 1926.

Conrad von Hötzendorf, Graf Franz. *Aus meiner Dienstzeit, 1906–1918.* Vol. 4. Vienna: Rikola, 1923.

Curtis, Monica, ed. *Documents on International Affairs 1938.* Vol. 2. London: Oxford University Press, 1943.

Deutschpolitisches Arbeitsamt in der Tschechoslowakischen Republik. *Rechte und Pflichten aller Personen deutscher Nationalität (Muttersprache) bei der Volkszählung 1930.* Prague: Deutschpolitisches Arbeitsamt, 1930.

Dvacet let zápasu o školství české. Paměti matice školské v Českých Budějovicích. Č. Budějovice: Matice školská / V. Matouš, 1893.

Dvořák, Lad. *Biskupský kněžský seminář v Č. Budějovicích.* Č. Budějovice: Diecésní spolek musejní, 1905.

Fehr, Götz. *Fernkurs in Böhmisch.* Hamburg: Hoffmann und Campe, 1977.

Fenzl, Karel. *Paměti Besedy česko-budějovické 1902–1912.* Č. Budějovice: Beseda č-budějovická, 1913.

———. *Beseda česko-budějovická v letech 1913–1922. K šedesátiletému trvání.* Č. Budějovice: K. Fiala, 1923.

———. *Beseda česko-budějovická v letech 1923–1932. K sedmdesátiletému trvání.* Č. Budějovice: Společenská tiskárna, 1933.

Festschrift der Deutschen Liedertafel in Budweis anläßlich ihrer 50 jähr. Bestandsfeier. Budweis: Selbstverlag, 1906.

Frýd, Norbert. *Hedvábné starosti aneb: Uprostřed posledních sto let.* Prague: Československý spisovatel, 1968.

———. *Vzorek bez ceny a pan biskup.* Prague: Československý spisovatel, 1966.

Fusek, Jaroslav. *Osvědčení o státní a národní spolehlivosti.* Brno: Zář, 1946.

Germanisirung oder Czechisirung? Ein Beitrag zur Nationalitätenfrage in Böhmen. Leipzig and Heidelberg: C. F. Winter, 1861.

Habel, Fritz Peter. *Dokumente zur Sudetenfrage.* Munich: Langen Müller, 1984.

Hácha, Emil, Jiří Hoetzel, František Weyr, and Karel Laštovka, eds. *Slovník veřejného práva Československého,* 4 vols. Brno: Polygrafia, 1929–1938.

Hanušová, Libuše. *Co s nimi?* Prague: Rebec, 1946.

Hašek, Jaroslav. *The Good Soldier: Švejk.* New York: Ungar, 1962.

Hlíza, František, ed. *Sedmdesát let trvání továrny na tabák v Čes. Budějovicích. 1872–1947.* Č. Budějovice: Společenské knihtiskárny, 1947.

Hoetzl, Jiří, and Václav Joachim, eds. *The Constitution of the Czechoslovak Republic.* Prague: L'Effort de la Tchéchoslovaquie, 1920.

Holeček, Josef. *Pero.* Vol. 1. Prague: Pražská akciová tiskárna, 1922.

Hubka, Antonín, ed. *Čes. Budějovice. Pamětní list slavnosti Praha—Čes. Budějovicům konané ve dnech 29., 30. června a 1. července 1906 v Praze.* Č. Budějovice: Slavnostní výbor, 1906.

———. *Naše menšiny a smíšené kraje na českém jihu.* Prague: Samostatnost, 1899.

Illing, Franz Xaver, and Franz Seyser. *Kurzgefasste Chronik der königlich privilegierten und freien Berg- und Kreisstadt Budweis (Budigowice) im Königreiche Böhmen.* Budweis: M. Zdarssa, 1841.

Jaksch, Friedrich [Bodenreuth, Friedrich]. *Alle Wasser Böhmens fließen nach Deutschland.* Berlin: Hans von Hugo, 1937.

Jaksch, Wenzel. *Europe's Road to Potsdam.* New York: Frederick A. Praeger, 1963.

Jihočeský kalendář. Schematismus a adresář na rok 1901. Č. Budějovice: Družstvo vydavatelské a nakladatelské, n.d.

Jirásek, Alois. *Z mých pamětí.* Prague: Mladá fronta, 1980.

Kaden, Helma, ed. *Die faschistische Okkupationspolitik in Österreich und der Tschechoslowakei (1938–1945).* Berlin: Deutscher Verlag der Wissenschaften, 1988.

Kaindl, Raimund Friedrich. *Der Völkerkampf und Sprachenstreit in Böhmen im Spiegel der zeitgenössischen Quellen.* Vienna and Leipzig: Braumüller, 1927.

Kárný, Miroslav, Jaroslava Milotová, and Margita Kárná, eds. *Deutsche Politik im "Protektorat Böhmen und Mähren" unter Reinhard Heydrich 1941–1942.* Berlin: Metropol, 1997.

Kennan, George. *From Prague after Munich. Diplomatic Papers 1938–1940.* Princeton: Princeton University Press, 1968.

Kohl, Johann Georg. *Austria.* London: Chapman and Hall, 1844.

———. *Hundert Tage auf Reisen in den österreichischen Staaten.* Vol. 1: *Reise in Böhmen.* Dresden and Leipzig: Arnold, 1842.

Kolmer, Gustav. *Parlament und Verfassung in Österreich,* 8 vols. [1902–14]. Graz: Akademische Druck- und Verlagsanstalt, 1972.

Král, Václav, ed. *Die Deutschen in der Tschechoslowakei 1933–1947.* Prague: Československá akademie věd, 1964.

———, ed. *Lesson from History. Documents concerning Nazi Policies for Germanisation and Extermination in Czechoslovakia.* Prague: Orbis, 1961.

Kratochwil, Karl, and Alois Meerwald, eds. *Heimatbuch der Berg- und Kreisstadt Böhmisch-Budweis mit einer Sammlung von alten und neueren Sagen.* Böhmisch-Budweis: Kratochwil, 1930.

Kudrnáč, Václav. *Úplný adresář hejtmanství Česko-Budějovického. Soudní okresy: Č.-Budějovický, Hluboký, Lišovský, Trho-Svinenský.* Turnov: Kudrnáč, n.d. [1904?].

Lemberg, Eugen. *Lebensbilder zur Geschichte der böhmischen Länder,* vol. 5: *Ein Leben in Grenzzonen und Ambivalenzen.* Munich: Oldenbourg, 1986.

Macháček, Jan. *Paměti 25 let. trvání c.k. č. gymnasia v Budějovicích (1868–1893) a seznam abiturientů, jejich nynější stav a bydliště.* České Budějovice: nákladem vlastním, 1894.

Masarykův slovník naučný, vol. 4. Praha: Československý kompas, 1929.

Matice školská v Čes Budějovicích. Její vzor a její pokračovatelé. Č. Budějovice: Matice školská / K. Fiala, 1925.

Mauthner, Fritz. *Erinnerungen*. Munich: Georg Müller, 1918.

Maysl, Albert. *Obchodní a průmyslová komora v Čes. Budějovicích 1850–1905*. Č. Budějovice: Obchodní a průmyslová komora, 1906.

Menger, Max. *Der böhmische Ausgleich*. Stuttgart: Cotta, 1891.

Mucha, Josef, and Karel Petrželka. *O některých problémech národnostně smíšených manželství*. Prague: Svoboda, 1946.

Müller-Guttenbrunn, Adam. *Deutsche Sorgen in Ungarn*. Vienna: Strache, 1918.

Neruda, Jan. "Eklogy." In *Menší cesty*. Prague: Grégr a Dattl, 1877.

Osmdesát let českobudějovické spořitelny. Č. Budějovice: K. Fiala, n.d. [1935?].

Österreichische National-Encyklopädie. Vol. 1. Vienna: Beck'sche Universitäts-Buchhandlung, 1835.

Otáhalová, Libuše, and Milada Červinková, eds. *Dokumenty z historie čs. politiky 1939–1943*. Prague: Academia, 1966.

Ottův slovník naučný. 28 vols. Prague: J. Otto, 1888–1909.

Palacký, František. *Idea státu rakouského*. Prague: I. L. Kober, 1865.

———. *Oesterreichs Staatsidee*. Prague: I. L. Kober, 1866.

[Palacký, Jan]. *Böhmische Skizzen, 1860. Von einem Landeskind*. Leitomischl: Anton Augusta, 1860.

Pamětní list jubilejní matični slavnosti v Českých Budějovicích, 28. a 29. června 1908. Budějovice, 1908.

Pisling, Theophil. *Nationalökonomische Briefe aus dem nordöstlichen Böhmen*. Prague: C. Bellmann, 1856.

Pucherna, Vojtěch J. *Paměti Besedy česko-budějovické 1862–1902*. Č. Budějovice: Přibyl, 1903.

Rádl, Emanuel. *Válka Čechů s Němci*. Prague: Čin, 1928.

Rauter, D. *Österreichisches Staats-Lexikon*. Vienna: Perles, 1885.

Der Reichsrath. Biographische Skizzen der Mitglieder des Herren- und Abgeordnetenhauses des österreichischen Reichsrathes. Vol. 1. Vienna: Fr. Förster und Brüder, 1861.

Renner, Karl. *Der deutsche Arbeiter und der Nationalismus*. Vienna: Brand, 1910.

———. [Springer, Rudolf.] *Der Kampf der Oesterreichischen Nationen um den Staat*. Leipzig and Vienna: Deuticke, 1902.

———. *Der nationale Streit um die Aemter und die Sozialdemokratie*. Vienna: Vorwärts, 1908.

Richter, Ernst Franz. *Kurzgefaßte Geschichte der k. befreiten allezeit getreuen Berg- und Kreisstadt Böhmisch-Budweis*. Budweis: F. Zdarssa, n.d. [1859?].

———. *Südböhmische Sagen und Geschichten. Mit einer kurzgefassten Geschichte der k.k. Berg-Kreisstadt Böhmisch-Budweis*. Korneuburg: Kühkopf, 1881.

Ripka, Hubert. *East and West*. London: Lincolns-Praeger, 1944.

———. *Československo v nové Evropě*. London: Lincolns-Praeger, 1945.

Rohmeder, Dr. "Der Budweiser Ausgleich." *Das Deutschtum im Ausland* 19 (1914): 88.

Roth, Joseph. *The Emperor's Tomb*. Woodstock, N.Y.: Overlook, 1984.

———. *Hotel Savoy*. London: Chatto and Windus, 1986.

————. *The Radetzky March.* Woodstock, New York: Overlook, 1974.
Sborník vydaný v 45. výročí založení Národní jednoty pošumavské. Deset let národní práce v jižních Čechách po převratu. Prague: NJP, 1930.
Scheu, Robert. *Wanderungen durch Böhmen am Vorabend der Revolution.* Vienna and Leipzig: Strache, 1919.
Schuselka, Franz. *Deutsch oder Russisch? Die Lebensfrage Oesterreichs.* Vienna: Jasper, Hügel und Manz, 1849.
Schweighofer, Leopold. *Die allgemeinen Verhältnisse im Bürgerlichen Bräuhaus in Budweis (Rede).* Budweis: A. Blaha, 1900.
Seipel, Ignaz. *Nation und Staat.* Vienna: W. Braumüller, 1916.
Sieghart, Rudolf. *Die letzten Jahrzehnte einer Grossmacht.* Berlin: Ullstein, 1932.
Skedl, Arthur, ed. *Der politische Nachlass des Grafen Eduard Taaffe.* Vienna: Rikola, 1922.
Slavnostní list Budivoje S.A.J. 1877–1927. Č. Budějovice: Budivoj S.A.J. / K. Fiala, 1927.
Smitka, František. *Státní převrat v Čes. Budějovicích a jihočeské sokolstvo.* Č. Budějovice: K. Fiala, 1928.
Somary, Felix. *Erinnerungen aus meinem Leben.* Zürich: Manesse, 1956[?].
Springer, Anton Heinrich. *Oestreich nach der Revolution.* Leipzig: Immanuel Müller, 1850.
Statuten des Militär-Veteranen-Vereines zu Budweis. Budweis: Josef Watzl, 1872 [?].
Štěpánek, Jan Nepomuk. *Čech a Němec.* Prague: M. Knapp, 1919. [1812].
Stifter, Adalbert. *Bunte Steine.* Munich: Goldmann, 1989.
————. *Der Nachsommer.* Munich: Deutscher Taschenbuchverlag, 1977.
————. *Witiko.* Leipzig: Insel-Verlag, n.d.
Stránský, Jaroslav. *Odsun Němců z ČSR z hlediska národního a mezinárodního.* 2 vols. London: Ústav Dr. Edvarda Beneše, 1953.
Strnad, Rudolf. *1884–1924. Čtyřicet let činnosti odboru Národní jednoty pošumavské v Č. Budějovicích.* Č. Budějovice: Odbor NJP, 1924.
————. *Dr. A. Zátka.* Č. Budějovice: Odbor NJP / K. Fiala, 1927.
————. *Sedmdesát let českobudějovické besedy 1862–1937.* Č. Budějovice: K. Fiala, 1937.
————, ed. *Padesát let odboru Národní jednoty pošumavské v Č. Budějovicích. 1884–1934.* Č. Budějovice: NJP, 1934.
————, ed. *Projevy a řeči dra. Augusta Zátky.* Č. Budějovice: Odbor NJP, 1935.
Tezner, Friedrich. *Handbuch des österreichischen Administrativverfahrens.* Vienna: Manz, 1896.
Trajer, Johann. *Historisch-statistische Beschreibung der Diöcese Budweis.* Budweis: F. Zdarssa, 1862.
Türk, Karl. *Böhmen, Mähren und Schlesien.* [*Der Kampf um das Deutschtum*, 6. Heft.] Munich: Lehmann, 1898.
Twain, Mark [Samuel Clemens]. "Stirring Times in Austria." In *The Complete Essays of Mark Twain.* Garden City: Doubleday, 1963, pp. 208–35.
Uhlich von Uhlenau, Gottfried. *Biographische Skizzen aus Budweis's Vergangenheit.* Budweis: F. Zdarssa, 1871.
————. *Thron, Bürger und Soldat.* Budweis: 1848.

Upomínka na slet sokolstva v Č. Budějovicích 1903. Program slavnosti a pokyny. Č. Budějovice: J. Přibyl, 1903.

Vodňanský, Fr. *Náš zápas o III. sbor.* Č. Budějovice: K. Stieflmaier, 1906.

Vondráček, Karel. *1884–1934. 50 let Národní jednoty pošumavské.* Prague: NJP, 1934.

Vondruška, Miloš, ed. *Jihočeská technická práce.* Č. Budějovice: Odbor spolku čs. inženýrů v Č. Budějovicích, 1938.

Weiss, Hugo. *Das Heimatrecht nach der Heimatgesetznovelle von 1896.* Vienna: Manz, 1906.

Whitman, Sidney. *The Realm of the Habsburgs.* Leipzig: Tauchnitz, 1893.

Wonesch, W. *Deutsche Liedertafel in Budweis 1856–1926. Ein geschichtlicher Rückblick.* B. Budweis: 1926.

Zeithammer, Leopold M. *České Budějovice a okolí. Přírodní, národohospodářské, kulturní a národnostní poměry, dějiny jakož i staré stavitelské a jiné památky.* Č. Budějovice: nákladem vlastním, 1904.

Zemmrich, Johannes. *Sprachgrenze und Deutschtum in Böhmen.* Braunschweig: Vieweg und Sohn, 1902.

———. "Josef Taschek." *Deutsche Erde* 11 (1912): 61.

Statistical and Demographic Studies

Austria. k.k. statistische Central-Commission. *Bevölkerung der Gemeinden mit mehr als 2000 Einwohnern in den im Reichsrathe vertretenen Königreichen und Ländern, nach der Zählung vom 31. December 1880.* Vienna: k.k. Hof- und Staatsdruckerei, 1881.

———. *Die Ergebnisse der Volkszählung vom 31. December 1890 in den im Reichsrathe vertretenen Königreichen und Ländern.* Vol. 1: *Die summarischen Ergebnisse der Volkszählung.* Vienna: k.k. Hof- und Staatsdruckerei, 1892.

———. *Die Ergebnisse der Volkszählung vom 31. December 1900 in den im Reichsrathe vertretenen Königreichen und Ländern.* Vol. 1: *Die summarischen Ergebnisse der Volkszählung.* Vienna: k.k. Hof- und Staatsdruckerei, 1902.

———. *Österreichisches Städtebuch. Statistische Berichte der grösseren österreichischen Städte.* Vol. 4. Vienna: k.k. Hof- und Staatsdruckerei, 1891.

Becher, Siegfried. *Statistische Uebersicht der Bevölkerung der österreichischen Monarchie nach den Ergebnissen der Jahre 1834 bis 1840.* Stuttgart und Tübingen: J. G. Cotta, 1841.

Bohmann, Alfred. *Bevölkerungsbewegungen in Böhmen 1847–1947.* Munich: Collegium Carolinum, 1958.

———. *Das Sudetendeutschtum in Zahlen.* Munich: Sudetendeutscher Rat, 1959.

Czechoslovak Republic. Státní úřad statistický. *Les élections à l'assemblée nationale en Avril 1920 et les élections communales en Bohême, Moravie et Silésie en Juin 1919.* Prague: Bursík et Kohout, 1922.

———. *Sčítání lidu v Republice Československé ze dne 21. února 1921.* Vol. 2, part 1. Prague: Bursík a Kohout, 1925.

———. *Sčítání lidu v Republice Československé ze dne 1. prosince 1930.* Prague: Bursík a Kohout, 1934.

————. *Die Volkszählung in der Čechoslovakischen Republik vom 15. Februar 1921.* Vol. 1. Prague: Bursík und Kohout, 1924.

Czoernig, Karl Freiherr von. *Ethnographie der österreichischen Monarchie.* 3 vols. Vienna: k.k. Direction der administrativen Statistik / k.k. Hof- und Staatsdruckerei, 1855–57.

Engelmann, Richard. "Österreichs städtische Wohnplätze mit mehr als 25,000 Einwohnern Ende 1910, ihr Wachstum seit 1869 und die konfessionelle und sprachliche Zusammensetzung ihrer Bevölkerung 1880–1910." *Statistische Monatschrift,* Neue Folge, 19 (1914): 413–510.

Ficker, Adolf. *Die Völkerstämme der österreichisch-ungarischen Monarchie, ihre Gebiete, Gränzen und Inseln. Historisch, geographisch, statistisch dargestellt.* Vienna: k.k. Hof- und Staatsdruckerei, in Commission bei August Prandel, 1869.

————. *Vorträge über die Vornahme der Volkszählung in Österreich.* Vienna: k.k. Hof- und Staatsdruckerei, 1870.

Hecke, Wilhelm. "Volksvermehrung, Binnenwanderung und Umgangssprache in den nördlichen Ländern Österreichs." *Statistische Monatschrift,* Neue Folge 19 (1914): 653–723.

————. "Volksvermehrung, Binnenwanderung und Umgangssprache in den österreichischen Alpenländern und Südländern." *Statistische Monatschrift,* Neue Folge 18 (1913): 323–92.

Jireček, Josef. *Národopisný přehled Králowstwí českého roku 1850.* Prague: W Komissí kněhkupectwí Řiwnáčowa, 1850.

Kárníková, Ludmila. *Vývoj obyvatelstva v českých zemích, 1754–1914.* Prague: Nakladatelství ČSAV, 1965.

Rauchberg, Heinrich. *Der nationale Besitzstand in Böhmen.* Leipzig: Duncker und Humblot, 1905.

Sommer, Johann Gottfried. *Das Königreich Böhmen: statistisch-topographisch dargestellt.* Vol. 9: *Budweiser Kreis.* Prague: F. Ehrlich, 1841.

Secondary Materials

Agnew, Hugh L. *Origins of the Czech National Renascence.* Pittsburgh: University of Pittsburgh Press, 1993.

Alderman, Geoffrey, ed. *Governments, Ethnic Groups and Political Representation.* New York: New York University Press, 1993.

Allmayer-Beck, Johann Christoph. "Die bewaffnete Macht in Staat und Gesellschaft." In *Die Habsburgermonarchie 1848–1918,* Vol. 5: *Die bewaffnete Macht.* Edited by Adam Wandruszka and Peter Urbanitsch. Vienna: Verlag der österreichischen Akademie der Wissenschaften, 1987, pp. 1–141.

Anderson, Benedict R. *Imagined Communities: Reflections on the Origin and Spread of Nationalism.* 2nd edition. New York: Verso, 1991; 1st edition. London: Verso, 1983.

————. *The Spectre of Comparisons. Nationalism, Southeast Asia and the World.* New York: Verso, 1998.

Applegate, Celia. *A Nation of Provincials: the German Idea of Heimat.* Berkeley: University of California Press, 1990.

Armstrong, John. *Nations before Nationalism*. Chapel Hill: University of North Carolina Press, 1982.

Bajerová, Anna. *Z české revoluce r. 1848*. Prague: F. Topič, 1919.

Barborová, Éva. "Jirsíkovo české gymnásium v Č. Budějovicích 1868–1953." In *Minulost a současnost Č. Budějovic. Studie a materiály I*. Č. Budějovice: M.N.V., 1969.

Barker, Ernest. "Emperor," and "Empire." In *The Encyclopaedia Britannica*. Vol. 9. Cambridge: Cambridge University Press, 1910, pp. 345–56.

Barkey, Karen, and Mark von Hagen, eds. *After Empire. Multiethnic Societies and Nation-Building*. Boulder, Colo.: Westview, 1997.

Barth, Fredrik, ed. *Ethnic Groups and Boundaries*. Boston: Little, Brown, 1969.

Bibó, István. "A kelet-európai kisállamok nyomorúsága." In *Válogatott tanulmányok*. Vol. 2. Budapest: Magvető, 1986, pp. 185–265.

Birke, Ernst. "Der Erste Weltkrieg und die Gründung der Tschechoslowakei 1914–1919." In *Handbuch der Geschichte der böhmischen Länder*. Vol. 3. Edited by Karl Bosl. Stuttgart: Hirsemann, 1968, pp. 274–446.

Bled, Jean-Paul. *Franz Joseph*. Oxford: Blackwell, 1992.

Bloomfield, Jon. *Passive Revolution: Politics and the Czechoslovak Working Class, 1945–1948*. New York: St. Martin's Press, 1979.

Böhm, Ferdinand, ed. *České Budějovice*. Č. Budějovice: Obchodní organisátor, 1928.

Borsody, István [Stephen]. *Beneš*. Budapest: Athenaeum, 1943.

———. *The Tragedy of Central Europe*. New Haven: Yale Concilium on International and Area Studies, 1980.

Boyer, Christoph. *Nationale Kontrahenten oder Partner?* Munich: Oldenbourg, 1999.

Boyer, John W. *Culture and Political Crisis in Vienna: Christian Socialism in Power, 1897–1918*. Chicago: University of Chicago Press, 1995.

———. *Political Radicalism in Late Imperial Vienna: Origins of the Christian Social Movement, 1848–1897*. Chicago: University of Chicago Press, 1981.

Brandes, Detlef. *Die Tschechen unter deutschem Protektorat*. 2 vols. Munich: Oldenbourg, 1969–75.

Bridge, F. R. *From Sadowa to Sarajevo: The Foreign Policy of Austria-Hungary, 1866–1914*. London: Routledge and Kegan Paul, 1972.

Brix, Emil. "Der böhmische Ausgleich in Budweis." *Österreichische Osthefte* 24, no. 2 (1982): 225–48.

———. *Die Umgangssprache in Altösterreich zwischen Agitation und Assimilation*. Vienna: Böhlau, 1982.

Brousek, Karl. " 'Ich verstehe heute nicht mehr, woher ich damals den Mut genommen habe. . .' Erinnerungen an eine Wehrdienstverweigerung im Zweiten Weltkrieg." In *Nationalitäten und Identitäten in Ostmitteleuropa*. Edited by Walter Lukan and Arnold Suppan. Vienna: Böhlau, 1995, pp. 85–96.

Brubaker, Rogers. *Citizenship and Nationhood in France and Germany*. Cambridge: Harvard University Press, 1992.

———. "Myths and Misconceptions in the Study of Nationalism." In *The State of the Nation. Ernest Gellner and the Theory of Nationalism*. Edited by John Hall. New York: Cambridge University Press, 1998, pp. 272–305.

————. *Nationalism Reframed*. New York: Cambridge University Press, 1996.
Brubaker, Rogers, and Frederick Cooper. "Beyond 'Identity.'" *Theory and Society*, vol. 29 (February 2000): 1–47.
Brubaker, Rogers, and David Laitin. "Ethnic and Nationalist Violence." *Annual Review of Sociology*, 24 (August 1998): 423–52.
Brügel, Johann Wolfgang. *Tschechen und Deutsche 1918–1938*. Munich: Nymphenburger, 1967.
Bugge, Peter. "Czech Democracy 1918–1938—Paragon or Parody?" *Phasen und Formen der Transformation in der Tschechoslowakei. Vorträge der Tagung des Collegium Carolinum in Bad Wiessee vom 23. bis 26 November 2000*. Edited by Christiane Brunner. Munich: Oldenbourg, forthcoming.
————. "Czech Nation-Building, National-Perception and Politics 1780–1914." Ph.D. diss. University of Aarhus, Denmark, 1994.
Calhoun, Craig. "Nationalism and Ethnicity." *Annual Review of Sociology* 19 (1993): 211–39.
Campbell, F. Gregory. *Confrontation in Central Europe: Weimar Germany and Czechoslovakia*. Chicago: University of Chicago Press, 1975.
Charmatz, Richard. *Das politische Denken in Österreich*. Vienna: Wiener Urania, 1917.
Chvojka, Jiří. *Město pod černou věží*. České Budějovice: Actys, 1992.
Cohen, Gary. "The German Minority of Prague, 1850–1918." In *Ethnic Identity in Urban Europe*. Edited by Max Engman. Volume 8 of *Comparative Studies on Governments and Non-Dominant Ethnic Groups in Europe, 1850–1940*. New York: NYU Press, 1992, pp. 267–90.
————. *The Politics of Ethnic Survival: Germans in Prague, 1861–1914*. Princeton: Princeton University Press, 1981.
Cornwall, Mark, ed. *The Last Years of Austria-Hungary*. Exeter: University of Exeter Press, 1990.
Cozine, Alicia. "A Member of the State: Citizenship Law and Its Application in Czechoslovakia, 1918–1938." Ph.D. diss. University of Chicago, 1996.
Deák, István. *Assimilation and Nationalism in East Central Europe during the Last Century of Habsburg Rule*. Pittsburgh: University of Pittsburgh Press, 1983.
————. *Beyond Nationalism: A Social and Political History of the Habsburg Officer Corps, 1848–1918*. New York: Oxford University Press, 1990.
————. "Comments." *Austrian History Yearbook* 3, part 1 (1967): 303–7.
————. "Comparing Apples and Pears: Centralization, Decentralization, and Ethnic Policy in the Habsburg and Soviet Armies." In *Nationalism and Empire: The Habsburg Empire and the Soviet Union*. Edited by Richard L. Rudolph and David F. Good. New York: St. Martin's Press, 1992, pp. 225–42.
————. *The Lawful Revolution. Louis Kossuth and the Hungarians, 1848–1849*. New York: Columbia University Press, 1979.
Dějiny jihočeských židů za okupace. České Budějovice: 1950.
Deutsch, Karl W. *Nationalism and Social Communication*. New York: John Wiley, 1953.
————. *Tides Among Nations*. New York: Free Press, 1979.
Doyle, Michael. *Empires*. Ithaca: Cornell University Press, 1986.
Eisenstadt, S. N. *The Political Systems of Empires*. New York: Free Press, 1963.

Fischel, Alfred. "Nationalitäten." In *Österreichisches Staatswörterbuch. Handbuch des gesamten österreichischen öffentlichen Rechtes*. Vol. 3. Edited by Ernst Mischler and Josef Ulbrich. Vienna: A. Holder, 1907, pp. 676–702.

Ford, Caroline. *Creating the Nation in Provincial France: Religion and Political Identity in Brittany*. Princeton: Princeton University Press, 1993.

Frommer, Benjamin. "Retribution against Nazi Collaborators in Postwar Czechoslovakia." Ph.D. diss.: Harvard University, 1999.

Galandauer, Jan. *Od Hainfeldu ke vzniku KSČ*. Prague: Svoboda, 1986.

Garver, Bruce. *The Young Czech Party 1874–1901 and the Emergence of a Multi-Party System*. New Haven: Yale University Press, 1978.

Gellner, Ernest. *Nations and Nationalism*. Ithaca: Cornell University Press, 1983.

Glaser, Kurt. *Czecho-Slovakia. A Critical History*. Caldwell, Idaho: Caxton Printers, 1961.

Glassl, Horst. *Der mährische Ausgleich*. Munich: Fides-Verlagsgesellschaft, 1967.

Gluckstein, Ygael. *Stalin's Satellites in Europe*. Boston: Beacon Press, 1952.

Gonda, Imre, and Emil Niederhauser. *A Habsburgok*. Budapest: Gondolat, 1987.

Graus, František, ed. *Naše zivá i mrtvá minulost*. Prague: Svoboda, 1968.

Gulick, Charles. *Austria from Habsburg to Hitler*. Berkeley: University of California Press, 1948.

Haas, Arthur. "Metternich and the Slavs." *Austrian History Yearbook* 4–5 (1968–69): 120–49.

Hájek, Jiří. *Setkání a střety*. Cologne: INDEX, 1983.

Hajn, Ivo. "Obchodní politika Českého akciového pivovaru v Českých Budějovicích v období před první světovou válkou." In Jihočeské muzeum. *Průvodce po budějovických hostincích a kapitoly z jihočeské pivní historie*. České Budějovice: Jihočeské muzeum, 1999, pp. 130–33.

Herrnritt, Rudolf Hermann von. *Nationalität und Recht*. Vienna: Manz, 1899.

Hirsch, Francine. "Empire of Nations: Colonial Technologies and the Making of the Soviet Union, 1917–1939." Ph.D. diss., Princeton University, 1998.

Hobsbawm, Eric J. *Nations and Nationalism since 1780*. Cambridge: Cambridge University Press, 1990.

Hojda, Zdeněk, and Jiří Pokorný. *Pomníky a zapomníky*. Prague: Paseka, 1996.

Horowitz, Donald L. *Ethnic Groups in Conflict*. Berkeley: University of California Press, 1985.

Housková, Hana. "Česká studentská knihovna a její přínos ke vzniku národního vědomí v Č. Budějovicích." In *Minulost a současnost Č. Budějovic. Studie a materiály I*. Č. Budějovice: MNV, 1969, pp. 75–85.

Hroch, Miroslav. *Die Vorkämpfer der nationalen Bewegung bei den kleinen Völkern Europas*. Prague: Univerzita Karlova, 1968.

Hroch, Miroslav. *Social Preconditions of National Revival in Europe: a Comparative Analysis of the Social Composition of Patriotic Groups among the Smaller European Nations*. New York: Cambridge University Press, 1985.

———. *V národním zájmu*. Prague: Lidové noviny, 1999.

Hugelmann, Karl Gottfried, ed. *Das Nationalitätenrecht des alten Österreich*. Vienna and Leipzig: Wilhelm Braumüller, 1934.

Huyer, Reinhold. *Geschichte des Bräuwesens in Budweis*. Budweis: Selbstverlag des Bräuausschusses, 1895.

Iggers, Wilma, ed. *Die Juden in Böhmen und Mähren. Ein historisches Lesebuch.* Munich: C. H. Beck, 1986.

Jacoby, Gerhard. *Racial State. The German Nationalities Policy in the Protectorate of Bohemia-Moravia.* New York: Institute of Jewish Affairs, 1944.

Janos, Andrew. *The Politics of Backwardness in Hungary 1825–1945.* Princeton: Princeton University Press, 1982.

Janoušek, Bohumír. *Město na soutoku. Vyprávnění o historii Českých Budějovic. Č.* Budějovice: Nový život, 1964–66.

Jászi, Oscar. *The Dissolution of the Habsburg Monarchy.* Chicago: University of Chicago Press, 1929.

Jenks, William. *Austria under the Iron Ring 1879–1893.* Charlottesville: University Press of Virginia, 1965.

———. *The Austrian Electoral Reform of 1907.* New York: Columbia University Press, 1950.

Jeřábek, Rudolf. "The Eastern Front 1914–1918." In *The Last Years of Austria-Hungary.* Edited by Mark Cornwall. Exeter: University of Exeter Press, 1990, pp. 101–16.

Jihočeské muzeum. *Průvodce po budějovických hostincích a kapitoly z jihočeské pivní historie.* České Budějovice: Jihočeské muzeum, 1999.

Judson, Pieter. *Exclusive Revolutionaries. Liberal Politics, Social Experience, and National Identity in the Austrian Empire, 1848–1914.* Ann Arbor: University of Michigan Press, 1996.

———. "Frontiers, Islands, Forests, Stones: Mapping the Geography of a German Identity in the Habsburg Monarchy, 1848–1900." In *The Geography of Identity.* Edited by Patricia Yaeger. Ann Arbor: University of Michigan Press, 1996, pp. 382–406.

———. "'Whether Race or Conviction Should Be the Standard': National Identity and Liberal Politics in Nineteenth-Century Austria." *Austrian History Yearbook* 22 (1991): 76–95.

Kann, Robert. *Dynasty, Politics and Culture: Selected Essays.* Boulder, Colo.: Social Science Monographs, 1991.

———. *The Multinational Empire. Nationalism and National Reform in the Habsburg Monarchy 1848–1918.* 2 vols. New York: Octagon, 1970.

Kappeler, Andreas. *Russland als Vielvölkerreich.* Munich: C. H. Beck, 1992.

Kautsky, John. *The Politics of Aristocratic Empires.* Chapel Hill: University of North Carolina Press, 1982.

Kazbunda, Karel. *České hnutí roku 1848.* Prague: Nakl. Historického klubu, 1929.

———. *Otázka česko-německá v předvečer velké války.* Prague: Univerzita Karlova, 1995.

Kestenberg-Gladstein, Ruth. "The Jews between Czechs and Germans in the Historic Lands, 1848–1918." In *The Jews of Czechoslovakia.* Vol. 1. Philadelphia: The Jewish Publication Society of America, 1968, pp. 21–60.

Kieval, Hillel. *The Making of Czech Jewry: National Conflict and Jewish Society in Bohemia, 1870–1918.* New York: Oxford University Press, 1988.

Kimball, Stanley. *Czech Nationalism: A Study of the National Theatre Movement, 1845–83.* Urbana: University of Illinois Press, 1967.

Kimball, Stanley. "The Matice Česká, 1831–1861: The First Thirty Years of a Literary Foundation." In *The Czech Renascence of the Nineteenth Century.* Edited by Peter Brock and H. Gordon Skilling. Toronto: University of Toronto Press, 1970, pp. 53–73.

King, Jeremy. "Austria vs. Hungary: Nationhood, Statehood, and Violence since 1867." In *Nationalitätenkonflikte im 20. Jahrhundert. Ursachen von inter-ethnischer Gewalt im europäischen Vergleich.* Edited by Philipp Ther and Holm Sundhaussen. Berlin: Harrassowitz, 2002, pp. 163–82.

———. "The Nationalization of East Central Europe: Ethnicism, Ethnicity, and Beyond." In *Staging the Past: The Politics of Commemoration in Habsburg Central Europe, 1848 to the Present.* Edited by Nancy Wingfield and Maria Bucur. West Lafayette: Purdue University Press, 2001, pp. 112–52.

———. Review of Hugh Agnew, *Origins of the Czech National Renascence* (Pittsburgh: Pittsburgh University Press, 1993). In *Nationalities Papers* 14, no. 4 (December 1996): 748–50.

Klabouch, Jiří. *Die Gemeindeselbstverwaltung in Österreich, 1848–1918.* Munich: Oldenbourg, 1968.

Klemperer, Klemens von. *Ignaz Seipel. Christian Statesman in a Time of Crisis.* Princeton: Princeton University Press, 1972.

Klíma, Arnošt. *Na prahu nové společnosti (1781–1848).* Prague: Státní Pedagogické Nakladatelství, 1979.

Kočí, Josef. *České národní obrození.* Prague: Svoboda, 1978.

Kohn, Hans. *The Idea of Nationalism: A Study in its Origins and Background.* New York: Macmillan, 1944.

———. *Pan-Slavism: Its History and Ideology.* Notre Dame: University of Notre Dame Press, 1953.

Kollar, Robert. "Sčítání lidu." In *Slovník veřejného práva Československého.* Vol. 4. Edited by Emil Hácha, Jiří Hoetzel, František Weyr, and Karel Laštovka. Brno: Polygrafia, 1938.

Kopáček, Jiří, ed. *Encyklopedie Českých Budějovic.* České Budějovice: Nebe, 1998.

Kořalka, Jiří. "Hans Kohns Dichotomie und die neuzeitliche Nationsbildung der Tschechen." In *Formen des nationalen Bewußtseins im Lichte zeitgenössischer Nationalismustheorien.* Edited by Eva Schmidt-Hartmann. Munich: Oldenbourg, 1994, pp. 263–75.

———. "Nationality Representation in Bohemia, Moravia and Austrian Silesia, 1848–1914." In *Governments, Ethnic Groups and Political Representation.* Edited by Geoffrey Alderman. New York: New York University Press, 1993, pp. 85–122.

———. *Tschechen im Habsburgerreich und in Europa 1815–1914.* Munich: Oldenbourg, 1991.

Kořalka, Jiří, and R. J. Crampton. "Die Tschechen." In *Die Habsburgermonarchie 1848–1918.* Vol. 3: *Die Völker des Reiches.* Edited by Adam Wandruszka and Peter Urbanitsch. Vienna: Verlag der österreichischen Akademie der Wissenschaften, 1980, pp. 489–520.

Korbel, Josef. *The Communist Subversion of Czechoslovakia 1938–1948.* Princeton: Princeton University Press, 1959.

————. *Twentieth Century Czechoslovakia*. New York: Columbia University Press, 1977.

Korostenski, Jiří. *Příspěvek k historii KSČ v letech 1928–1938 na Českobudějovicku*. České Budějovice: KSČ, 1981.

Král, Václav. *Otázky hospodářského a sociálního vývoje v českých zemích v letech 1938–1945*. Prague: Nakl. Československé akademie věd, 1957.

————. *Pravda o okupaci*. Prague: Naše vojsko, 1962.

Křen, Jan. *Konfliktní společenství*. Toronto: 68 Publishers, 1989.

Krinsky, Carol. *Synagogues of Europe*. New York: Architectural History Foundation, 1985.

Kubeš, Milan, and Ivana Šustrová, eds. *Češi ve střední Evropě*. Munich: Tschechischer Nationalausschuß in Deutschland, 1988.

Kulisch, Max. "Gemeinden: Gemeindewahlen." In *Österreichisches Staatswörterbuch. Handbuch des gesamten österreichischen öffentlichen Rechtes*. Vol. 2. Edited by Ernst Mischler and Josef Ulbrich. Vienna: A. Holder, 1906, pp. 335–47.

Kural, Václav. "Češi a Němci v čs. státě 1918–1948." In *Kapitoly z dějin Střední Evropy. Češi a Němci*. Edited by Rudolf Kučera. Munich: Tschechischer Nationalausschuß, 1989, pp. 188–230.

Laitin, David. *Language Repertoires and State Construction in Africa*. Cambridge: Cambridge University Press, 1992.

Lass, Andrew. "Romantic Documents and Political Monuments: The Meaning-Fulfillment of History in 19th-Century Czech Nationalism." *American Ethnologist* 15, no. 3 (August 1988): 456–471.

————. "What Keeps the Czech Folk 'Alive?'" *Dialectical Anthropology* 14 (1989): 7–19.

Lemberg, Eugen. *Nationalismus*. 2 vols. Reinbek bei Hamburg: Rowohlt, 1964.

Lipscher, Ladislav. *Verfassung und politische Verwaltung in der Tschechoslowakei: 1918–1939*. Munich: Oldenbourg, 1979.

Luft, Robert. "Die Mittelpartei des mährischen Grossgrundbesitzes 1879 bis 1918. Zur Problematik des Ausgleichs in Mähren und Böhmen." In *Die Chance der Verständigung: Absichten und Ansätze zu übernationaler Zusammenarbeit in den böhmischen Ländern 1848–1918*. Edited by Ferdinand Seibt. Munich: Oldenbourg, 1987, pp. 187–244.

Luža, Radomír. *Odsun. Příspěvek k historii česko-německých vztahů v letech 1918–1952*. Vienna: 1953.

————. *The Transfer of the Sudeten Germans: A Study of Czech-German Relations, 1933–62*. New York: New York University Press, 1964.

Macartney, C. A. *The Habsburg Empire, 1790–1918*. New York: MacMillan, 1969.

MacDonald, Callum. *The Killing of SS Obergruppenführer Reinhard Heydrich*. New York: Free Press, 1989.

Macura, Vladimír. *Český sen*. Prague: Lidové noviny, 1998.

————. *Masarykovy boty a jiné semi(o)fejetony*. Prague: Pražská imaginace, 1993.

————. *Šťastný věk: symboly, emblémy a mýty 1948–1989*. Prague: Pražská imaginace, 1992.

————. *Znamení zrodu. České národní obrození jako kulturní typ*. 2nd edition. Prague: H&H, 1995.

Mamatey, Victor, and Radomír Luža, eds. *A History of the Czechoslovak Republic, 1918–1948*. Princeton: Princeton University Press, 1973.

Markovits, Andrei. "Empire and Province." In *Nation Building and the Politics of Nationalism. Essays on Austrian Galicia*. Edited by Andrei Markovits and Frank Sysyn. Cambridge: Harvard Ukrainian Research Institute, 1982, pp. 1–22.

Martin, Terry. *Affirmative Action Empire: Nations and Nationalism in the Soviet Union, 1923–1939*. Ithaca: Cornell University Press, 2001.

Mastný, Vojtěch. *The Czechs under Nazi Rule*. New York: Columbia University Press, 1971.

———. *Russia's Road to the Cold War*. New York: Columbia University Press, 1979.

May, Arthur. *The Hapsburg Monarchy 1867–1914*. Cambridge: Harvard University Press, 1951.

Menzel, Wolfgang. *Die nationale Entwicklung in Böhmen, Mähren und Schlesien. Von der Aufklärung bis zur Revolution 1848*. Nuremberg: Preussler, 1985.

Mešt'an, Antonín. "Böhmisches Landesbewußtsein in der tschechischen Literatur." In *Die Chance der Verständigung: Absichten und Ansätze zu übernationaler Zusammenarbeit in den böhmischen Ländern 1848–1918*. Edited by Ferdinand Seibt. Munich: Oldenbourg, 1987, pp. 31–38.

Mezník, Jaroslav. "Dějiny národu českého v Moravě: nárys vývoje národního vědomí na Moravě do poloviny 19. století." *Český časopis historický* 88, nos. 1–2 (1990): 34–62.

Mischler, Ernst, and Josef Ulbrich, eds. *Österreichisches Staatswörterbuch. Handbuch des gesamten österreichischen öffentlichen Rechtes*. 4 vols. Vienna: A. Holder, 1905–9.

Mommsen, Hans. *Die Sozialdemokratie und die Nationalitätenfrage im habsburgischen Vielvölkerstaat*. Vienna: Europa, 1963.

Moritsch, Andrej. " 'Slovenci' in 'Nemci' v koroških mestih 1850–1940." *Zgodovinski Časopis*, 46, no. 1 (1992): 13–32.

Moritsch, Andreas, ed. *Vom Ethnos zur Nationalität*. Munich: Oldenbourg, 1991.

Motyl, Alexander. "From Imperial Decay to Imperial Collapse: The Fall of the Soviet Empire in Comparative Perspective." In *Nationalism and Empire: The Habsburg Empire and the Soviet Union*. Edited by Richard L. Rudolph and David F. Good. New York: St. Martin's Press, 1992, pp. 15–44.

Myant, Martin R. *Socialism and Democracy in Czechoslovakia 1945–1948*. New York: Cambridge University Press, 1981.

Němec, Ludvík. "Solution of the Minorities Problem," in *A History of the Czechoslovak Republic, 1918–1948*. Edited by Victor Mamatey and Radomír Luža. Princeton: Princeton University Press, 1973, pp. 416–21.

Niederle, Helmut. "Es war sehr schön, es hat mich sehr gefreut." Vienna: Oesterreichischer Bundesverlag, 1987.

Nikrmajer, Leoš. "Vznik Národního souručenství v Českých Budějovicích a jeho činnost do vypuknutí druhé světové války." *Jihočeský sborník historický* 65 (1996): 106–19.

Novotný, Jan. *Slovanská lípa 1848–1849*. Prague: Muzeum hlavního města Prahy, 1975.

Paikert, Géza Charles. *The German Exodus*. The Hague: M. Nijhoff, 1962.

Pasák, Tomáš. *Pod ochranou Říše.* Prague: Práh, 1998.

Paterson, Thomas, ed. *Major Problems in American Foreign Policy. Documents and Essays.* Vol. 2: *Since 1914.* Lexington, Mass.: Heath, 1978.

Pech, Stanley, *The Czech Revolution of 1848.* Chapel Hill: University of North Carolina Press, 1969.

Pecha, Miloslav. *Státní převrat v říjnu 1918 v Českých Budějovicích.* České Budějovice: Gabreta, 1999.

Pecha, Miloslav, Stanislav Šmíd, and Václav Vondra. *Protifašistický odboj 1938–1945 na Českobudějovicku.* Č. Budějovice: Okresní národní výbor Č. Budějovice, 1986.

Pecháček, Jaroslav. *Dvacet let svobody.* Munich: Národní politika, 1988.

Pelinka, Anton. *Karl Renner zur Einführung.* Hamburg: Junius Verlag, 1989.

Petráň, Josef, ed. *Počátky českého národního obrození.* Prague: Academia, 1990.

Petráš, Jiří. "Konec soužití Čechů a Němců v Českých Budějovicích." *Jihočeský sborník historický* 66–67 (1997–98): 147–72.

Pichlík, Karel, Vlastimil Vávra, and Jaroslav Křížek. *Červeno bílá a rudá.* Prague: Naše vojsko, 1967.

Pithart, Petr, Petr Příhoda and Milan Otáhal. ["Podiven"]. *Češi v dějinách nové doby.* Prague: Nakladatelství A. Tomského, 1991.

Plaschka, Richard. "Zur Vorgeschichte des Überganges von Einheiten des Infanterieregiments Nr. 28 an der russischen Front 1915." In *Österreich und Europa. Festgabe für Hugo Hantsch zum 70. Geburtstag.* Universität Wien, Institut für österreichische Geschichtsforschung. Graz: Styria, 1965, pp. 455–64.

Pletzer, Karel, and Oldřich Šeda. *Měšťanské i městské pivovarství a dvě stě let Prvního českobudějovického pivovaru Samson.* České Budějovice: Jihočeské pivovary, 1995.

Poggi, Gianfranco. *The State: Its Nature, Development and Prospects.* Stanford: Stanford University Press, 1990.

Preuss, Hugo. *Die Entwicklung des deutschen Städtewesens.* Vol. 1. Leipzig: Teubner, 1906.

Prinz, Friedrich. *Geschichte Böhmens 1848–1948.* Gütersloh: Langen Müller, 1988.

Procházka, Theodore. *The Second Republic: The Disintegration of Post-Munich Czechoslovakia.* Boulder, Colo.: East European Monographs, 1981.

Przedak, A. G. *Geschichte des deutschen Zeitschriftenwesens in Böhmen.* Heidelberg: Carl Winter, 1904.

Pulzer, Peter. *The Rise of Political Anti-Semitism in Germany and Austria.* New York: Wiley, 1964.

Rachamimov, Alon. "Diaspora Nationalism's Pyrrhic Victory: The Controversy Regarding the Electoral Reform of 1909 in Bukovina." In *State and Nation Building in East Central Europe: Contemporary Perspectives.* Edited by John Micgiel. New York: Columbia University Institute on East Central Europe, 1996, pp. 1–16.

—— "Imperial Loyalties and Private Concerns: Nation, Class, and State in the Correspondence of Austro-Hungarian POWs in Russia, 1916–1918." *Austrian History Yearbook*: 31 (2000): 87–105.

Rada, František. *Když se psalo c.k. Ze života Č. Budějovic na počátku století.* Č. Budějovice: Nakladatelství Č. Budějovice, 1966.

Rada, František. *Když se psalo T.G.M. České Budějovice v prvním desetiletí republiky.* České Budějovice: Růže, 1970.

Rak, Jiří. *Bývali Čechové: české historické mýty a stereotypy.* Jinočany: H&H, 1994.

Redlich, Josef. *Das österreichische Staats- und Reichsproblem; geschichtliche Darstellung der inneren Politik der habsburgischen Monarchie von 1848 bis zum Untergang des Reiches.* 2 vols. Leipzig: P. Reinhold, 1920–26.

———. *Das Wesen der österreichischen Kommunal-Verfassung.* Leipzig: Duncker & Humblot, 1910.

Richtr, František. "Minulost pivovarství v jižních Čechách a v Č. Budějovicích." *Kvasný průmysl* 16, no. 6 (1970): 129–33.

Rothschild, Joseph. *East Central Europe between the Two World Wars.* Seattle: University of Washington Press, 1974.

———. *Return to Diversity. The Political History of East Central Europe since World War II.* 2nd edition. New York: Oxford University Press, 1993.

Roubík, František. *Bibliografie časopisectva v Čechách z let 1863–1895.* Prague: Česká akademie věd a umění, 1936.

———. *Časopisectvo v Čechách v letech 1848–1862.* Prague: Duch Novin, 1930.

Sahlins, Peter. *Boundaries: The Making of France and Spain in the Pyrenées.* Berkeley: University of California Press, 1989.

Santifaller, Leo, ed. *Österreichisches biographisches Lexikon 1815–1950.* Graz-Köln: H. Böhlau Nachf., 1957–present.

Šantrůček, Bohuslav. *Václav Klofáč.* Prague: Mladé Proudy, 1928.

Schödl, Günter. "Varianten deutscher Nationalpolitik vor 1918. Zur politischen Organisation und Programmbildung deutscher Minderheiten in Ost- und Südosteuropa." *Südostdeutsches Archiv* 22–23 (1979–80): 109–12.

Schorske, Carl. *Fin-de-siècle Vienna: Politics and Culture.* New York: Vintage, 1981.

Šeda, Oldřich. "Kalendárium vývoje českého a amerického piva 'Budweiser.'" In *Jihočeské muzeum. Průvodce po budějovických hostincích a kapitoly z jihočeské pivní historie.* České Budějovice: Jihočeské muzeum, 1999, pp. 140–65.

Sedlmeyer, Karl Adalbert, ed. *Budweis. Budweiser und Stritschitzer Sprachinsel.* Miesbach: Verlag Bergemann & Mayr, 1979.

———. "Adalbert von Lanna." In *Lebensbilder zur Geschichte der böhmischen Länder.* Vol. 4. Edited by Ferdinand Seibt. Munich: Oldenbourg, 1981, pp. 165–90.

Seton-Watson, Hugh. *Nationalism and Communism. Essays, 1946–1963.* New York: Praeger, 1964.

———. *Nations and States: An Enquiry into the Origins of Nations and the Politics of Nationalism.* Boulder, Colo.: Westview Press, 1977.

Sigl, Franz. *Die soziale Struktur des Sudetendeutschtums, ihre Entwicklung und volkspolitische Bedeutung.* Leipzig: A. Lorentz, 1938.

Slezkine, Yuri. "The USSR as a Communal Apartment, or How a Socialist State Promoted Ethnic Particularism." *Slavic Review* 53, no. 2 (Summer 1994): 414–52.

Smelser, Ronald. "German-Czech Relations in Bohemian Frontier Towns: The Industrialization and Urbanization Process." In *Studies in East European Social History.* Vol. 2. Edited by Keith Hitchins. Leiden: E. J. Brill, 1981, pp. 62–87.

———. *The Sudeten Problem 1933–1938. Volkstumspolitik and the Formulation of Nazi Foreign Policy.* Middletown, Conn.: Wesleyan University Press, 1975.

Smutný, Jaromír. *Němci v Československu a jich odsun.* London: Ústav dr. Edvarda Beneše, 1956.

Sobota, Emil. *Co to byl protektorát?* Prague: Kvasnička a Hampl, 1946.

———. *Republika národní či národnostní?* Prague: Čin, 1929.

Šolle, Zdeněk. *Dělnické hnutí v Českých zemích koncem minulého století.* Prague: Rovnost, 1951.

Spiegel, Ludwig. "Heimatrecht." In *Österreichisches Staatswörterbuch. Handbuch des gesamten österreichischen öffentlichen Rechtes.* Vol. 2. Edited by Ernst Mischler and Josef Ulbrich. Vienna: A. Holder, 1906, pp. 809–43.

———. "Wahlen: Landtagswahlen." In *Österreichisches Staatswörterbuch. Handbuch des gesamten österreichischen öffentlichen Rechtes.* Vol. 4. Edited by Ernst Mischler and Josef Ulbrich. Vienna: A. Holder, 1909, pp. 894–927.

Spunda, Johanna. "Die verlorenen Inseln. Ein Beitrag zur Erforschung der nationalen Auseinandersetzung und Umvolkung in Mittelmähren." *Bohemia* 2 (1961): 357–413 and 3 (1962): 273–359.

Starzyński, Stanislaus Ritter von. "Wahlen: Reichsrathswahlen." In *Österreichisches Staatswörterbuch. Handbuch des gesamten österreichischen öffentlichen Rechtes.* Vol. 4. Edited by Ernst Mischler and Josef Ulbrich. Vienna: A. Holder, 1909, pp. 871–94.

Steenson, Gary. *After Marx, Before Lenin: Marxism and Socialist Working-class Parties in Europe, 1884–1914.* Pittsburgh: University of Pittsburgh Press, 1991.

Steger, Manfred. "Victor Adler and Austrian Social Democracy, 1889–1914." In *Vienna: The World of Yesterday, 1889–1914.* Edited by Stephen Bronner and F. Peter Wagner. Atlantic Highlands, N.J.: Humanities Press, 1997, pp. 204–20.

Stölzl, Christoph. *Die Ära Bach in Böhmen.* Munich: Oldenbourg, 1971.

———. *Kafkas böses Böhmen. Zur Sozialgeschichte eines Prager Juden.* Munich: Edition Text + Kritik, 1975.

———. "Zur Geschichte der böhmischen Juden in der Epoche des modernen Nationalismus." *Bohemia* 14 (1973): 179–221, and 15 (1974): 129–57.

Storch, Franz. "Preßrecht." In *Österreichisches Staatswörterbuch. Handbuch des gesamten österreichischen öffentlichen Rechtes.* Vol. 3. Edited by Ernst Mischler and Josef Ulbrich. Vienna: A. Holder, 1907, pp. 973–83.

Stourzh, Gerald. "Die Gleichberechtigung der Volksstämme als Verfassungsprinzip 1848–1918." In *Die Habsburgermonarchie 1848–1918.* Vol. 3: *Die Völker des Reiches.* Edited by Adam Wandruszka and Peter Urbanitsch. Vienna: Verlag der österreichischen Akademie der Wissenschaften, 1980, pp. 975–1206.

———. "Problems of Conflict Resolution in a Multi-ethnic State: Lessons from the Austrian Historical Experience, 1848–1918." In *State and Nation in Multiethnic Societies.* Edited by Uri Ra'anan. New York: Manchester University Press, 1991, pp. 67–80.

Sturm, Heribert, ed. *Biographisches Lexikon zur Geschichte der böhmischen Länder.* 3 vols. Munich: Oldenbourg, 1974–present.

Sutter, Berthold. *Die Badenischen Sprachenverordnungen von 1897.* 2 vols. Graz-Cologne: Böhlau, 1960, 1965.

Táborský, Edward. *President Edvard Beneš: Between East and West 1938–1948.* Stanford: Hoover Institution Press, 1981.

————. "Politics in Exile, 1939–1945." In *A History of the Czechoslovak Republic, 1918–1948.* Edited by Victor Mamatey and Radomír Luža. Princeton: Princeton University Press, 1973, pp. 322–42.

Theisinger, Hugo. *Die Sudetendeutschen: Herkunft, die Zeit unter Konrad Henlein und Adolf Hitler, Vertreibung.* Buchloe: Obermayer, 1987.

Tilly, Charles, ed. *The Formation of National States in Western Europe.* Princeton: Princeton University Press, 1975.

Tilly, Charles, and Wim P. Blockmans. *Cities and the Rise of States in Europe, A.D. 1000 to 1800.* Boulder, Colo.: Westview Press, 1994.

Tobolka, Zdeněk. *Politické dějiny československého národa od r. 1848 až do dnešní doby.* Vol. 4: *1914–1918.* Prague: Čsl. Kompas, 1937.

————, ed. *Česká politika.* 5 vols. Prague: J. Laichter, 1906–13.

Ulbrich, Josef. "Böhmen." In *Österreichisches Staatswörterbuch. Handbuch des gesamten österreichischen öffentlichen Rechtes.* Vol. 1. Edited by Ernst Mischler and Josef Ulbrich. Vienna: A. Holder, 1905, pp. 530–611.

Ullmann, Walter. *The United States in Prague, 1945–1948.* Boulder, Colo.: East European Quarterly, 1978.

Urban, Otto. *Česká společnost 1848–1918.* Prague: Svoboda, 1982.

Ústřední matice školská České Budějovice. 1872–1925. Inventář. České Budějovice: Okresní archiv, 1963.

Verdery, Katherine. *National Ideology under Socialism. Identity and Cultural Politics in Ceausescu's Romania.* Berkeley: University of California Press, 1991.

————. *Transylvanian Villagers.* Berkeley: University of California Press, 1983.

————. "The Unmaking of an Ethnic Collectivity: Transylvania's Germans." *American Ethnologist* 12 (February 1985): 62–83.

Veselý-Štainer, Karel. *Cestou národního odboje. Bojový vývoj domácího odbojového hnutí v letech 1938–45.* Prague: Sfinx, 1947.

Wandruszka, Adam, and Peter Urbanitsch, eds. *Die Habsburgermonarchie 1848–1918.* Vol. 3: *Die Völker des Reiches.* Vienna: Verlag der österreichischen Akademie der Wissenschaften, 1980.

Weber, Max. "Politics as Vocation." In *From Max Weber: Essays in Sociology.* Edited by H. H. Gerth and C. Wright Mills. New York: Oxford University Press, 1946, pp. 77–128.

Whiteside, Andrew. *Austrian National Socialism before 1918.* The Hague: Martinus Nijhoff, 1962.

Wingfield, Nancy, and Maria Bucur, eds. *Staging the Past: The Politics of Commemoration in Habsburg Central Europe, 1848 to the Present.* West Lafayette: Purdue University Press, 2001.

Wiskemann, Elizabeth. *Czechs and Germans.* 2nd edition. New York: St. Martin's Press, 1967.

————. *Germany's Eastern Neighbors.* London: Oxford University Press, 1956.

Wurzbach, Constant von, ed. *Biographisches Lexikon des Kaiserthums Oesterreich.* 60 vols. Vienna: L. C. Zamarski, 1856–91.

Za obnovu státu Čechů a Slováků 1938–1945. Prague: Státní pedagogické nakladatelství, 1992.

Zacek, Joseph. "Czechoslovak Fascisms." In *Native Fascism in the Successor States, 1918–1945.* Edited by Peter Sugar. Santa Barbara, Calif.: ABC-Clio, 1971, pp. 56–62.

———. "Nationalism in Czechoslovakia." In *Nationalism in Eastern Europe.* Edited by Peter Sugar and Ivo Lederer. Seattle: University of Washington Press, 1969, pp. 166–206.

Žákavec, Theodor. *Lanna.* Prague: 1936.

Zeman, Zbynek. *The Breakup of the Habsburg Empire, 1914–1918.* New York: Oxford University Press, 1961.

Zinner, Paul E. *Communist Strategy and Tactics in Czechoslovakia 1918–1948.* New York: Praeger, 1963.

Index

Adler, Viktor, 88–90, 151
Alsace and Lorraine, 42, 152
Anderson, Benedict, 20
Anheuser, Eberhard, 2, 107
Anschluss, 25, 26, 27, 160, 173
anti-Semitism. *See* Jews
Anzeiger aus dem südlichen Böhmen (newspaper), 3, 4, 34, 35, 38, 53
Aryan "race," 73, 112, 180
associations, 25–26, 50–51, 53–54, 56–57, 102, 106, 109, 161, 190
  laws concerning, 30, 34–35, 37, 70, 141, 148, 179, 205
  socioeconomic composition of, 23, 46–47, 51, 57, 65–67, 69, 72–73, 86
  See also *Beseda*; *Böhmerwaldbund*; *Deutsches Haus*; *Liedertafel*; *Turnverein*; *Sokol*
Austria. *See* Austria, Republic of; Habsburg Monarchy
Austria, Republic of, 148, 155, 157, 159–60, 173
Austria-Hungary. *See* Habsburg Monarchy
Austrian Social Democratic Party. *See* Social Democratic Party
Austro-Prussian War, 36–37, 45, 55, 75, 174
autonomy. *See* federalization

Badeni, Count Casimir, 90
Badeni decrees (1897), 92–93, 96–97, 99–100, 129, 134
beer, 2, 106–11
  See also Burghers' Brewery; Czech Shareholders' Brewery
Beneš, Edvard, 175, 176, 186–87, 190, 193, 196, 202, 204–8, 249n.2
Bernatzik, Edmund, 143
Beseda, 4, 34, 35, 42, 44, 47, 49, 51, 54, 63, 65–67, 78, 83, 86, 97–98, 108, 126, 148, 205
  army officers in, 77, 104, 127
Beseda of Artisans and Tradesmen, 68
Beseda, "Civic-Political," 84
Beseda of the People, 67–68, 69
Beseda, Workers', 88, 90

Better ... than ..., 43, 47, 83, 109, 136
Bibó, István, 207
bilingualism
  in associations, 53–54, 65, 88, 102
  in municipal government, 61, 133, 141, 158, 166
  of population, xiii, 1–4, 7, 10, 16–18, 21, 63–65, 144, 166, 184, 210
  state policy of, 19–20, 37–38, 56–57, 92–93, 162–63, 166, 183
  See also Badeni decrees; census; schools; state; Stremayr decree; utraquism
Bismarck, Otto von, 36, 41, 55, 70, 79, 112, 163, 169, 171
blood, 114–15, 132, 179–80, 200
Bohemia, Kingdom of
  linguistic composition, 20, 72
  Habsburg acquisition of, 15
  linguistic border of, 15–16
  maps of. *See front map section*
  See also Czechoslovakia; Germany; Habsburg Monarchy
Bohemian Compromise. *See* compromise
Bohemian/Czech National Party, 32, 36, 56, 68, 97, 135
  Catholics and, 41, 52, 66, 67, 73–74
  great landowners and, 32, 40, 42, 46, 55, 62, 66, 74, 92, 134, 160, 209
  Young Czechs and, 73–74, 81–86, 91–94, 131
Bohemian Diet, 21, 23–27, 29, 32, 36–37, 40–43, 69, 139, 147, 221n.37
  See also boycotts; elections; Zátka, August
Bohemian Forest, 15, 35, 157, 205. See also *Böhmerwaldbund*
Bohemian governor, 1–2, 26, 43, 47, 50, 61, 240n.56
Bohemian lands, xiii, 12, 19, 20, 22
  maps of. *See front map section*
Bohemian politics, structure of, xiv, 4, 11, 13–14, 55, 75–82, 112–15, 124, 130, 145–46, 151–54, 160, 162, 169–70, 177–78, 189–90, 206–11
Bohemian state rights, 10, 32, 40, 48, 74, 82, 92, 134, 135, 154, 159–61